D1223307

Building **the Cold War**

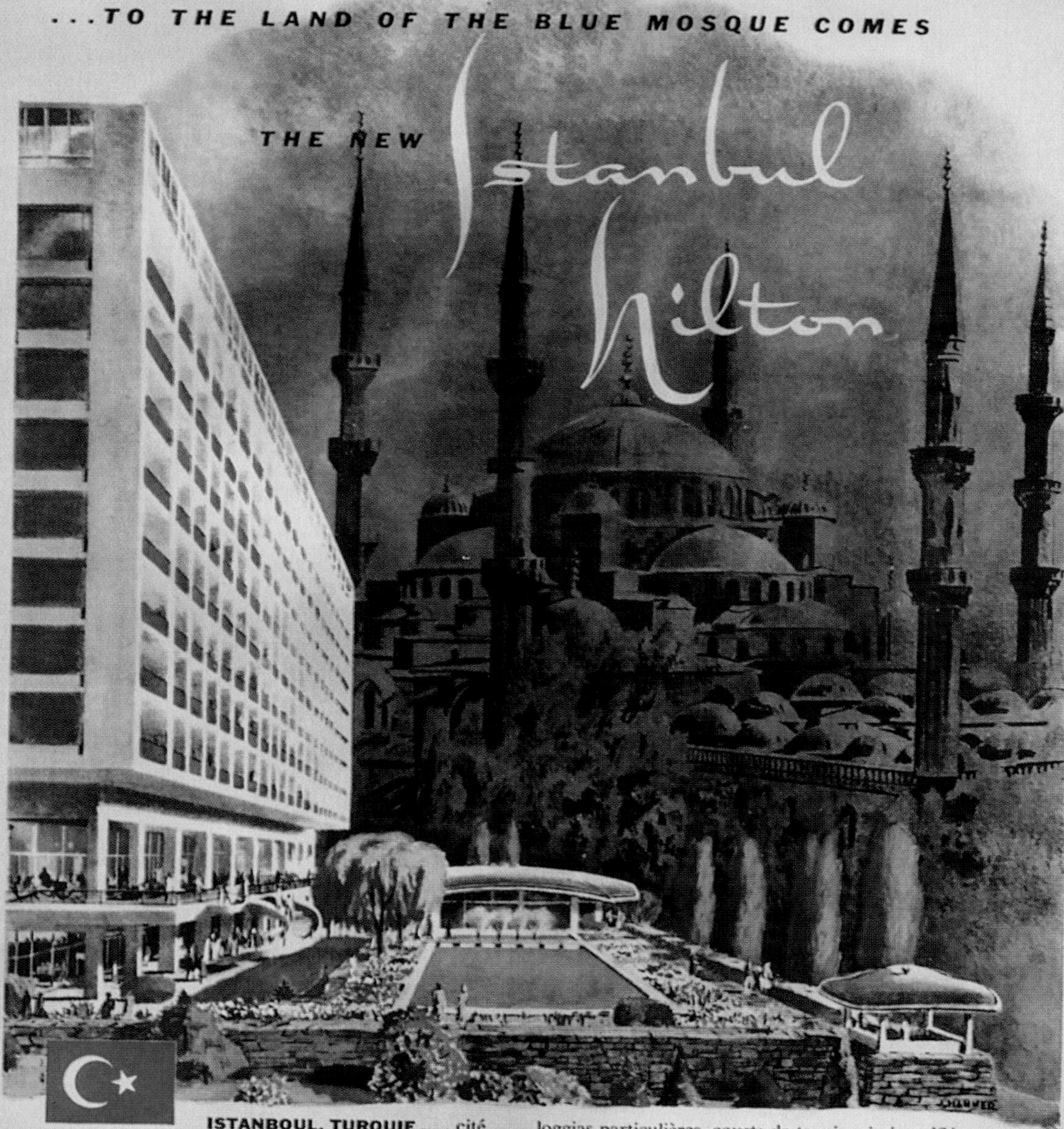

...TO THE LAND OF THE BLUE MOSQUE COMES

THE NEW *Istanbul Hilton*

ISTANBOUL, TURQUIE . . . cité à la beauté légendaire . . . offre un site féerique pour ce nouvel Hôtel Hilton, le second, déjà, en Europe. Dominant le Bosphore, ce magnifique hôtel de 300 chambres, conçu d'après les tout-derniers perfectionnements du confort et de la technique moderne, est un attrait nouveau pour les visiteurs de l'Orient. Jardins panoramiques, terrasses, loggias particulières, courts de tennis, piscine réfléchissante, telles sont les innovations qui viennent rehausser encore l'éclat du modernisme à Istanbul. Fidèle à la haute tradition Hilton, l'Istanbul Hilton offre à ses hôtes, un accueil aimable, une fine cuisine et des appartements gais et agréables.

Consultez votre Agence de Voyages ou adressez-vous directement à: Hilton Hotels International, c/o Comptoir International de Publicité, 3, rue de Stockholm, Paris 8e. Téléphone: LABorde 57.50, LABorde 48.59.

Conrad N. Hilton, President

Building **the Cold War**

Hilton International Hotels and Modern Architecture

Annabel Jane Wharton

The University of Chicago Press
Chicago and London

Annabel Jane Wharton is professor of art history at Duke University. Her books include *Refiguring the Post-Colonial City: Dura, Jerash, Jerusalem, and Ravenna* and *Art of Empire: Painting and Architecture of the Byzantine Periphery.*

The University of Chicago Press, Chicago 60637
The University of Chicago Press, Ltd., London

Printed in the United States of America

10 09 08 07 06 05 04 03 02 01   1 2 3 4 5
ISBN: 0-226-89419-3 (cloth)

Library of Congress Cataloging-in-Publication Data

Wharton, Annabel Jane.
Building the Cold War : Hilton International hotels and modern architecture / Annabel Jane Wharton.
p. cm.
Includes bibliographical references and index.
ISBN 0-226-89419-3 (cloth : alk. paper)
1. Architecture, Postmodern—Middle East. 2. Architecture, Postmodern—Europe. 3. Hotels—Middle East—History. 4. Hotels—Europe—History. 5. Hilton International (Firm)—History. I. Title

NA7850.M628 W48 2001
728'.5'09045—dc21   00-048409

This book is printed on acid-free paper.

Frontispiece: Istanbul Hilton, advertisement, 1956. Courtesy of Conrad N. Hilton College Archives and Library, University of Houston.

To Hilton workers

Contents

Illustrations

Take a cheap room if you have to, but always stay in the best hotel in town.

—H. JEROME WHARTON

Preface

Books, no matter how scholarly, are always biographies of their authors. My parents lived for some time in the Middle East. My father's corporation paid for me to visit them twice a year. Often we met somewhere between Pittsburgh and Teheran, in London, Rome, Istanbul, or Athens. Hiltons luxuriously accommodated these family encounters. In my research as a graduate student and then as a professor of early Christian and Byzantine architecture and painting, I spent considerable time in these same cities. I never stayed in the Hilton. Just as I disdained my fellow travelers as tourists, I disdained Hiltons as sites of institutionalized inauthenticity. To me they represented a retreat from the real experience of difference. They were also, of course, too expensive. Now I acknowledge that I am myself a tourist, as much when I work as when I travel. All historians are tourists in a past where they may visit but where they will never belong. This project has made me particularly aware of my foreignness. I am an American writing about Europe and the Middle East; I am a medievalist writing about Modernity. My observations are very much those of a historical tourist. Now, too, I allow myself to be nostalgic for the time I spent with my family in Hiltons. This study is my means of coming to terms with the ambivalence toward Hiltons that I experienced, an ambivalence that proceeded from a sense that Hiltons powerfully represented America where America did not necessarily belong.

I have contracted many more debts in pursuing this project then I ever did in my research on early Christian and Byzantine topics. And I enjoyed incurring every one of them. As a medievalist, the challenge is to revive the long dead. There are no artists, architects, producers, or consumers to interrogate. With this project I interviewed architects, designers, managers, executives, engineers, and workers. My book is dedicated to them. Their narratives provide the human core of this volume. From Seham Abdul Khalek, the telephonist in the Nile Hilton who over twenty years ago left her job as a teacher to become a waitress in the new hotel, to Kurt Strand, the former president of Hilton International, I had the satisfaction of talking with people of wit, intelligence, commitment, and passion. I acknowledge individuals whose comments contributed to specific chapters in the endnotes. Here I recognize those who helped me understand the history of Hilton International more broadly. Kenneth J. Sailor, present director of architecture and interior design, Hilton International, was my first official contact with Hilton. He provided me with the names and addresses of possible contacts and requested of David Jarvis, former chief executive of Hilton International, that he facilitate my visits to those Hilton hotels that are the subject of this study. David Jarvis and Dieter H. Huckestein, executive vice president of Hilton Hotels Incorporated, were both instrumental in arranging my reception at Hiltons both in the United States and abroad. Cathleen Baird, director of the Conrad N. Hilton Archives and Library at the University of Houston, facilitated my work in the Hilton Archives and shared her own rich historical understanding of the Hilton with me. Curt Strand, former president of Hilton International, Charles Bell, a former vice president, and Frank Bemiss, long-time director of technical services, provided valuable insights into the early history of the corporation. Charles Warner of WBTL Architects, Val Lehr of Lehr Associates Engineers, David Williams of Interior Design Associates, and David Leavitt of the Hilton's architecture department, helped me understand the design processes and the problems of architectural execution. I am also grateful to my editor at the University of Chicago Press, Susan Bielstein, and to the two exceptionally careful and insightful reviewers whom she chose to read my manuscript. I was fortunate enough to have Maura High again as my copy editor; she found every error and infelicitousness in the text, though I insisted that some be put back. I am also deeply in debt to the staff of the Duke Department of Art and Art History, particularly William Broom, who introduced me to the mysteries of PhotoShop and digital imaging, and Betty Rogers, who helped me with the final preparation of the manuscript.

A major grant from the Graham Foundation for the Advanced Studies in the Fine Arts supported the travel necessary for this study. I am also indebted to the Trent Foundation and to the Research Council of Duke University for additional travel funds. Acknowledged in various chapters are the friends and colleagues who have read and critically commented on them. Two friends, Andrew Jacobs and Ken Wissoker, have read most of the manuscript. One person, Kalman Bland, has read the whole thing. To him I am indebted for much more than his critical readings. Finally, I am grateful both to my daughters, Andrea and Nicole Epstein, for giving me time to write this book by going away to college and law school, and to this book for giving me something to do in their absence. The work also gave me time to think about my parents, Janey and Jerry Wharton, who introduced me to Hilton Hotels.

"Each of our hotels," I said, "is a 'little America.'"

—CONRAD HILTON, *BE MY GUEST*

Individual consciousness is not the architect of the ideological superstructure, but only a tenant lodging in the social edifice of ideological signs.

—V. N. VOLOSINOV, *MARXISM AND THE PHILOSOPHY OF LANGUAGE*

Introduction

Remains of the Kaiser-Wilhelm-Gedächtniskirche.

Ground. This book considers the inscription of power in the urban landscape. The city is a palimpsest: new meanings overlie old ones. Marking the surface of the city inevitably involves the erasure of one set of social relations by another, the superimposition of an altered structure of authority over an older system. Just as inevitably, the residue of prior patterns is visible in the forms that replace them. The rebuilt site constructs its signification within the web of a preexistent civic order. The debris of that which is destroyed—whether remnants remain on the site or in the memory of those who once lived it—affects new production and its consumption. An American luxury hotel built in a public parkland, over a colonial barracks, or on the graves of the dispossessed realizes a revision of spatial politics, but not the emptying of history. My book is, itself, a trace of that which seems to be lost.

Figure. In post–World War II Europe and the Middle East, the Hilton hotel was quite literally "a little America." The Hilton's success in representing America—its iconic authority—depended on the rich mix of its sources. American postwar wealth produced the upper-middle-class travelers who staged their business or pleasure activities in the Hilton. The Hilton provided this elite with a familiar environment. From American suburbs and country clubs came the Hilton's lawns, swimming pools, and tennis courts. From American upper-middle-class social practices came its cocktail lounges and rooftop supper clubs. From American popular culture came its cheeseburgers, milkshakes, and soda fountains. From American technology came its ice water tapped to individual guest rooms, its direct-line telephones, its radios, its air-conditioning, and, most fundamentally, the architectural form of the building itself.

For the economically exhausted local populations, these same features lent the Hilton a utopian aura. The Western European city welcomed Hilton as a vehicle for the revival of tourism and as proof of American confidence in its economic potential. In the East the newly decolonized state sought a Hilton hotel along with a national airline as an index of its revised status. The Hilton was a space of modern luxury and technological desire, a space that effected, with pomp and prominence, the new and powerful presence of the United States. The building dramatically marked the city with the difference between its traditional culture and desired American modernity and named that desire Hilton.

History.

Hilton was incorporated in 1946; in 1947 Hilton Hotel Corporation became the first hotel chain to be listed in the New York Stock Exchange.[1] Conrad Hilton, founder and president of the organization, had begun buying hotels in Texas in 1919. In the 1930s he established a dominant presence in the hotel business by collecting hotels built by others. Among his "great ladies" were the Stevens Hotel in Chicago, the largest hotel in the world at the time of the sale, and the Waldorf-Astoria, arguably the best hotel in the world at the time of the sale.[2] In 1954 Hilton Hotel Corporation bought the Hotel Statler Company, realizing the largest hotel merger in history. In 1949 Conrad Hilton established Hilton International as a wholly owned subsidiary. The project of the new corporation was to build new hotels abroad. Between 1949 and 1966 Hilton International constructed seventeen luxury hotels in foreign countries.[3]

The three decades after World War II, the time frame of this book, coincided with the escalation of the cold war.[4] It was an age in which the threat of an unspeakable world holocaust was continuously named in advertisements for nuclear blast shelters and practiced in school air raid drills.[5] It was an era of conservative values, McCarthyism, and segregation. It was a time of economic growth, corporate expansion, and CIA interventions abroad. It was a moment in which the real excesses of Cadillac fins contrasted with the pseudoausterities of the glass curtain wall. It was an epoch when the apparent conformity of Levittown contrasted with the apparent originality of Jackson Pollock.[6] Hilton gave American values and practices of the 1950s and 1960s a material form. A Hilton International hotel was as eloquent a sign of those times as *I Love Lucy*.[7]

The first five chapters of this work investigate the economics and politics of form as the vehicle by which Hilton International inscribed the new and alien presence of the United States in the landscapes of several of the world's most important cities. I limit my selection of sites to three capitals of former colonizers in the West—London, Berlin, and Rome—and to five principal cities in the countries that they had earlier colonized, literally or culturally—Cairo, Tel Aviv, Jerusalem, Athens, and Istanbul.[8] With the exceptions of Tel Aviv and Jerusalem, these buildings represent the first generation of hotels planned if not built in the 1950s. In his expansion outside the Western hemisphere, Conrad Hilton initially focused on Europe and the Middle East.[9]

The observer outside.

The Hilton was often the first significant Modern structure in its host city, as well as its finest hotel. A number of Hilton hotels were constructed by distinguished American architectural firms such as Pereira and Luckman or Skidmore, Owings and Merrill. Other Hiltons were designed by a local architect working with an American consulting firm. All were planned according to the Hilton program and styled as American Modern.[10] The Hiltons introduced a striking visual contrast to the vernacular fabrics of Istanbul, Cairo, and Athens, where the impact of the new architecture was amplified by the hotel's unprecedented siting and scale. Even in cities familiar with the Modern, the new Hilton often dominated the urban landscape by its height. The London Hilton was the first structure in the city higher than St. Paul's Cathedral. At the time of their construction, the Istanbul, Jerusalem, and Cairo Hiltons were each described as the highest building in their respective cities. The Hilton changed the look of the city for the observer outside.[11]

To understand the ways in which the Hiltons remapped their sites, I have sketched the histories of the great cities in which they were constructed. These political landscapes have taken lessons from urban critics like Michel de Certeau and Mike Davis, social geographers like David Harvey, and materialist sociologists like Henri Lefebvre.[12] Novelists like Orhan Pamuk and Henry James and observers like Theodore Herzl and Federico Fellini also contributed to my descriptions of urban spectacle.[13] I offer these impressions of cities as a historical tourist, an American in an alien location and in the unfamiliar territory of the nineteenth and early twentieth century. But historical topographies, however naive, enable a record of the early effects of American globalization on the urban fabric of established cities. The grand hotels displaced by the Hiltons provide one index of the shifts—both topographic and architectural—that were introduced in the second half of the twentieth century. The Pera Palas in Istanbul, Shepheard's in Cairo, the Grand Bretagne in Athens, the Savoy in London, the Adlon in Berlin, the Excelsior in Rome, and the King David in Jerusalem each functions as a control both for identifying the spatial innovations introduced by the new Hiltons and for marking shifts in urban landscape. The contrasts between the grand hotel of the past and the Hilton of the mid-twentieth century register the transformation of consumable space. The changed locations of the city's most prestigious transient address map the social and economic drift in the urban plan. The establishment of the Hilton—sometimes in conjunction with a new American embassy—modified the civic order. With the exception of Rome, the nineteenth- and early twentieth-century programs of the cities in this book were rearticulated by the introduction of the Hilton. I argue that the commercial success of these early Hiltons corresponded to the degree to which the hotel changed the look of its host city.

I do the basic empirical work on the consumption, production, and politics of Hilton space within the frame of this historical topography. European-language newspapers and Hilton workers—men and women who had served the corporation since the fifties and sixties—provided a perspective on the astonishingly enthusiastic reception of Hilton hotels in Istanbul, Cairo, Athens, Tel Aviv, and Berlin.[14] Newspapers and interviews also gave me a sense of local hostility to the Hilton project in London, Rome, and Florence. I try to document as fully as possible the arrangements made between Hilton International and the local institutions or entrepreneurs who wanted to own Hilton hotels. In every instance, negotiations engaged politics at the highest level—from Gamal Abdel Nasser to the London County Council. In Rome, the Hilton was at the center of a scandal that caused a political crisis. The differences in the Hiltons and their status, East (here the Middle East) and West (Western Europe), proceed from the terms of the corporation's contract; the contractual base determined the hotel's quality, topography, and social location. The best Hiltons were in the East.

The observer within.

Those best Hiltons were marked by their brilliant transparency. The program of the space was immediately legible to those who were paying for it. The principal route from entrance to registration to elevator to room to balcony was clear. Signage was unnecessary. Diversions—shops, restaurants, bars, the swimming pool—were distinctly diversions, however attractive. Not only were the patterns of guest circulation unambiguous, but the anatomy of the building was exposed. Vertical piers of the superstructure were displayed. Typically, posts took the form of box-framed uprights; they are not all encased in continuous walls or costumed as columns or arches. The horizontals were treated as the slabs that they were. Floor coverings did not draw attention to themselves; carpets tended to be earth-toned and monochromatic. Also avoided along the main circulation route were ornamental ceiling treatments—moldings, coffers, trompe l'oeil vaulted forms—which might have suggested a plasticity and depth not intrinsic to construction methods. Similarly, walls were presented as arbitrary dividers. Polished marble, tile, neutral paint described a series of logical surfaces. Walls worked as depthless ground. Nothing architectural drew the observer's attention away from the patrons for whom the building was a backdrop.

Certainly, the Modern space of the Hilton International hotel was carefully coded as foreign by its decoration. Like the great hotels of the colonial era in the Middle East, the postcolonial Hiltons embodied the cultural values of home veiled with references to the local. Interior design bore the burden of representing the host site. In Berlin, Athens, and Tel Aviv—cities associated with the West and its culture—works by well-known local artists were commissioned and prominently displayed. In Cairo and Istanbul ancient artifacts and indigenous crafts were deployed to provide Hilton interiors with their regional essence. These crafts might subsequently also be retailed in the hotel's mini-mall, itself a Hilton innovation.[15] The use of local artistic and craft production in the hotel's decoration was intended to provide guests with the pleasure of an effortless experience of the alien. Indigenous decorative motifs were tokens that allowed consumers to distinguish among the Hiltons that they encountered. The limited, ornamental role of the local subordinated it within a hierarchy of an American economy of signs. The buildings themselves—their forms, technologies, and landscaping—were trenchantly American.

Of all the ingredients that contributed to the Hilton's Modernity, the preeminent medium of the building's transparency was plate glass. Glass was the essential means of the building's effacement as well as its most notable sign. Glass allowed the building to be literally seen through. Glass was not only the principal source of the hotel's look, but it was also an essential contributor to its elevated status as high-tech spectacle. The vast expanse of plate glass was the newly available product of multiple modern technologies—not only in glass manufacture and transportation, but also in the heating and cooling mechanisms that were necessary to compensate for the thermal inefficiencies of the medium. Glass was economically profligate.[16] More than the polished neutrality of the hotel's marble walls and floors, the unmarked and unmarkable surface of glass was an extravagance. The traditional heavy, gilt frame of an oil painting was replaced in Modernity with the unobtrusive strip frame or framelessness. The edge defers to the ground without pretence of participation. So the Hilton marks the shift from an architecture of sumptuous involvement to an architecture of refined circumscription. Glass was the ultimate material index of the Hilton's utopian technology.

Glass dematerialized the building; simultaneously, glass supplemented the substance of the bodies framed by the building. The transparency of the structure fixed the opacity of the body within. The glass walls of the hotel prescribed a double visibility—the viewing subject was simultaneously the viewed object. Within the hotel the audience was the entertainment. No truly private space was produced. Even the guest room was like every other and had a balcony dictating the anticipated appearance of the occupant. The grand hotel had always functioned as a place to be seen. But in the nineteenth and early twentieth centuries, characters competed with the architecture for attention, just as they did in Nathaniel Hawthorn's novels. Patrons in these hotels were also only seen by one another.[17] In contrast, the structure of the Hilton gave visual cues of a sumptuous setting without itself inviting the look of the observer. Glass also implied, if it did not actuate, an anonymous audience outside the elite domain of the hotel, recognizing without sharing the aura of those within its diaphanous bounds. Guests were meant to be conspicuous. The Hilton transformed the anxiety of being observed into a pleasure.

The Hilton was a machine for viewing. In the foreground that it framed was the body of the guest; in the background was the immediate source of the patron's status, the foreign panorama. The extended vista opened through the plate glass windows, offering visual control of an alien urban landscape from an entirely secure site of observation. The Hilton provided a haven from exotic difference. In a popular article revealingly titled "The View from a Tall Glass Oasis: The Subliminal Pleasures of Hilton Hotels," which appeared in *Vogue* in 1965, George Bradshaw smugly described the Hilton as a Western oasis in the East:

> [T]he network of Hiltons acts as a balm, a salve, a glass of Alka-Seltzer. . . . . One morning in Istanbul I was having breakfast in a glass-walled room looking out over the Bosporus. At a table nearby was an American businessman. . . . He peered through his glasses at his native [i.e., traditional American] breakfast: fresh orange juice, wheat cakes and maple syrup, and plenty of good hot

> coffee. . . . At that very instant, a few miles away in the Blue Mosque, there were going up calls to heaven which might well have appalled his soul. But did he notice them? Not he. He felt safe in his oasis.[18]

1. Istanbul Hilton, advertisement, 1956. Courtesy of Conrad N. Hilton College Archives and Library, University of Houston.

This quote manifests the arrogance of conventional travel writing. The author ensures his own authority as sophisticated traveler through hyperbolic ridicule of his fellow touristic businessman. A muezzin's call to prayer from the Sultan Ahmet Camii could never have been heard from the hotel. But more to the point, the passage also conveys the sense of cultural insulation staged by the hotel. Bradshaw provides a textual equivalent of an advertisement for the Istanbul Hilton published in 1956 (fig. 1). The sleek white hotel slices into the picture plane. The mysterious Blue Mosque, icon of the exotic East, floats behind the hotel as its backdrop. American Modernity dominates an alien territory. As I argue in the first chapter, this advertisement promises the visual control of the unfamiliar from a familiar location. Advertisements marketed the architecture of the hotel; they also marketed the imaginary view from the hotel. The vista was always, its seems, a little out of focus. Enough is seen to know that the building dominates the landscape. And enough is glimpsed to know what might be seen. This advertisement sells entitlement; it suggests how the landscape was meant to work for the observer within.[19]

Architecture, the market, and government.

Hilton hotels aestheticized technological efficiency. Describing Hilton's place in the development of an American aesthetic of efficiency is the project of my final chapter. American hotels from the nineteenth through the mid-twentieth centuries map the progressive commoditization of American space. I have used the uncanny term "commoditization" to identify the force of the entrepreneurial economy in shaping space.[20] From Benjamin Latrobe's plan for a hotel in Richmond at the end of the eighteenth century to the Beverly Hilton in 1956, American hotels were distinguished from their European counterparts by the advanced engineering of their building technology and service equipment. American hotels introduced novelties from self-operated elevators to servidors.[21] These innovations were both the product and the promoter of an expanded consumer market. Efficiency became a significant object of desire between the World Wars. After World War II, efficiency was promoted to the level of Art. This was the space of aestheticized efficiency that Hilton International exported to Europe and the Middle East twenty years before McDonald's thought about franchising fast food abroad.[22] The final chapter further proposes that leisure migration, like hotel space, was informed by the same commodity values. The urban view was restructured for sale to an ever increasing number of tourists as panoramic spectacle. Hiltons, moreover, did not package these views of the Bosphorus, the pyramids, and the Acropolis, but produced them.

Hilton's Modernity was the product of the dazzling standardization of the commodity that radically changed American society from the end of the forties through the fifties. Hilton contributed to that Modernity by giving it an elite form. Like abstract expressionism, Hilton hotels refined the elementary and the efficient and sold it to American and foreign elites. The local owners insisted on Modernity, sometimes in opposition to Hilton executives and designers, who desired more vernacular forms. Hilton made less more costly than more. Making the Modern abroad was, after all, not so easy. Indeed, the effort required in the realization of a monumental Modernity where none had previously existed was heroic. Basic building materials like concrete and steel were difficult to obtain in Europe after World War II; they were completely lacking in the Middle East. The clarity and transparency of the building, its efficient plan, and manifest structure gave eloquent spatial utterance to the supple forms of American entrepreneurial expansion.

This representation of America was not paid for by Hilton. Hilton International did not own hotels abroad as Hilton Hotels Corporation did at home. Hilton did not provide the monies for the construction of its foreign hotels. Investment capital came from local institutions (pension funds, joint stock companies, magnates). Moreover, foreign legislatures were persuaded to pass acts allocating prime public property, usually park land, for the hotel's site. If hard currency was wanting, it was generally not the Hilton Corporation that provided it. Rather, it came, at least on occasion, through the U.S. government on the authority of the Economic Cooperation Administration (ECA) from Marshall Plan funds. The Marshall Plan was announced in 1947 by George Marshall, the United States secretary of state. The plan, intended to promote political stability in Europe, was prompted by a growing fear of Soviet expansion.[23] Although used primarily for agricultural and industrial stabilization in its early years and later for military development, Marshall Plan funds have been linked to the cultural politics of the post–World War II era—particularly the sponsorship abroad of abstract-expressionist exhibitions and Hollywood films.[24] Perhaps less familiar are the ways in which development funds were also used for the promotion of certain architectural forms. The political role of architecture was, nevertheless, recognized at the time as advancing American interests abroad. An anonymous article published in *Arts and Architecture* in 1953 refers to American buildings abroad as the "architectural calling cards" of the U.S. government.

> The United States Government is making modern American architecture one of its most convincing demonstrations of the vitality of American culture. The credit for this accomplishment goes to FBO—the State Department's Foreign Buildings Operations program—directed by Leland W. Ding, and to the outstanding American architects chosen to represent America abroad. . . . Financing of the program was met largely by utilization of foreign currency credits. The cost of the FBO's program is unusually low. The plan devised by Frederick Larkin, Leland King's predecessor in the Department of State and by King himself, allowed foreign governments to pay for buildings and sites and thus reduce their debts to the United States (from Lend-Lease, Surplus Property and Marshall Plan). This method of financing our buildings enables our allies to discharge some of their obligations without touching their limited hard-currency reserves. It also enables the State Department to acquire valuable property abroad, and it allows the Foreign Service to reduce its office rentals and quarters allowances to Foreign Service personnel. Of the 1946 appropriation of $110 million, 97% has been met by our allies. . . . 3% was met by new dollar appropriations. FBO is responsible for buildings in 272 cities in 72 countries. . . . As Henry-Russel Hitchcock has said, "By the middle of the twentieth century American architecture has come to occupy a position of special prominence in the world."[25]

That Marshall Plan funds were also used to support American corporate interests abroad is nearly forgotten. Also almost unrecognized are the international effects of American corporate building programs.

Extravagant galas marked the openings of the new Hiltons: Pan American clippers were chartered for the importation of American notables—movie stars, columnists, politicians, government officials, and business figures—to celebrate the occasion with their counterparts among the local elites. These lavish pageants displayed as spectacle the convergence of architecture, politics, the media, and international enterprise that constituted Hilton. They were moments of excess that collapsed politics into pleasure.

Politics.

That Hilton International hotels were political is not my hypothesis, but Conrad Hilton's claim. Hilton explicitly represented his international hotels as ideological, in the popular sense of ideology as propaganda.[26] He repeatedly reported that Hilton International Hotels were constructed not only to produce a profit, but also to make a political impact on host countries.[27] In his autobiography he wrote: "Let me say right here, that we operate hotels abroad for the same reason we operate them in this country—to make money for our stockholders. . . . However, we feel that if we really believe in what we are all saying about liberty, about Communism, about happiness, that we, as a nation, must exercise our great strength and power for good against evil. If we really believe this, it is up to each of us, our organizations and our industries, to contribute to this objective with all the resources at our command."[28] Or again: "[A]n integral part of my dream was to show the countries most exposed to Communism the other side of the coin—the fruits of the free world."[29] In the corporation's in-house publications for all employees, Conrad Hilton made similar assertions: "We mean these hotels as a challenge—not to the peoples who have so cordially welcomed us into their midst—but to the way of life preached by the Communist world. Each hotel spells out friendship between nations, which is an alien word to those who try to reduce friends to slaves. To help fight that kind of thinking and that kind of living we are setting up our hotels of Hilton International Across The World."[30] And most explicitly:

> Now, why is Hilton International building hotels in all these key spots around the world? . . . Because there is a job to be done there. And I will tell you frankly, satellites and H-bombs will not get that job done. I do not disparage the West's armament program; we must keep our defense superior to the Communist world. I insist, however, that it is a defense and will not work as an offensive to destroy Communism across the world. . . . I say that . . . a far higher dividend is likely to follow from industrial assistance in Asia, Africa and the Middle East, than from military aid. . . . There you have the reason why, in Istanbul and Baghdad, we are pushing close to the Iron Curtain. We are in Cairo because it is the center of the Moslem world and holds the key to Africa and the Middle East. . . . We are in Berlin because Germany holds the key to the containment of Europe.[31]

Conrad Hilton's anticommunism was not of the American-chauvinist variety. In the confidential correspondence between Hilton and the executives commissioned to negotiate abroad, there is a complete absence of that which might be expected in the politically incorrect 1950s and 1960s—condescension, or worse, toward the Other. Hilton's lack of prejudice is also suggested in his corporate structure, which included Jews among the top executives of Hilton International. Jews were as uncommon in corporate America in the 1950s and early 60s as they were in universities.[32] Though not jingoistic, Hilton's patriotism expressed his deep commitment to two American habits: religiousness and capitalism. Hilton's personal investment in religion was registered in his autobiography. It was also recorded in his will. Hilton bequeathed the bulk of his holdings in Hilton Corporation to a foundation supporting Roman Catholic nuns.[33]

Hilton's belief that religious faith was critical in the battle against communism was also, quite literally, publicized. In 1956, an article in the trade magazine *Sales Management: The Magazine of Marketing*, noted: "The recent rise of Hilton International has coincided with Conrad Hilton's personal fight against Communism. One of his speeches, 'Blueprint for Freedom,' received a Freedom Foundation award. A prayer which climaxed another [speech] was reproduced in several national magazines and on the air, and 500,000 reprints of it were distributed."[34] Indeed, Conrad Hilton regularly substituted prayers for advertisements. At Christmas time, Hilton offered an inspirational religious message accompanied only by the Hilton logo. For example, in 1958 there appeared in *Life* a full-page Hilton "advertisement" showing a traditional shepherd with his sheep looking with some surprise toward a five-pointed star in the heavens (fig. 2). The painting of the shepherd and his small flock is overlaid with a ghostly columnar text cataloging the catastrophes that occurred that year between January and October: "Violent Peru quake kills 21. . . bacteria kills 16 . . . Russ launch 1½ ton sputnik . . . U.S. ships rush toward Lebanon . . . Rome stirred by communist riot . . . Russ warns U.S. of destruction . . . Jewish synagogue dynamited." In bolder type below is a prayer beginning, "Be not afraid."

Conrad Hilton was a passionate Catholic. He also had a respect for other religions, working closely with Jews and Muslims. He abominated atheists and demonized communists. Establishing his intention to construct hotels as a political intervention is no problem. Conrad Hilton believed his hotels made a significant contribution to America's struggle against communism in the cold war. This project suggests how right he was.

Making the case for Conrad Hilton's personal political intent is easy. Demonstrating how Hilton hotels functioned as the materialization of politics is both more significant and more difficult. In the core chapters of this book, I narrate the histories of specific sites in order to argue that the politics of Hilton International hotels, as well as their status and profitability, were indistinguishable from their Modernity. The early success of Hilton International can be attributed to a remarkably effective formula of corporate action. This formula was complex, involving the style and decoration of buildings as well as a distinctive set of business practices. The Modernism of Hilton hotels, their privileged sites, and their depthless incorporation of the exotic local embodied the company's remarkable political and commercial enterprise. The effectiveness of Hilton's architecture and the efficiency of the company's political and corporate performance produced an American spectacle abroad.

The Modernity of the Hiltons, though demanded by local owners, was a physical expression of an American assurance in the truth, righteousness, and stability of its economic and moral values at the beginning of the cold war. The erosion of this confidence in the continuing encounter with the

2. Hilton Prayer, advertisement, 1958. Courtesy of Conrad N. Hilton College Archives and Library, University of Houston.

complexities of global power is one piece of the postmodernity alluded to in the epilogue. Just as the changed form of the hotel marked the shift from colonial to postcolonial, so the hotel is an equally sensitive indicator of the cultural shift from the modern to the postmodern. After all, the Bonaventura stands at the core of Fred Jameson's authoritative definition of postmodernity.[35] As an epilogue, I remark on the postmodern remodelings of the Hiltons in relation to changes in the hotels' social meaning. Hilton International is now owned by Ladbrokes, a British corporation best known for its gambling interests. Hilton International has become one among many contemporary worldwide hotel chains serving a broader, less elite traveling public. With the end of the cold war, Hiltons have lost their initial ideological referent at the same time that they have been stripped of their Modernity. Hiltons no longer encode vision and remake urban landscapes.

I hope that this book provides its readers, as it did its author, with a newly critical grip on the space they occupy away from home. A part of that understanding depends on recognizing the ideological traits of both built space and the gaze that it engineers. Much interesting work has been done on the function of texts and images in the construction of Otherness and ideology.[36] Work has just begun on the similar work of architecture. This study considers the contribution made by architecture and by the view that it framed to American identity and self-representation in post–World War II Europe and the Middle East. It thereby participates in the broader acknowledgment of the materiality of ideology. Politics are embodied in the built environment just as they are in texts and movies, but architecture, like legislative actions, continue its effects when you aren't looking. This assessment of early Hilton International hotels documents the contribution that architectural representations of the West make to the construction of its continuing economic and cultural dominance.

Pera Palas Hotel, Istanbul (detail).

The night is yellow and trickles with gold. All the marble statuary of all the palaces of Byzantium is there, as well as all the treasures of sultans and all the gems of the Seraglios! A solid gold Venus and a Ceres stand at the head of the Phanal, the stairway of Justinian's palace, leading to the water. Lying in the sand at the promontory of the Seraglio are bronze cannons decorated in gold and big solid gold rings like those that they—the divine, thrilling odalisques—used to wear around their naked ankles and arms like serpents. . . . But enough of this wretched yellow. . . . I want Stamboul to sit upon her Golden Horn all white, as raw as chalk, and I want light to screech on the surface of domes which swell the heap of milky cubes, and minarets should thrust upward, and the sky must be blue. Under the bright light, I want a city all white.

—LE CORBUSIER, *JOURNEY TO THE EAST*

On the last day when the waters [of the Bosphorus] suddenly recede, among the American transatlantics gone to ground and Ionic columns covered with seaweed, there will be Celtic and Ligurian skeletons open-mouthed in their supplication to gods whose identities are no longer known . . . [and] mussel-encrusted Byzantine treasures, forks and knives made of silver and tin, thousand-year-old barrels of wine, soda-pop bottles, carcasses of point-prowed galleys.

—ORHAN PAMUK, *THE BLACK BOOK*

1 Gaze to the East: Istanbul

The city. The advertisement designed to promote the new Istanbul Hilton shortly after its opening in 1955 features a wash drawing by J. Hammer (see frontispiece and fig. 1). It depicts in dramatic perspective the brilliant white east façade of the hotel with its sunlit terraces and reflecting pool in the foreground. From the dark mists of the backdrop emerges the Sultan Ahmet Camii, the Blue Mosque. The rationality of the Hilton's neat rectilinearity contrasts with the brooding mass of the mosque's multiple domes. The picture does not pretend to a photographic realism. The guest did not see the Sultan Ahmet Camii from the hotel's terrace. Rather, the advertisement promised the familiar space of American modernity as the secure vantage point from which to view the exotic domain of the East.

For the advertisement's American and Western European audiences, the forbidding mosque evokes the old city in which it is found—Byzantium, Constantinople, Istanbul. That old city occupies a peninsula formed by the Sea of Marmara to the south and the Golden Horn and the Bosphorus to the north and east (fig. 3). Its seven hills are swollen by massive, domed monuments that celebrated the political ascendancy of the city's successive imperial patrons.[1] Hagia Sophia, Holy Wisdom, Justinian's cathedral and the sacred center of the Byzantine Empire, still dominates the skyline from the first hill. Further asserting the ancient prominence of the eastern tip of the peninsula is Topkapi Palace, the successor of the Great Palace of the Byzantine emperors, and the mosque of Sultan Ahmet I, the Blue Mosque, Hagia Sophia's magnificent pendant. On the fourth hill, Fatih Camii, the foundation of Mehmet the Conqueror, replaced Constantine's burial church, the Holy Apostles, shortly after the Ottomans' occupation of the city in 1453. Hagia Sophia was the archetype of the Conqueror's great structure, whose architect, it is said, had his hands cut off for making it a lower height than its model.[2] Mahmut Pasha Camii, built a few years later by the Conqueror's grand vizier, a converted Byzantine aristocrat, and the later, seventeenth-century Nuruosmaniye Camii, share the second hill. The great Süleymaniye Mosque, built by Süleyman the Magnificent in the mid-sixteenth century, stands before the third hill. However Istanbul is first seen, it is best remembered as a distant view, approached across the Bosphorus. Le Corbusier, one of the masters of Modern architecture, describes the scene:

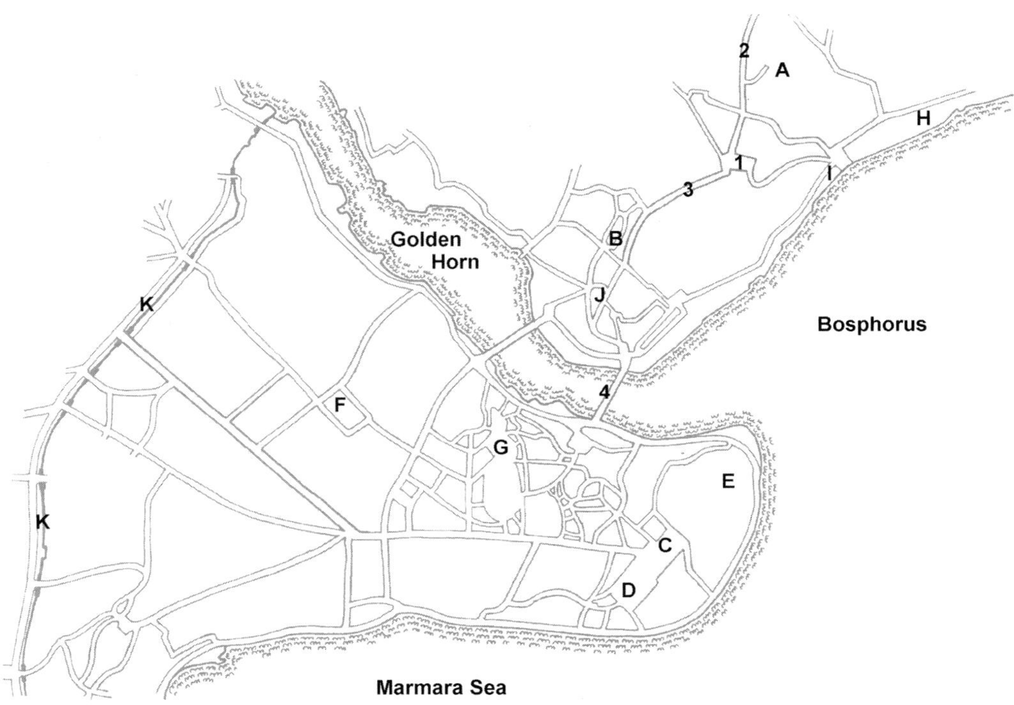

3. Sketch plan of Istanbul, by author: *A*, Istanbul Hilton; *B*, Pera Palas; *C*, Hagia Sophia; *D*, Sultan Ahmet Camii, the Blue Mosque; *E*, Topkapi Palace; *F*, Fatih Camii, site of the Holy Apostles; *G*, Süleymaniye Mosque; *H*, Dolmabahçe Palace; *I*, Dolmabahçe Camii; *J*, Galata Tower; *K*, Land Walls; *1*, Taksim Square; *2*, Cumhuriyet Caddesi; *3*, Istiklal Caddesi; *4*, Galata Bridge.

> Sails were playing with the wind ahead of us and became the harbingers of the apparition that led us to the point where Asia, in an unforgettable spectacle, abruptly withdraws from Europe. The light was behind Stamboul, giving it a monolithic appearance. . . . Beyond the prow the rooftops of the Seraglio rose in tiers between the cypresses and the sycamores—a palace of poetry, a creation so exquisite that it cannot be dreamed of twice. The mist of light upon the sea was dissolving into this great back lighting that extended as far as Mihrimah outlined against a sky annihilated with brightness. I don't believe I shall ever again see such *Unity*![3]

The old city of the peninsula was shaped by the eastern empires of the Byzantines and Ottomans. It was an object of Western desire, though only the Venetian-led crusaders, from 1204 to 1261, managed actually to occupy the city. In the nineteenth and early twentieth centuries, the Ottoman

Empire seemed to many to invite colonization. Just after the turn of the century, John Stoddard envisioned Istanbul as a beautiful hostage enslaved by the oriental infidel:

> The Turk, by nature and religion, belongs not to Europe, but to Asia; and when sufficient unanimity is found among the jealous European nations to insure united action, to Asia will the Sultan and his evil government depart. Such thoughts recurred to me with special force, as, on a recent visit to the Bosphorus, I saw again the form of fair Stamboul, stretched out in indolent repose. . . . For, whether it be Russia, Austria, Germany, England or a joint protectorate of nations, some Christian power must ere long occupy this site, and lift it to the rank designed for it by destiny,—that of the immortal Queen of the East, throned on the Eden of the world, and holding as a scepter in her hand the Golden Horn.[4]

Turkey avoided military occupation. The West made do with making a part of the city—the suburbs of Galata and Pera on the north shore of the Golden Horn—in their own image. From the end of the tenth century the Byzantines had given trading concessions and parcels of land to Genoa, Venice, Pisa, and Amalfi. The privileges and wealth of the Latins were sources of resentment among Byzantine Greeks. In a horrific massacre of the Latin population of Constantinople in 1182, they vented their frustration with the growing economic power of the Italians without preventing its escalation. Galata became a virtually independent, walled Genoese city. Established during the Byzantine Empire, the Europeanness of the north shore of the Golden Horn, including Galata and Pera, further up the hill, was sanctioned and extended by the Ottomans.[5] By the nineteenth century, not only the Europeans but also the Turkish elites preferred to dwell on the northern side of the Gold Horn. In 1853, Dolmabahçe Palace in a suburb north of Galata superseded Topkapi Palace as the imperial residence. Resort-like villas in filigree rococo and *horror vacui* Victorian settled in gardens on the banks of the Bosphorus. By the turn of the century, Pera's vineyards and orchards had been transformed into the most fashionable shopping district in the city. Its architecture, like its merchandise, was produced by Europeans. Edwin de Leon, a late-nineteenth-century traveler, characterized the built environment: "The Grande Rue of Pera . . . is now . . . a really fine street. For about two miles, which is traversed by a tramway, it is a street which would be creditable to any European town; and its club-houses, shops, hotels, and private residences, are suggestive of Paris."[6] He also described its produce: "Pass from the bridge into Galata, and your disenchantment is complete. . . . From 'The East,' of our early memories and dreams . . . into the mean traffic of Maltese and Sicilian and nondescript hucksters of European products, such as bacon, sausages, brandies, and other articles which stink in the nostrils of the faithful."[7]

The Sixth District of the city, a district which included Pera, Galata, and Tophane, was the site of wealth and status. A report of 1857 by the Commission for the Order of the City identifies this district as the principle object of urban innovation: "Since to begin all things in the above-mentioned districts [the thirteen districts excluding Galata] would be sophistry and unworthy, and since the Sixth District contains much valuable real estate and many fine buildings, and since the majority of those owning property or residing there have seen such things in other countries and understand their value, the reform program will be inaugurated in the Sixth District."[8] The first streetcar lines and the newest harbor facilities were constructed in Pera and Galata. Here were the embassies of the Western powers and the mansions of European commercial magnates. By the turn of the century, Pera was the modern Istanbul; the old city remained largely medieval in its facilities and its form.[9]

The contrast between the modern and the antique represented in Hilton's advertisement perpetuated a nineteenth-century European understanding of Istanbul into the mid-twentieth. For Robert Hichens, a turn-of-the-century traveler, Istanbul was a city with two natures:

> One was to me hateful—Pera, with Galata touching it. The other was not to be understood by me . . . —Stamboul. . . . Pera is a mongrel city . . . a city of tall, discolored houses not unlike the houses of Naples; of embassies and churches; of glaring shops and cafés glittering with plate-glass, through which crafty, impudent eyes are forever staring out upon the passers-by; of noisy, unattractive hotels and wizened gardens. . . . Stamboul is a city of wood and of marble, of dusty, frail houses that look as if they had been run up in a night and might tumble to pieces at any moment, and of magnificent mosques, centuries old, solid, huge, superb, great monuments of the sultans. . . . Old Stamboul wraps itself in a black veil and withdraws where you may not follow.[10]

For Hichens, Pera was unsuccessfully European. Its Western façades only served to mask an ominous oriental gaze. Stamboul, as an enigmatic, veiled woman, was unknowably Other. Its beauty was disturbingly potential and not possessable.[11] The Hilton advertisement in figure 1 suggests that the darkness of the old city described by Hichens in the nineteenth century was still part of the city's attraction in the mid-twentieth.

Pera was the principal site of hotels. An imperial order of 1865 identified Pera, Büyükdere, Üsküdar, and Prinkipo of the Princes' Islands as the sections of the city in which hotels for foreigners might be built.[12] Among the hotels constructed in the late nineteenth century in response to the opening of the Orient Express railway line from Paris to Aleppo was the famous Pera Palas (figs. 4 and 5). Here Agatha Christie reportedly worked on her *Murder on the Orient Express*, and here too she mysteriously disappeared for eleven days, an event celebrated in the film *Agatha*, with Dustin Hoffman and Vanessa Redgrave.[13] In 1998 the Pera Palas was the setting of a fine off-Broadway play.[14] The doors of its rooms are marked with plaques bearing the name of its most distinguished inhabitant, mostly dispossessed royalty: "Reza Pahlevi, Former Shah of Iran," "Edward VIII, Former King of England," "Pierre, Former King of Serbia." The site of the Pera Palas, as is the case with all hotels, was integral to its status. It was located two blocks west of the lower end of Istiklal Cadessi, the old Grande Rue de Pera, *the* shopping street of Istanbul, in the neighborhood of Western embassies. Around the corner was the U.S. Consulate, formerly the Palazzo Corpi, our country's first diplomatic property in Europe. To the southwest, the city dropped away, providing the Pera Palas with an exceptional view of the Golden Horn and of the old city beyond.

The Pera Palas was not, however, designed to frame the spectacle that its site provided. It was a massive block with a generic neo-Renaissance wrapping on the outside and a remarkable multistoried oriental court on the interior (fig. 6). This was a space of sumptuous oriental carpets, luxurious palms, and elaborate furnishings. The lowest level of the exotic core was defined by piers of striped green and beige faux marble supporting segmental arches of complexly profiled voussoirs of alternating pink and cream. The upper reaches of the court were intricately wooden: an elaborate

4. Istanbul, Pera Palas Hotel, exterior view. Photo by author.

5. Istanbul, Pera Palas Hotel, main entrance, photographed probably in the 1920s. Photo courtesy of Pera Palace Archive, Istanbul.

mashrabiyyah-enclosed gallery below massive beams separating six domes that vaulted the interior space. This great hall was the focus of the structure. On the ground floor the court opened to the entrance of the building through a low loggia with white marble balustrades and verde antico columns. To the back was the sumptuous lounge and writing room with a view of the street life of Meşrutiyet Cadessi; to the right a bar and tea room opening in the summer to a marble terrace above the same busy boulevard. To the left was a three-person lift and monumental staircase to the guest rooms. The most privileged of the guest rooms opened into the gallery that surrounded the central oriental court. Reception was a tiny desk located down three steps in the corner of the entrance hall.

The Pera Palas was characteristic of the remarkable development of the new Istanbul in the later nineteenth century and early years of the twentieth. The hotel was built in 1892 and managed by a European travel firm, the Compagnie Internationale des Wagon-lits et des Grands Expresses Européens.[15] Designed by the French architect Alexander Vallaury, it represented the eclecticism of Western European practice imported to the continent's eastern edge. Though for the most part the new buildings of Istanbul took some form of the neoclassical, eclecticism allowed experiments with more exotic local motifs. In his Office of Public Debt Administration of 1899, Vallaury ironically chose neo-Turkish details for a structure "that symbolized the absolute economic control wielded by Western powers over

6. Istanbul, Pera Palas Hotel, interior of the central oriental hall. Photo courtesy of Pera Palace Archive, Istanbul.

7. Istanbul, Sirkeci Train Station, 1889. Photo by author.

the Ottoman Empire."[16] The same thing might be said of the façade of the Sirkeci Train Station of 1889 (fig. 7). A German architect named Jachmund or Jasmund provided the conventional symmetry of the beaux arts plan of this terminus of the Oriental Express with a richly ornamental Moorish envelope.[17] Only the technology and craft of these new buildings were local; their architects were European and their expression of the oriental was European. The Western military occupation of Turkey may have been expected, but it was never realized. Colonization remained economic and cultural. European dominance was articulated in the look of Istanbul's prestigious neighborhoods as well as by their amenities. When new construction in Istanbul began again after the World Wars, the city's buildings similarly attested to a new American hegemony.

The Istanbul Hilton.

In April 1951 Hilton International and the Turkish government announced their agreement to construct a new hotel in Istanbul.[18] The Istanbul Hilton was inaugurated with a gala celebration a little over four years later, in June 1955 (figs. 8, 9, and 10).[19] The building received international coverage in architectural trade journals before and after its official opening.[20] Gordon Bunshaft, a principal of Skidmore, Owings and Merrill (SOM) and an acknowledged second-generation Modern master, worked on the design in conjunction with the distinguished Turkish architect Sedad H. Eldem.[21] In his memoirs, Nathaniel Owings of SOM recalled the collaboration:

8. Istanbul, Istanbul Hilton, view from the northeast. Photo by author.

9. Istanbul, Istanbul Hilton, view from the southeast at night, June 1955. Photo courtesy of Conrad N. Hilton College Archives and Library, University of Houston.

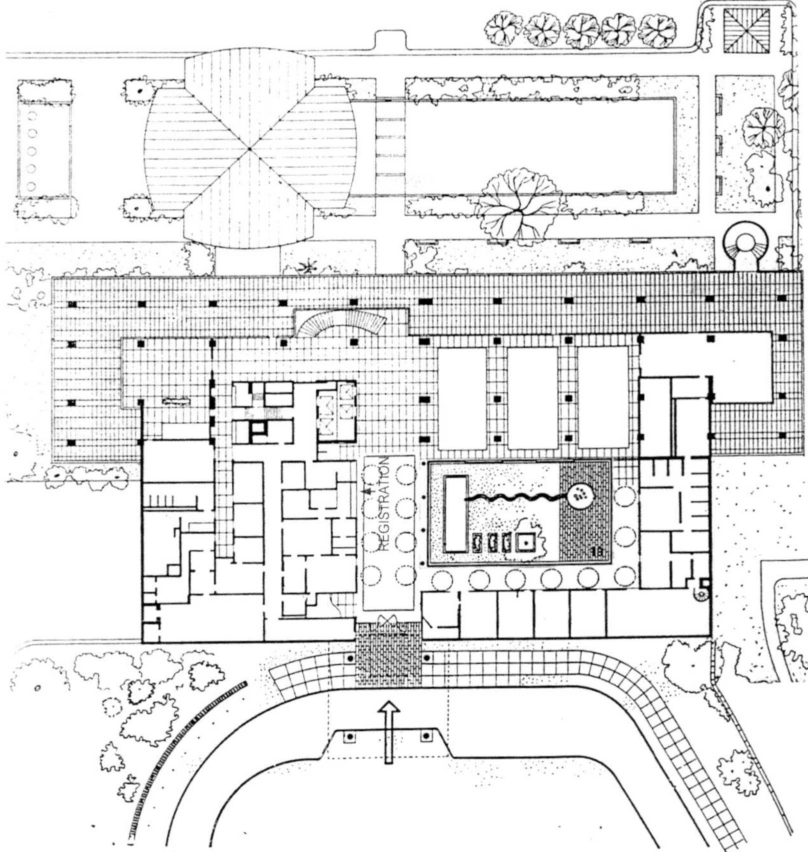

10. Istanbul, Istanbul Hilton, plan of the lobby level. Modified from "Hotel in Istanbul," *Architectural Review* 118 (November 1955).

> [L]ike a meteor in the sky came an Arabian Nights' job: the Istanbul Hilton Hotel on a promontory overlooking the Dardanelles in the magic city of Istanbul. With the Santa Sophia and the Bosphorus for inspiration, we had to do a great building. The result is a salubrious blend of strong Turkish architectural motifs and American plumbing and heating. Sedad Eldem, our associate, a resident of Istanbul, master of five languages, proved that the legendary toughness of the Turks extended to the character and fiber of their architects. Sedad Eldem is famous for having defeated Bunshaft on his own ground, maintaining the supremacy of rich, lush, romantic Turkish architecture over Bun's more classic international predilections. The resulting building is considered by both Sedad and Gordon as a satisfactory compromise between two worlds of culture.[22]

An alternative history is proposed by two Turkish practitioners. Ali Kolsal studied in Turkey with Eldem before going to the School of Architecture at Columbia University and working for a number of years at the New York architectural office of Hilton International.[23] Yavuz Erdem, who received his engineering degree from the Technical University in Istanbul, has worked on the Istanbul Hilton since 1954.[24] Both observe that Bunshaft's Modernity was not only left intact, but that subsequently it deeply affected both Eldem's practice and all Turkish architectural performance more broadly. The building corroborates their version of the narrative.

The Istanbul Hilton was a heroically scaled white slab constructed of reinforced concrete, scaled by a regular grid of balconies and lifted off the ground by slender white *pilotis*, or piers.[25] The mass and purity of its abstract exterior made it a remarkably compelling structure. The Modernity of the

Hilton resided in the lucid rationality of its form. Like a Sol Lewitt sculpture, the building embodied an ideal of a pure geometry generated by multiplying clearly articulated, identical blocks. Descriptions of the Istanbul Hilton tend to emphasize its similarities to the buildings of Le Corbusier. "The somewhat Corbusian character of SOM's work in these early years of the 50's is further evident in the Istanbul Hilton Hotel in Turkey, designed in 1951 and opened in 1955; for that is raised on concrete *pilotis*, faced with box-like balconies, and capped with shaped equipment housings and a domed nightclub."[26] The Istanbul Hilton, in any case, initiated the whitening of Istanbul that Le Corbusier desired.

The new Hilton was a monumental structure enshrined as an elite art object by its exceptional site. The hotel was prestigiously located, positioned at the edge of the wealthiest part of Istanbul, high above Galata. It was ten minutes' walk from Taksim Square, the commercial hub of Istanbul in the 1950s. The centrality of Taksim Square, the upper terminus of Istiklal Cadessi, the old Grande Rue de Pera, indicated the progressive migration of capital toward the city's northern periphery. This development has continued through the second half of the century; the Hilton is now in the midst of Istanbul's business district. Further, the hotel was set in a natural preserve in the midst of the dense urban fabric: it was strikingly situated in the upper quadrant of Democracy Park, which fell away unimpeded from Cumhuriyet Cadessi, the main boulevard running north from Taksim Square, down a steep slope to the edge of the Bosphorus (fig. 11). This site—reportedly occupied previously by an old Armenian cemetery—allowed the powerful Modernity of the hotel to be dramatically displayed to the outsider. The site also allowed the spectacle of the city to be dramatically displayed to the insider.

The idyllic isolation of the Hilton in the midst of the city was announced by its Modernist entrance from Cumhuriyet Cadessi. Like a triumphal arch marking admission to the privileged space of an imperial forum, the access drive opened through a sleek structure of marble and glass (fig. 12). The flat roof of this portal-pavilion with its square-profile, white marble cornice was suspended between the parallel glass-walled offices occupied by companies like Pan American Airlines and American Express. Within the enclosure was a driveway with Olmsted rhythms amid meticulously kept country-club lawns (fig. 13). Lawns were popularized by the English and elevated to obsession by middle-class Americans.[27] Introduced in the Middle East with colonialization, expanses of grass in the Mediterranean basin remain fundamentally unnatural. Even more alien in this urban milieu were the swimming pool and tennis courts just visible through screens of shrubbery. Suburban United States was thus imported to the core of urban Istanbul. The pool particularly, with its colorful cabanas and interesting bodies, became a source of pleasure not only for those who swam, but also for those who looked. To enter the Istanbul Hilton compound was to gain admission to a "little America."[28] For the American guest, the hotel's site and landscape design reproduced the familiar security of the suburban. For others, it contributed to a sense of the building's uncanny utopic difference. For both, the space promised an experience of America.

The interior order of the Istanbul Hilton, analogous to its exterior, looked like a photograph from the handbook of American Modernism, Hitchcock and Johnson's *The International Style* (fig. 14).[29] Like Johnson's Glass House or Mies's Crown Hall, the hotel was transparent. Entering the building, the observer looked beyond it, through the glass curtain wall to the Asian shore of Turkey. The space of the lobby was uninhibited by the cool, naked

11. Istanbul, view from the air. The Istanbul Hilton is at the center of the image; Asia is visible across the Bosphorus. Photo courtesy of Conrad N. Hilton College Archives and Library, University of Houston.

12. Istanbul, Istanbul Hilton, entrance from Cumhuriyet Cadessi. Photo by author.

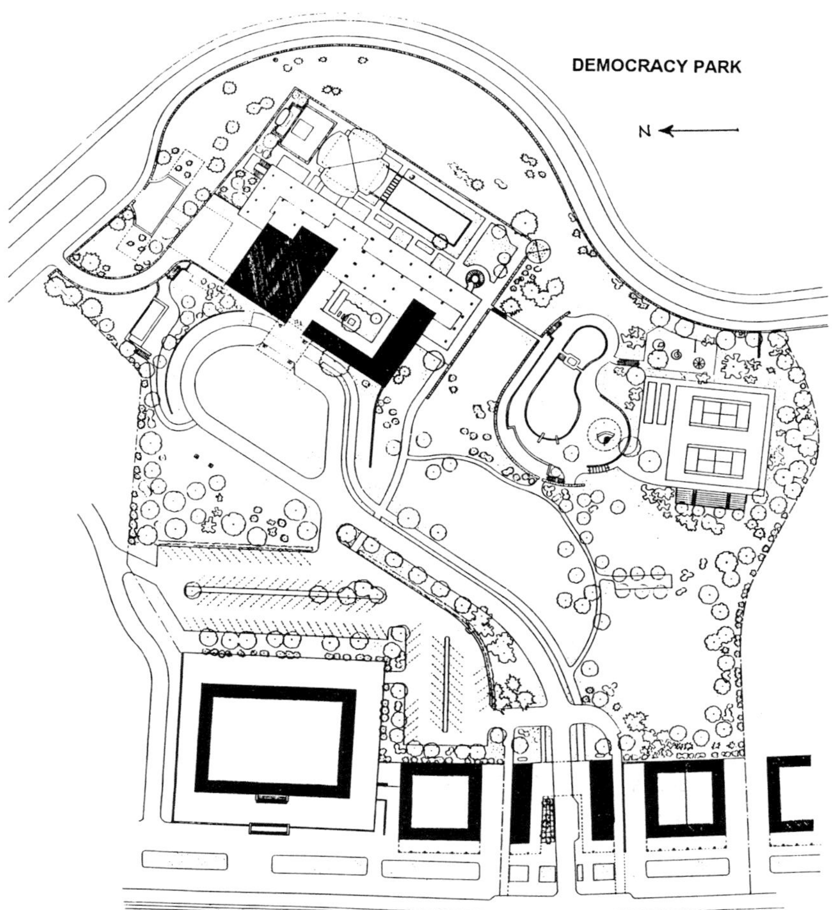

13. Istanbul, Istanbul Hilton, plan of the grounds. Modified from Paul Bonatz, "Hilton-Hotel Istanbul," *Baumeister: Zeitschrift für Baukultur und Bautechnik* 53 (August 1956).

piers of its structure and unconfined by the sheets of plate glass that replaced conventional masonry walls. Glass also opened into the atrium; its fountain was a three-dimensional version of a witty Paul Klee drawing. The two dramatic Le Corbusier–inspired staircases linking the entrance level of the hotel with a lower-level lobby and dining spaces emblematically expressed the spatial freedom of the structure's building technology. Neither staircase, however, functioned as a sculptural centerpiece, displaced as both were to the sides of the main block. The hotel's dominant aesthetic was refined austerity. Molding-free ceilings, recessed lights, naked piers, undifferentiated space contributed to the linear purity of the interior. Polished marble floors and walls and strategically positioned art works identified this purity as elite. Even in 1970 Ada Louise Huxtable, the distinguished architectural critic, could write of the Istanbul Hilton: "Built sixteen years ago, it has become a modern classic."[30]

The only architectural interventions that suggested the hotel's location in the East were its vaults, which Kolsal ascribed to Eldem. The vault is a profoundly structural element. Historically, the domical vault generated Istanbul's urban profile and fixed its architectural character. In the Hilton, vaults were either peripheral or purely decorative. At the entrance to the hotel, the prominent marquee was an elaborate vault of multiple double curvatures appropriately referred to as the "flying carpet" (fig. 16).[31] Equally flamboyant vaults were deployed in the hotel's other spatial accessories, the

14. Istanbul, Istanbul Hilton, view of the modern lobby from the entrance of the hotel, 1955. From "Hilton's Newest Hotel," *Architectural Forum* 103 (December 1955).

15. Istanbul, Istanbul Hilton, view of the postmodern lobby toward the entrance of the hotel, 1997. Photo by author.

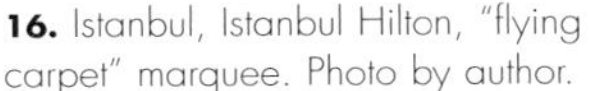

16. Istanbul, Istanbul Hilton, "flying carpet" marquee. Photo by author.

pleasure pavilions at its margins. Voluptuous vaults covered the large nightclub to the rear of the building, the cocktail lounge of the roof restaurant, and the kiosk overlooking the swimming-pool area. There, curvilinearity and brilliant color produced a visual opulence avoided elsewhere in the building. Complexly lighted cupolas, the curved glass walls and sculptured bars offered visual entertainment worthy of the sensual East. Ornamental only were the "domes" puncturing the otherwise flat ceilings of the entrance hall and of the shopping arcade around the atrium. These convex forms imitated cupolas, but they were spatial motifs, not structures. The oriental dome was also the principal subject of the original decorative panels in each of the guest rooms. The domical motifs appearing in the architectural margins of the hotel functioned as signs of the pleasures offered by the building's location. Intentionally or not, they also accentuated, through contrast, the Modernity of the refined rectilinear structure to which they were attached.

There were other ornamental details that indicated that this American space was located in the exotic Turkish city. Teakwood screens referenced the *mashrabiyyah* work of vernacular Ottoman architecture. Sumptuous Turkish carpets with their elaborate geometries and rich color periodically relieved the severity of the marble floors while reinforcing their planarity. Turkish tiles did the same for selected dividing walls. These tiles raise questions of authenticity. Conrad Hilton boasted that the Hilton reinvented the Turkish art of tile making: "[G]enerations ago the Turks had been famous tile-makers but the art had largely died out. Evidence of their handiwork, however, abounded in the old Sultan's Palace. When we wanted to use similar tiles, a local architect searched out a few old men who could teach the younger ones and today, long after the completion of the hotel, tile-making is again a thriving business."[32] The claim was further elaborated in an account that appeared in the *Hotel Gazette:* "At the Istanbul Hilton, the organization revived the making of brightly colored Kutahya tiles which centuries ago went into such structures as the Suleiman Mosque. Hilton rounded up the few artisans who could still make these tiles—in effect, created a factory for them, put the tiles into the hotel's lobby, and has developed demand for them abroad."[33] Local informants remember that the Turkish tiles in the Istanbul Hilton were produced in traditional factories to new specifications and with new designs. Whether these tiles were modified or reinvented, they were deployed as a sign of the Other within a dominant aesthetic of American Modernity.

The site of greatest orientalist display was a section of the public space reserved for women (fig. 17). The "'Tulip Room' off [the] main lobby has all the rich trappings of an Arabian Nights harem. Used as a ladies' sitting room, it can be screened off for private parties."[34] The curtains of this room were lavishly draped to refer to a sultanic tent; bedlike divans with great cushions and large, tasseled pillow-stools, and locally produced hand-painted furniture inform the peculiarly eroticized Otherness of this space. Western assumptions of the location of women in the East are as clearly articulated in the Tulip Room as in contemporary popular accounts of Turkish women: "Americans visiting Turkey these days inevitably express surprise at the modern Turkish woman. No longer is she hidden in a harem, nor is she constantly veiled and chaperoned. Many Turkish girls now have jobs in business and industry, just like American women. Some fly airplanes professionally, nearly 100 sit on the judicial benches of Turkish courts. American visitors to the new Istanbul Hilton hotel opened recently in Istanbul were impressed by the efficiency and beauty of Turkish girls employed as members of the hotel staff."[35] The space of the hotel was themed as oriental. Long before Disney constructed Epcot's World Showcase, the Istanbul Hilton reproduced the experience of the alien within the controlled environment of the Modern. Like later Disney, Hilton theming involved not only architectural decoration but also costuming and food.

> One of the numerous striking features of the Istanbul Hilton is the beauty of the uniforms worn by some of the personnel. I know the word "beauty" may sound exaggerated, but I use it advisedly because it truly fits the case. Each uniform was decided upon with great care and study. The aim was to make it both functional and attractive and, at the same time, lend dignity to the wearer. The most beautiful are those worn by the hostesses in the Bosphorus Terrace (an American snack bar, coffee shop and soda fountain all rolled into one) and by the coffee girls, who prepare coffee in the Turkish manner, in the presence of the guests. These uniforms, in bright colors, were inspired by authentic, ancient Turkish national costumes, and are exquisitely designed and embroidered.[36]

17. Istanbul, Istanbul Hilton, view of the Tulip Room. From "Hilton's Newest Hotel," *Architectural Forum* 103 (December 1955).

Efforts were also made to provide "authentic" cuisine.[37] The framing of the hotel as a site of oriental luxury was persuasive. A travel description of Istanbul in the *Saturday Evening Post* enthusiastically referred to the Hilton as "Conrad's Seraglio."[38]

Markers of the Otherness of the Hilton's location supplemented rather than contradicted the hotel's most Modern and most American aspect—its astute commoditization of space. In its scale, its program, and its management of the gaze, the design of the hotel is distinct from the grand hotels of the late nineteenth century. Those contrasts reveal the reconceptualization of space as profit.[39] The Hilton sold beds in unprecedented numbers. When it was built, the eleven-story Istanbul Hilton with its 244 rooms was the largest hotel in eastern Europe and the Middle East. Work on an extension of 150 rooms, included in the original plans, was begun in 1957, though because of the delays caused by a military coup, the addition was only completed in 1965.[40]

The Hilton marketed food as well as space innovatively. Grand hotels had always offered expensive food expensively; the Hilton also offered cheap food expensively. The Hilton, like the Pera Palas, served its guests haute cuisine. But the Hilton also sold popular American foods, such as hamburgers and milkshakes, as pop cuisine. Homesick Americans and curious locals desirous of a taste of America made the soda fountain a prominent and profitable part of Hilton's catering. Marketing was not, however, limited to the dining room. There was little to buy in the Pera Palas outside the bar and the restaurant. In contrast, immediately to the right of the entrance in the Hilton was an enclosed, elite shopping court with stores arranged around the atrium. These shops offered locally produced luxury items—leathers, jewelry, and carpets—as well as expensive imported goods. The Hilton mini-mall afforded travelers access to those cultural artifacts which would later, after their return home, furnish proof of their alien encounter. At the same time, the arcade provided tourists protection from the ordeal of experiencing the mysterious practices of the local market. The tourist might thus be saved from the disorienting experience of the oriental bazaar and the disempowering trial of haggling—though at considerable cost.[41] At the Pera Palas, as in many other grand hotels, reception seemed something of an embarrassment. Relegated to a corner niche, reception there was treated as though it compromised the representation of the hotel as the guest's own palatial residence. In contrast, at the Hilton, reception parallels the axis of entry. It is dramatically staged against a backdrop of spacious public rooms, a broad terrace and a panoramic view of the Bosphorus. The place of buying and selling the space of the hotel is not hidden but exhibited (fig.14).

The most axiomatic shift from old to new was registered in the treatment of the gaze. The importance of the view was most dramatically effected at the Hilton's entrance. Grand hotels were conventionally ordered in such a way as to concentrate the observer's attention on the hotel itself, usually by means of a dramatic architectural gesture at its core. The oriental court of the Pera Palas was such a gesture. In the Hilton there was no architectural object for the gaze. The building itself offered minimal visual resistance. Entering the Hilton, the guest was presented not with the hotel itself but with the East beyond. The landscape, not the building, was displayed for the patron's consumption.

The force of this view was indicated by its consistent determination of the hotel's program. The hotel escaped the block of the urban grid so that it might be oriented according to the prospect offered by the landscape. The public, profit-producing spaces were generated by the view that they were to frame. The rooftop cocktail and dancing lounge opened to the Bosphorus, as did the café–soda fountain and lounge on the lobby level and the dining room on the lower level. The offices, kitchens, and service areas of the "back of the house," as well as the cheaper rooms, were located at the front, city side of the structure. The guest room also focused on the landscape; the view was its dominant feature. In older European hotels, luxury was coded by lavish furnishings and artworks in the guest rooms. A deluxe suite might have a balcony, but individual rooms often had neither a private balcony nor a private bath. In the Hilton, each guest room had both. Except for the corner suites, the guest rooms of the Hilton were identical, representing a new American aesthetic of efficient space.[42] Differentiation was in location and room rate. Guest rooms were large, approximately five by six meters (about sixteen by twenty feet), and provided with all the current amenities, including excellent mattresses, an efficient bathroom with a bidet as well as a toilet, and an endless supply of hot water. In addition, rooms had specifically American features, such as a telephone, radio, and, most peculiarly, ice water on tap. This last feature had long been an American hotel amenity, apparently first introduced by Ellsworth Milton Statler.[43] The American dependence on drinking water, even with meals, was much commented upon by Europeans. That this third spigot represented a cultural threat outside the United States is revealed by the hysterical response of the Terminus Hotel in Dijon, France, where both red wine and white were piped to individual rooms: "The red wine comes through the tap at room temperature, the correct way to serve the red; the white wine is delivered through the pipes properly chilled. Posted in each room in English and German is a sign advising guests that: 'All the countries of the world have their riches. Burgundy has its wine. You will be happy all day if upon awakening, you drink a glass of wine.' . . . The hotel manager explained the new plumbing thus: 'In America hotel rooms have three taps—hot, cold and ice water. In Burgundy, we consider ice water should be replaced by wine.'"[44]

Furniture in the guest rooms was English-made Danish-American-Modern: simple lines rendered in teakwood with a dark varnish and upholstered in high-quality, abstractly patterned fabric. Hilton had as much of the furniture as possible made locally. "A substantial part of all upholstered furniture was produced under the direction of the Design Office by the Teacher's Technical College in Ankara. This is a government-sponsored project to train teachers to help advance the technical industries throughout the country. All other furnishings, including textiles and lamps, were imported from fourteen different countries."[45] Rooms were carefully designed to look like living rooms rather than bedrooms. Beds were disguised as couches during the day. Lighting was provided by table and floor lamps of vaguely Bauhaus ilk. The Hilton requirement of wall-to-wall carpeting was met, in the absence of local machine-made carpet, with 15,000 square yards of carpeting handwoven in Konya. A Hilton publication proudly announced its role in the entrepreneurial development that produced these carpets. "Each of the 1,200,000,000 carpet tufts have been hand-knotted by women workers. All this under the watchful eye of Kemal Seli, an American-trained business executive who, several years ago, returned to his homeland especially to carry out a planned revitalization of the Turkish carpet industry which once commanded the whole world market in luxury carpets."[46] The unornamented simplicity of these hallway and guest room carpets made no explicit reference to the great tradition of carpet making in Turkey, but their depth and richness was unparalleled in the Hilton chain. The color schemes tended to the light earth tones. Care was taken so that the palette of adjacent rooms was complementary, but not identical. Pictures favoring orientalizing architectural motifs—notably domes—produced by an Italian designer named Fornasetti decorated the walls. The anonymous character of the room and its decoration offered no distraction from the view, to which the entire outer wall of the room was devoted. Floor-to-ceiling sliding glass doors in aluminum frames opened to the balcony and the view beyond.

Architecture, politics, and profit.

If the view determined the program of the hotel, the hotel also constructed the view. The view framed was not the view that was provided by the traditional grand hotel in the Middle East, which opened through the windows of the tearoom or from the raised platform of the terrace on to the immediate theater of oriental life.[47] The Hilton was located to insulate its occupants from the sensorial assaults of the city—the cacophonies of urban congestion; the pungencies of people, animals, vended food and refuse; the images of poverty and decay. Its suburban setting distanced them from the city; its air-conditioning and double-pane plate glass excluded noise and odor. Vision was also protected. The view presented was the view from above. At the time of its construction, it was claimed that the Hilton was the highest building in the city.[48] The height of the structure enhanced the elevated topography on which it was sited. Bellevue Park (now Democracy Park) fell away to the shore of the Bosphorus and its architectural adornments, the delicate Dolmabahçe Camii, which looked more interesting from a distance than it did up close, and Dolmabahçe Sarayi, which replaced Topkapi Sarayi as the Imperial Palace in 1855. Beyond was the generous sweep of the Bosphorus and the shore of Asia Minor.

This superb vista was no doubt what most tourists who occupied the rooms of the Hilton desired to see. But to some observers the hotel presented a political topography; it produced and delivered visual control of a vast landscape between West and East. This landscape was not merely aesthetically pleasurable but ideologically potent. According to *Architectural Record*, the hotel offered a commanding view of an East, a view that was both exotic and "strategic": "The overall design [of the Istanbul Hilton] takes full advantage of a site difficult to match in any of the tourist centers of the world. Bellevue Park, on the top portion of which the hotel will stand, is a high promontory overlooking the *strategic* Bosphorus, with views and breezes to give the steamship and airlines much copy for their tourist folders."[49] Conrad Hilton was more deliberate: "The Istanbul Hilton stands thirty miles from the Iron Curtain. . . . Here, with the Iron Curtain veritably before our eyes, we found a people who had fought the Russians for the past three hundred years and were entirely unafraid of them."[50] Conrad Hilton was explicit about the ideological importance of the hotel's location; for him the Hilton's proximity to the Soviet Union was central to its function. The claim of geographic proximity was dramatic; it was also fictional. No part of the Soviet Union was found within three hundred miles of Istanbul. Hysteria over the threat of communism in the United States in the fifties was manifest in maps of the creeping Red Menace. The sense of the physical immediacy of the Russian peril was pervasive. The soberly objective *New York Times* exaggerated the Hilton's adjacency to the Soviet Union even further, stating that its site was "within ten miles of the Russian border."[51] The importance to Conrad Hilton of the hotel's nearness to the Soviet Union had to do not only with the view it provided of the "Iron Curtain," but also with the antithesis of this perspective. If Russia was "veritably before our eyes," it followed that the Hilton, the representation of America, was veritably before the Soviets' eyes. The view was potentially contested and certainly confrontational. The view that the Hilton framed for the guest, no less than that which the Hilton itself presented to the outsider, was deeply political.

Texts from the Hilton Archives further document the ideological character of the corporation's Istanbul project. They also nuance an understanding of its politics by adding economic and cultural factors to the mix. One of the earliest sources is a letter written by John W. Houser, vice president of Hilton International, from the Park Hotel in Istanbul on August 27, 1950:

> Dear Mr. Hilton:
>
> Well, it looks as though you can have Istanbul and Athens if you want them. Both will take a few weeks to fully work out but are ready for the taking. I wrote you briefly about Athens, now let me tell you the set up in Turkey.
>
> Our Ambassador and the ECA [Economic Cooperation Administration] people are definitely on our side and have helped a great deal. Went from here to Ankara, the Capital, by train, to see the Turkish officials. Met with the Director General for Tourism, Press, etc. Also the Minister of State and his deputies. It developed that Pan American has had a man there for two years working on the hotel project and he was very busy while I was there. I took the position that we were interested only if they wanted us very much and would work out the financing quickly. They were quite surprised at my leaving for Istanbul the second day but it was the right approach as it turned out. They flew the Director General up here for more meetings and they have decided in principle to build a fine hotel with us. They have agreed to a 300 room hotel for $5,000,000 which is a lot of money here. $3,000,000 of local currency is to be provided by the Turkish Government and $2,000,000 is to be used from ECA funds. The ECA fellows are clearly

in favor of it, and I know will approve the use of the $2,000,000 for purchases abroad. The only worry on the part of the Government is as to political repercussions, since there are so many things needed for the country.

But I have held to the idea that if we touch it, the hotel must be one of the best hotels in the world and that we must be able to build a fine building with all modern facilities. They like the idea since it appeals to their pride. They will have more cabinet meetings and finally settle the matter in the next week or so.

Istanbul is a large sprawled out city, mixing the Orient and Occident. There are many Mosques with Minarets and you definitely get a feeling of mystery and strangeness. The city is on the Bosphorus and the Golden Horn and there are beautiful views of water and islands. There is a bazaar in an old Monastery that is a natural place for tourists. In brief, I believe this place offers great attractions for the tourist and of equal importance is the obvious growth of foreign businesses. Business men from all countries are here.

The so-called hotels here now are small and usually old and bad. The only really good one is the Park, with 75 rooms and plans for doubling in size. It would require ECA funds and if we go ahead there won't be any money for them. Rooms run around $6.00 but you could charge more with a hotel that is good. Wages are terribly low. The wage of the headwaiter here is 100 lira a month, or less than $40. Waiters get 50 to 75 lira. . . . We would have to pay more to get good men, but wages still would be very favorable.

One of the ideas of interest to the Government is our training of a Turkish staff in the United States. I am going to talk to ECA in Paris to see if they will finance it just in case we go ahead.

There are plans for a national celebration in 1953 and the hotel would have to be finished by the beginning of that year. They will agree to American architects and I believe contractors as well, if we feel they are needed.

This is the real crossroads of the East and West and if there isn't a war [Turkey] will be in for a great advance and development. The ECA fellows believe that we could fill the hotel with rich Turks and Egyptians if we never saw a tourist from Europe or America. It's hard to say, but certainly the combination of customers would be of real interest.

I haven't forced an answer on convertibility of currency into dollars since they know we want it and some way of our getting our return must be provided. I felt it better to get their commitment to us for the hotel first. With the Government owning it, we won't have to worry about restrictions. Also, they will agree to make any site we want available. The one Pan Am agreed to is a secondary location and we can do much better. There is one outstanding place that will command a beautiful view but we should have to tear down a bunch of houses—it can be done, I gather.

Anyway, the Government has it before them for a final decision and I have kept the door open for us to move either way. Istanbul with Athens mightn't be too bad a start in Europe.[52]

The first couple of paragraphs of this letter presented Hilton's entrepreneurial interest in Turkey in the language of territorial occupation. The principal adversary in the conflict was not, as in the colonialist enterprise, the host state, but rival corporations. Rather than competing in the direct exploitation of the host country, corporations competed for the opportunity to develop profit-making enterprises. Hilton's prime antagonist was Pan American, the holding company of the Intercontinental Hotel chain. Pan American was at the time the flagship of American international aviation.

Its executives recognized the intimate relation of international air travel to business and tourism and sought to promote the expansion of all three by hotel construction, first in South America and then in Europe and Asia.[53] Local hotel owners apparently offered little resistance in Istanbul, though they were vocal in other countries. The Soviet Union apparently also entered the competition. In a letter written the following year, Houser reported that the Russians had countered the Hilton offer of a hotel for Istanbul with plans for a massive structure of a thousand rooms modeled on New York's Waldorf-Astoria. Ironically, the Waldorf-Astoria, opened in 1931, had been bought by Hilton in 1949.[54] Houser commented, "[I]t was interesting to sit discussing the new [Istanbul] Hilton Hotel with the drawings from Moscow on the next table. The moral to me is that anyone who thinks hotels aren't part of this cold war doesn't understand the struggle."[55]

Houser's letter emphasizes the government role in the Hilton undertaking. The U.S. State Department was certainly aware of the role hotels might play in the expansion and stabilization of capital after World War II. Its involvement in the corporation's expansion was acknowledged in Conrad Hilton's autobiography:[56] "Both the State Department and the Department of Commerce suggested that the Hilton organization could make a substantial contribution to the government program of Foreign Aid by establishing American-operated hotels in important world cities. These hotels could stimulate trade and travel, bringing American dollars into the economies of countries needing help. Besides, and this pleased me most especially, they felt that such hotels would create international good will."[57] Another letter from John Houser to Conrad Hilton articulates the close, but not identical interests of the State Department and the Hilton corporation. This text also conveys the pervasive fear of imminent war:

> Arrived in Istanbul last night and came straight on through to Ankara. Am staying with McJenkins (Deputy Chief ECA here) whom you met in New York. . . . We need a good business man to deal with to keep away from government red tape. I find that all the hesitation of our government in including Turkey in the Atlantic Pact has had serious repercussions in their attitude here. Also they feel we haven't helped them enough in solving their basic economic troubles and apparently believe our efforts and help is aimed only at creating a fighting force which we may or may not back up in case of trouble. There is growing talk of standing neutral particularly since they apparently aren't to be included in the Atlantic Pact in spite of our finally purposing it. It is serious and I feel our uncertainty of approach has perhaps lost an important close alley. On the other hand they are a powerful military force and will direct a sizable force at Russia if we do come to war. And also we may be able to win them again as closer allies. The change of attitude is not openly recognized but is reported in whispers. In spite of the deteriorating government position, ours seems untouched. McJenkins is giving a cocktail party for me and inviting the cabinet. It will be a good chance to strengthen our relations.[58]

Istanbul was the most populous city of Turkey, itself the most Westernized state in the Middle East and closest cold war ally of the United States in the region apart from Israel.[59] The U.S. government strengthened its alliance with military and monetary aid. In an address to the American-Turkish Society in New York in October 1950, George C. McGhee, assistant secretary for Near Eastern, South Asian, and African affairs, commented: "I am glad to be able to say that, in the economic, as well as in the military field, the United States is re-enforcing the efforts which Turkey has been making on her own behalf. . . . As of June 30, 1950, Turkey had received approximately 185 million dollars in ECA aid. . . . They are being used to purchase tractors, plows, combines, and other types of agricultural equipment so that great areas of land can be brought under cultivation. They are used to modernize and expand the principal coal mines. . . . They are used for road-building. . . . They are used to increase the country's power facilities."[60] The U.S. government did not limit its financial assistance to Turkish agriculture and industry. It complemented its moral support of the Hilton with dollars. The State Department authorized the use of ECA dollars for the purchase of equipment unavailable in Turkey, mainly from the United States. These materials and technologies had to be bought with hard currency, of which the Turks had very little. Though not included in the ECA's official publications, the U.S. government's contribution to Hilton construction was by no means clandestine. The *New York Times* of March 30, 1951, for example, matter-of-factly reported ECA financing for Hilton. According to their account, Hilton announced that his trip to Europe resulted in contacts that would lead to the building of hotels in Rome, Istanbul, and elsewhere. The total cost would be $50 million. "Part of the money will be supplied by the Economic Cooperation Administration."[61]

State support came from the Turks as well as the Americans. Houser's letter of August 27, 1950, documents the Turkish government's stake in the project. The Turkish government in the guise of the Turkish Pension Fund provided the land, the building, and the maintenance costs of the hotel. Even this money was, however, underwritten by the Americans. According to the *New York Times*, the FOA (Federal Operations Administration) guaranteed the Bank of America loan to Turkish Pension Fund for the hotel.[62] The Turkish government's desire for a Hilton was greater than its anxiety about potential protests against a luxury hotel from an economically pressed populace. In other locations such concerns proved to be well founded. There were hostile responses to the Hilton in Berlin, Rome, Florence, and London.[63] Criticism in Turkey was muted, in part because of the United States' relative popularity in the country in the early 1950s. Through the decade, Turkey was increasingly closely allied with the United States.[64] A virulent anti-Americanism emerged only in the 1960s.[65] Turkey's involvement with corporate America was a corollary of the country's progressive dependence on American military assistance.

As Houser's letter indicates, the Hilton Corporation had no intention of investing its own capital in the Istanbul Hilton. Indeed, Hilton International neither financed nor owned its earliest hotels outside the United States. Rather, the construction and equipage of a building was typically paid for by the host state or by private investors in the country, frequently with a subsidy of American foreign aid or loans guaranteed by the United States. Hilton's favored international contract gave the corporation complete control of the management of the hotel and oversight of its design and construction, but little financial obligation.[66] In return for their oversight and advertising, Hilton received a third of the hotel's profits. When Hilton hotels were confiscated, as they were during the revolutions in Cuba and Iran, Hilton International Corporation lost access to future profits.[67] It did not forfeit significant investment moneys. The Hilton International management contract became a popular model for management leases. In 1990, for example, it served as a template for the agreement form promoted by the United Nations in negotiations between "third world" countries and "first world" hoteliers.[68]

Houser's letter further indicates the corporate concern with both the quality and Modernity of the hotel structure and its site. Hilton's desire to appoint an architect is notable. In most later contracts the selection of the architect was left to the hotel owners, though Hilton continued to maintain control of the building design and quality through its own architectural office in New York. It seems that the principal criterion for the location was the view. Istanbul's exoticness was presented as contributing to its potential as a site of tourism. Its position between East and West also made it a locus of enough business activity that the project would be successful even in the absence of tourism. The central concern with potential commercial success was explicit. The bottom line, literally, was that wages were low, promising a favorable profit margin.

The Istanbul Hilton was opened in June 1955. The official scrapbook marking the occasion contains a set of texts that locate the social imaginary of the hotel:

> *The Magic Carpet*
> An international galaxy of 113 celebrities from the American and European world of movies, radio, television, press, national magazines, news wire and picture services, and feature syndicates, left from New York International Airport June 8 on board two chartered Pan American airliners to attend the formal, gala opening of the eleven-story, 300-room, 500-bed new Istanbul Hilton Hotel.
>
> The huge planes, nicknamed The Flying Carpet and The Magic Carpet, will get the guests to Istanbul in plenty of time for the colorful, five-day program. . . . Aside from the many functions scheduled to be held in the beautifully decorated public rooms of the hotel itself, the entertainment planned for Istanbul's guests includes the presentation of honorary citizenship papers to Conrad N. Hilton by Istanbul's Mayor Dr. F. K. Gokay, sightseeing tours of Turkey's Magic City, receptions and special programs of Turkish folk dancing and folk music at historic Yildiz Palace, special trips up and down the glamorous Bosphorus with a garden party at Beylerbeyi Palace, exhibits of Turkish design and hand-embroidery and other arts and crafts, demonstrations of horsemanship and horse mastership by teams costumed in ancient and authentic uniforms of Ottoman Turkish cavalry, military bands playing the instruments of past centuries borrowed for the occasion from Turkish museums, and a hundred and one other treats.

The scrapbook conveys something of the spectacularity of the early International Hilton Hotels. The oriental city was the stage setting for exotic traditional entertainments, witnessed by those who are themselves spectacle. Among the celebrities was Bob Consignee, the popular columnist, who subsequently wrote "Glamour Rides a Flying Carpet":

> The Turkish people love Americans. . . . [But they] reserve their utmost spirit of welcome for American movie people. It was with great difficulty that police hacked a channel through the solid wall of humanity that reached from the steps of the plane to the terminal building. Through that channel graciously swam Irene Dunne, Merle Oberon, Ann Miller, Diana Lynn, Sonja Henie, Mona Freeman, Carol Channing, June Falkenberg and other belles. The applause was deafening, the faces of every strain of blood known to the crossroads of Europe and Asia alighted with delighted recognition. Leo Carrillo (on whose Spanish ancestors' estate Hilton is building the Beverly Hilton Hotel) responded to the cries of "Seesko Keed, Hallo!" with waves of his own

> Panama sombrero. The stars have responded with a warmth that has made hosts of new friends for themselves, their industry and their country in a land that rubs shoulders hostilely with Russia.[69]

The scrapbook also included a statement made by His Excellency Mayor Gokay: "I sincerely hope that very soon you will again invite us to assist at the opening of a new Hilton Hotel in Cairo and in Athens, and thus the three old civilizations, the Byzantine, the Egyptian and the Greek, will be linked by Hilton Hotels, and in that way attract a great number of tourists from all over the world." The address by Conrad Hilton that followed put the expansion of Hilton in a more political frame:

> For the western world, the transforming events of 1923 have been of supreme importance. The old, imperial Ottoman dynasty, though continuously and unreservedly hostile to the Russian encroachments over the centuries, had lost its earlier vitality, and was commonly referred to as "the sick man of Europe". Then came 1923; then came Mustafa Kemal Ataturk and the revitalization of that latent energy; and today, Turkey is once more a respected member of the family of nations. It was indeed fortunate for the Western world that the new republic chose to continue one element of the foreign policy of the Sultans—a deep and very sound mistrust of its great northern neighbor. This common opposition to Communism has done much towards educating Americans to the pressing existence and survival problems of the republic of Turkey. . . . We view our international hotel ties as a first-hand laboratory where men of Turkey and Egypt, Rome and Madrid, and of other world capitals may inspect America and its ways at their leisure. . . . We mean these hotels too as a challenge—not to the peoples who have so cordially welcomed us into their midst—but to the way of life preached by the Communist world. Each hotel spells out friendship between nations which is an alien word in the vocabulary of the Iron Curtain. The Marxian philosophy with its politically convenient dialectic has a way of reducing friends to slaves. To help fight that kind of thinking and that kind of living we are setting up our hotels of Hilton International across the world.[70]

Conrad Hilton repeated the same message in his autobiography. "Standing before the assembled guests at the opening ceremonies, I felt this 'City of the Golden Horn' was a tremendous place to plant a little bit of America. Here was the site that had known the Persian hordes, become Constantine's capital, seen the invading Crusaders, been the center of the old Ottoman Empire, and where in 1923 Mustafa Kemal Ataturk had fostered a young Republic. . . . 'Each of our hotels,' I said, 'is a "little America."'"[71] The commercial, entertainment, and government elites coalesced in the celebration of a site which inscribed urban space with the presence of an anticommunist America. The event's specifically political content was made clear by its organizer. The Istanbul Hilton was part of the bulwark of the Free World against the threatened encroachments of communism. It did its work through spectacle—not only the panoramic spectacle that it packaged but also the cultural spectacle that the hotel itself enacted.

The Hilton project involved the Hilton International Corporation, the United States Department of State, and the highest levels of the Turkish government. The Hilton was not imposed on Istanbul; on the contrary, as Houser's letter of August 1950 makes clear, the Turkish government embraced the project. Turkey was understandably anxious to distance itself from the "sick man of Europe" image, to promote identification with American and European enterprise, and to share in the economic benefits of modernity. Not only did the Turkish government in large part pay for the Istanbul Hilton, but it promoted its hotel in remarkable ways. It was noted in the Hilton newsletter that the "Istanbul Hilton, the first hotel in the world to be portrayed on a postage stamp, has now been honored by the Turkish Government with a postmark of its own, two unique distinctions held by no other commercial organization."[72] The popularity of the Istanbul Hilton with the Turks was also reported in the *Reader's Digest*, suggesting something of the hotel's propagandistic value in the home market:[73]

> How do the Turks feel about this ultramodern building dominating a hilltop in their ancient city of crumbling walls and historic mosques? "Proud and happy," they will tell you. "It is *our* building, owned by us, co-designed by a Turkish architect, financed by the Turkish Republic Pension Fund and staffed more than 95% by Turks. It is the most dynamic showcase in this part of the world of the modernization we are desperately trying to achieve. This is not a Communist-propaganda promise of better things to come—this is a Free World achievement here and now. We can see it, walk through it, eat in it, drink in it, sleep in it. Here we can entertain distinguished visitors from all over the world and be proud of it."[74]

The choice of Skidmore, Owings and Merrill as the American designers of the new Hilton was appropriate for the hotel's broader project. SOM was a major player in development of American Modernity.[75] The firm was associated with the Modern as early as the 1940s. They produced their first hotel, the Terrace Plaza in Cincinnati, in 1949, for an owner who disliked the Modern, but regarded it as an aesthetic imperative for profitable commercial construction: "The commission arose from the desire of Jack Emery of Cincinnati to build a truly modern hotel, not, he admitted, out of any deep conviction of the essential value of the modern style, but out of the sound commercial feeling that in spite of his lack of sympathy with it, a hotel of the forties should look to be of the forties. To this end he retained as architects Skidmore, Owens [*sic*] and Merrill. They had never built a hotel before, but had a reputation for modernity."[76] The Terrace Plaza was bought by Hilton in 1959.

The United States Air Force Academy, perhaps SOM's most controversial undertaking, indicates its privileged position as a representative of both Modernity and the American establishment. This commission was one of the biggest and most ideologically charged government building projects of the post–World War II years.[77] Moreover, criticism of SOM's work on the Academy mirrors the progress of Modernism from a style denounced by architectural conservatives in the early 1950s as alien to America to one condemned by architectural radicals at the end of the decade as overidentified with the military-industrial complex.[78] SOM was also involved in the venture that consolidated the association of America with the Modern in the postwar years—the construction in American Modern of U.S. embassies and consulates abroad: "[F]ollowing World War II the increased foreign responsibilities and the substantial accrued foreign currency assets of the United States stimulated a vastly expanded embassy construction program. From 1946 through 1953 the Foreign Buildings Office (FBO) of the State Department executed over 200 projects in 72 countries: the results were in the modern corporate idiom."[79] The benchmark corporate structures of SOM from Lever House to the Sears Tower are well known. The firm's early and continuous link with the government is perhaps less familiar. From Atom

City, Oak Ridge, Tennessee (1942–1946), through the U.S. Consulate at Düsseldorf (1954), the Air Force Academy, and the U.S. Embassy in Moscow (1985), SOM has worked extensively at home and abroad for the U.S. government. The centrality of SOM in the emergence of the Modern as the architectural expression of American corporate and state power is suggested by the range and scale of its commissions. The Istanbul Hilton, like the State Department's new consulates and embassies, gave the emergent American presence in Europe, Asia, and South America a material form. The Hilton's success made it a model for subsequent luxury hotels.[80]

The results of the Hilton project surpassed even John Houser's expectations. The hotel was immediately extremely profitable, both for the Turkish Pension Fund and for Hilton International.[81] Further, the Hilton was given "large credit for an electrifying 60% increase in tourism [in Turkey] that took place in the hotel's first year of operation."[82] The hotel also had a significant impact on local architectural practice, contributing to the reconfiguration of Istanbul's urban landscape. It introduced building materials and building techniques previously unused, if not unknown, in Turkey. The contractors, Dickerhof Widman and Julius Berger, were German, but the labor and on-site engineers were Turks. The hotel was constructed with speed and efficiency. Yavuz Erdem, the engineer who acted as controller for the project and who still works in the architectural office of the Pension Fund, insisted that no problems were encountered during construction. The German contractors worked very well; construction progressed without any delays or difficulties. Sedad Eldem took care of all on-site problems. "It was really unusual construction, unusual design, and an unusual interior concept for Turkey at that time. . . . [A]ll the other architects in Turkey learned Modern architecture from this building. Every one here today [in the architectural office of the Pension Fund] agrees with me."[83] The Hilton was a training ground in Modernity for both Turkish architects and Turkish workers (fig. 18).

18. Istanbul, Istanbul Hilton under construction, September 26, 1953, view from the northeast. Photograph from the private collection of Yavus Erdem, engineer.

All the critical construction materials for the Istanbul Hilton were imported: white cement, glass, and the necessary structural steel came from Germany; aluminum window casings and most of the technical equipment such as elevators and air-conditioning units came from the United States; marble and ceramic fittings came from Italy.[84] By the time of the new addition, only the plate glass windows and their aluminum casings were imported. In the intervening years a factory that produced white cement was established in Turkey and new marble quarries were being exploited. The buildings constructed in Istanbul in the wake of the Hilton were significantly shaped by the experience of its technologies. They were also profoundly affected by its form. The Modern, which before the Hilton had been realized only in small projects in Istanbul, became the dominant mode of architectural expression in the city. The cheap concrete tenements on the periphery of the city, no less than the massive Belidiye (Municipality), the headquarters of civil government at the center of Istanbul, trace their genealogy to the Hilton and raise questions about its aesthetic consequences.

In the aftermath of World War II, the Modern was the shape of dreams. It promised an escape from poverty and dislocation. The Istanbul Hilton, the first elite, large-scale Modern structure in the city, changed the urban landscape. The experience of the Hilton was utopic. And it was American. Through the early 1970s, the Hilton itself remained a utopic site of desire, both for Turks and for foreigners. But just as American popularity began to wane in Turkey in the late 1960s, the Modernism that the hotel so brilliantly embodied became increasingly an architecture of bureaucracy and despair. The utopic vision of the Modern was lost at the very site of its production. The Istanbul Hilton, though still a prestigious hotel, no longer functions as a compelling sign of a specifically American ideology. Le Corbusier's dream of whiteness is now part of Orhan Pamuk's urban nightmare.

Modern Athens ought to be removed. It is a very clean, bright, well-built, regular, enterprising town, and therefore one wouldn't really wish to see it destroyed, but it certainly ought to be removed. It is dreadfully in the way of ancient Athens and seriously injures the effect of the old ruins. . . . [The contemporary buildings] are an impertinent intrusion of the utilitarian upon the poetical by no means to be tolerated.

—SAMUEL WHEELOCK FISKE, *MR. DUNN BROWNE'S EXPERIENCES IN FOREIGN PARTS*

[W]ith the polo, the balls, the races and the riding, Cairo begins to impress itself upon you as an English town in which any quantity of novel oriental sights are kept for the aesthetic satisfaction of the inhabitants, much as the proprietor of a country place keeps a game preserve or deer park for his own amusement.

—WILLIAM MORTON FULLERTON, *IN CAIRO*

2 Appropriating Pasts: Cairo and Athens

Athens Hilton as viewed from the Parthenon.

Cairo. One of the more serious series of archaeological guide books in English is the *Blue Guide*. The *Blue Guide: London* begins with Parliament, symbol of the origins and durability of English democracy. The *Blue Guide: Florence* begins with San Giovanni in Fonte, the great baptistery in which the newborn Florentine became a citizen.[1] The first building named in the *Blue Guide: Egypt* is the Nile Hilton.[2] It is cited not for its architectural significance, but as the marker of the center of Cairo, the point from which an English-speaking visitor organizes an understanding first of the city, then of the country. The site is known as the Qasr al-Nil (Fortress or Palace on the Nile). Before it became the locus from which tourists planned their forays into Egypt, it had functioned as a center of political control. Qasr al-Nil was named for the royal residence built there in the mid-1850s by Sa'id Pasha, son of the formidable Muhammad'Ali.[3] During the British occupation of Egypt between 1883 and 1952, it became the barracks of British troops.

The British confiscation of the Qasr al-Nil was part of a wider appropriation of the already Europeanized, elite periphery of Cairo (fig. 19). This new Cairo had been developed by Isma'il Pasha, the grandson of Muhammad'Ali, to the west and north of the old city, absorbing the space added to the city by the significant shift to the west of the Nile's flow. Isma'il Pasha's model was Haussmann's Paris, which he visited during the Exposition

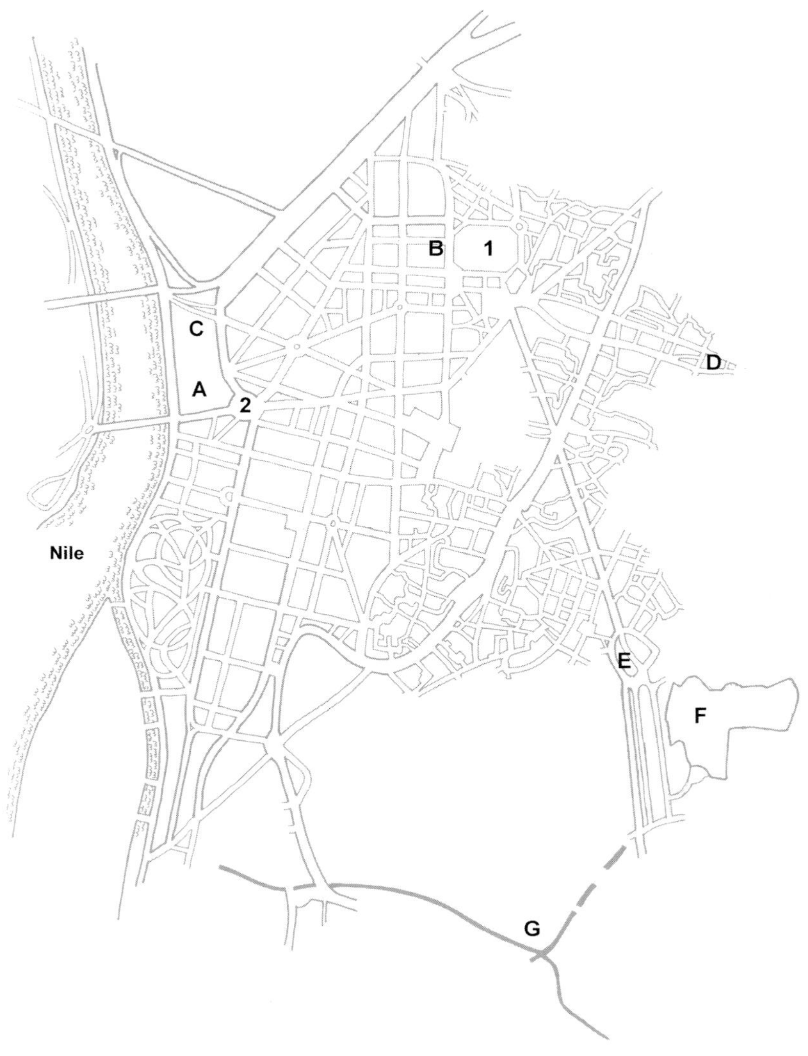

Universelle of 1867.[4] New Cairo had everything the old city did not: sewage systems, gas streetlights, public gardens, boulevards with wheeled traffic, and foreigners. It had multistory structures with ornate eclectic façades and urban villas built by European architects. Old Cairo was a labyrinth of narrow streets tangled around its great mosques. An apotropaeic evil eye painted on the mud-plastered façade protected the inhabitants in the absence of street lamps. Colonial power settled in new Cairo, which superseded and masked the native, impoverished, medieval Cairo further east. The conventional asymmetry between West and East was reproduced in the new and old cities.

19. Sketch plan of Cairo by author: *A*, Nile Hilton; *B*, Shepheard's Hotel; *C*, National Museum; *D*, Al-Azhar Mosque; *E*, Mosque of Sultan Hasan; *F*, Citadel; *G*, Old Walls of Cairo; *1*, Azbakiyyah Gardens; *2*, Tahrir Square.

New Cairo replaced the old even in the imagination of some of its residents. In his *Journey to the East*, Le Corbusier recounted his shock at such an understanding:

> A Greek dentist we met in Constantinople who had been practicing for many years in Cairo said: "Ah, Cairo? It is a hundred times more beautiful than here! Oh, but certainly, because they *have the English over there*. By all means, go there. It's just like a European city. You'll love it there, you'll see lots of paved streets. And then there are the streetcars, and the hotels, fifty or a

> hundred times bigger than this one here. . . . " Dumbfounded, I inquire about the Arab city, the white city with mouchorabies and polychrome minarets, and then about the museum in which everything of Egypt will soon be housed. "Yes, yes, I know all that, but after all it's not the real Cairo!" On the other hand, he knew about the Pyramids.[5]

A similar, though more sinister distinction between the new and old Cairos was provided by the professional English tourist, Douglas Sladen, in his book, *Oriental Cairo: The City of the "Arabian Nights,"* published in 1911: "It is the custom of the swallows of London Society, who go to Cairo for the season, and spend their entire time between the hotels, the Turf Club, and Ghezira, to complain that Cairo is almost as European as London or Paris. You would gather from their conversations that the one thing they really yearned for in Egypt was to see unspoiled native life. . . . [But in truth there is another Cairo,] a city as Oriental as Granada was in the days of the Moors, and not totally different to the Baghdad of the *Arabian Nights*."[6] Sladen's stated object is to chart for the "amateur photographer [the] endless opportunities of securing humorous subjects" in the old city of Cairo. He identifies with breathtaking arrogance the nature of those subjects: "I was never tired of watching [and photographing] the life of the really poor, whether I was rambling in the Arab city at Cairo or in the villages of Upper Egypt . . . [where] the poor are as natural as animals."[7] Sladen was not the only Western observer to compare the Egyptians to animals, as the quote from William Morton Fullerton at the head of this chapter indicates. Sladen's and Fullerton's subjects were constructed of poverty and Otherness for the amusement of the Western viewer.[8]

The distinction made in these travelogues between the viewer and his object was also encoded in the urban landscape of turn-of-the-century Cairo. The subject occupied the hotel and the Turf Club of the new, Europeanized Cairo. The object was located in the oriental street. In his chapter, "Street Life in Cairo as Seen from the Continental Hotel," Sladen described this difference explicitly:

> There is one great advantage in staying at the Continental Hotel for the two or three months of the Cairo season: you can see, without dressing to go out, the most roaring farce ever presented off the stage. The great hotel has a nice sunny terrace with a balustrade which looks out on the Street of the Camel—the Regent Street of Cairo—and the Eskebiya [Azbakiyyah] Gardens and a regular museum of touts. It is doubtful which could be satirized more successfully as a human Zoological Gardens, the people who sit on the terrace behind the railings, Americans chiefly . . . —or the extraordinary collection of parasites in the street below.[9]

For Sladen, as for many European travel writers, particularly English ones, the American tourist is almost as rich a source for ridicule as the local. Sladen and his bourgeois English readers elevate their own project of looking by caricaturing the gaze of the American.

The most famous hotel in Cairo for such looking was not the Continental, but Shepheard's. Shepheard's Hotel was, "by all accounts the oldest, as it is the most romantic, of all Egyptian inns," wrote Robert Ludy, in his book, *Historic Hotels of the World: Past and Present*, of 1927.[10] Shepheard's was established in 1841 by Samuel Shepheard, an ambitious ex-apprentice pastry chef whose undistinguished background hindered his ambitions less in Egypt than in England. Abbas I Pasha gave Shepheard, his hunting companion, the Palace of Alfi Bay, overlooking the Azbakiyyah gardens. Reflecting the two principal colonialist contenders for Egypt in the nineteenth century, the French and the English, the hotel initially had an appropriately ambivalent name, Hotel des Anglais. Later it was renamed, renovated, rebuilt. Through the nineteenth and first half of the twentieth century, Shepheard's was perhaps the most consistent site of elite Western patronage in Cairo.[11]

At the turn of the century, Shepheard's was an Italianate block with an interior courtyard adorned with a central fountain and palm trees.[12] The hotel's ballroom was ornately Louis XVI.[13] In addition to luxurious carpets and fine furnishings, a collection of paintings of Egypt by English artists adorned its walls. Guarding the entranceway were sphinxes brought from the Temple of Seraphis at Memphis. The unscenic squalor behind the hotel's garden was hidden by a sixty-foot-high lattice-work screen. A raised terrace in the front of Shepheard's staged the popular Azbakiyyah Gardens as exotic theater for the hotel's guests (fig. 20). Another early description gives some sense both of what was present and what was absent in the view of the city:

> In front of the Hotel . . . was to be seen the old Ezbekieh [Azbakiyyah], planned and planted by Mehemet Ali, the primitive Hyde Park of Cairo, with its gigantic trees and thick shrubbery, with Arab cafés and cafés chantants at intervals, filled nightly with Egyptians of every rank and race . . . chattering like a flock of magpies. . . . There you saw men of all shades of color, different types of race, and varieties of costume; the half-naked Fellah or peasant, the stark-naked Santon or saint, the richly clad Turk, the Arnaut soldier, a walking arsenal, the coal black Nubian, the coffee-colored Abyssinian, the

20. "Shepheard's Hotel, 1914." Print by an anonymous artist for a promotional brochure of the late twenties. Courtesy of Shepheard's Hotel Archives, Cairo.

> copper-colored Arab and the straight-laced European. All mingled and fused together, conversing together in a perfect Babel of every known dialect of Eastern and Western tongues. The absence of all women, save of the lowest class, rendered the scene still more unique and remarkable. The guests at Shepheard's had thus an 'Arabian Nights Entertainment': improvised for them always without care and without cost, in this Egyptian Champs Elysées.[14]

The variously colored and potentially uncovered male body is the authentically exotic, made more alien by the absence of the woman. The Other was readily available, close enough to hear, smell and touch, as well as see. For Sladen and other tourists, looking at the exotic began at the hotel.

During the anti-British riots of January 16, 1952, Shepheard's Hotel was burned down, along with a number of other elite sites associated with the British occupation. Shepheard's was relocated and rebuilt in 1957 as a modern hotel.[15] Its new site, further west on the east bank of the Nile River, marks modern Cairo's continued growth in that same direction. The new Shepheard's, however, never reassumed the social mantle of the old Shepheard's. The Nile Hilton took its place as the site of foreign and local entitlement.

The Nile Hilton.

On November 12, 1953, the *New York Times* announced that Hilton was to build a new hotel in Cairo: "A luxury hotel that will take the place of the famous Shepheard's in Cairo will be constructed with Egyptian funds and operated on a twenty-year lease by the Hilton Hotels Corporation. Plans for the 400-room, $6,000,000 air-conditioned hotel were announced in Washington yesterday by Conrad N. Hilton, president of the corporation, and Dr. Ahmed Hussein, Egyptian Ambassador to the United States."[16] The agreement signed by Hilton in Cairo reproduced the formula employed in Istanbul. Hilton was the managing company. In exchange for its third of the profits, Hilton provided the specifications for construction of a modern deluxe hotel as well as managerial executives and training for local staff.[17] Hilton was responsible for the running costs, but those were repaid from income before profits were calculated. Hilton also linked the hotel to a growing network of travel agencies and a sophisticated reservation apparatus. For its two-thirds of the profits, the local owner provided the site for the hotel. It was also responsible for the construction of the hotel to Hilton's specifications and for the building's maintenance costs.[18] Again, as in Turkey, this project succeeded only through government sanction and support. Hilton International Corporation, the embodiment of the American entrepreneurial spirit, depended on state sponsorship.

In Cairo, as in Istanbul, the relation between Hilton and the state was direct. Misr (Egypt) Hotels Company, with whom Hilton signed the contract, was a holding corporation established by Gamal Abdel Nasser's Revolutionary Council after Egyptian independence had been achieved in 1952.[19] Conrad Hilton emphasized the role of the Egyptian government in the undertaking: "The national government of Egypt has been a prime motivating factor in the creation of this hotel and set aside the beautiful site upon which it is being constructed. The investment of the Misr Hotels Company in this enterprise will enable the Nile Hilton to become a reality.

Its officials have worked in magnificent cooperation with us toward that goal."[20] Nasser, leader of the revolutionary Republic, spoke at the ceremonial laying of the foundation stone of the new hotel in 1955. According to Conrad Hilton, Nasser publicly committed himself to both capitalism and the United States. Hilton quoted Nasser as saying, "I am very happy to participate in this ceremony because it symbolizes cooperation between government and private enterprise and, more particularly, because it symbolizes cooperation between private enterprise in Egypt and private enterprise in the United States."[21] Hilton himself was characteristically open about the company's commitments:

> As businessmen, we in the Hilton organization do not attempt to portray that this splendid hotel will be an idealistic operation with no thought for financial return. At the same time, to deny any concern for its good-will impact would be equally misleading. We are certain that the Nile Hilton will be a financial success and that its extensive advertising and publicity programs will increase travel to Egypt and business to other hotels and industries. . . . In our current expansion, Hilton Hotels International views itself as a medium for bettering the understanding of peoples by extending the best we have to offer in the American enterprise system to other countries.[22]

Hilton took pride both in making a profit and in showcasing the benefits of capitalism. Just as the hotel offered more than luxury accommodation to its guests, it provided more than touristic profits to its managers. For Hilton, the hotel served an important ideological function. The hotel also worked on a variety of levels for its owners.

The Egyptian government was centrally concerned with the profits the hotel would generate. Like all countries after World War II apart from the United States, Egypt was desperate to attract hard currency. Reestablishing tourism in postrevolutionary Egypt provided one important means of generating foreign exchange. In addition to revenues, the hotel offered a spectacle of glamorous modernity. The Modern form of the structure was the materialization of the modern social practices that it housed. The building rendered public certain aspects of Nasser's new Egypt. It monumentalized Egypt's ambition to acquire international political status through modernization. It also demonstated the new Egyptian commitment to secularization. In old Cairo, women were enclosed. They could witness the public sphere only from the private one. In *Palace Walk*, Naguib Mahfouz describes the emotions of a woman who ventures out with her son to pray at the shrine of a holy martyr while her husband is absent:

> As she crossed the threshold of the outer door and entered the street, she experienced a moment of panic. . . . She had an oppressive feeling of doing something wrong. . . . She was gripped by intense embarrassment as she showed herself to the eyes of people she had known for ages but only through the peephole of the enclosed balcony. Uncle Hasanayn, the barber, Darwish, who sold beans, al-Fuli, the milkman, Bayumi, the drinks vendor, and Abu Sari', who sold snacks—she imagined that they all recognized her just as she did them. She had difficulty convincing herself of the obvious fact that none of them had ever seen her before in their lives. . . . She turned to look at her latticed balcony. She could make out the shadows of her two daughters behind one panel. . . . Then she hurried along with her son down the desolate alley, feeling almost calm. Her anxiety and sense of doing something wrong did not leave her, but they retreated to the edges of her conscious emotions.

> Center stage was occupied by an eager interest in exploring the world as it revealed one of its alleys, a square, novel buildings and lots of people. She found an innocent pleasure in sharing the motion and freedom of other living creatures. It was the pleasure of someone who had spent a quarter of a century imprisoned by the walls of her home.[23]

In a domestic loge, from behind the *mashrabiyyah* screens, women watched without self-consciousness. The open balconies of the Hilton on which viewers displayed themselves offered a manifest contrast to the shuttered compartments of old Cairo in which viewers hid themselves. The Hilton represented alternative cultural practices.

Correspondingly, the Hilton offered one of the first venues in Egypt where women from good families might work in public. Suliman Kahoul remembered his early days at the Hilton:

> I came in 1958, before the Hilton opened. . . . They collected athletes from the University. I represented Egypt in the Davis Cup. They wanted the right people to work in the hotel. At first I worked the elevators for the workers, moved furniture, did everything. Then they needed about 600 people to work here and they received 66,000 applications. They selected me as a bellboy. . . . The staff came from the best families. Members of the Farouk family worked here, the sons and daughters of the ministers. The hostess used to be dropped off by a chauffeur, and he would come and pick her up again. . . . Housekeepers were all women from high families. They could speak English and French and German.[24]

Seham Abdul Khalek, who left her job as a teacher to become a waitress at the Hilton when it opened, told me that the hotel, even at the service entrance, "smelled beautiful, like perfume. I don't know how. It is not the same now. But perhaps it was because I loved so very much my job."[25] The prestige of the Hilton attached to its staff as well as its guests, managers, and owners. The affectionate memories of Seham Abdul Khalek, Suliman Kahoul, and Mohammed Saleh suggest the Nile Hilton's success in representing the social practices of modernity.

The Nile Hilton not only displayed modernity to the public, but also presented itself as a stage for the display of local and international elites to one another. Its function was inscribed from its opening. The Nile Hilton opened in February 1959. The gala celebration was depicted in a promotional brochure: "Conrad Hilton's 'Jewel on the Nile' opened with great fanfare and a cast of several dozen Hollywood celebrities and journalists. . . . This momentous occasion was honored by the presence of . . . President Gamal Abdel Nasser and President Tito of Yugoslavia, who were besieged by a group of autograph-seeking Hollywood film stars."[26] Art Buchwald, columnist for the *New York Herald Tribune*, also described the event: "Things have been done on such a heroic scale that a group of guests almost expected Cleopatra to sail up the Nile in a golden sampan."[27]

The hotel's function as spectacle continued after its opening. Suliman Kahoul, who was hired the year of the Hilton's opening as a bellboy and who retired as its health club manager, described the hotel's local significance: "[The Nile Hilton] was a very important hotel. All the most important people came here—movie stars, politicians, businessmen. If they didn't find a place here, they canceled their trip until they could get a room. The lobby was like a railroad station. Until the seventies, the lobby was filled all night and all day. All the newspapers concentrated on it. President Nasser used this hotel as a presidential palace. All the big conferences were held here."[28] Suliman Kahoul's comment reflects on the hotel's appeal to an affluent clientele. From its opening until the middle of the 1970s, the Nile Hilton was the most prestigious location in Cairo for local as well as foreign elites. The number of wedding receptions held at the Hilton was symptomatic of the hotel's popularity. Mohammed Saleh, who was hired as a waiter during the hotel's first year of operation and who is now assistant manager of food and beverage, recalled: "We were famous for making weddings. In the good old days, we had a wedding every day. Since 1970, people are shifting, they want something new. But many couples who were married here want to have their children's weddings here. We have also had men get married here more than once. One guy, very rich and well known, was married here three times."[29] The Nile Hilton was the social center of the rich and powerful, both Egyptian and expatriate, in Cairo, as well as the most popular hotel for tourists in the city.

The effect of the Nile Hilton on its users depended on its effect on Cairo. The hotel was described by Richard Joseph in his *Hilton Hotels Around-the-World Travel Guide*: "The four-hundred-room, twelve-story, completely air conditioned Nile Hilton is Cairo's largest and most modern hotel, and one of the most spectacular in the entire Hilton International chain. It was opened in 1959 on a magnificent site overlooking the Nile on one side, and the Egyptian Museum and Liberation Square on the other. The striking beauty of its contemporary architecture contrasts with the time-honored antiquity of its surroundings."[30] The site of the new Nile Hilton, Qasr al-Nil, positioned the hotel at the center of new Cairo. Despite its location at the very core of the modern city, its landscape presented it as the culmination of a generous vista. The hotel was framed by the Nile River to the west and, to the east, the immense Tahrir Square and the Hilton's own gardens (fig. 21). At the time of its opening, the twelve-story Hilton was the tallest building in the city, looming over its closest neighbor, the neoclassical Egyptian Museum. The structure was not, however, an urban vertical high-rise, as might be expected from its central location. Rather, the white-skinned Nile Hilton took the form of a suburban horizontal slab. It resembled the Istanbul Hilton, despite lacking the earlier hotel's peripheral, parkland setting. Even now the Nile Hilton's real-estate-consuming horizontality conveys an immediate sense of opulence. The Nile Hilton did not, however, take the purist form of its predecessor in Turkey. Its guest room slab was not a precise block, but rather an expansive wedge pointing west. The pure geometry of the Istanbul Hilton established it as static and fixed it as a city monument. In contrast, the subtle triangulation of the Cairo Hilton gave it a plastic capacity, allowing the building to mold urban space. It functioned as a giant screen. From the heights of the medieval citadel the hotel deflected the sight line to the pyramids. From the Nile, its mass, exaggerated by its reflection in the river, curtained the city behind it. Before the building boom of the 1970s, the Hilton was a felt presence in Cairo from both the east and the west.

If the Hilton displayed itself equally to all parts of the city, the hotel itself presented the city unevenly to its guests. The hotel faces resolutely west. "From nearly any floor in the hotel guests have a panoramic view to the west that includes the Great Pyramids."[31] The view promoted in Hilton's advertising offers the sweep of the Nile, the new suburbs on its opposite bank, and, in the desert beyond, the pyramids. The gaze of its highest-paying guests was directed to the most modern and the most ancient parts of

21. Cairo, Nile Hilton, view from the east. Photo by author.

Egypt's historical topography. The Nile Hilton turned its back on the old city. The rooftop bar and dance club opened exclusively to the west. A formal dining room and a dining terrace opened over the Nile at the front of the structure. The ballroom at the back of the building had no windows at all opening to the city. The more expensive rooms and all the suites had western exposures. As was the case with the Istanbul Hilton, the privileged face of the building was as manifest in the regularity of its exterior articulation as in its higher room rates. The Nile façade presented a uniform grid. There were no deviations from the regular lattice of the guest room balconies—again, every room had its own loge overlooking the landscape of historical spectacle. In contrast, the city side of the structure was interrupted by blank passages masking the stairwells and elevator shafts. Like the Istanbul Hilton, the Nile Hilton was given a specific orientation. The Istanbul Hilton looked to the east across the Bosphorus. The choice of view in the case of Istanbul was obvious: the alternative was nondescript commercial. In Cairo the reasons behind the ordering of the gaze to the west, away from the old city, are less self-evident. The medieval citadel to the east, with its surrounding mosques and minarets, would seem to lend itself to orientalist romanticization, particularly before the overbuilding and pollution problems of the 1970s. Such a landscape of exotic eastern picturesqueness might appear to vie with a scene of the very modern and the very ancient as an attraction for the Western observer. But it did not. Perhaps the stable, transparent deep past embodied in the pyramids provided a source of security and self-confirmation as well as aesthetic interest. Perhaps in contrast, the medieval city manifested a disturbing religious and political Otherness. Perhaps resonances of the continuing Arab struggle for independence from the West made the medieval city an uncomfortable object to contemplate.[32]

The Hilton's displacement of medieval Egypt in favor of ancient Egypt was not limited to its control of the view. The decoration of the hotel was consistent with the building's physical orientation to the pharaonic past. The guest room block was floated above a broad, two-story base of public spaces and service areas. The lower level was almost entirely glazed to both the east and the west. The dining room overlooking the Nile formed a porte cochere for the main entrance to the hotel. It was adorned with a mosaic frieze of figures in conventional pharaonic partial profile bearing offerings of the land's produce. Above the pedestrian entrance on the city side of the hotel, filling the external blind wall of the ballroom, were monumental panels of hieroglyphic symbols in the saturated pastels of the late 1950s palette. These Egyptian symbols, claimed to be "the world's largest Venetian glass mosaic," had the scale if not the irony of a Claes Oldenberg.[33] Sacred magic became a billboard.

The interior decoration maintained the pharaonic theme. The broad entrance lobby had reception on one side and a massive reproduction of a stone relief from the Egyptian Museum on the other: a colossal pharaoh hunting the wildlife of the Nile (fig. 22). In the guest rooms the brass lamp stands were inspired by the lotus and the draperies were hand-blocked with a stylized version of the same flower (fig. 23). The furniture was reportedly "entirely hand-styled by Egyptian craftsmen, with designs and motifs reminiscent of the pharaonic past. These modern designs [were] based upon the XII Dynasty and the Tutankhamun XVIII Dynasty. The 'art feature' of each room [was] a reproduction of an ancient bas-relief selected from the Cairo museum and cast under their supervision."[34] In the elite shops of the lobby mall, ancient artifacts and their reproductions were available for purchase, the ultimate form of touristic consumption. Trips to the desert were promoted as the object of sightseeing pleasure: "Camping in the desert is one of the real high spots of a visit to Cairo," wrote Richard Joseph, who treated this escape from the city in far greater detail than an investigation of old Cairo itself.[35] His further comment, "You'll get an excellent sampling of Egyptian shopping specialties *first* at the many smart and *dependable* shops right at the Nile Hilton," implies that the bazaar of the old city is both undependable and secondary, and therefore unnecessary.[36] The Egypt marketed by the Nile Hilton was pharaoh's Egypt, the Egypt that was the birthplace of Western Civilization. This was the same Egypt that was promoted by *Life* magazine's "Epics of Man" series in the mid-fifties, by Helen Gardner's popular textbook, *Art through the Ages*, and by the official Egyptian tourist bureau.[37]

22. Cairo, Nile Hilton, lobby interior. Photo courtesy of Nile Hilton Archive, Cairo.

23. Cairo, Nile Hilton, guest room. Photo courtesy of Nile Hilton Archive, Cairo.

The Nile Hilton, like the Istanbul Hilton, was programmed for the distant view. The concentration on the street and its display that characterized the order of the old Shepheard's Hotel or the Pera Palas was relocated. The pathetic body of the passing Other, the object of such nineteenth- and early twentieth-century amusement, was displaced not only by the beautiful body around the swimming pool but also by the safe pleasure of the distant landscape. The reordering of hotel space documents a shift after World War II

in touristic attention. The object of the tourist's search for authenticity was no longer found in the dangerously proximate social, but rather in remote and passive historical artifacts and their commodifiable renderings as souvenirs. This alteration in site might be identified as the mid-twentieth century "look" of American Modernity. How Modern is bracketed with "American" is suggested in the following passage. In it, the American, though unnamed, is defined through reference to the two traditionally dominant tourist nationalities: "Cairo has held a strong attraction for Western tourists for more than a century now, but up until fairly recently it was invaded mostly by British pukka sahib types in pith helmets who sailed up and down the Nile completely surrounded by nice cups of tea and whisky and soda; and by dead serious German *wandervolk* who tumbled down the steps of the Great Pyramid as they checked the number against the listing in their always-open Baedeker. Now, though, Cairo has entered the province of the modern [e.g., American] traveler."[38] In the 1950s, Western European colonialist tourism was replaced by American postcolonial tourism.

If the Nile Hilton's orientation and ornamentation signified an Americanization of the touristic experience, so did its form. Its style was similar to the Istanbul Hilton, though its shape was a less purist expression of the Modernist aesthetic. In contrast to the austerity of Istanbul, the Nile Hilton had a slightly baroque sensibility. Not only did the angled superstructure of the hotel deviate from the ideal geometry of Istanbul, but its interior was theatricalized. The drama was most marked in the treatment of the entrance (fig. 24). There the wedge of the plan opened symmetrically at its hinge. A wide, slightly flared porte cochere below the dining terrace flowed seamlessly through glass doors into the lobby. The plan continued to taper toward the opposite side of the hotel where it focused on a narrow reflecting pool beyond another set of glass doors. The narrowing of the lobby as it receded, complemented by the decreasing diameter of the piers, worked to exaggerate the depth of the space. But this Albertian perspective was frustrated. The observer was displaced from the remarkable axis of the building by a series of columns. The sight line was surrendered to the support system. It was further disrupted by a grand staircase that occupied the center of the structure. This accessorized version of the suspended stairs of Le Corbusier's Domino House suggested that the uneasy American mannering of the Modern was not limited to the plan of the building.

The particular Americanness of the Nile Hilton was in part the responsibility of its architect, Welton Becket and Associates, who controlled the interior decoration as well as the building plan.[39] Welton Becket was West Coast–born, –bred and –trained. He began his architectural career building Tudor, neo-Georgian, and classical mansions for such Hollywood stars as Robert Montgomery, Cesar Romero, and James Cagney. Welton Becket was a golfer. As the eulogist of the firm observes, "Welton Becket found very early that he could move easily among the top executives of great corporations. . . . As time went on, Becket attracted into the firm other people who had innate abilities or aptitudes for contact with clients . . . on the highest level."[40] For these CEOs he built a series of department stores and corporate structures in various appropriated forms of Modernism. In an article suitably titled "Portrait of the Artist as a Businessman," and suitably appearing in *Fortune*, a magazine for corporate executives, Becket's eclecticism was given a positive spin. "Throughout the panorama of Becket's good-looking, superbly functional, and often innovative work, which has contributed to the skylines of five continents, no single style is discernible. On coming

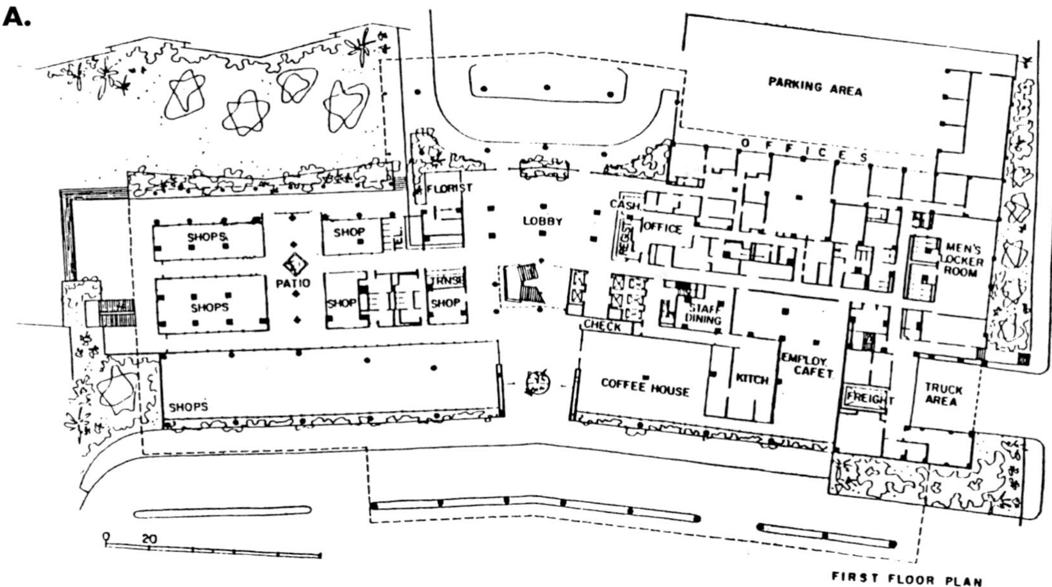

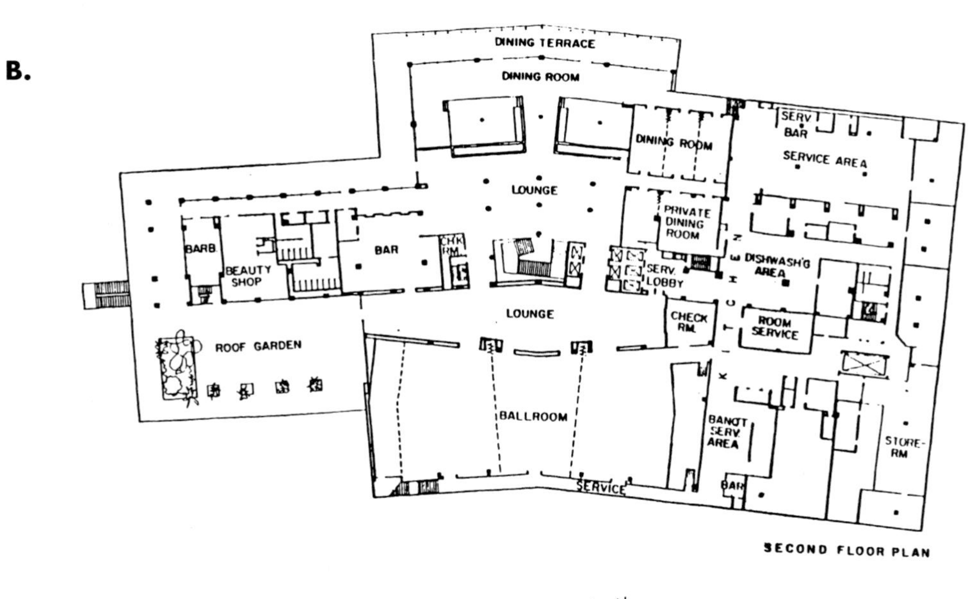

24. Cairo, Nile Hilton: A, plan of the entrance level; B, plan of the second level. Modified from "Hotels," *Architectural Record* 121 (May 1957).

upon any example of it no viewer is likely to exclaim, 'Ah, a Welton Becket building!'" Or again, "It is impossible to characterize the style of Becket's work, and for good reason. Some of it is conventionally sleek and of cellular form, like the Humble Oil Building in Houston. Some is boldly sculptured in dark-grained poured-in-place concrete, like the Xerox Building design. And at least one example—the Los Angeles Music Center—is an earnest attempt to achieve a contemporary expression of classical architecture."[41]

Becket's first job for Hilton was the corporation's Los Angeles administration building. In 1952, he designed the Beverly Hilton, in Beverly Hills, California.[42] The Beverly Hilton also had an angled guest room block floated above a base of public and service spaces and capped with a roof-top bar, though the view was different: "Crow's nest for well-heeled birds is 'L'Escoffier,' Hilton's version of the Top of the Mark and the top of Cincinnati's Terrace Plaza. Here eighty-eight gourmets may sit on ivory leather banquettes, choose delicacies from a menu without prices on it, or look out to an unmatched view of movie studios, oil wells and general suburban sprawl." The view on ground level was, however, the same as that of the Nile Hilton: "In back, the customary palm trees and bathing girls adorn the customary king-size, free-form pool nestled in a rainbow of *cabanas*."[43] Hilton's exportation of the American hotel abroad is assessed in chapter 6. Here it is enough to note that the view of the pyramids did not dictate the form of the Nile Hilton. Rather, the form of the Nile Hilton overdetermined the view of the pyramids. The object of the gaze was exotic, but the means by which it was framed was familiar, at least to Americans.

Athens.

The marble Kritios Boy was reconstructed from fragments found on the Acropolis in the third quarter of the nineteenth century (fig. 25).[44] This athlete or young Theseus was a votive offering made around 480 B.C.E. to the temple complex at the sacred center of ancient Athens. An innocent modern viewer may see the boy as an ideal rendering of adolescence, the transformation from innocent to adult. For art historians, the marble marks another transition—a shift in the form of ancient Greek art from the relative abstraction of the archaic style and idealized naturalism of the classical. The poignancy of impermanent beauty, accentuated by the sculpture's fragmentary state, is enduringly rendered in marble. The boy is a particularly powerful embodiment of the Greek Ideal. The Greek Ideal might be defined crudely as "The Greeks got it—literature, art and politics—right, and that rightness was the origin of Western culture." How the Greek Ideal works and how the Kritios Boy has been used as its sign is suggested by an image and text that appeared in 1992 in the *Washington Post*. An extraordinary exhibition of ancient Greek art, titled *The Greek Miracle*, was mounted at the National Gallery in Washington and sponsored in part by the Philip Morris Company. The corporation publicized their support in an advertisement that featured the bust of the Kritios Boy and a long caption (fig. 26):

> "We are all Greeks," the poet Shelley said. Born of democracy. Invention. Philosophy. Theatre. History. Sciences. And art, born from that democracy makes us so. For out of the fifth-century Greece, modern man was given life. Now the art of the Golden Age of Greece is here, to explore, embrace and revel in. An historical event—of great importance to all of the western world—a study of man and democracy through art. . . . Art as evolution. As mankind. As free. As all. For now, as in the age of Perikles, politics flower. History writes itself anew. Man challenges his world. Art tells the story. And we, in awe, muse over the miracle of democracy.[45]

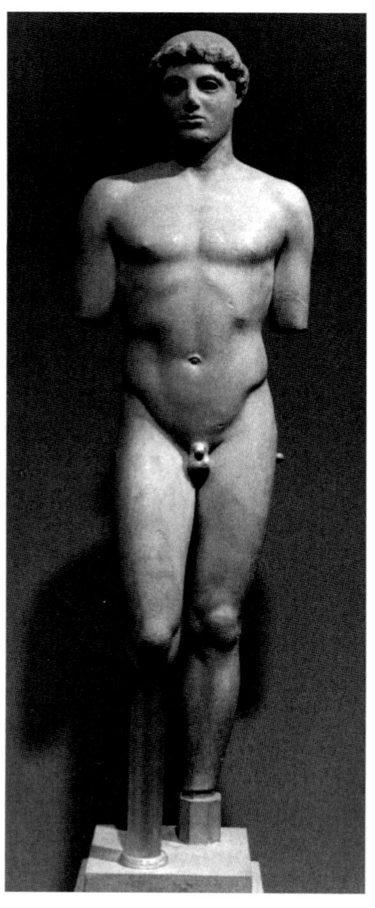

25. Athens, Acropolis Museum, Kritios Boy. Photo courtesy of Jeffrey M. Hurwit.

This Philip Morris advertisement is symptomatic of the location of ancient Greek culture in the self-understanding of the West since the eighteenth century. With its affected syntax and rhetorical clichés, this text voices a popular understanding of the relationship that exists between modern Western democracies and ancient Greek artifacts. Greek art, brought to us by Philip Morris, explicitly makes us Greek. Implicitly, Greek art, which is progress ("evolution"), individualism ("free"), and universal truth ("all") also makes us democratic. The work's spiritual aura is put to political work. The great art of Greece translates the abstract notion of democracy into a

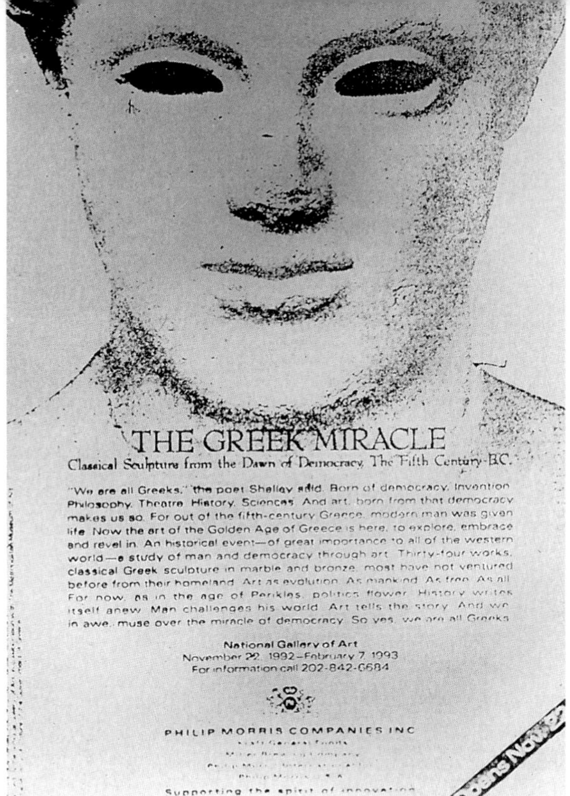

26. Kritios Boy, from an advertisement by Philip Morris for the exhibition The Greek Miracle, from the *Washington Post*, November 22, 1992.

beautiful physical presence. The naturalism of Greek art literally naturalizes Western democracy. The material immediacy of the work serves to obscure the problematic aspects of both the ancient and modern democracies and magically to connect them.[46]

Much has been written on the Western construction of the Greek Ideal.[47] This ideal forms the core of the West's secular soul. It tends to be expressly democratic and rational and tacitly masculine, elite and triumphal. But it comes in a variety of other forms, depending on the historical circumstances in which it is needed. From the eighteenth through the twentieth centuries, the ideal has been malleable enough to be put to very different uses by Enlightenment thinkers, by Romantics, and by revolutionaries.[48] But certain features of its appropriation seem to be relatively constant. Two of these elements were articulated by Nicholas Biddle, a precocious young American, who traveled to Greece at the beginning of the nineteenth century: "The soil of Greece is sacred to Genius & to letters. The race of beings whose achievements warm our youthful fancy has long disappeared. But the sod under which they repose; the air which listened to their poetry & their eloquence; the hills which saw their valor are still the same."[49] The Greek Ideal typically had nothing to do with postclassical Greece, except perhaps in terms of degenerative contrast. Medieval Greece was disdained. The rational humanism of antiquity stands in opposition to the superstitious irrationality of the Byzantine Middle Ages. There was also a widespread aversion to modern Greeks. Nineteenth- and twentieth-century travel accounts commonly express the distress of their authors at the failure of the contemporary population to live up to the cultural standards established by their ancient forebears.[50] For Biddle the Greek Ideal is characteristically absent in Greece's postclassical history and population. The true inheritors of the Greek Ideal are not modern Greeks. By default the Greek Ideal becomes the patrimony of Western Europe and the United States. The same passage suggests that the Greek Ideal is, nevertheless, characteristically preserved in the materiality of Greece.[51] Antiquity could be recovered in the country's landscape. Alternatively, as suggested by the Kritios Boy, it could be recuperated in its art. Indeed, the passion for ancient Greece was inseparable from an appreciation and appropriation of its art.[52] The spoils of Lord Elgin and the writings of Winckelmann both manifested the centrality of art to the construction of the Greek Ideal.[53]

The special aura of the Kritios Boy was effected by its embodiment of the Greek Ideal. This marble is a beautiful fragment of a larger whole—the Acropolis in Athens. Still rising above the city of Athens, the Acropolis literalizes the elevated status of Greek art in Western European consciousness. In the West's construction of its identity, the Acropolis is the only sight on the periphery of Euro-American power that has been more widely appropriated than the Egyptian pyramids. Just as Philip Morris deployed a representative vestige of an aestheticized past in its advertising promotion, so Hilton International presented its guests with a framed icon of an originating site of Western culture. And just as the Kritios Boy was removed from the debris in which it was found, cleaned, and presented with exquisite theatricality in the National Gallery, so the Acropolis has been freed of any history not relevant to the Western production of its meaning.

The Acropolis was not always as purely classical as it is now. Through the first decades of the nineteenth century, it was a palimpsest of classical, Byzantine, Turkish, and Frankish cultures. But to function effectively as the originating site of Western identity, the Acropolis had to be rewritten. Western archaeologists eliminated all of the postclassical structures on the site: Byzantine churches, Ottoman mosques, and crusader fortifications were excavated to bedrock. The medieval and early modern histories of the Acropolis were thoroughly eradicated. The preeminence of the site continues to necessitate its purification. Erasure still takes place in most, if not all, of the textual representations of the Acropolis.[54] A recent scholarly book entitled *Architecture and Meaning on the Athenian Acropolis* is symptomatic. "Meaning" is singular. The only "meaning" of interest to the author is that produced by antiquity. The terms "Byzantine" and "Ottoman" are not in the index. In the introduction to the book the author writes:

> The Periclean acropolis is one of the most elaborate examples and perhaps the purest expression of classical form ever created, and the primary goal of this book is to speak of the meaning of its individual buildings and of the program as a whole, within the immediate context of Classical Greece. . . . Why our attraction to classical architectural form? . . . The Parthenon, in its historical context, its mathematical refinement, its sculptural narrative, its international style, is a celebration of victory, a celebration of culture, a celebration of Athens as cosmopolis; it speaks to us in intentional, unambiguous terms of the value of humanity in this world. . . . Is this the power of classical architecture? Or is its power derived from a less historically specific source? Is there something in its appeal more basic, less intellectual—even, the gods forbid, primally religious?[55]

As in the Philip Morris ad, the staccato syntax suggests that the experience of the Greek site exceeds grammar. By stripping the Acropolis of its histories, the cultural power of its classical monuments works more effectively. The Acropolis becomes available for Western contemplation as the embodiment of a nostalgic, pseudoreligious memory, as well as a democratic presence.[56]

The elimination of other pasts is not limited to the Acropolis. In contrast to most cities, the threat to Athen's fabric has come not just from Modern construction. The city has also been under constant threat from antiquity. From the Middle Ages through Ottoman rule, Athens was a small, provincial town.[57] The Turco-Byzantine walled city, with its two- or three-story buildings and complex narrow streets, occupied the north and east slopes of the Acropolis (fig. 27). During the War for Independence (1821–1833), Athens was besieged and hideously damaged. In 1835, after gaining its freedom from the East, Greece received a king from the West: Prince Otho of Bavaria. A plan for an appropriate capital also arrived from the same source. The new Athens was invented by King Otho's German-trained architects, Stamatios Kleanthes and Eduard Schaubert. The plans for the city, as modified by Leo von Klenze and numerous planning committees, imposed a rational, beaux arts–classical order on the city. The plan's dominant boulevard, appropriately named Athinas Street, pointed toward the Acropolis. Its originating center was Omonoia Square, the commercial focus of the city. Another major square, the Plateia tou Syntagmatos (Constitution Place), was the site of elite residences, including the Royal Palace and the best hotels, most notably the Grande Bretagne.[58] These two centers were connected by Panepistimious Street, the cultural axis of the new city. Constructed there in good neoclassical style were the university, the academy, and the national library. These buildings "contributed to the first national aspiration [of the state]: the architectural transformation of Athens into a

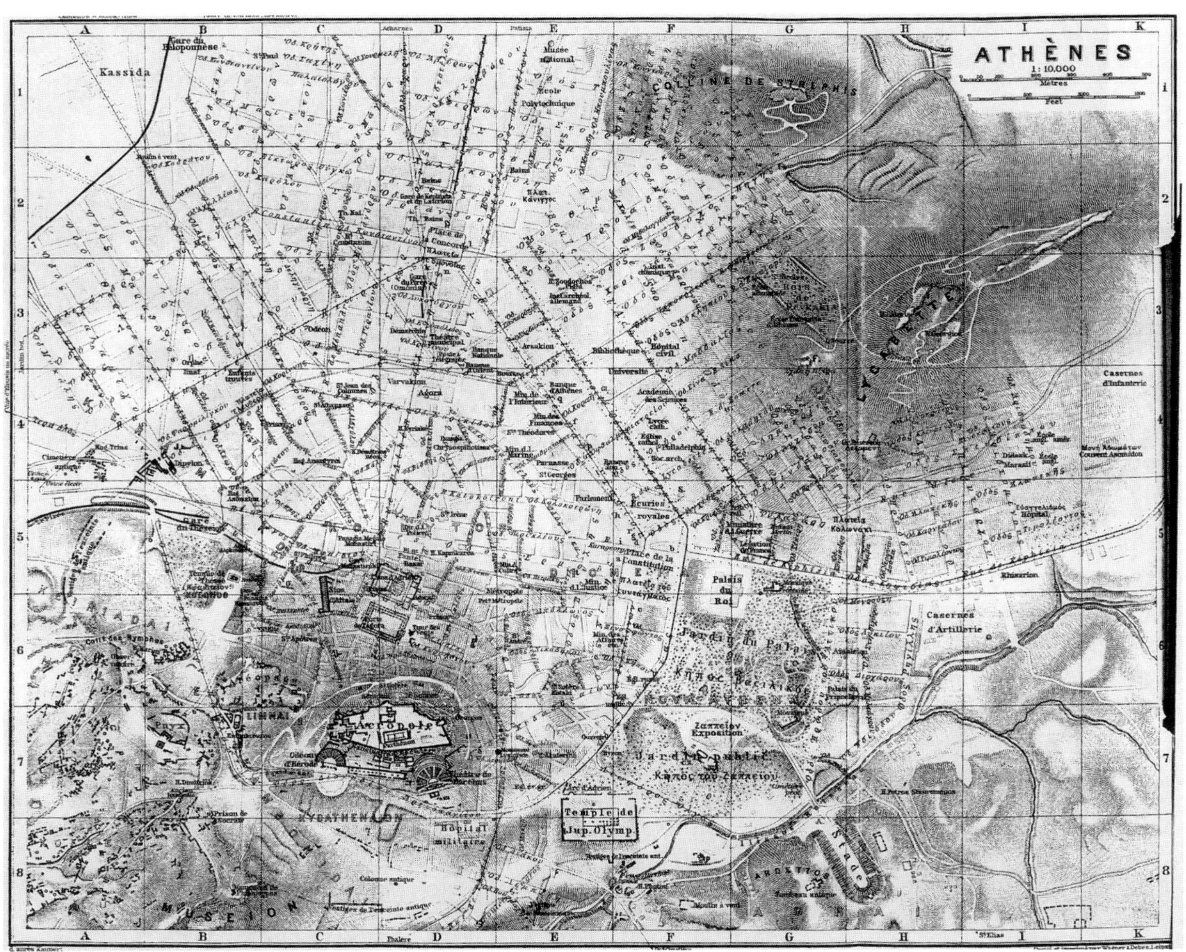

27. Plan of Athens. Modified from Karl Baedeker, *Greece: Handbook for Travellers*, 4th ed. (Leipzig: Baedeker, 1909).

European-style capital. . . . The creation of these institutions was intended to address not so much the country's practical needs at the time, but rather its projected image as the cultural beacon of the Balkans and the Middle East."[59] The beaux arts regularity of the plan of the new Athens as well as the neoclassicism and imposing scale of its public and many of its private buildings reveals the political aspirations of the city. Athens had the trappings if not the power of a European capital.

The nineteenth-century invention of a new Athens occupied the space beyond the walls of the medieval town. The reconstruction of the old section of the city after the war was, in contrast to the beaux arts order of the new city, unsystematic. It included surviving fragments of the medieval and early modern town. Families built anew the shops and houses that had been destroyed. The irregular plan of the old town remained intact. Its old order was not newly rationalized. The complex plan and domestic scale of the past was reproduced in a rich vernacular version of the then-current neoclassical style. This space in Athens is known as Plaka (fig. 28). In the twentieth century, the threat to the beaux arts neoclassical capital of Greece came from the new construction of the Modern. In contrast, the threat to the medieval and vernacular neoclassical old city came from the new construction of antiquity.

28. Athens, a street in Plaka. Photo by author.

The Western traveler's disdain for the post–War of Independence Athens was perfectly articulated in 1857 by the American tourist Samuel Wheelock Fiske, quoted at the beginning of this chapter. The bantering threat voiced by Fiske was carried out by archaeologists, sometimes on a small scale, sometimes on a large scale. There were the individual plunderers. Ludwig Ross, an early archaeologist, described the devastation wrought on Athens by the War for Independence and recorded the vandals, both local (the reusers of ancient stone) and foreign (artifact seekers), who robbed the city of its ancient monuments. But he also took advantage of destruction for his own appropriation of the past. The ruination of medieval churches provided him particular satisfaction because they offered the richest yield in his search for ancient inscriptions.[60] It is said of another classical epigrapher, the Frenchman Michel Fourmont, that he smashed inscriptions once he had transcribed them so that no later scholar might dispute his authority.[61]

In the long term, state-sanctioned institutions committed to antiquity represented an even more serious threat to Plaka. Plans for the elimination of Plaka were already in place in the first modern schemes for the city. Plaka was to be treated as the extension of the Acropolis and cleared of its postclassical structures as an archaeological zone first for an excavation of antiquity and then for its display. The limited funds of the Greek government restrained its earliest attempts to erase the district. The infusion of American moneys from the 1930s through the 1950s did allow the systematic expropriation of much of the ancient Agora.[62] Archaeological work on the site was particularly intense after World War II. It culminated in the reconstruction of the Stoa of Attalos (fig. 29). This project was approved by the ministers of education, finance, and coordination; supervised by the Department of Restorations in the Ministry of Education; and executed by the architectural firm of W. Stuart Thompson and Phelps Barnum of New York.[63] The work was initiated by the American School of Classical Studies with a substantial contribution by John D. Rockefeller Jr. The pristine monumentality of the Stoa dominated the bricolage of ruins of the ancient Agora in much the same way as the Modernist U.S. Embassy and the Hilton initially controlled the more prosaic urban clutter of their surroundings.

29. Athens, Stoa of Attalos, 2nd century B.C.E., reconstructed between 1953 and 1956 by the American School of Classical Studies in Athens. Photo courtesy of the American School of Classical Studies in Athens.

The Stoa remains as much a monument to the American School and to Rockefeller as to Attalos.[64]

If Plaka was threatened by American investment in Athens's past, the new city was reordered by American investment in Athens's present. The Agora and the area below Lykabettos, the highest hill in Athens, were the two sites in the city most radically changed by American investment in the 1950s. The promotion of tourism transformed both spaces. No less than the reconstituted Agora, the Athens Hilton was a product of the fetishization of Athens's classical past. It also contributed significantly to the subversion of the city's other histories.

Athens Hilton.

Hilton began negotiations for a hotel in Athens in 1950. A letter of February 1951 from John Houser to Conrad Hilton conveys a sense of the parties and issues involved.

> Bill Irwin spent a week in Athens and we should have the answer from them within the next two weeks as to whether we are going ahead there. We are dealing with the Military Pension Fund whose representatives you met.
>
> You remember they had a site they wanted us to use but they have complied with our wishes and have taken an option on the Italian Embassy site and adjoining land which is across from the Royal Park. Bill went over the full lease contract with them which they are now studying. The proposal is for a 200 to 250-room first-class hotel with a total cost of the project of around $3,000,000.00.
>
> The oral understanding is that they will enter into the agreement with us conditioned upon a 70% loan arranged through ECA [Economic Cooperation Administration] (already agreed to by ECA) and ability to purchase the properties we selected at a fair price. I will advise you as soon as we hear from Athens.[65]

In addition to local officials, American agencies were intimately involved in discussions of the Athens Hilton, just as they had been in the early negotiations for the Istanbul Hilton. A later letter from Houser to Hilton, dated June 1951, made this clear.[66]

> Left Athens with the situation unclear. Discovered their figuring of costs was not based on realistic facts. They had figured $10,000 per room fully furnished

> and equipped. Checked cost on the two new hotels being built in Corfu and it is clear the Pension Fund estimate is low. I figure it will cost at least $15,000 a room and asked for their financing to be adjusted to that figure. The land will cost about $1,100,000 so that the 250 room hotel discussed will cost close to $5,000,000 total. It was a shock to them but I think it would be a mistake to accept anything but a very outstanding hotel. Suggested decreasing it to 200 rooms if necessary which apparently satisfied them. The Pension Fund, however, still wants some protection from risk and since we won't give it—it is up to their government. They are having meetings in the next day or so to decide it. Believe the course is wise, for the Military Pension Fund is powerful and if we didn't earn enough for them to meet fixed charges we would be in trouble. The guarantee of the government if given will give us protection too in that way. It would be easy to talk them into a deal, but it [is] so unattractive to us commercially that [I] decided it was better to have everything out on the table and be sure our partners won't be hurt. If they get the government guarantee and assurance from ECA, they are to send me a cable so I will stop for a short stay on the way back to Rome.
>
> The enclosed government cables are very confidential. The long one is the one sent by the ECA in Rome and the short one the reply from Paris our friends are trying to get cleared. They were given to me by mail in secrecy but thought you would want to see them.[67]

The references to the Economic Cooperation Administration might suggest that it was interested in subsidizing the Hilton project, but was hesitant about making public its support of a luxury American hotel. In its own bulletins, the ECA provided the rationalization for such a subvention. Soon after its establishment, the ECA issued a series of reports on the conditions of the countries to which Marshall funds were directed. Tourism is not mentioned in the pamphlets dealing with Italy and Turkey. For Greece, however, tourism seems to offer the primary hope for economic recovery.

> Among the country's most important assets are its historical interest and its fine climate and scenery. Tourist traffic has contributed substantially to its foreign exchange earnings in the past, and with the annexation of Rhodes, which has already been developed as a tourist resort by the Italian Government, its potential earnings from tourists are still greater. . . . Funds available for this object will be spent to improve hotels and to build new ones; and modest sums will also be spent for the preservation and better display of historical monuments. Granted restoration of order throughout Greece, it appears that the expenditures for tourism will reap quick and rich returns.[68]

Apparently the financial and site problems suggested in Houser's correspondence could not be resolved. Much later, in April 1957, an agreement was reached between Hilton and Apostolos Pezas, the Greek shipping magnate. Apparently Apostolos Pezas, like John D. Rockefeller Jr., was committed to constructing a monument in Athens that would write his memory into the landscape.[69] Nevertheless, financial exigencies caused Pezas to sell his shares to Ioniki Hotel Enterprises, a subsidiary of Ioniki Bank, in February 1960, well before the hotel's opening in April 1963. Although the local owner of the Athens Hilton was, in the end, not directly linked with the Greek government, the state's intimate involvement in the negotiations for the hotel are suggested by the owners' ability to procure prime real estate and to elude restrictions in the building code.[70] "[T]he architect in charge of the Town Planning Directorate, Mr. P. Vassiliadis—who also happened to be one of the associated architects who designed the building—managed, under existing laws relative to buildings of public utility and tourism, to procure a waiver from the Ministry of Public Works, permitting the violation of the Athenian building code: the provision relative to height. . . . [T]he hotel is well over twice the legal maximum of twenty-four meters."[71] In Athens, as in Istanbul and Cairo, the local owners' wealth and influence assured the Hilton of the most advantageous site and highest quality building. The owners did not, however, always get exactly what they wanted. A story from the time of the hotel's construction told by Eric Pick, one of the consulting American architects, suggests that the building's significance was sometimes greater than that of its possessors:

> When I heard that Vice President Lyndon Johnson was visiting Athens, I thought it would be great publicity to have him visit the construction site. The embassy said that would be fine; he would stop on his way from the airport between 10–11 AM. Well, the manager and owners were present, the bank president and their staffs, and a ceremonial stand was set up and carpets were laid out. The cavalcade was sighted, but they drove right by. I called the Embassy to ask what was the matter. They answered, "There wasn't anyone out there; Johnson expected a thousand workers." I said, "Well, the owners and manager were there!" They said, "Johnson doesn't care about them. He didn't see any workers, so he didn't stop." When I said that I could get workers out, they allowed that he might stop on the way back to the airport. It was lunch time; I got several hundred workers to come out and line-up in front of the hotel. And sure enough Johnson stopped and started to make a speech. He talked for a half an hour or forty-five minutes. He had been a road worker and loaded and driven trucks at construction sites. He insisted on going into the raw building with all these workers and talking with them. The bankers were upset, but Hilton was happy. And Johnson was happy.[72]

The Athens Hilton was opened in April 1963.[73] The architects responsible for the construction of the Athens Hilton were Greek nationals. Prokopios Vassiliadis, E. M. Vourekas, and Spyros Staikos were the principals of the undertaking; the American firm of Warner, Burns, Toan and Lunde was the consultant.[74] (Charles Warner had already contributed to the design of the Caribe Hilton.)[75] No claims had been made for the Egyptian character of the Nile Hilton by Welton Beckett, its American architect.[76] The Nile Hilton was patently Modern with a pharaonic gloss and an American subtext. Nathaniel Owings of SOM remembered the Istanbul Hilton as Turkish, but the Turks working on the project regarded it as essentially American Modern. The Athens Hilton, in contrast, was claimed to be identifiably Greek. Spyros Staikos, one of the architects, maintained that the Athens Hilton was conceived as a Greek building:

> The general idea of the design was with the type symmetrical bilateral ATRIUM of the main body of the building which were surrounded by columns ("pteron" in ancient Greek temples) with construction of partitions of clostra walls. From a decorative aspect the inlaid depictions of the PANATHENIAN and other Greek motifs (Greek Key, triglyphs, etc.) which were designed by the Greek artisans, J. Moralis and J. Tsarouhis, maintain in the decor the exterior appearance. Generally the materials which have sustained the exterior and interior lobbies are marble, mosaic, and bronze.[77]

Although Hilton International's contract with the Greek architects of the Athens Hilton required them to visit the Hiltons in Montreal, Istanbul, and, later, Cairo, Spyros Staikos insisted that this experience had no effect on their thinking. The Istanbul Hilton, he observed, was Turkish, the Nile Hilton Egyptian, and the Athens Hilton essentially Greek. For Mr. Staikos, the Greek architectural form of the building distinguished it clearly from its predecessors.[78] The two Americans who worked on the project were more circumspect about the structure's Greekness. Charles Warner, a principal of Warner, Burns, Toan and Lunde, was modest in his ascription of Hellenic qualities to the Athens Hilton: "The only Greek thing about the building was the base on which it was set and the landscaping, with horizontal, plateau-terraces. These were 'acropolytic' (not apocalyptic)—a place for people to gather, like the ancient agoras. We did a simple building, with a base and columns, not modeled on ancient columns, but creating a classical rhythm. With an entablature, which is the bar and terrace on the roof. Greek in spirit, but not narrowly Greek."[79] Eric Pick, the on-site American architect, similarly attributed the building's Greekness to its social spaces: "It had a Greek quality in terms of planning. The Greeks like to socialize in open, park-like surroundings, like the ancient agora. The hotel acted as a forum. It was in a green area, it had atria surrounded by shops, with olive trees and a big pool at the back, and all that opened to a big lobby with several levels."[80] As did Mr. Staikos, the advertising for the hotel emphasized its Greek character: "ATHENS, ANCIENT CAPITAL OF CULTURE. Treasure-trove of antiquity and a modern, vibrant city, entrusted with the architectural wonders of the centuries. . . . [T]he majestic Athens Hilton, twelve stories high, entered through a series of descending stages in ancient Greek amphitheater style, classic lobbies, gallery terraces, gardens, superb swimming pool, health club, garden rooms. Interior courts in the manner of old Greek atria, surrounded by fascinating shops."[81] The Athens Hilton was treated as a new ancient monument, worthy of the great tradition of classical architecture in which it participated.[82] Locally this understanding of the Hilton has apparently been broadly accepted. In a recent poll asking, "Is the Parthenon a monument?" "Is the Parliament (formerly the Royal Palace of King Ludwig of Bavaria) a monument?" and "Is the Athens Hilton a monument?" over half the respondents answered yes to the last question.[83]

30. Athens, Athens Hilton, exterior view from the west. Photo by author.

31. Athens, Athens Hilton, interior view through the lobbies toward the front entrance. "The lobby ceiling has been lowered. The chandeliers have all been changed. The carpets used to be blue-gray, now they are flame red, changing the atmosphere completely." Elly Hadziotis, director of public relations, Athens Hilton, interview, November 27, 1997. Photo by author.

For the uninitiated, however, the Athens Hilton might not seem so different from its predecessors in Istanbul and Cairo. The hotel was again a luminous horizontal mass poised over an extended base. As in the Istanbul and Nile Hiltons, it was assumed that guests would arrive by automobile. And indeed, they were driven in from the broad avenue Leoforos Vasilissis Sofias (figs. 30, 31, and 32). They were deposited under the porte cochere covering the drive, then entered a lobby flanked by open courtyards surrounded by shops. Parallel with their line of vision was reception. Beyond were a series of descending lobby and lounge levels. Like the Hiltons of Istanbul and Cairo, the hotel was one of the highest buildings in its city at the time of its construction. As in the case of the Nile Hilton, the Athens Hilton was presented as a site from which the city could be controlled: "A preliminary look out over the city from the balcony of your room or from the terrace of the Galaxy Roof and Bar will help you lay out your excursions throughout the city."[84] Again like the Nile Hilton, the guest room block responded to a spectacular view, though by embracing it with a gentle curve rather than by pointing at it with a flat angle. This block was once more perforated by a regular grid of balconies. The familiar amenities of Hilton modernity were included: radios, telephones, and ice water on tap in each room, air-conditioning, and wall-to-wall carpeting (fig. 33). The customary assortment of boutiques and restaurants were part of its program: a dinner-dance club promoted the remarkable view at the top of the building; a soda fountain–snack bar and other eateries at lower levels along with shops with luxury goods. There was the expected swimming pool and cabanas. The symmetrical pairing of boutiques around the two atria flanking the main entrance to the Athens Hilton appeared to be a multiplication of the single cluster of luxury retailers around the garden courtyard in Istanbul. Similarly, the pumpkin-domed restaurant of the Athens Hilton had the same volup-

tuous effect as the domed cocktail lounge in Istanbul. The greater flow of lobby area in Athens might have looked like a natural development of Becket's space-modeling introduction of a grand central staircase in the Nile Hilton. The new Athens Hilton appeared to contribute to the distinctive Hilton International formula rather than to diverge from it.

Part of this Hilton formula was the construction of the local by employing indigenous materials and by historical reference in the ornamentation. The Athens Hilton takes full advantage of the superb local marble that distinguished ancient Athenian monuments. Marble was used to clad much of the structure as well as to provide its details. The bathroom floors of the guest rooms, for example, were monolithic slices of white marble. As in Istanbul and Cairo, the hotel was decorated with local crafts and its fixtures simulated ancient artifacts. The guest room lamp stands, for example, evoke

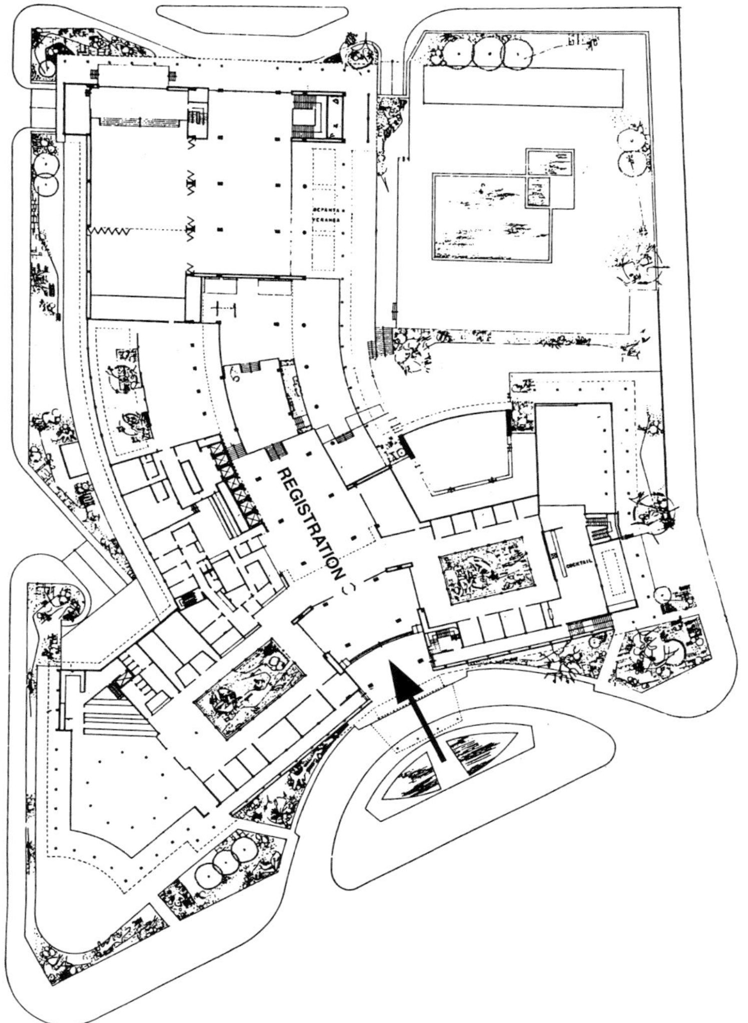

32. *Left* Athens, Athens Hilton, plan. The guest room block rises above the paired piers at the core of the ground plan. Modified from "Athens Hilton," *Architektonike* 15–16 (May–August 1959).

33. *Above* Athens, Athens Hilton, view below the sink in a guest room showing the third water cock that controlled the flow of ice water. It is now disconnected. Photo by author.

Archaic horse figurines (fig. 34). The Hilton also displayed the work of contemporary Greek artists. The most impressive contribution appeared on the monumental slabs closing the narrow ends of the curved guest room block. These massive blank panels provided an imposing surface for a monumental work by the well-known Greek artist Yannis Moralis.[85] On the entrance side of the structure, Moralis depicted the Panathenaic procession in a contemporary interpretation of Greek archaic forms. A colossal Athena in the upper right received the ranks of maidens and warriors who brought her the city's offerings. The figures were constructed of a few lines of black shadows caught in taut incisions in the stone. The back face of the building was enlivened with staccato registers of incised vertical lines and small squares aligned with the floors of the guest room block. The Hilton again avoided kitsch, though here it is not only through quality reproductions of the ancient as in Cairo but also by the deployment of contemporary works. Guests were met with the serious pleasure of Art.[86]

For all its Hiltonesque elements, the feature of the Athens Hilton that most marked it as a Hilton and simultaneously identified it as uniquely Greek was its relation with the landscape. The Hilton was sited in the hollow below the Lykabettos outcrop, in a zone made available for development in the fifties by infilling the Ilissos River with a major urban motorway (fig. 35). This new extension of Athens to the northeast was quickly occupied with high-class buildings. Alexander Papageorgiou-Venetas described the nature of the expansion:

> This privileged area situated on the eastern edge of the inner city, between the Royal Garden and Lykabettos and tangential to the main arteries of Dephissias Avenue and Vasileos Konstantinou Avenue, was destined to fulfill some representative urban functions. Some important new buildings were already under construction or planned in the vicinity of this area: the American Embassy designed by Gropius and built in 1957–1958 at the north; the Athens Hilton designed by Vassiliadis, Vourekas and Staikos, built in 1958–1962, in the center. Others were to follow in the east: the National

34. Athens, Athens Hilton, guest room lamp stand, an original fixture still in use. Photo by author.

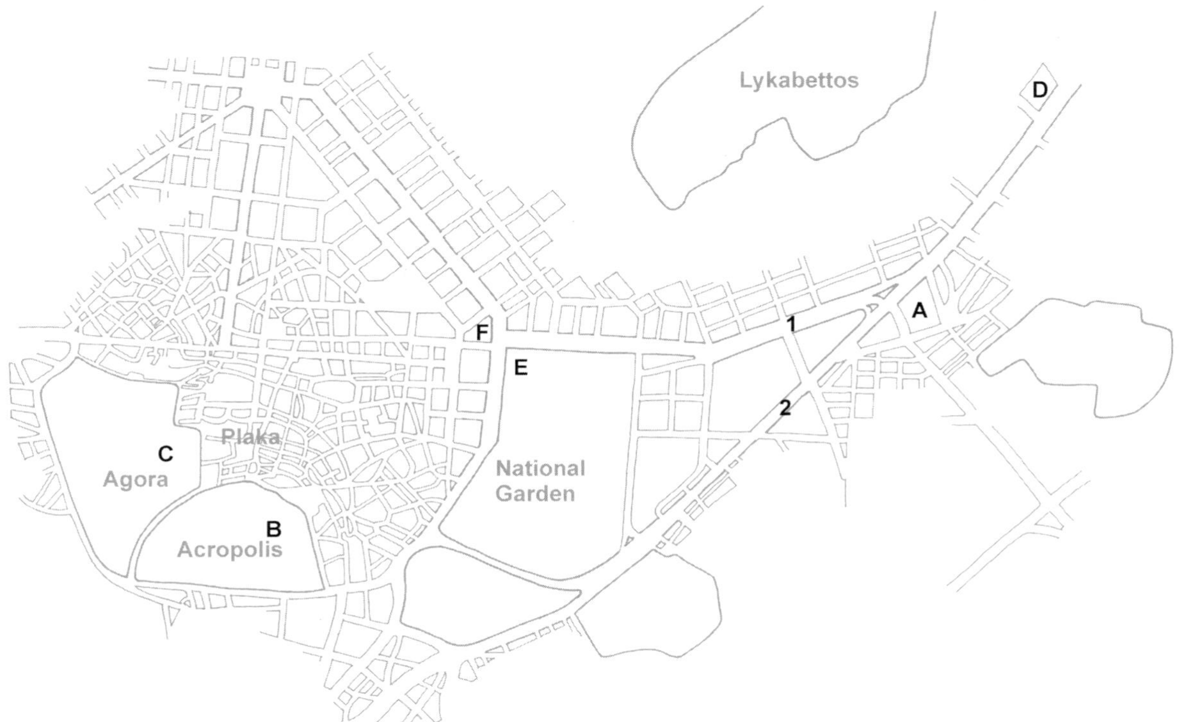

35. Sketch plan of Athens, by author: *A*, Athens Hilton; *B*, Parthenon; *C*, Stoa of Attalos; *D*, U.S. Embassy; *E*, Royal Palace, now the Parliament; *F*, Grande Bretagne; *1*, Vasilissis Sophias Avenue; *2*, Vasileos Konstantinou Avenue.

> Gallery, designed by Mutsopoulos, Fatouros and Mylonas, built in 1968–1973; the National Research Foundation, designed by Doxiadis Associates, built in 1965–1967; the Friends of Music Concert Hall designed by Keilholz and Vourekas, recently completed.[87]

Charles Warner, the principal of the American architectural firm involved in the project, explained the hotel's relation to its urban setting: "The site was in a depression amongst brownish-beige, four- or five-story apartment blocks of apartment buildings. . . . The idea was to do something white and marble, to form an anchor in the city. Surrounded by the monastery hills, we needed a little height, something to lift the heart of the city. The problem was to lift it out of that depression."[88] The Hilton helped lift this space out of more than a physical depression. The Athens Hilton, like the Nile Hilton, was popular with the rich, famous, and powerful. "Young King Constantine and Queen Anne-Marie often dropped in at the coffee shop (he is a spaghetti and sundae fan) during their courtship and before his accession to the throne. And for some reason or other, Greek film star Melina Mercouri has chosen the spacious landscaped grounds of the hotel as a favorite walking spot for her black poodle."[89] In Athens as in Istanbul and Cairo, the building of the Hilton confirmed and contributed to the status of its location. In a city desperately undersupplied with accessible parks, the Hilton provided the well-to-do with a central-city playground. Admission to its large pool and tennis courts was available for a fee.[90] Electric streetcars were introduced to Athens first in this area. Property values increased dramatically.

The discrepancy between the luxury of the Hilton and the poverty of nearby neighborhoods was locally recognized and satirized. The *New York Times* noted that the Hilton, built not far from "the working class district known as Pangrati, is the subject of a musical revue called 'Hilton and Pangrati.' . . . The verse, written by Napoleon Eleftheriou, goes:

> Hilton and Pangrati
> Here live the rich and the poor
> What you need to pay for a Hilton room
> Would pay for a house in Pangrati."[91]

Moreover, some Greeks regarded the Athens Hilton as an obvious locus of the overprivileged alien. In May 1969, a bomb was exploded in the hotel by opponents of the right-wing military regime in retaliation for American support of the Colonels.[92] But the resentment of the contrast between the conspicuous expenditure of the American Hilton and the poverty of Greece was remarkably rarely expressed. More characteristically, the hotel was described with veneration, as in this note from a local journal: "Yes, here is good taste, daring prodigality and imagination. There is no place for discussion, criticism or humor. Here, the quality of the most perfect American product, the shining Cadillac, has been coupled with the added luxury of the European taste and the Greek marble."[93] Most Greeks, like the critic just quoted, seemed to see the Hilton as a promise of their own modernist possibility. The Hilton presented to the Greeks, as it had to the Turks and Egyptians, modernity's technical utopia. In any case, both those Greeks who liked the building and those Greeks who disliked it apparently looked at the Hilton and reacted to its Modernity, luxury, and internationalism as a sign of American technology and wealth, not as an autochthonous piece of architecture.

Americans, in contrast, tended to gaze out from the Hilton to Athens's past greatness. The importance of the site was the spectacle that it allowed the hotel to present to its consumers. The object of the guest's historically laden gaze was, of course, the Parthenon, the crowning feature of the Acropolis. It was the promise of that look that sold the Athens Hilton. A typical advertisement was headed: "THE MOST FAMOUS VIEW IN HISTORY!"[94] The broad west face of the Hilton directly confronted the east façade of Athena's temple. The plan of the building was determined by the view that it would in turn produce. Charles Warner commented, "We weren't trying to match the Acropolis, though the building looks right at it."[95] Whatever the architects' intentions, the Hilton did establish a new and dramatic visual axis in the city. In Cairo, the Hilton was ubiquitously prominent. In Athens, the Hilton was particularly present when viewed from the Acropolis. The Parthenon was made the ancient foil of the modern Hilton.

The effect of the Athens Hilton's reconstruction of the Acropolis is nowhere more dramatically represented than in the images illustrating an article in *Architectural Forum* by Vincent Scully, Yale professor and highly respected architectural historian.[96] The article begins with a full-page photograph of the Hilton in the distance framed by the columns of the Parthenon. The viewer assumes the position of Pheidias's goddess looking out of her *cella* not at the sacred mountain of Hymettos, but at the Hilton (fig. 36). A final full-page telephoto image shows the Hilton in such a way that it appears to be set on its own, competing acropolis. The essay also has a Le Corbusier–like heading-sketch. The Parthenon, an oblong of brief verticals with a pediment occupies the foreground; a second, similarly sized form made up of horizontals usurps the background. Scully vitriolically denounces the Athens Hilton as "vandalism." Scully begins: "Once [Greece] demonstrated what Camus called a 'pact of friendship' between men and the earth. . . . Now she represents . . . the opposite: the destruction of the earth by men. She . . . is fouling her nest in most of the time-honored contemporary ways. It is peculiarly bitter and instructive to watch, in a landscape once regarded as holy."[97] Scully's anger resulted from the failure of modern Athenians in their priestly obligation to maintain their ancient and sacred panorama. The consecrated space for Scully involved much more than an archaeological site: "[T]he Parthenon and its sacred mountain Hymettos, have always acted together as one architecture. . . . Together they have stated the facts of human life upon the land. . . . They have managed to sustain that demonstration of ultimate reality throughout all the spectacular vicissitudes of approximately twenty-five hundred years."[98] For Scully, the Greek's unconscionable neglect of a landscape essential to the human understanding of spatial reality was epitomized by the construction of the Athens Hilton:

> This Hilton must surely be the best yet of its numerous clan, since it makes those that did similar though vastly less critical jobs on Istanbul and Cairo seem comparatively innocuous. The Athens building is both over scaled and arrogantly sited for its clients' bleary view (the architecture of the *voyeur* come into its own at last); it is at once too big, in too important a place, and indefensibly sited in that place. . . . [I]f one takes a position in the Parthenon where Pheidias' ivory and gold statue of Athena once stood, it will be seen that the temple, once orientated directly toward its appropriate sunrise over the mountain, is now oriented toward the sun and the Hilton—whose egg-crate facade leers up on axis between the two central columns. . . . The effect

36. Athens, Athens Hilton as viewed from the Parthenon. From Vincent Scully, "The Athens Hilton: A Study in Vandalism," Architectural Forum 119 (July 1963). Reprinted with permission from Vincent Scully.

> may most accurately be described as obscene. . . . [T]he *Hilton* is not entirely lacking in importance, being so conspicuous an example of what can happen when men build on the earth without intelligence, reverence, or love.[99]

Scully condemns all aspects of the Hilton with a ferocity rarely encountered in the balanced discourse of the *Architectural Forum*. Some parts of the structure might understandably be mocked. He caustically describes the Byzantine Café as one of those "charmingly oriental, Hilton-trade-mark-wavy slab-lunchroom-kiosks." But Scully is equally vicious in his criticism of parts of the project that perhaps deserve a more circumspect assessment. He characterizes Moralis's mural, for example, as "the giant graffiti on the building's northern flank [that] call to mind the last palsied scratchings of a dying civilization."[100] Scully's anger over the Hilton's desecration of the sacred landscape verges on the hyperbolic.

In his anger, Scully supplements Hilton advertising. The Hilton's special relation to the Parthenon, promoted in the corporation's commercials, is confirmed by Scully's denunciation. Both Hilton and Scully exaggerate the hotel's proximity to the Acropolis—Hilton in advertising texts, and Scully with images. The Le Corbusier–like sketch aggrandizes the Hilton's scale. The drawing also implies that the Hilton has desecrated the great architect's vision as well as the topography of the city. Moreover, Scully's final photograph appears to be a collage.

Hilton and Scully's textual and visual hyperboles come from the same source. As Le Corbusier wrote in 1911: "Hymettus and Pentelicus, two very high mountain ranges, like two wide adjoining screens, are located behind us, orienting our sight in the opposite direction, toward the estuary of stone and sand, the Piraeus. The Acropolis, whose flat summit bears the temples, captivates our attention, like a pearl in its shell. One collects the shell only for its pearl. The temples are the cause of this landscape."[101] Le Corbusier's observation is persuasive. The classical architecture of Athens, not its geology, consecrates the city. But the sacred panorama so central to the Greek Ideal was a space created by American and Western Europeans in the nineteenth and early twentieth centuries through the restoration of the Parthenon and the elimination of competing histories. Both Scully and Hilton accepted the truth of this construction. Hilton successfully commoditized that truth by packaging its view. Scully was infuriated by the hotel's disruption of the same truth. Scully is, of course, correct. The imposition of the Hilton, a visually demanding building, in this setting changed the meaning of the landscape. Had the great palace of Ludwig I designed by Karl-Friedrich Schinkel for the Acropolis been constructed, the site would have been written instead as a document of German nineteenth-century cultural imperialism.[102] The Hilton introduced its text of an American twentieth-century presence with greater subtlety. The object that gave Athens its mid-twentieth-century cultural and touristic value—the Acropolis—was maintained intact only for those viewing it from the source of the site's rewriting, the Hilton. The raw nerve that the Hilton laid bare in an exemplary historian of the Western architectural tradition was symptomatic of the depth of the Euro-American intellectual's stake in the Greek Ideal and its aesthetic materialization. Scully's article is the proverbial other-side-of-the-coin of Phillip Morris's advertisement for *The Greek Miracle*.

The Athens Hilton was the product of the same veneration of Greek antiquity that occasioned both Scully's wrath and Philip Morris's advertisement. The hotel was the response of capital to cultural demands for the spectacle of a reassuring past, a past that confirmed the viewer's faith in the present. Like the Nile Hilton, the Athens Hilton remade an ancient landscape in the process of packaging it for our consumption.

Berlin Hilton advertisement (detail), 1959.

"We just call it [Strasse des 17 Juni and Unter den Linden] Big Street," said the American as Johnny moved into the fast lane. In the distance the statue on the [Brandenburger] Tor glinted gold in the afternoon sun, beyond it in the Soviet sector a flat concrete plain named Marx-Engels Platz stood where Communist demolition teams had razed the Schloss Hohenzollern. We turned toward the Hilton.

—LEN DEIGHTON, *FUNERAL IN BERLIN*

Forty years ago I predicted that the foolish mistakes of other countries would be imported everywhere and all cities would become equally ugly and equally devoid of individuality. My prophecy has come true so far as London is concerned. It has been spoiled by a number of meaningless skyscrapers.

—STEEN EILER RASMUSSEN, *LONDON: THE UNIQUE CITY*

3 Appropriating the Present: Berlin and London

Berlin.

The Berlin Hilton on Budapester Strasse was built on the grounds of the Berlin Zoo at the edge of the Tiergarten and the banks of the Landwehr Canal (fig. 37).[1] The Tiergarten is Berlin's Central Park. Walter Benjamin, one of the great cultural critics of the twentieth century, claimed that his first memories of urban space were formed there.[2] The Landwehr Canal, constructed between 1845 and 1850, was part of the water transportation system linking the Elbe and the Oder Rivers. These urban waterways transformed Berlin into a trading metropolis. The mutilated bodies of Rosa Luxemburg and Karl Liebknecht, leaders of the German Communist Party, were recovered from the Landwehr Canal after they had been executed by right-wing militia members in 1919. The Hilton, like Berlin itself, was framed by a history of refined intellect and political violence.

Before 1945, Berlin must have felt like a coherent urban space. The city center that had been defined by its seventeenth-century fortification walls survived their demolition. The center's axis was the grand boulevard idyllically named Unter den Linden (Under the Linden Trees). This broad avenue had the expansive Tiergarten (Game Park) and the Brandenburg Gate at one end and the royal palace with its more formal Lustgarten (Pleasure Garden) at the other. Here was the core of the city, where its political ascendancy was displayed as high culture. Berlin, along with London and

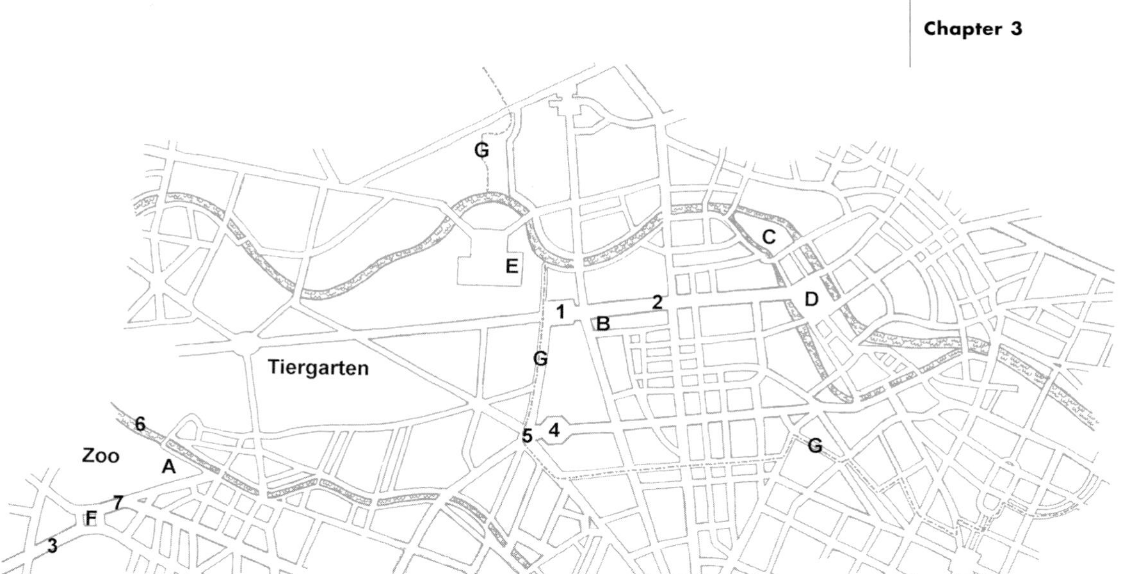

37. Sketch plan of Berlin, by author: *A*, Berlin Hilton, now the Hotel Inter-Continental Berlin; *B*, Adlon Hotel; *C*, Museumsinsel; *D*, Lustgarten, later Marx-Engels Platz; *E*, Reichstag; *F*, Kaiser-Wilhelm Gedächtniskirche; *G*, Route of the Berlin Wall; *1*, Brandenburg Gate; *2*, Unter den Linden; *3*, Kurfürstendamm Strasse; *4*, Leipziger Platz; *5*, Potsdamer Platz; *6*, Landwehr Canal; *7*, Budapester Strasse.

Paris, was a showplace of the Western tradition. Appropriated pasts were exhibited in affirmation of the city's dominion. The Pergamon Museum reproduced the Attalid's great sanctuary of Zeus from Asia Minor and the monumental Istar Gate of Nebuchadnezzar, just as the British Museum reconstructed the Temple of Athena from Periclean Athens. These spoils were complemented by the intellectual structures that rationalized their confiscation. Humboldt University did for the modern university what the University of Paris had done for higher education in the thirteenth century. Institutions devoted to music and books were housed in grand buildings. The classical forms of these buildings embodied the rarefied status of their contents. Resplendent churches and synagogues evidenced the moral and spiritual basis of Germany's cultural accomplishments. No. 1 Unter den Linden was the Adlon, Berlin's most renowned hotel.[3]

Within this urban space, as in other metropolises, memorials of powerful men performed as monuments to great ideas. Berlin, like all great cities, was ordered for display. Berlin's particular urban pageant was preponderantly military. The autocratic Hohenzollerns suppressed civilian self-governance between 1442 and 1918.[4]As the foremost city of Prussia and then, with the nation's unification in 1871, as the capital of imperial Germany, the stage was set for Hitler's Third Reich. Berlin was the center of a sequence of militaristic states. From Frederick William I's use of the Tiergarten as a parade ground in the eighteenth century to the refiguring of "the Big Street" as a military processional by the Nazis in the twentieth, Berlin was a theater for martial performance. This city of high culture and military might was destroyed by Allied bombing in 1945. After World War II, two very different Berlins were reconstructed. These two Berlins offered an unparalleled spatial experience of conflicting ideologies.

On April 30, 1945, two days after Hitler killed himself in his bunker in the grounds of Speer's Reich Chancellery, Berlin capitulated to Soviet troops. The Allies had already agreed that Germany was not going to remain independent and united, as after World War I. Rather, it would be divided and occupied by the British, French, Americans, and Soviets. The territory of greater Berlin, though located deep within the Soviet zone of Germany, was to be jointly controlled by all four Allies as a symbol of their own victorious identity of purpose. At stake, however, was something more than a symbolic gesture. West Berlin soon reinstated itself as one of Germany's significant industrial cities, employing some 285,000 industrial workers. The male workforce in Berlin, decimated by the war, was in part regenerated by the immigration to West Berlin of German youth escaping the mandatory conscription of the rest of the country.[5] It is even claimed that West Berlin exported more per year than Portugal.[6] The first troops of the Western Allies entered the city on July 1, 1945. The Soviet plans to reunify the city as the capital of East Germany required the withdrawal of French, English, and American forces. To force a military evacuation, the Soviets blockaded the city in June 1948. This action precipitated the famous airlift in support of the troops and civilians in the western sectors of Berlin and forced an acknowledgment of the city's division. Berlin, center point of the cold war, was two cities, not one.

The Soviet sector, known to the West as East Berlin, retained the lion's share of old Berlin's important cultural monuments and elite social sites. It encompassed the old city center, including Unter den Linden with its ranks of cultural buildings, Museumsinsel, Wilhelmstrasse with its governmental structures, and Potsdamer Platz, along with Leipziger Platz, where the most elegant cafés had been located. Despite deeply stressed economic resources, the public buildings and monuments at the core of the old capital were restored, including the Brandenburg Gate, the Alte Bibliothek, parts of Humboldt University, the Neue Wache, St. Hedwigs-Kathedrale, and the Berlin cathedral. Enough of the splendid Oranienburger Strasse Synagogue was retained to allow its late reconstruction (fig. 38). The buildings of the

38. Berlin, Oranienberger Strasse Synagogue. Photo by author.

Museumsinsel were also reopened. The reconstructed neoclassicisms of these early modern and nineteenth-century edifices complemented the party's preferred mode of architectural expression. The East promoted a vaguely classicizing architecture planned and executed by architectural collectives.[7] "It was a sincere struggle to form an authentic architecture with which to represent and enhance the promise of proletarian culture. Modernism in all its forms was the product of bourgeois intellectualism. Classical architecture alone would build upon German heritage, would mirror democracy from its roots in ancient Greece, and would mirror socialism by providing unambiguous symbols of equal meaning to all."[8] The most celebrated project in (East) Berlin was the building of Stalinallee, later renamed Karl-Marx-Allee. Widened into a grand proletarian boulevard to complement Unter den Linden, it was to be defined by the continuous neoclassical (sometimes named neofascist by Western architectural critics) façades of solid, traditionally constructed, medium-rise apartments. The finished flats were rented to workers for a pittance. The old Soviet Embassy had occupied an eighteenth-century palace in the city center. After the war its ruins were cleared. The new Soviet Embassy complex was much larger, but it was rendered in a state-renaissance style that conformed reasonably to its nineteenth-century neighbors on Unter den Linden. The German Democratic Republic, or GDR, attempted to produce a Berlin that preserved the semblance of nineteenth-century bourgeois cultural institutions for the new proletariat.[9]

(East) Berlin, capital of the GDR, was shaped not only by reconstruction and new construction, but also by destruction. Buildings that were deeply implicated in fascism were destroyed. For example, Albert Speer's monstrous Reich Chancellery, which was begun in January 1938 and virtually complete by Kristallnacht, on November 10 of the same year, was razed soon after the occupation began. The ideological significance of this destruction of Hitler's headquarters was reified in the Soviet Memorial in the Tiergarten, in the British sector of the divided city, a massive work constructed of marble salvaged from the demolished Nazi structure. This Soviet Memorial was, in turn, noticeably neglected in many Western guidebooks.[10] Rewriting (East) Berlin as socialist also required the redefinition of its old aristocratic center. The imperial palace, Schloss Hohenzollern, culmination of Unter den Linden, was razed. The clearing of the site of the royal palace and its Lustgarten opened the new expanse of the Marx-Engels Platz for proletarian demonstrations. This gesture of erasure allowed commentators in the West to ignore the attempts in the East to preserve most of the old monuments of bourgeois culture. The passage from Len Deighton's *Funeral in Berlin*, quoted at the beginning of this chapter, is typical. It deploys this one act of destruction to characterize the East. The elimination of the Schloss Hohenzollern did ideological work on both sides of the ideological divide.[11]

The most extensive destruction in (East) Berlin, however, occurred on its periphery. There, the city was redescribed in an effort to forget West Berlin.[12] Parts of the old city that had been important social centers now were recoded as unsocial edges. The locus of fancy shops and fashionable cafés around Potsdamer Platz was abandoned. Here Erich Mendelsohn's Columbus Haus, having remarkably survived fascism and Allied bombing, was destroyed in 1957 because of its anomalous location between East and West.[13] The GDR's insistent masking of West Berlin culminated violently in the construction of the "antifascist protective rampart" in 1961. Like the early modern fortifications which had originally defined the city, the new Berlin Wall marked the official boundary between social order and its lack.[14] At the same time that the officials of the GDR worked hard to ignore the existence of West Berlin, they constructed (East) Berlin in competition with it. A government-produced pamphlet, published in English, entitled *Successful Path of Developing an Advanced Socialist Society in the GDR: Facts and Figures*, describes (East) Berlin in terms that sound suspiciously like those used in the West for West Berlin:

> Berlin is the capital of our flourishing socialist state, the German Democratic Republic. The people of the GDR are proud of their capital, which is continuing to be systematically extended as their political, economic, intellectual, and cultural center. The development of Berlin is the concern of the whole republic. Our capital is a city of peace. It attracts millions of visitors from all over the world. Berlin is the political center of our state. In this city one finds the seat of the Central Committee of the Socialist Unity Party of Germany, the People's Chamber, the Council of State and other central bodies and institutions, as well as diplomatic missions.[15]

(East) Berlin, rebuilt at the expense of the whole of the impoverished GDR, was the showplace of the socialist state in the same way that West Berlin came to be presented as the display case of the West.

But if for communist officialdom there was no West Berlin, for (East) Berliners, West Berlin was forever present. If the Wall was erected to block the view of the West, it functioned as a proof of the delights that lay beyond it. As a curtain, it attracted attention to what was hidden; as a built monument it maintained the memory of what once was and titillated the imagination about what might be. In West Berlin, the Senate and the Allied powers appropriated the Wall as propaganda and ignored it in long-range planning. Urban planning schemes commissioned in West Berlin inevitably assumed the reunification of the city. An international design competition held in 1957 invited architects to redesign the center of the city, an area that included a significant portion of the Soviet sector.[16] This competition epitomized the differences between East and West. Rather than obliterating its opposite, the West incorporated the East. Rather than trusting bureaucracies and collectives, the competition promoted famous architects and idiosyncratic designs. Rather than consolidating the neoclassical past, the competition entries refigured Berlin as Modern. Rather than ending in construction, the project stopped with plans and models.

Much, of course, was built in West Berlin, but not to a municipal building plan. Old Berlin was not allowed to impede unduly the shaping of a new city. There were fewer cultural monuments left in the western sectors of Berlin than there were in the east. And the West attended less to their preservation. Perhaps the symbolically most significant structure in the West was the Reichstag. In 1957 local authorities dynamited what remained of the dome of the building. After much debate, reconstruction of the Reichstag began, but neither the original decoration of the structure nor its domical crown were restored. The remains of the Kroll Opera opposite the Reichstag were also demolished. The Anhalter Bahnhof, an outstanding example of the Berlin round-arched style, was blown up in 1959–1960, despite preservationists' protests. Only the portico was preserved as a ruin. The same was true of the magnificent synagogue on Fasanenstrasse, which is pathetically recorded only by the domed porch of the central entrance attached to the undistinguished Modern Jüdisches Gemeindehaus.[17] In contrast to (East) Berlin churches like St. Hedwigs-Kathedrale, the Französische Kirche, or the cathedral, neither of the formidable memorial churches in the western sector of the city were restored. The Kaiser-Friedrich-Gedächtniskirche was replaced with a conventional modern church. The Kaiser-Wilhelm-Gedächtniskirche, an elaborate, mosaic-adorned neoromanesque church built at the end of the nineteenth century, was damaged by Allied bombing. Rather than reconstructing the structure, only some of its fragments were preserved as a memorial to the war. Egon Eiermann, who would have preferred razing the site, instead framed the ruins with a broad, modern, octagonal church and a tall bell tower (fig. 39). The campanile has been aptly described as an exquisitely exaggerated hi-fi speaker. The triad of buildings became the symbol of the new West Berlin. In apparent perfect opposition to (East) Berlin, the largest restoration project in West Berlin was the Charlottenburg Palace. If the great palace at the center of the city had been destroyed, the one at its periphery would be rebuilt. The Charlottenburg Palace was scrupulously restored inside and out. The history to be remembered in the West was different from that in the East. The only past seriously reconstructed in the West was the aristocratic past erased in the East. The East German government was made up almost exclusively of acknowledged antifascist exiles. The West Berlin government included, in contrast, many de-Nazified National Socialists. The willingness to eliminate most of the past in the West perhaps suggests that they had more to forget than their counterparts in the East.

39. Berlin, remains of the Kaiser-Wilhelm-Gedächtniskirche (1891–1895), flanked by the octagonal church and bell tower by Egon Eiermann (1959–1961). Photo by author.

If (East) Berlin was an incomplete old city, West Berlin was an artificially created new one. It lacked a center. The center that emerged was defined not by government urban planners, but rather by the exigencies of free enterprise, incited by the Federal Republic's incentive packages.[18] In a recent letter to me, Richard Dill, former vice president for international affairs, German Public Television, described West Berlin as he remembered it from the 1960s:

> It was the biggest brothel, the biggest bar mile (Berlin hat immer geöffnet), the center of drug and gay communities [in Germany]. At the same time [Berlin was] the site of highly subsidized culture, museum life and (alternative) education structures. Glitz and broads around Kurfürstendamm, poverty, crime and decay in many other areas. Kreuzberg was the biggest Turkish town apart from Istanbul. Germans went to Berlin like Americans go to Vegas. Touristic artificiality coupled with escapist chaos. Not a single first class restaurant ever succeeded in Berlin. Their beer is awful. The "alternatives" . . . clustered there, evading the draft, practicing "free love" in WGS (Wohngemeinschaften), studying and displaying Marxist attitudes in the sixties (Kommherunter vom Balkon, unterstütz den Vietcong!). . . . West Berlin was never interested in East Berlin, and is not to this very day. But West Berlin was the dream of everybody on the Eastern side. Only foreign visitors gazed to the East.

Capital settled at the top of Kurfürstendamm Strasse. Like the Champs-Élysées, with which it is often compared, Kurfürstendamm Strasse was laid out in the eighteenth century to connect the ruler of the city to his hunting lodge in the country.[19] The western end became associated with the grand houses of the rich and powerful. In the late nineteenth and early twentieth century, the eastern end of the street, near the Kaiser-Wilhelm-Gedächtniskirche, became a popular social center. Its luxury boutiques and popular cafés began to compete with those around Potsdamer Platz. After the war, this space attracted banks and corporate buildings as well as new boutiques and cafés. The ruins of the memorial church with its modern additions served to center the new city of high-rises. The cultural and administrative sites, rather than being at the center of this synthetic urban complex, were at its margins. The Free University was constructed to the northwest and the Culture Forum to the east. All of the significant new buildings were Modern. The newness of this Berlin was articulated in the contemporary shape of its architecture. The pivotal site at the end of Kurfürstendamm and at the edge of the Culture Forum was occupied by the Hilton.

Berlin Hilton.

Hilton's plans to build in Berlin were announced in the *New York Times* on April 10, 1955: "Mr. Hilton has proposed, they [American authorities] said, that [the new Berlin Hilton] be financed jointly by German money and United States counterpart aid funds. . . . East Berlin disclosed earlier this week that it was planning to complete reconstruction of pre-war Berlin's most famous hotel, the Adlon."[20] The Hilton was completed in three years, opening on November 30, 1958. The East Germans' proposed reconstruction of the Adlon was realized only after Berlin's reunification. The new Adlon opened only in

1997 as a faux version of the old building.[21] In the same way that the postcolonialist Nile Hilton superseded the colonialist Shepheard's as the space of glitz in Cairo, the West's Hilton replaced the East's Adlon in Berlin.

In the rubble of Berlin, amidst the material hardship of Germany's first postwar decade, the announcement of a new American luxury hotel for West Berlin was not universally welcomed. Opposition came from a variety of sources. In his autobiography, Hilton claimed that protests came from the East because of what the East might see: "That the Communists are aware of the danger to them of having the fruits of democracy displayed in their own backyard was very evident recently. In reporting the ground-breaking ceremonies for the Berlin Hilton now being erected in free Germany, the Communist press headlined: LOOK HERE—WHAT A HELL OF A BUSINESS and HOTEL KING ON PLUNDER CAMPAIGN."[22] Polly Houser, wife of the executive vice president of Hilton Hotels International, John Houser, wrote to her friends suggesting that protests came from the East because of what the West might see: "The East Berlin press blasts us almost weekly. Among other names, they call us 'the laughing hyena' because of our proximity to the Zoo. What they really fear is the Hilton giraffe peeking over into the Russian sector, allowing Americans to see the dramatic contrast of life for the same peoples behind the iron curtain and in a western democracy."[23]

Less acknowledged but more serious opposition came from within West Berlin. Nine days after the original announcement of a Berlin Hilton, Berlin hoteliers complained to the city's Senate about the construction of the Berlin Hilton. The *New York Times* reported the hotel association's protest: "The Association of Hotel and Restaurant Owners wrote to Mayor Otto Suhr, charging that the new hotel would bankrupt many of them. They contended that during the course of a year, only half of their beds are occupied. The pensions—a European form of boarding house—are even worse off, they said. Allied authorities, however, are eager to have foreign investments made in Berlin to increase the morale of the city and to raise employment. The new building would cost about $5,000,000."[24] The protest was also, of course, described in the West German press:

> The Berlin Hotel Association [Berliner Gastwirte-Innung] appealed against the construction of a large hotel, the commission of the American hotel company, Hilton, in a resolution to the Senate. As the chair of the Hotel Association, Zellermayer, said yesterday in a press conference, the new building would seriously endanger the existence of Berlin hoteliers and their investment of between DM 30 and 40 million. At mid-year the largest operators were only about 60 percent full and the smaller ones only 30 percent. The announced support of the Senate for this new building was unreasonable, so long as Germany remained ununited and therefore tourism could not be raised to its former heights. As the Senate Committee on Business and Investment made clear, it sees in the new hotel a stimulation for tourism and a proof of confidence in Berlin.[25]

At least one city official, Dr. Paul Hertz, the Social Democratic senator in charge of business and credit, was particularly vocal in support of the project.[26] The protest elicited sympathy in the East. An article in *BZ am Abend* was titled "Ein Hertz für Hilton," perhaps punning on the senator's name.[27] The objections of Hilton's competitors were not, however, given much credence in other quarters.[28] *Bauwelt*, a major German architectural journal, lamented the fact that the hotel's considerable financial cost and propagandistic presentation had elicited a not altogether friendly reception.[29]

The hoteliers' opposition to the project was not simply a reaction to new competition. It was a response to competition that seemed to them unfair. They were privately funded enterprises competing with a state-owned operation.[30] Ironically, the Berlin Hilton, publicized as the ultimate entrepreneurial ratification of capitalism's commitment to West Berlin, was financed by the government of Berlin. The Berlin Hilton's owner was the Hotel Corporation of Budapester Strasse, Ltd. (Hotelbaugesellschaft Budapester Strasse mbH), a corporation founded by the Berlin Senate specifically for the purpose of owning the new hotel. By 1955 Berlin was no longer governed by the Kommandatura, the council of the four Allied commandants. It had a democratically elected parliament of nearly 150 seated members, which, among other things, elected the Berlin Senate. The Senate, consisting of the mayor, his deputy, and no more than sixteen senators, administered the city. The Senate procured the Berlin Hilton.

Hilton apparently had been seeking U.S. support for the construction of a hotel in Germany as early as 1952.[31] A letter from John Houser to Conrad Hilton on May 21, 1954, provides the backdrop of the negotiations between Hilton International and the civic authorities in Berlin:

> It is becoming increasingly clear that the Sheraton chain is trying very hard to break into the European picture. . . . [I] just learned from a friend of mine who is head of TWA [Trans World Airways] in Germany that one of the Sheraton representatives called on him recently, looking into the possibilities of putting up a hotel in Frankfurt or other places in Germany. I think that we are far enough along that knowing of this added competition we can in time match them any place they go in, but it does mean that we cannot sit back in any areas of particular interest to us. Along that line, I am working with Bruno Foa for the possibility of a hotel in Berlin. . . . I suppose that before too long, either I or someone representing us should go to Germany to have first-hand discussions. I shall try to set it up so that we have a firsthand invitation from the German Government.[32]

Hilton's close relationship with Dr. Paul Hertz had been established during his visit to the United States in the spring of 1955.[33] *Der Spiegel* reported that Hertz secured for Hilton 30,000 square meters of the best real estate in the city. This property on Budapester Strasse was appropriated by a decree of the Senate. Hertz also organized the financing for the Senate's owning company, the Hotel Corporation of Budapester Strasse, Ltd.[34] In the end, the hotel, including the over DM 7 million or the interior decoration, cost DM 27.2 million, of which DM 19 million came from American counterpart funds and the rest was secured through mortgages.[35] In view of the Senate's involvement in the project, it is hardly surprising that the Berlin Senate approved construction of the new hotel a mere three weeks after the hoteliers' protest had been mounted.[36] The next day, the details of the project were disclosed:

> Plans for a $4,500,000 hotel in Berlin, Germany—the first major new one since World War II—were disclosed here yesterday. Work on clearing the rubble on the site is scheduled to start as soon as feasible. . . . Construction is being made possible, Mr. Houser said, by an agreement between his company and the Berlin Senate. The basic points of the agreement provided for the establishment of the German owning company and the financing of the building, furniture and equipment through a mortgage loan supplemented by counterpart funds. The Berlin Senate and the Federal German Government,

> as well as United States authorities, have approved the plan, Mr. Houser added. . . . Conrad N. Hilton, president of the Hilton Hotels Corporation, said the hotel would provide "a dramatic symbol of West Berlin's steadfastness and progress as a dynamic center of the free world."[37]

Work on the building was executed with proverbial German efficiency. The foundation stone was laid on April 6, 1957; the Richtfest (festivity for the workers when the roof is complete) was celebrated on January 15, 1958; the gala opening was held on November 30, 1958; and the hotel was opened to the public on December 2, 1958.[38]

The Berlin Hilton, like the Istanbul Hilton, was the product of Hilton's creative use of the state. American moneys subsidized the enterprise of a German municipal government, which in turn paid a portion of its profits to Hilton International Corporation. Important differences between the Berlin Hilton and the Istanbul Hilton are a result of the relative power of their respective state owners in their negotiating positions with Hilton International. Apparently, the more authoritarian state apparatus of Turkey allowed Hilton to dictate the terms of its contract with the assurance that the government would not suffer from criticism. Hilton demanded and got for Istanbul the best building that money could buy. The more sensitive political conditions of West Berlin seriously curtailed the standards that Hilton could set for the Berlin hotel. Polly Houser's description of the Berlin Hilton makes its limitations very clear: "[Y]ou will not find the Berlin Hilton the sophisticated luxury hotel that we have in Istanbul, Puerto Rico, Cuba or even in Montreal. The economic struggle here made it difficult to build at all, and the German Socialist government insisted that the rooms be minimum in size, with no fancy do-dads such as balconies. Their first demand was that only half the rooms have private baths, but upon that we balked and each room has its own bath, most with tubs and showers, some with just showers."[39] The hotel had three hundred guest rooms with baths, and twenty with only a shower.[40] The dramatic improvement of the economic environment in West Berlin between the time of the contract negotiations and the beginning of construction allowed the further improvement of some facilities. "John convinced the Berlin hotel company that these changing conditions warranted a few more suites (which can still be done) as only two had been allowed in this economy hotel. . . . The public areas are more spacious and elaborate as the government decided that in areas which could be used by persons other than guests of the hotel, visiting Germans who wished to buy dinner or just a drink, this was permissible."[41] There was, however, no swimming pool and, despite protests from the Hilton International, guest rooms were not air-conditioned. Air-conditioning was limited to the public areas.[42] The "back-of-the-house" space was less generous than that of the Nile and Istanbul Hiltons. The staff cafeteria, kitchens, and utility rooms were smaller. The language with which the hotel was presented also exposed the problematic politics of luxury. The Berlin Hilton took its place among the roster of luxury hotels in Hilton's advertisements and in its presentation in architectural journals (fig. 40). In contrast, the hotel's opulence was minimized to its local public. *Die Zeit* reported that "the hotel's administration claims that the Hilton was not a luxury hotel, but rather 'a first-class hotel according to international standards.'"[43]

The Berlin Hilton was designed by the well-known Los Angeles firm of Pereira and Luckman (fig. 41).[44] Pereira visited Berlin in early spring 1955.

40. Berlin Hilton, now the Hotel Inter-Continental Berlin, advertisement, 1959. Courtesy of Conrad N. Hilton College Archives and Library, University of Houston.

Fourteen months later, Luckman brought the preliminary plans for the hotel to Berlin. Schwebes and Schoszberger of Berlin did the working drawings, which were finished the following year.[45] Schwebes and Schoszberger also oversaw construction. Apart from the notable absence of such luxuries as a swimming pool, balconies, air-conditioning, and generously scaled guest rooms, the program of the Berlin hotel broadly conformed to the pattern established by the Hilton International hotels that had preceded it. The expansive lower level of the building centered on a generous and transparent lobby of floor-to-ceiling plate glass made more luminous by polished Italian marble floors. The lobby space was rather conservatively ordered.

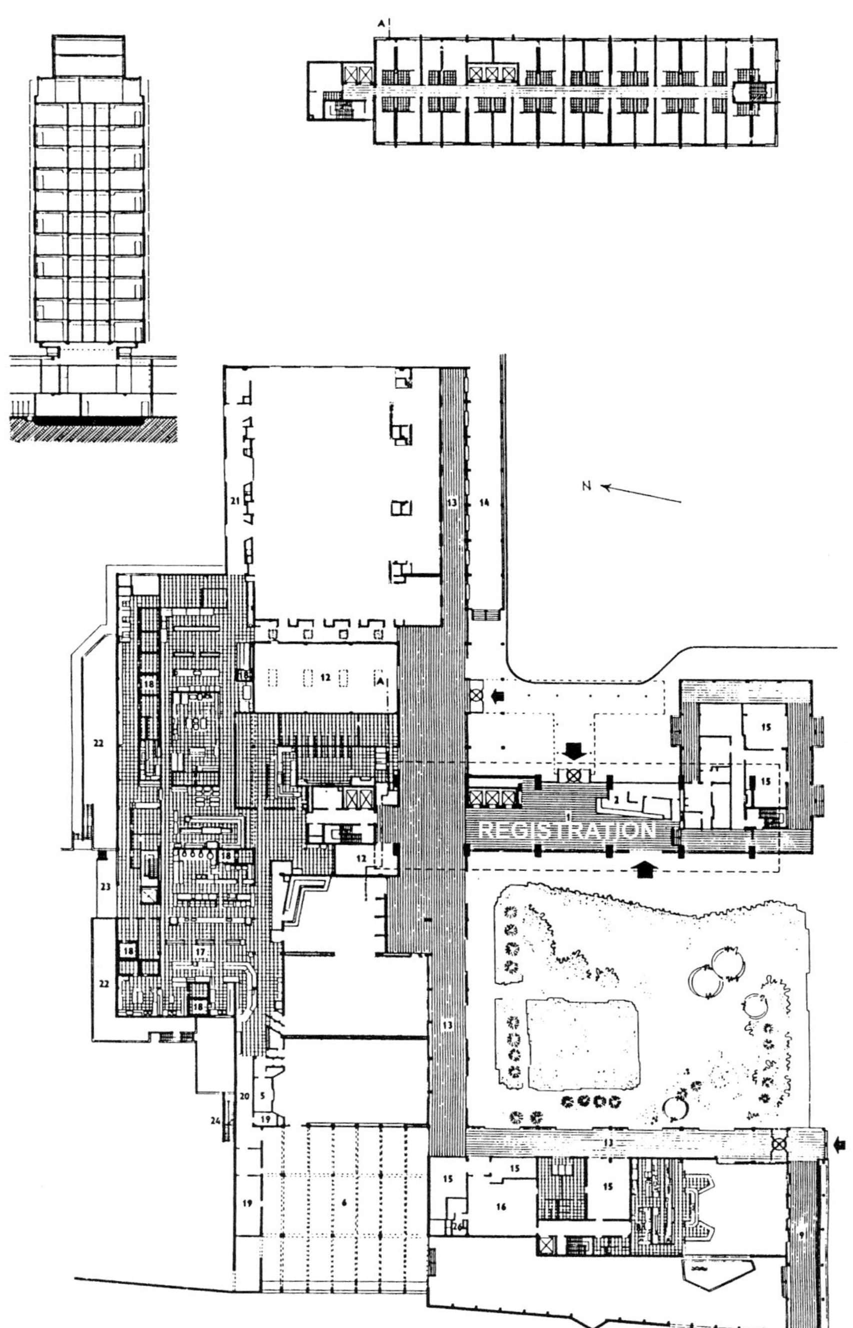

41. Berlin, Berlin Hilton, plans of the entrance level and typical guest room floor with a section of the guest room block. Modified from "Hotel Hilton à Berlin," *L'Architecture française* 211–12 (March–April 1960).

Reception and the elevator bank were not positioned in front of the entering patron, but rather behind her, on either side of the façade's interior wall. The hi-tech profile of the Hilton was nevertheless maintained by registration's remarkable gadgetry, as described by Peter J. Meyer, a concierge who had been in the hotel since 1962.[46] A section of the desk opened as a screen for an overhead slide display of the rooms available to the guest so that she might choose her accommodation. Another technology simultaneously registered the guest at the reception desk and in the chambermaids' office.

Apart from the location of the reception desk, the entrance level of the hotel was characteristically Hilton in its arrangement and decoration. The *Hotel Monthly* describes classic Hilton:

> Upon entering the hotel, the guests can view through lobby windows a plaza around which the hotel's restaurants and bars are grouped. Huge glass windows from floor to ceiling have been used. A marble terrazzo floor continues through lobby and promenades. Groups of seating furniture on hand-woven rugs are used in the spacious lobby. An open grille in marble and metal and groups of plants add color. All restaurants are entered from the lobby and the promenade as are the various shops. The coffee shop, especially the soda fountain, is something quite new to Berliners. Diners can look out on the plaza, the street and the Zoological Garden. A mosaic frieze around the room consists of stylized animals in tones of golds, blues and greys set into a white plaster wall.[47]

The view from the lobby was externalized, as usual. In this instance, the focus was a large, semiprivate garden. The administration offices, grand ballroom, private dining rooms, conference rooms, a bar, and three restaurants were all accessible from the lobby. Among those restaurants was the Hilton signature soda fountain–café, where milkshakes and hamburgers provided Berliners a taste of America. The roof-garden restaurant featured elegant dining, drinking, and dancing. Shopping was also a prominent part of the program. Within the hotel were a hairdresser's salon with a beauty parlor, a Dutch flower shop, a drugstore, a tobacco shop, and a travel agency.[48] Further, a file of twenty-four boutiques and airline offices was connected to the lobby by a covered arcade. Promotional materials for this Hilton, as for others, suggest that penetrating the city in search of its commodities is unnecessary. "You can do a good part of your Berlin shopping without leaving the grounds of the Berlin Hilton—a great convenience in inclement weather—as some of the finest shops in town are situated in the hotel's colonnade."[49] Raised above the lobby area was the neat oblong of the guest room block. It contained 350 rooms, including 22 apartments and 2 luxury suites. The names of the two suites, "The President" and "The Senator," seem to suggest the clientele that were sought for these suites. All guest rooms had telephones from which patrons could dial directly anywhere in Berlin. Not to be routed through a switchboard was still a novelty. Rooms also featured a radio and a television connection. Televisions were available for an additional charge. Characteristically, the German commentators were particularly fascinated by the technological innovations that were found in the bathroom:

> Technical devices of all types have always played a large role in the hotel business. It is therefore hardly surprising that in the Hilton Hotel they are found in masterful, if inconspicuous, form. . . . In tastefully appointed bathrooms, outfitted by the Berlin supplier Bergmann and Franz Nachf., one finds a completely novel, solid, squared porcelain washbowl with a continuous working surface cast as a single piece, a masterwork of ceramic technology (Keramag AG, Ratingen); a further innovation is the toilet with a soundless flush (Georg Rost & Söhne). In the side wall is a built-in, cast iron bathtub which has a profiled bottom to protect against slipping (Ahlmann & Co., Andernach). The cold douche, which has startled so many when the wrong handle was mistakenly turned on, is a thing of the past. . . . [At the Hilton] both hot and cold water runs together from the same valve, so that the guest can no longer make a mistake (Triton-Belco Armaturenfabrik, Hamburg). The whole bathroom is dominated by a great mirror (N. Kinon GmbH., Aachen) which is let into the wall over the sink.[50]

Again, as in the earlier Hiltons, the local was inscribed on the surface of the hotel, in its decoration and ornamental features, rather than in its form or program. Art, as in Athens, instead of craft, as in Istanbul and Cairo, was deployed in the hotel as a sign of the site. The Berlin Hilton represented Berlin's tradition of high culture by displaying works by Berlin artists:[51] "In order to capture the local atmosphere, the work of native [einheimischer] artists was introduced extensively into the decoration. All artworks—pictures in the guest rooms, paintings in the halls, mosaic works, the Pan statue in the roof-garden (Professor Erich G. Reuter), etc.—with the exception of the glass-fantasy in the roof-garden bar were produced by West Berliners."[52] But the high culture of Berlin was not thematized. There was no Bertolt Brecht Bar or Karl Friedrich Schinkel Neoclassical Lounge. Indeed, the incoherence of the Berlin Hilton's decoration suggests the city's uncanniness, the discomforts and instabilities of its meanings and its histories. It lacked the theming consistency that characterized the spaces of Istanbul, Cairo, and Athens. Bits of the decoration seemed to follow the pattern of the earlier Hiltons, rendering the hotel local through reference to the history of the place: "If you have a room on the west side, you have a view of the zoo. On the east, you have the Landwehrkanal at your feet; the Victory Column, Reichstag, Brandenburg Gate and the silhouette of the old Berlin Rathaus in your gaze. And many of these motifs turn up again on the curtains and wall paintings with which the rooms are decorated. It is a Hilton tradition that the interior of every hotel is typical of the city in which it is located."[53] The local-historical was also deployed in the naming and decoration of the hotel's four private dining rooms, each identified with one the region's palaces—Charlottenburg, Pfaueninsel, Rheinsberg, and Sanssouci. Each site was abstractly rendered on the back of its respective door in mock wood-inlay. When the partitions between the dining rooms were removed, the four chateaux appeared as a unified mural, a continuous reference to Germany's romanticized aristocratic past.[54]

The hotel also thematized a utopian future. The dream of complete disengagement from the threats of a fascist history and a communist present was expressed most powerfully in the Golden City Bar: "The main decorative characteristic of the bar is an abstract, three-dimensional wall panel behind the bar showing a modern city in golden metal." This was a city of gilded steel skyscrapers, a city in which history was entirely eliminated.[55] The utopian modernity of the decoration was like the utopian competition plans for the city itself. The most ubiquitous theme for the hotel, the animals of the zoo, escaped Berlin's contemporary tragedy and its inadmissable past by retreating to an imagined childhood. Inge Bech's beasts were rendered in the style of children's book illustrations. A mural of playfully untamable animals adorned the back wall of the coffee shop. Camels, zebras, and giraffes also decorated the elevator lobbies on each of the hotel's guest room floors. There was even talk of a parade of zoo beasts for the opening of the hotel.[56] The wild animal, domesticated by cheerful color and naive form, seems a pure expression of the metaphoric desire to tame the bestialities of Berlin's present and past.[57]

The building, like its decoration, distinguished the Berlin Hilton from earlier members of the chain. There were, however, structural similarities. The Berlin Hilton was a ferroconcrete structure. Its guest room slab also floated above a transparent lobby of plate glass and slender supports. But the surface treatment of the high-rise block, the visually most dominant part of the building, was radically different. The slender, fourteen-story guest room slab rose like a giant inlaid checker board, folded and upended. The white façades of the Nile and Istanbul Hiltons were functionally gridded by the shadows of their balconies. In contrast, the Berlin façade was treated as a "decorated shed."[58] The white *Mittelmosaik* of the façade was interrupted by dark window bays with blue recessed parapets and blue vertical window dividers. Projecting blue concrete slabs dramatize the checkerboard effect.[59] The earlier Hiltons were conspicuous because of their scale, their eminent location, and their Modernity. In contrast, Modernism was nothing new to Berlin. Germany was, after all, an inventor of Modernity, not one of its recipients. But the Hilton's American Modernity superseded the avant-garde Modernism of the 1920s and 1930s. The surviving fragments of Erich Mendelsohn's Columbus Haus of 1931–1932, a monument of early Modernism, were destroyed as the Hilton was built. The conspicuous checkerboard treatment of the hotel's surface was the Berlin Hilton's compensatory means of self-promotion. The building could not attract attention as a Modernist "duck," as it did in Istanbul, Cairo, and Athens; rather, the façade served as a billboard promoting the hotel's presence and literally authorizing the site with Hilton's signature at its apex.[60] The billboard advertised the hotel to both the West and the East. It arrested the attention of an observer standing at the center of West Berlin, glancing east from the Kaiser-Friedrich-Gedächtniskirche. Equally, the Berlin Hilton made its presence known in the East. *Die Zeit* noted: "[F]rom the border streets of the Soviet sector one sees the uppermost of the fourteen-stories that rise above the Tiergarten."[61]

The façade's double appeal to both the East and West characterized the look toward the hotel. Doubleness also described the look from it. In contrast to the directed orientation of the gaze in Istanbul, Cairo, and Athens, the Berlin Hilton offered its occupants panoramas both to the east and the west of the city: "The Roof Garden and El Panorama, with its sliding roof which can easily be opened in the summer time, provide a matchless view of both West and East Berlin. From this vantage point you'll be able to plan a series of excursions, some of them on foot, to cover the sight-seeing high spots of the city."[62] The arrangements of the public rooms and guest rooms revealed no privileged view. The rooftop restaurant and bar opened to both the East and the West. The elevator shafts were sunk at the core of the building. Their location did not define the "back" of the structure, as they did in the earlier hotels. Although the building itself equally valued the view to the East and the view to the West, the written descriptions of the hotel featured the special access to the East afforded by the hotel. Contemporary accounts presented the hotel as offering a satisfying penetration of the Soviet sector: "From the large window wall in the section, guests can see the Congress Hall, the famous Brandenberg Gate and *far into* East Berlin, the Russian sector of the city."[63] Or again: "From the hotel one looks East over the Brandenburg Gate *deep* into East Berlin."[64] The Berlin Hilton pretended surveillance and, in consequence, some control of the East. At the same time, it facilitated for its patrons the comparison of the East and West, of the communists and capitalists, which framed Conrad Hilton's rhetoric of international expansion.

Although the look of the Berlin Hilton—internally and externally—was treated differently from the earlier buildings of the chain, the experience it offered remained essentially the same. The hotel presented to the Berliners of the West an encounter with America at the same time that it suggested to the Berliners of the East what they were missing. Dieter Werner, who is still a concierge at the hotel, worked in the Hilton from the time of its opening. He nostalgically described the importance of the hotel in its early years: "The building of the Hilton hotel was at that time a great event in Berlin. It was the first hotel built after the war. Hundreds of Berliners came through the hotel every day just to look at it; and that went on for months. I was there from day one and it makes me so happy that I am still there today. All who had status and prestige stayed with us. And because we had a great ballroom, all high-society events happened at our hotel."[65]

The gala opening of the Berlin Hilton on November 30, 1959, defined its social location. Chartered Pan Am clippers imported Conrad Hilton, Hilton family members and executives, newspaper columnists, and entertainment celebrities to Berlin for the occasion.[66] Invited guests also included the American ambassador, David K. E. Bruce, as well as local dignitaries, military figures, and government officials, of whom Willy Brandt, mayor of West Berlin, was perhaps the best known. Tickets were also available; they were sold out for weeks before the occasion.[67] The timing of the event was both socially and politically significant. For West Berlin, the hotel's opening marked the beginning of the Berlin ball season. Local newspapers reproduced sketches of the ball gowns that would be worn.[68] The theme of the gala was medieval Germany. "Promptly at 8:30 four men costumed as knights blew the fanfare and opened the festival. The actor Wolfgang Lukschy, fashioned as a late-Burgundian seneschal, unrolled a sealed parchment and welcomed the knights and ladies to the candlelit festival hall, which the set designer H. W. Lenneweit with the support of the Ufa-Studios had changed into a Riesen-Dinkelsbühl with galleries and balconies for the orchestra and photographers. Towers, pennants, arches, so far as the eye could see, only here and there a lonely enamel shield with 'Trink Coca Cola.'[69]

The moment had a powerful political content. The opening of the Hilton countered the alternative political celebrations held on the same day in East Berlin. On November 30, 1948, the so-called Magistrat von Gross-Berlin was constituted under the communist Friedrich Ebert after a putsch by the Socialist Unity Party (SED) had caused the flight of the West-leaning mayor, Dr. Friedensburg, from the New Rathaus in East Berlin to West Berlin. The tenth anniversary of this division of the city was commemorated in East Berlin by a variety of events, including a great demonstration march of thirty thousand men.[70] The ideological implications of these celebrations were exaggerated by escalating political tensions. The launching of Sputnik in October 1957 had undermined the West's sense of military superiority and security. Then, less than three weeks before the opening of the Hilton, anxieties about a war with the Soviet Union were aggravated by Khrushchev's "Berlin ultimatum," issued on November 10, 1958. The Soviet leader announced a treaty with the East German government that would allow them to sever access to West Berlin. The Allies were given six months to remove all occupying forces from the city. The confrontational mood of the moment is inflected in the rhetoric around the Hilton. The *New York Times* published this account:

> The United States Army commander in Europe said today that any action against the United States garrison in Berlin would be "an action against the United States.". . . General Hodes held his news conference during a two-day visit he described as "routine.". . . The senior United States diplomat in West Germany, Ambassador David K. E. Bruce, arrived in West Berlin today, also informally to "show the flag." His official purpose was to attend the gala opening of the Berlin Hilton Hotel, a joint project of the West Berlin gov-

> ernment and Conrad Hilton, United States hotel man. Willy Brandt, governing Mayor of West Berlin, said the construction of the $6,500,000 hotel was a demonstration by "our friends in America to prove their confidence in Berlin." "No power on earth will be able to force us from our chosen way of peaceful construction work," the Mayor said in the presence of celebrities brought to Berlin by Mr. Hilton and of a group of Berliners.[71]

A local newspaper represented the affair in much the same terms: "The mayor, Willy Brandt, named the new hotel, which numbers among the most modern buildings in Europe, a proof of Berlin's belief in the future. The construction of the hotel is a demonstration of the will to life of the city and a mark of the confidence of good foreign friends in the future of Berlin. At the same time it represents the building of a new bridge of friendship between America and Berlin. 'The *Berlin Hilton Hotel* is an indication of our will to rebuild Berlin, from which task we shall let no power deter us,' said Brandt."[72] Another newspaper listed the movie stars in attendance at the gala, then recorded further comments made by the mayor: "Willy Brandt praised the construction of the Hilton Hotel as a new link between Berlin and its American friends. Further, he noted that Conrad Hilton, when asked by telephone about Moscow's threat [Khrushchev's 'Berlin ultimatum'], had responded that if Berlin did not already have a Hilton, they would have had to start building one now."[73]

Conrad Hilton had recorded his thoughts on the matter at the time the hotel was first announced: "The new hotel will provide a dramatic symbol of West Berlin's steadfastness and progress as a dynamic center of the Free World. It will attract tourists, business people, additional cultural activities, exhibitions, professional and business conventions and thus attract new foreign and German investments. By bringing visitors from abroad into direct contact with Berlin and its people, the hotel will develop a better understanding of the role played by West Berlin in furthering the hopes and objectives of the Free World."[74] He reiterated these same ideas when the hotel was completed: "[With the new Hilton] we have hit upon a new weapon with which to fight Communism, a new team made up of owner, manager and labor with which to confront the class-conscious Mr. Marx. Incidentally, Karl Marx never owned, managed or worked an enterprise in all his life. But from this world of inexperience he has managed, for a whole century, to convince hundreds of millions of people that we are all at each other's throats. I am happy to say that the project we are dedicating here today gives the lie to Marx, Communism and all they stand for."[75]

The Berlin Hilton functioned as Hiltons did elsewhere in Europe and the Middle East: it was a piece of American experience that yielded ideological and political effects. But the Hilton's political operation was more explicit in Berlin than it was in other sites. Indeed, the symbolic force of the hotel is unambivalently observed in *Die Zeit:* "Who in Berlin these days does not speak of the Soviet threat or of the Stadtautobahn speaks of the Hilton Hotel. Most commonly, indeed, the Berliners speak of these three things together, as themes interrelated in a meaningful way. For the shadows cast by the Soviet threat give all the more brilliant contours to the city's two special structures and endow them with additional symbolic power of a truly concrete 'Now it is finally right.'"[76] Of course, it was not "finally right." Both constructions contributed to a city that had to be remade after the fall of the Berlin Wall. Since reunification in 1989, two cities, rebuilt after World War II to be different, have had to be made the same. The claim of 1958 that "it is finally right" seems hollow, not only for the time it was made but also for the present. Since the elimination of the Wall, a new corporate Berlin has been imagined and is being built.[77] The problem confronting the previous planners was not so much how to memorialize the good memories and purge the bad from the landscape, but rather how to decide which was which. Now memory seems a memory.

London.

London is an unwieldy city (fig. 42).[78] Samuel Wheelock Fiske, a travel writer of the mid-nineteenth century, complained: "I am compelled to say, London is entirely too big. And yet the infatuated inhabitants, far from acknowledging and seeking to remedy this defect, go on adding house to house, and street to street, till one begins to feel that it is by a wise dispensation of Providence, England is an island, so that a limit must come some time to the growth of this monster."[79] At the beginning of the twentieth century the same observation was made more poetically by Ford Madox Ford: "If [the young provincial] were intent upon getting a complete picture of London . . . we might imagine him setting out self-consciously, his eyes closed during the transit, to climb the heights of Hampstead, the top of the Monument, the Dome of St. Paul's. But he will not. London, with its sense of immensity that we must hurry through to keep unceasing appointments, with its diffuseness, its gatherings up into innumerable trade-centers, innumerable class districts, becomes by its immensity a place upon which there is no beginning."[80]

Neither London's topography nor its governments much disciplined its growth.[81] Disasters provided occasions for imposing order on the city. In 1665 the Great Plague killed at least 100,000 Londoners; the following year, the Great Fire destroyed most of the medieval walled city.[82] Before the fire was out, thirty-four-year-old Christopher Wren presented to King Charles II a plan for rebuilding London.[83]Having experienced Paris and admired Bernini, Wren proposed a rational grid overlaid with diagonals emphasizing the social centers of London.[84] His plan indicated the relative importance of institutions: the Royal Exchange was framed with a great oval plaza at the hub of ten streets; St. Paul's Cathedral occurred at a triangular intersection. Wren's ideal plan of broad thoroughfares and monumentally embellished perspectives suggested Versailles and the new parts of baroque Rome. But with neither Louis XIV nor the pope as a patron, Wren's plan could not be imposed on the powerful burghers of London. The spatial language of absolutism was unacceptable. Bankers, merchants, and guildsmen were unwilling to give up any part of their real estate for the sake of a vista. And the king was unwilling to test the loyalties of those who contributed most to his coffers. The City of London retained its medieval complexity because of the property rights of the rising bourgeoisie. Urban forms remained expressive of the individual entrepreneurs who created the city's wealth. Those forms were uneven, complex, and irregular. The building codes, however, changed after the fire. Most notably, brick and stone replaced wattle and daub. Old London, characterized by narrow streets framed by half-timbered buildings, some with thatched roofs, was reconstructed in masonry. But the pattern of possession remained essentially the same.[85]

The Great Plague and Great Fire did precipitate the development of less crowded, healthier residences beyond the city walls. One of the most attrac-

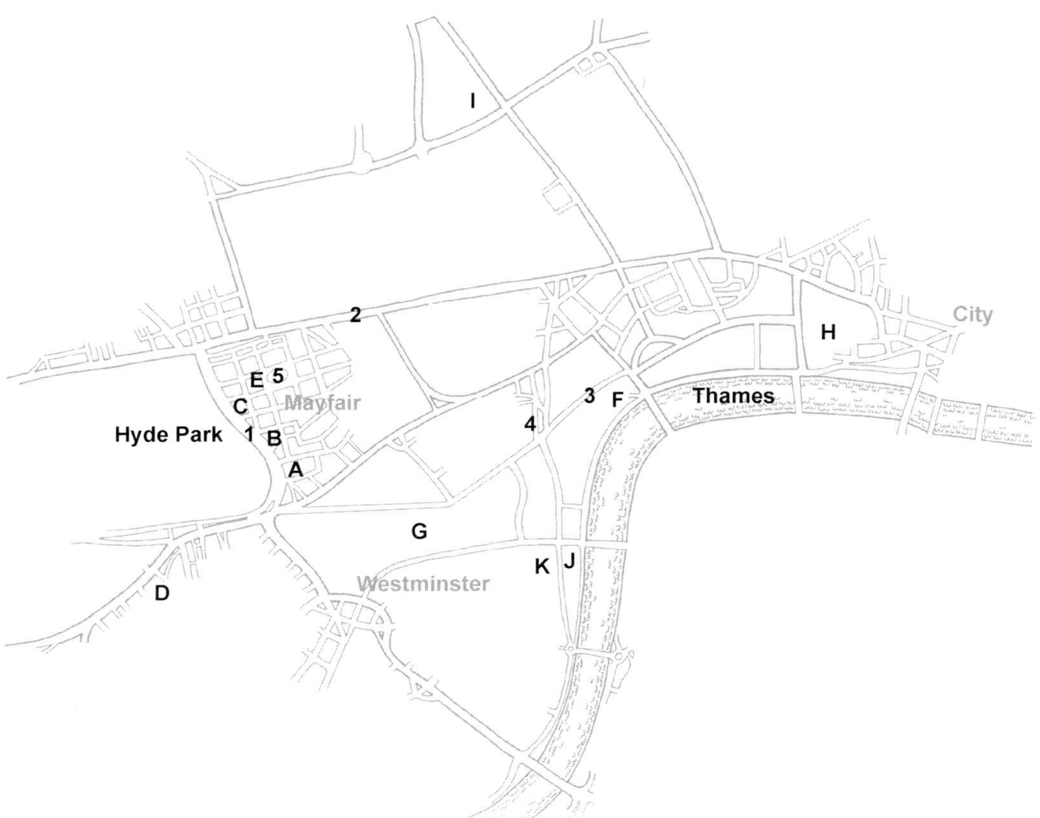

42. Sketch plan of London, by author: *A*, London Hilton; *B*, Dorchester Hotel; *C*, Grosvenor House; *D*, Harrods; *E*, U.S. Embassy; *F*, Savoy Hotel; *G*, Buckingham Palace; *H*, St. Paul's Cathedral; *I*, St. Pancras Station and the Midland Grand Hotel; *J*, Houses of Parliament; *K*, Westminster Abbey; *1*, Park Lane; *2*, Oxford Street; *3*, The Strand; *4*, Trafalgar Square; *5*, Grosvenor Square.

tive spaces for high-end housing lay between the City of London, the center of merchants and bankers, and Westminster, the City's neighbor upstream on the Thames, the traditional locus of government and the aristocracy. The West End, the space in between, might be regarded as the product of royal pleasure and aristocratic speculation. The great open spaces, Hyde Park and Regency Park, were originally royal hunting and gaming parks. They were surrounded by estates awarded to the secular and ecclesiastical favorites by the crown. The dissolution of the monasteries provided the king and his minions with more land. Especially in the eighteenth century, landowners developed elite residential sites, often around garden squares, which were either oriented to the established throughways, like Bath Road (now Oxford Street), or established boulevards of their own, like Portland Place.[86] The development of this land as high-quality housing around generous open squares created a sense of order. The programmatic regularity of the scheme was complemented by the restraint of its architecture. Named "Georgian" for the kings George I to George IV, who occupied the throne of England from 1714 to 1830, this architecture is characterized by its classically articulated planar surfaces. These separate, well-ordered pieces of London were not, however, related to one another by any larger systematic plan. London's expansion outside its walls was thus distinct from that inside them, but it also was remarkably idiosyncratic.

London became industrial and imperial in the nineteenth century. The nineteenth century was England's "most prosperous and socially regressive period," to quote one of her more notable architects, Peter Smithson.[87] The working-class housing of the period was notoriously shoddy. Middle-class residences expanded into such suburbs as Hampstead and Highgate. London's new elite buildings—clubs, mansions, and commercial establishments—tended to the pretentious: monumental in scale and elaborate in ornament. The City's exchanges and markets were rebuilt to conform to contemporary fashion as were the great estates that had been developed in the eighteenth century. But ownership remained remarkably intact through the extensive use in England of the peculiarly English system of leasehold. Property and whatever had been built upon it reverted to its ground landlord at the end of its lease, which might be as long as ninety-nine years. The texture of London was changed and its edges expanded, but the irregular property patterns of its center endured. The city's eighteenth-century structure remained largely unchanged. John Summerson, the consummate architectural historian of London, puts it simply: "The very first thing to realize and remember about Victorian London is that the whole of its center and much of its perimeter was, in fact, Georgian. Victorian London *was* Georgian London and remained substantially Georgian till near the end of the century. It is only in our own time that the Georgian body has become fragmentary and residual."[88] The disintegration of the Georgian body was not natural, but political. Death duties were instituted in England in 1893. The great estates of London could not be sustained; by the end of World War I many had been sold. World War II further mutilated that same Georgian body and precipitated its reconfiguration. In the Blitz of 1941–1942, as much as a third of the City and the East End were destroyed.[89]

The destruction of London by German bombing, like the destruction of the city by fire in 1666, has been regarded as a lost opportunity for rationalizing the city. Roy Porter, author of the most important recent study of London's social and material history, comments: "If the post-1666 rebuilding was a chance missed, that judgment applies all the more to the post-1945 era. London's fabric was patched up, but no fresh start was made with respect to street plans, transport or the siting of employment. And there was no Wren."[90] There certainly was no "Wren," an architect of genius, commissioned to rebuild the churches of London in a contemporary style. But there was Patrick Abercrombie. Abercrombie was the efficient envisioner of urban order who prepared a plan for post–World War II London that was persuasive and practical.[91] His outline for the rebuilding of the city has a narrative lilt. It was purposely published in an attractive format before the end of the war with the ideological intent of inspiring in an exhausted and impoverished populace some confidence in the future. It was also projected as the necessary foundation of an immediate and full postwar recovery. It could be argued that, in its way, Abercrombie's project was as ideal and rational as Wren's plan. Its idealism and rationality lay not with abstract geometries of discipline and with the visual drama of the architectural tableau, but with the social engineering of haptic, healthy space. Abercrombie was a committed Garden City advocate.[92] He sought to save the metropolis by reducing its population. Density was to be decreased by carefully regulating the reconstruction of London and by rapidly developing New Towns for heavy industry well beyond its edges. Fresh air and open leisure grounds, along with good housing for all classes, were essential to the revival of London. Further, whereas Wren had been interested in creating a new city, Abercrombie was committed to retaining as much of the old as was possible.[93] In addition to promoting preservation, Abercrombie explicitly advocated that important structures be appropriately framed: "[S]afeguards should be introduced in the vicinity of many of London's historic buildings which, at the present time, are detrimentally affected by inappropriate surroundings."[94] Abercrombie was aware of the potential threat of the high-rise to London's texture and panorama. "The height of buildings is one of the more important aspects of the control of development, affecting as it does (a) the density and intensity of the use of land, (b) the consequent value of land, and (c) the architectural appearance of the town."[95] But Abercrombie was not an idealist. His desire to be practical, not utopian, is revealed in his retreat from *strict* height limitation codes:

> [T]here are many sites where the maximum of 80 or 100 feet has been regarded, by would-be developers and others, as unduly restrictive. . . . While we wish to avoid overcrowding, and in certain areas, such as the surroundings of squares, to maintain a reasonable uniformity, we should like to encourage greater intensity of use and designed variety of skyline where the situation justifies it. It is appreciated that the Council has opposed the exploitation of sites overlooking publicly maintained open spaces by high buildings when these were likely to prejudice amenity, but there are numerous situations in the County of London where, subject to proper safeguards, buildings considerably higher than are provided for under the present height tables, would enhance rather than detract from the general view.[96]

Though Abercrombie's practical plan was broadly applauded, it was only partially implemented. Specific historical sites were for the most part salvaged, but the human scale of the city was often compromised and the distant view lost. Abercrombie had assumed that after the war resources would be diverted from the military to reconstruction. But England was bankrupt. He also assumed that new legislation would limit the rights of individual property owners for the public good. But he was mistaken. Building codes were egregiously circumvented by powerful developers and colluding politicians. The multiplicity of local and regional planning authorities made circumvention relatively easy.[97] The Greater London Plan provided an intention, but failed as a template. The traditional contours of London, in contrast to Washington or Paris, were not preserved by strict adherence to the height restrictions. Thomas Hall, in a comparative study of European capital cities, notes: "[W]hat does distinguish London from most other capital cities is the lack of any overall plan. . . . The absence of an overall plan can be explained in part by the fragmentation of the city's administration and the non-interventionist tradition which was characteristic of English public. . . . The passive attitude of the English government to conditions in the capital city contrasts sharply with the situation in many other countries, in particular of course with France, where the national government took it upon itself to see that comprehensive changes were accomplished."[98] The disasters of 1665–1666 had not led to a reordered London. Though Wren's churches certainly contributed to London's adornment, his plan for a geometrically coherent city never materialized. The growth of London in the nineteenth century was also left largely to speculators. The state was not willing to contest the rights of individual property holders. In the twentieth century, the Blitz made a doily of the city's fabric, but disturbed property boundaries even less than had the Great Fire. The traditional English reverence for individuals' rights of possession remained in place. Cautious respect for private property frustrated Abercrombie's plan as it had Wren's nearly four hundred years earlier. Indeed, the change in the look of London occurred not despite the individual's rights to exploit his possessions, but because of them. Speculation remodeled London.[99]

The boardgame Monopoly is the ludic manifestation of property speculation. It is a game about buying hotels, commercialized and mythologized by Parker Brothers during the Depression.[100] In the English version of Monopoly, Mayfair and Park Lane are the equivalent of Boardwalk and Park Place. They are the dark blue sites of entrepreneurial desire. The game makers chose well: Mayfair and Park Lane are symptomatic of speculation in London from the eighteenth to the twentieth centuries.[101] Mayfair, which got its name from the annual festival May market established by James II in 1686, is bordered on the west by Hyde Park and Park Lane. To the north lay what is now Oxford Street and what was then Tyburn Gallows. At Tyburn heinous traitors to the crown, like John Southworth, a self-confessed Catholic priest, were hanged, drawn, and quartered for the edification of an audience of all classes.[102] To the south was St. James' Palace and the royal realm. Mayfair, which was higher and more healthful than the City, provided particularly attractive land for privileged residential development after the Great Plague and Great Fire. In the seventeenth century, a great estate, which included among other properties most of Mayfair, was inherited by an infant, Mary Davies.[103] She was the main asset of her mother. She was bartered at the age of twelve to Sir Thomas Grosvenor in exchange for the settlement of her mother's debts. It was a good deal for the Grosvenor family. In 1720, Mary's son, Sir Richard Grosvenor, began to develop the northern portion of his mother's inheritance as a speculative venture in prestigious residences. Stately four- and five-story Georgian houses, their planar surfaces articulated with discreet classical members, were built facing a large rectangle. At the square's six-acre core was a grand oval garden accessible only to residents. Sir Richard's fealty to the new Hanoverian dynasty was demonstrated by the gilded equestrian statue of George I as a Roman emperor that served as the garden's centerpiece. The Grosvenor family was awarded the dukedom of Westminster in 1874.[104]

The square attracted the elite, as intended. Residents even included foreign governments. The American ambassadors John Adams and W. H. Page lived in the square. Leaseholders could rebuild their mansions, under the ground landlord's supervision. Consequently, by the mid-nineteenth century, Grosvenor Square, still part of the Grosvenor Estate Trust, was Georgian only in its basic shape. Not only did Grosvenor Square lose its architectural integrity in the nineteenth century, it also lost its ideological sign. The statue of George I, on which antimonarchists had periodically vented their spleen, was dismantled. This symbol of English royalty's German connections and imperial pretensions was, in the twentieth century, superseded by monuments to the new power in Europe. A statue of Franklin D. Roosevelt by Sir William Reid Dick was erected. Also added was the predatory thirty-five-foot American eagle that surveys the square from its perch high above its main axis. More effectively than F.D.R., this huge bird replaced George I as the Grosvenor Square's political referent. Its perch is the U.S. Embassy. The embassy occupies, literally *en bloc*, the entire west side of the square, a space once defined by the exquisite Derby House (no. 23) built by Robert Adam and other residences.

The U.S. Embassy, built between 1958 and 1961, is one of Eero Saarinen's few ugly buildings (fig. 43). Because of the acknowledged importance of this particular embassy and its site, the State Department held a limited competition in order to select its architect. Directions suggested that "to the sensitive and imaginative designer," the project represented "an invitation to give serious study to local conditions of climate and site" and "to understand and sympathize with local customs and people and to grasp the historical meaning of the particular environment in which the new buildings must be set."[105] Saarinen's competition sketch of the façade shows a well-mannered, Georgian-proportioned four-story block, diapered with Georgian-proportioned windows, and raised on a glazed podium.[106] The building lost its good manners during construction. The gilded, anodized aluminum facing was a big mistake. It gave the building its appearance of cheap glitz. R. Furneaux Jordan's reaction was typical of the structure's critical reception: "For all its sham politeness this building had also to be American, new, crisp, and glamorous. Hence the rather aggressive, staccato modeling of the façade, the perpetual gilding, the costume jewelry that overbedecks it all."[107] The building was also criticized for failing to fill the entire width of Grosvenor Square. Instead of completing the square, as would a disciplined row of houses, it allowed the space to siphon off toward Park Lane.[108] But the basic embarrassment of the building lies in its display of an aggressive American control of a quintessentially English space.[109] Its temple-like isolation exaggerates its scale. The three other sides of the square appear to be made up of multiple, if relatively homogeneous structures. The embassy, in contrast, is mammothly monolithic. Its control of the axis of the square is marked by the giant eagle that possesses the garden through its gaze. The anti-tank bulwark with which the embassy is surrounded makes the eagle's perch unassailable and marks its presence as ominous. Reyner Banham put the appearance of the American Embassy in London into a broader political context:

43. London, U.S. Embassy in Grosvenor Square. Photo by author.

> Saarinen has produced a building that is modern when seen in raking views along the front, but contradicts itself when seen from further away. . . . Saarinen in designing a building that looks one thing from one viewpoint and something else from another, has given the State Department the architecture it deserves. . . . When the US diplomatic building program first began, it favored straight modern as the best vehicle of its intentions—and produced Ralph Rapson's exemplary work in Stockholm, Copenhagen and Paris, for instance. But as the Dulles line hardened in the mid-fifties, and Kruschchev reversed the Russian line on architecture, there was a change in State Department policy, even a change in the make-up of its architectural advisory panel, and a new regime appeared that seemed bent on extracting the utmost pomposity from even the most self-effacing architects—as witness Gropius's tame little office-block in Athens ridiculously wrapped in a faintly classicizing peristyle.[110]

44

An imperative presence was what was wanted.

By the mid-twentieth century, governmental and commercial interests had became more lucrative than individual leaseholders. Recognizing that the attractiveness of the property depended in part on its associations with an architecturally distinguished past, the Grosvenor Trust drew up a master scheme of neo-Georgian façades which were to be imposed by covenant on leaseholders. The Georgian character of Grosvenor Square, lost in the nineteenth century, was thus reinvented in the twentieth. The north side is now occupied by the London Marriott (formerly the Europa Hotel), constructed by Lewis Solomon, Kaye and Partners in 1963–1964.[111] Another big neo-Georgian hotel, the Britannia, built by the notorious R. Seifert and Partners, followed on the south.[112] Transient foreigners replaced upper-class Londoners as the principal residents of Grosvenor Square. Park Lane was also converted from luxury housing to hotels. Grosvenor House, the early nineteenth-century mansion of the Grosvenor family, located on Park Lane a few blocks away from its eponymous square, was replaced by the Grosvenor House Hotel in 1930. Its near neighbor, Dorchester House, was also demolished in 1930 for the sake of a new hotel, the Dorchester. Property development in the area accelerated after the war especially in the 1950s.[113] The Regency terraces at the Hyde Park Corner end of Park Lane were bought by a consummate speculator for a new, American hotel.[114] The London Hilton now dominates Park Lane in the same way that the U.S. Embassy dominates Grosvenor Square.

45

London Hilton.

"The London Hilton on Park Lane rises high above its rivals. Located in Mayfair with stunning views of the capital the hotel offers the perfect vantage point for London."[115] Like the Dorchester and Grosvenor House, the Hilton was adjacent to Hyde Park, one of the great urban playgrounds of Europe (figs. 44, 45, and 46). But the Hilton was closer to the Royal Academy and, probably more importantly, to Harrod's, the world's most famous department store. More fundamentally, it was on a different scale than its neighbors. When the London Hilton was opened on April 17, 1963, it was the tallest structure in London—the first building in the city to overtop St. Paul's Cathedral (fig. 47).[116] It was then also Europe's largest postwar hotel. It had

44. London, London Hilton, view from Grosvenor Square. Photo by author.

45. London, London Hilton, view from Hyde Park. Photo by author.

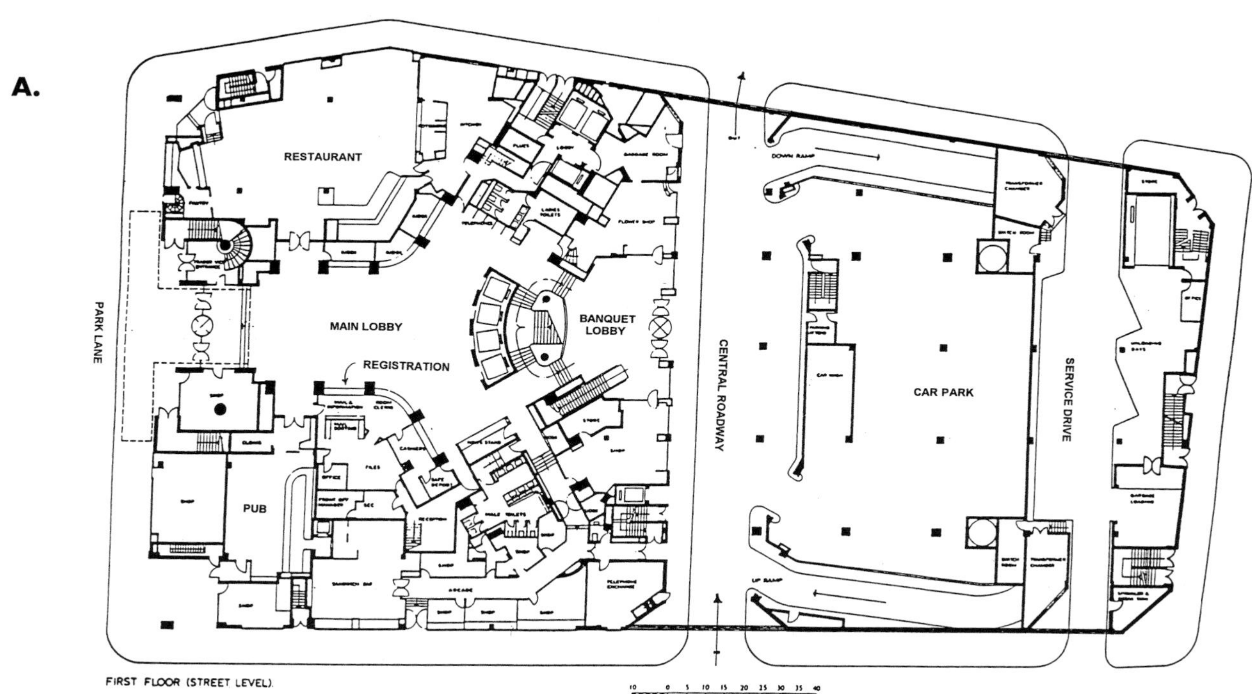

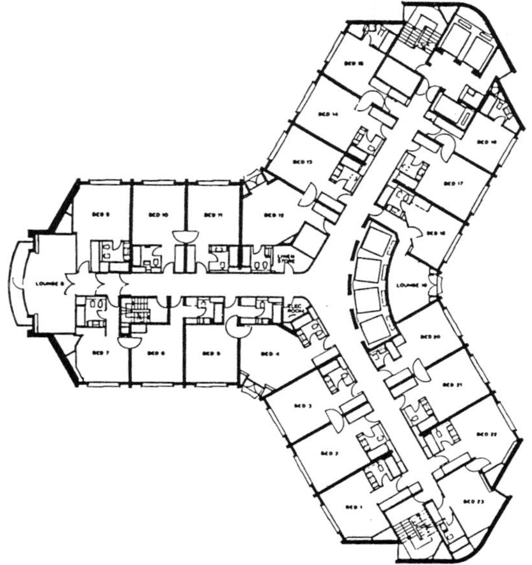

46. London, London Hilton: *A*, plan of the ground floor; *B*, plan of a typical guest room floor. Modified from a plan provided by Ray Pask, chief engineer of the London Hilton.

47. London, London Hilton, view from a guest room window toward St. Paul's Cathedral. Photo by author.

512 guest rooms, five restaurants, five bars and cocktail lounges, seven private dining rooms, and one of Europe's largest ballrooms.[117] In the luxury hotel range, it was the first in Britain to be fully air-conditioned and it was the first in London to have a partial kosher certificate.[118]

A baroque, thirty-story guest room tower was the most prominent part of the building. It was rendered as an equal-armed Y with large balconies swelling from the main foot that faced Hyde Park and small ones protruding from the junctures of its appendages. The steel-frame structure was clad in contrasting materials. An off-white Portland stone was used on the verticals. Prominently deployed at the ends of the wings, this pseudostone gave the illusion of functionally buttressing the superstructure. The window bays between the verticals were faced with a gold-and-black anodized-finished aluminum.[119] The skin bore a resemblance to that used on Saarinen's U.S. Embassy. This voluptuous pile sprang from a clean Miesien-modern base made up of a low entrance floor and a double-story second level that was glazed in large vertical panels. The original incongruity of the hotel's two principal parts is now disguised by awnings and an elaborate marquis. Below the building were four innovatively constructed basement levels.[120]

The divide between the interior and the exterior of the building was minimized. The entrance wall and doors were plate glass. The crispness of the podium façade design was maintained in the simple lines of the lobby (fig. 48). The Botticino marble wall revetment and floor paving continued on either side of the glass doors. Interior and exterior detailing was in rosewood. Retail sites also overlapped the boundaries between interior and exterior. The International Shopping Arcade led from the south side of the lobby through to the Hertford Street side entrance. It culminated in the Scandinavian Sandwich Bar, which opened to both the street and the hotel's interior. At the Park Lane entrance and in the lobby there were three shops and multiple sales desks for airlines, travel agents, newspapers, and the like.[121] Unfortunately, however, the lobby did not escape the discrepancy between the tower and its base that disturbs the hotel's exterior.

The busy lobby was too small and too low. Its dominant feature, a ballooning bank of four elevators, intruded on the space. The commercial outlets and the aggressively convex arrangement of the elevators left the patrons no leisure space. The design of the elevator bank was also functionally unfortunate. The curve made it difficult for guests to see the arrival of the side elevators. Even now the side elevators are switched off late at night because the convexity of the elevator bank frustrates surveillance. Finally, four elevators, even the latest high-speed Otis elevators, which ran at five hundred feet per minute, were from the very beginning inadequate to the traffic of the building. The design precluded the addition of further shafts.

American imports included design features as well as Otis elevators. Originally the floors were numbered beginning with the ground level as "one," following American practice. Confusion among guests attempting to find the second-floor ballroom required that the numbering system be changed.[122] Because in the 1950s and 1960s Americans conventionally did their drinking before dinner, with cocktails, and had water with their meal, the banquet facilities were planned with only a small dispensing bar in the middle of the kitchen. In London people expected wine with dinner. As a consequence, waiters with bottles and glasses had to get through the confusion of those carrying food. Later, a part of the banquet hall foyer had to be reconstructed as a dispensing bar.[123] In addition to planning details, the interior decoration of the London Hilton combined American modernity with the imagined local, as had other hotels in the chain. For the lobby, ballroom, and guest rooms, as an in-house document noted, "the keynote of the decor is elegant simplicity."[124] High-quality materials were used to finish rooms in a simple, modern style. Bathrooms had terrazzo floors and floor-to-ceiling marble revetment. All bathrooms had tapped-in ice water, the ultimate American feature, but only fourteen suites, on the twenty-sixth and twenty-seventh floors, had bidets, the mark of Europeanness.

In contrast to the understated modernity of the most private and most public spaces of the Hilton, the settings for dining and drinking were elaborately thematized. The London Tavern on the ground floor was inspired by "the architecture of the Shakespeare country." Its "traditional London char-

48. London, London Hilton, lobby interior.

acter" was emphasized by the use of "shields and coats of arms of the London Boroughs." St. George's Bar was also decorated à la Olde English. Behind the polished rosewood counter were panels that mimed the glass etching of late Victorian pubs. Represented on them were scenes of a middle-aged St. George attempting unsuccessfully to do more than save the partially nude, bound damsel in distress from the dragon. Rumor has it that St. George's features satirize those of a flirtatious Hilton International executive (fig. 49). A little later, the most popular locus in the Hilton was the 007 Bar, which was decorated with artifacts from James Bond movies. The 007 Bar was so popular that people would queue for standing space.[125] Most elaborately decorated was the International Restaurant, the main dining room of the hotel, located on the second floor overlooking Hyde Park. A memorandum issued by Hilton describes it: "[T]he entire character of the restaurant can be changed to present cuisine from five different parts of the world. The change will affect the decor itself, the lighting, the waiters' uniforms, and the menus themselves. To achieve a change in appearance, four sets of vertical sliding panels have been incorporated, which depict different areas of the world. In addition to a Northern American background, the restaurant can present a feeling of the Mediterranean, the Orient, or Central and South America. . . . [and] changes can also be effected by varying the intensity and color of the lighting behind the plastic molded ceiling."[126] The same document suggested that the most striking of the Hilton's uniforms were the pink silk Raja tunics worn by the waiters of the International Restaurant when it was displaying its oriental decor.[127] British colonialism is thus thematized within a globalizing American context.

49. London, London Hilton, St. George's Bar, etched-glass mirror with one of a series of representations from a satiric version of the St. George narrative. The tree to which the maiden is tied and the dragon on which the triumphant George places his foot are hardly visible. The can opener in George's hand suggests that he is unable to get out of his armor. Photo by author.

The most spectacular restaurant-bar in the Hilton occupied much of the twenty-eighth floor.[128] The Roof Restaurant was the first restaurant in London to offer an elevated panorama of the city. Its design, by Sir Hugh Casson, featured a free-standing fireplace surrounded by a circular leather sofa and a dropped bar so that bartenders would not obstruct the sight-lines of patrons sitting at the counter. Lighting was also recessed in such a way as not to reflect on the windows that opened the space from floor to ceiling. The transparency of the glass was not to be compromised. The designer judiciously acknowledged that it was not the decoration of this restaurant that made it dramatic, but rather the view it offered of London.

Although one of the earliest of the Hiltons to be projected, the London Hilton was one of the last of the first generation to be built. As early as 1950, Hilton was negotiating for a hotel in London.[129] In a letter written to Conrad Hilton from an international hotel congress in Nice, John Houser, executive vice president, described his search for a site:

> As it turns out, the time here at the Congress was fairly well justified. First I believe we now have an answer for London. I believe I told you in my last letter that the Board of Trade has decided that only one hotel will be built in London and that one must go ahead fast. They want us, but realized it was difficult to obtain and clear a site in time (the law prevents eviction unless the tenant has a provision in his contract permitting recapture with notice). Also they realize the hotel owners may try to prevent our coming in. So since Sir Francis Towle has a project well along, and he is the head of the hotel association, they asked me off the record to try to get him to turn his land and financing over to us and to get him to sponsor our project. I have spent a lot of time with him here, and he agreed today.
>
> His site has over 80,000 square feet and zoning changes have been cleared

> with the London County Council. The land is owned by Prudential Insurance Company (not related to our company) and they are willing to provide it on a 99-year lease at ten thousand pounds a year—very cheap for London. Also they are willing, according to Sir Francis, to loan at least 60% of the cost of the project. Some more equity money will be needed but I feel sure we can get Lord Nathan's group to furnish it. The loan, incidentally, is tentatively agreed to at 4% interest and 1% sinking fund. Sir Francis has just cabled his London office to get the plot plan, etc. ready and to bring it to me at the airport next Sunday on my way through. Sir Francis wants a voice, but he is willing to have us lead all the way through and to take over the operation by ourselves. He has considerable knowledge, you know, and should be of real help. I hadn't realized he built the Dorchester Hotel, did you?[130]

This document does not locate the property in question, but suggests something of the mixture of the personal and the political involved in obtaining prime real estate in London. The British government's Board of Trade seems to have favored Hilton International, but there was never a possibility that the British government itself would finance a new Hilton. The need for an established local sponsor both to obtain the necessary building site, funds, and code permits and to avert effective local hotel opposition was assumed. The complexity of this terrain is suggested both in the length of time it took to break ground and in the absence of Sir Francis in the final project.[131] His place was taken by Charles Clore.

Charles Clore was the son of a Jewish émigré who had fled the Russian pogroms and successfully established himself as a textile manufacturer in London. Clore himself made his fortune through speculation, buying low and selling higher. He became one of the first post–World War II asset-strippers. He bought controlling stock in companies undervalued on the market and then resold their most lucrative parts at a remarkable profit. His business interests were eclectic, ranging from motion pictures and theaters through tankers and quarries to footwear and beer.[132] In the early 1950s, Clore had expressed an interest in hotels. He unsuccessfully attempted a take-over of the Grosvenor House Hotel on Park Lane. In late 1953, Clore and Harold Samuel moved to gain a controlling share of the stock of the Savoy Group—Claridges, the Berkeley, and the Savoy—probably the world's most prestigious set of hotels.[133] Frustrated in his efforts to buy into London's established luxury hotels, he apparently decided to build one of his own.

Indeed, Clore may already have been in negotiations with Hilton. Hilton announced its plans for a 550-room hotel overlooking Hyde Park in the *New York Times* in October, 1953.[134] Evidently, negotiations between Clore and Hilton over the contract were complex and prolonged. Clore would not accept a management agreement on the model of Istanbul; Hilton was forced to share in the cost of the project. By 1957, Clore and Hilton had a contract and a set of drawings for a hotel on Park Lane.[135] A description of the proposed hotel and a sketch of the structure appeared in the London *Times* in July, 1957: "The building itself as at present envisaged is a crescent-shaped tower structure of 32 storeys, resting on a two-storey podium. . . . Apart from aesthetic considerations, the curved front of the building would enable the maximum number of bedrooms to overlook the park. In effect, a frontage of 180 ft. could be turned by this means into the equivalent of about 216 ft." The sketch shows a dramatically convex tower on a square podium.[136]

The proposed Hilton elicited an angry response. The protests were not directly economic, like those from the members of the Berlin Hotel Association. The text of the objections was aesthetic, though their subtext may have been a resentment of American and Jewish capital. The height of the structure offered the greatest affront. The hotel flagrantly infringed on the building code height limits for Mayfair. It would tower over its neighbors on Park Lane and disrupt the human-scaled frame of Hyde Park. Perhaps most egregiously, the panoramic view of London that the building's height presented for its guests included Buckingham Palace. The queen was to be looked down upon by American tourists.[137] Outrage precipitated a public inquiry.[138] In May, 1958, London County Council voted against granting building permission for the Hilton. The *New York Times* carried the story:[139] "The British Government refused permission today for a thirty-five-story Hilton Hotel to be built on London's fashionable Park Lane. The 700-bedroom skyscraper, designed to overlook Hyde Park, would have been London's tallest building. Housing minister Henry Brooke turned down the application in a letter to New City Properties Ltd., agent for the hotel group. Mr. Brook conceded that hotels need to be built high nowadays and acknowledged that Park Lane was a good spot for them. But he said he preferred a building that "would present a less massive appearance from the park."[140] The hotel was redesigned with a lower, less massive, Y-shaped tower. The new plan called for over a hundred fewer guest rooms. But resistance continued. In April 1959, the London *Times* reported: "The Royal Fine Arts Commission are still opposed to the revised design for a new hotel. . . . [They] informed the county council that the site was not one on which a building much above the normal height of about 100 ft. should be permitted. . . . The council feel that if permission were given for an exceptionally high building in this case they do not see how it would be possible to refuse permission for others at different points on the perimeter of the central parks. 'The final result would be the destruction of that sense of remoteness from the atmosphere of a big city which is one of their unique assets.'"[141] In 1959, despite on-going protests, the London County Council's decision was unexpectedly reversed. The Conservative Macmillan government apparently overruled the objections of the Labour-controlled LCC.[142] The project was immediately announced to the public.[143] Construction was begun with dramatic rapidity. One retired Hilton executive expressed the shock of the reversal by suggesting that someone in the government must have been paid off. The queen has never been seen in the London Hilton.

The construction companies used on the project were largely Clore-owned firms.[144] The architect for the project was Sidney Kaye, with William B. Tabler acting as a consultant. Kaye had worked for Clore before. He was, for example, involved in Clore's speculative development in Kingsway. Shirley Green describes that project:

> The only reason the West End's theaters survive in architectural terms is that they are protected from demolition and redevelopment. The days have gone when a property speculator could use the ploy of redeveloping an old theater with a block of offices that incorporated a new theater, and then, when the anonymous new theater proved unsuccessful, get planning permission to convert it into something like a conference center. The late Charles Clore was one of the first to use this technique. He demolished the old Stoll Theater in Kingsway and replaced it with 90,000 square feet of offices, forty-six underground car-parking spaces, and a small new theater called the Royalty. When

> the theater failed to catch on with the public, it was converted to a television studio, which is now owned on a long leasehold by Thames Television. Ironically, in view of their role as custodian of most of London's historic buildings, the offices are let to the Department of the Environment's Property Services Agency.[145]

It has been difficult to find material on Kaye.[146] The librarian at the Royal Institute of British Architects was apologetic when she gave me his file. It contains but a single sheet, noting his birth in 1915, his education at Brixton School of Building and the London Polytechnic, the firms in which he worked and five buildings.[147] The only project specifically mentioned in his obituary, written by his last partner, Eric Firmin, was the London Hilton: "Sidney specialized in hotels and commercial developments. . . . During his period as senior partner, Sidney was, rightfully, particularly proud of the dozen or so major hotel projects completed world-wide. Not least of his achievements was gaining the commission for the London Hilton Hotel, Park Lane, against strong North American competition. To this day, some thirty years later, it remains one of the most financially successful hotels in the world."[148] The phrasing of this obituary is peculiar. "Not least" must mean "greatest." Kaye is represented as proud of the Hilton commission, but not of the building itself. Apparently the structure's merit resided in its profits rather than in its aesthetic presence.[149]

The London Hilton was, indeed, bitterly criticized. The critic of the *Architect's Journal* wrote scathingly of its appearance on the London scene:

> [T]he harmonica-cluster of the Hilton Hotel is the largest architectural disaster to hit London so far. By all accounts Hilton hotels abroad are not too bad, in a brash American way, so why should we in particular be inflicted with such vulgar design? . . . Why did Hilton—or was it developer Clore—feel impelled to use a firm of British architects whose buildings are largely unknown and certainly unremarkable apart from the dreary Bowmaker House, St. James's Street? After all, Americans are supposed to be able to teach us a thing or two about high buildings. . . . But, in compensation, remember that some people put up a fight against the Hilton design. The LCC rejected it, and the Royal Fine Arts Commission supported the council. They were both overruled by tasteless, insensitive thugs at the Ministry of Housing. . . . Rumor says that the dollar-hungry Board of Trade browbeat the ministry.[150]

The building continues to get bad press.[151] The entry on the London Hilton in the *Guide to the Architecture of London* comments: "An early arrival of Manhattanism. The chief attraction of the view from the rooftop restaurant and bar, one of the earliest in London (by Casson, Conder and Partners) is that this particularly inept building is for once absent from the skyline (as Victor Hugo remarked of the Eiffel Tower)."[152] The London Hilton's promotional brochures include numerous large images of London seen from its windows, but nothing over postage-stamp size of the building's exterior. Like all of the early Hilton International hotels, the London Hilton on Park Lane occupied prime real estate. But its ground lot was very small, only one and a quarter acres. A vertical structure was, for Hilton, the only economic possibility. It took eight years to leverage out each of the 170 bodies with some claim on the location and to acquire the necessary building permits.[153] And though the London Hilton has been a great financial success, it remains an aesthetic failure.

The early Hilton International hotels tended to be good buildings. The London Hilton is one exception. The aesthetic and the political problems of the London Hilton issue from its speculative conception and its ideological associations. In London, in contrast to Istanbul, Cairo, and Berlin, Hilton was not dealing with a government-sponsored organization and public park land. In London the Hilton Corporation had to do business with the private and the entrepreneurial. The London Hilton was confronted with much greater competition from a significant number of well-established, extremely prestigious, and utterly British hotels, two of which were on the same block. Though hotels like the Savoy and the Dorchester still suffered in the 1950s from shortages of materials for refurbishing and still resisted such modernizations as showers and in-room radios (much less ice water spigots in every bathroom), they still offered unsurpassable personal service, generously scaled rooms, and English tradition.[154] This circumstance aggravated a more fundamental problem: Hilton was not dealing in London with a government agency imbued with a desire for a great international hotel and with relatively little experience in negotiation. Rather, the Hilton architectural office presented its demands to an owner skilled in profit making. Corners were cut: an unnotable architect was appointed, facing materials were not of the highest quality, lobby space was ungenerous and oversold. The commitment of the owner to economic efficiency seems to be related to the aesthetic inadequacies of his building. I must, in consequence, accede to a comment made by a eulogizer of Britain's multimillionaires: "Mr. Clore has already left a permanent mark on British industry, both by his development of his own great group of companies and by acting as a pioneer of new financial methods that have now been generally adopted throughout the field of industry; when his new hotel is completed, with its night club and restaurant overlooking Hyde Park from the top of a twenty-five-story building, he will also have altered London's sky line and left a most characteristic memorial to his own energy and enterprise."[155]

With the construction of the Hilton, Rasmussen's prophecy, quoted at the beginning of this chapter, came to pass. Many views along London streets terminate in massive superstructures, as the look east down Oxford Street is curtained by Seifert's politically and aesthetically grotesque Centre Point. Further, the panorama of London offered by the Hilton when it was first constructed presented the great dome of Christopher Wren's St. Paul's as majestically isolated, framed by Senate House of London University to the far left and by the clustered towers of Big Ben and Westminster Abbey to the right. Now that sweep "has been spoiled by a number of meaningless skyscrapers," many constructed on economic principles similar to those that produced the London Hilton.[156]

The Hilton was disliked because it was ugly. It was also not English. The Americanness that made the Hilton popular in Berlin, Athens, Cairo, and Istanbul seems to have made it an object of contempt and envy in London. A member of the board of British Petroleum expressed to an American executive of the Gulf Oil Corporation the utter disdain that he and his wife felt for the new hotel shortly after it opened. The American was subsequently surprised to see his British colleague dining with his spouse in Hilton's Roof Top Restaurant a few evenings later. The Englishman's rhetorical contempt for American culture had apparently been mastered by his actual fascination with it. During the heated discussion of the building in the House of Lords before its construction, Lord Blackford violently denounced the Hilton. His comments, reported in the London *Times* described the effect of the building on the London skyline: "[T]o the east a lovely structure symbolizing Almighty God [St. Paul's]; to the west, a massive structure symbolizing the almighty dollar. He deplored the prospect of London's architecture being Americanized. . . . [He stated that if] we allowed this massive pillar to be erected in Park Lane we should never be able to get away from it."[157] The "it" to be gotten away from was apparently not only an architectural monument to a local Jew made good, but also to the American supersession of Britain as the major power in the postcolonial world.

Hilton International Conference and Banqueting Facilities

AMERICAS	EUROPE	AFRICA—WEST ASIA	THE ORIENT
Barbados	Amsterdam	Istanbul	Hong Kong
Cartegena	London, Park Lane	Cairo, Nile	Shanghai
Caracas	Royal Berkshire	Cairo, Ramses	Bangkok
Margarita	Paris	Luxor	Tokyo
New York	Corfu	Isis and Osiris	Tokyo Bay
San Juan	Athens	Fayrouz Village	Seoul
Honolulu	Malta	Tunis	Singapore
Ojai	Rome	Nairobi	Australia
Chicago	Wien	Salt Lick	Sydney
Toronto	Wien Plaza	Taita Hills	Cairns
Montreal	Budapest		
	Geneva		
	München City		
	München Park		
	Tel Aviv		
	Jerusalem		

—HILTON INTERNATIONAL,
INCENTIVE DESTINATIONS

4 Spectacle: Tel Aviv and Jerusalem

Jerusalem Hilton under construction.

Jaffa/Tel Aviv. In 1902, Theodor Herzl published *Altneuland* (translated in English as *Old New Land*), a novel that projected the Zionist politics of contemporary Europe into a future Palestine.[1] In the novel, a young Jewish lawyer contemplates suicide because of his lack of prospects in anti-Semitic Vienna. Instead he goes into amnesia-like seclusion on a South Sea island. Twenty years later, on his return journey to Europe, he finds love and economic security in a New Society. The New Society is a commonwealth established in Palestine by Jews escaping European racism: "At the end of the nineteenth century and at the beginning of the twentieth, life was made intolerable for us Jews. . . . The persecutions were social and economic. Jewish merchants were boycotted, Jewish workingmen starved out, Jewish professional men proscribed. . . . They were humiliated everywhere in civil life. It became clear that, in the circumstances, they must either become the deadly enemies of a society that was so unjust to them, or seek out a refuge for themselves. The latter course was taken, and here we are. We have saved ourselves."[2] If the New Society is the issue of European intolerance, it is also the product of Western culture, technology, and commerce. The New Society invents nothing. Its scientific, technological, and institutional features are adapted from Europe and America and imposed on the East. In the novel, Joe Levy, the founding executive director of the New Society as a liberal capitalist enterprise, makes this clear: "I do not claim that we created anything new. American, English, French, and German engineers had done the same things before us, but we were the first heralds of technical civilization in the Orient."[3] In the novel, the imposition of the West on the East is materially demonstrated in the urban landscape:

> Before them lay an immense square bordered by the high-arched arcades of stately buildings. . . . [These structures] housed colonial banks and the branch offices of European shipping companies. It was for that reason that the square was called "The Place of the Nations." The name was apt not only because the buildings were devoted to international commerce, but because the "Place of the Nations" was thronged with people from all parts of the world. Brilliant Oriental robes mingled with the sober costumes of the Occident, but the latter predominated. There were many Chinese, Persians and Arabs in the streets, but the city itself seemed thoroughly European. One might easily imagine himself in some Italian port. . . but the buildings were much cleaner and more modern.[4]

One Europeanism not imported to Herzl's New Society was racism. Indeed, Herzl represents the New Society as providing Europeans with a model in this particular domain: "Only when the Jews, forming the majority in Palestine, showed themselves tolerant, were they shown more toleration in all other countries."[5] The New Society was liberal and open. Jews, Arabs, and Christians enjoyed equal rights within the community. The New Society was a reconstruction of European society in an inert East by liberal, middle-class professionals. The founders of the New Society were not opposed by the local Muslim population, who embraced European innovation; they were, however, deeply opposed by a conservative, opportunist rabbi who uses bigotry to manipulate the proletariat. In the novel, the secular, enlightened leaders come out on top.

In some ways, Herzl's projection was tragically accurate. As Herzl predicted, Jewish colonization of Palestine was the product of Western racism. European anti-Semitism motivated migration, from the first colonists at the beginning of the twentieth century to the mass influx of the 1930s with the rise of fascism. Herzl's presentiment of the conflict between the secular, liberal Jews and the religious right also has proved dismally correct. In other ways, Herzl's presentiments of a utopian Jewish community in Palestine were tragically wrong. The liberal, middle-class professionals have not won the struggle for power. Israel has not abandoned European racism but reproduced it. In 1998, nearly a century after Herzl predicted a free and open society, a rally in Jerusalem to celebrate a victorious soccer season, with then prime minister Benjamin Netanyahu presiding, ended with the great mass of Israeli Jerusalemites chanting "death to the Arabs."[6] In contrast, at the same moment in Tel Aviv, people were hooting their car horns in the streets celebrating the triumph of Dana International, the popular Israeli transsexual entertainer, in the 1998 Eurovision Song Contest. Tel Aviv and Jerusalem are two very different places.

Tel Aviv was the title given to the Hebrew translation of Herzl's novel. Tel Aviv was also the name given to a Jewish suburb founded northeast of Jaffa in 1909 (fig. 50). Jaffa was an ancient port city which, over the centuries, had vied for commerce with other harbors, like Caesarea, along the coast of Palestine. In the nineteenth century, it was the principal anchorage between Alexandria and Beirut. In *Innocents Abroad*, the account of his pilgrimage of 1867, Mark Twain describes Jaffa as a city "buried" in "noble"

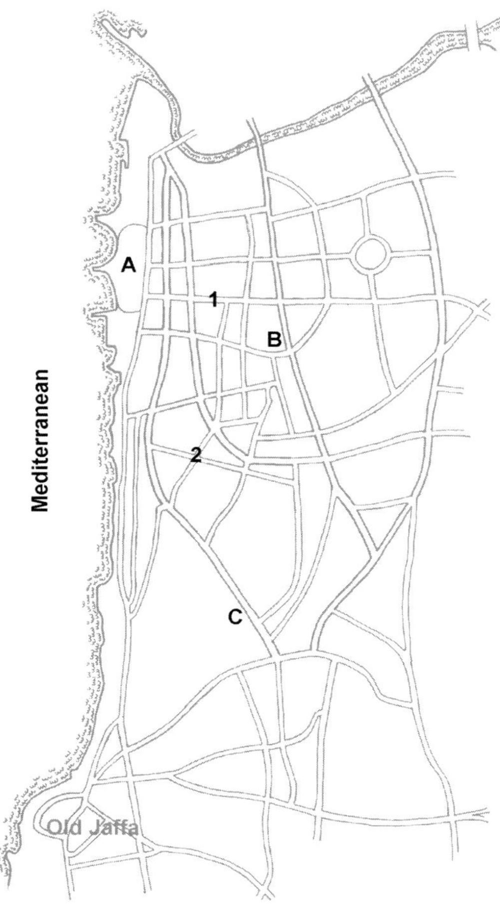

50. Sketch plan of Old Jaffa and Tel Aviv, by author: *A*, Tel Aviv Hilton; *B*, Municipal Center; *C*, Shalom Mayer Tower built on the site of the Gymnasia Herzliya; *1*, Arlozorov Avenue; *2*, Dizengoff Circle.

orange groves and as Palestine's "only good seaport."[7] By the turn of the century, there was in Jaffa a small Jewish community of merchants and craftsmen that attracted increasing numbers of Jewish immigrants. Secularized colonists found the Orthodox establishment in Jerusalem hostile to nonreligious Western European Jews.[8] So when a group of middle-class Jews of Jaffa founded a building society in 1907, they were responding to a strongly felt need to establish a separate community. The suburb imagined at the first meeting of the Achusat-Bayit [Home] Association suggests that in some ways life follows art: the new community was to realize Herzl's desire for a secular European city in the East. Early Tel Aviv, produced for middle-class Jews of European origin, gave Herzl's imagined space a material form.[9]

In his novel Herzl depicts the planning of the New Society's towns as exclusively Western: "The town plans for Haifa, Jaffa, Tiberias and other places had been prepared by Steineck [the architect of the New Society] before he left London. Steineck had also made several model plans for pretty middle-class homes."[10] The residence of David Littwak, one of the novel's protagonists, was described as "a large, pleasant mansion in the Moorish style, set in gardens." The drawing room was "a high-vaulted room containing magnificent works of art. Rose-colored silk covered the walls. Furniture was of the delicate English style."[11] Inscribed in Herzl's vision are the general symmetries of beaux arts planning and the eclectic taste that characterized European architecture in the last years of the nineteenth century.

The founders of Tel Aviv realized Herzl's vision by imitating Germans. The embarrassing contrast between the gentile German Quarter and the earliest Jewish settlements in Jaffa informed the conception of Tel Aviv. In 1907, a Jewish settler, Ze'ev Smilansky, commented:

> Passing through the neighborhood of the Germans near Jaffa, as well as the small German quarter [Valhalla] opposite Neve Zedek, it is a pleasure to see pretty, tastefully built houses embellished by courtyards full of trees and flower gardens which blossom almost all year long. In contrast, when we come to [the Jewish sector of] Mishkneot Yaakov in Jaffa, it is saddening and shaming to find something akin to a new version of the ghetto. . . . [Further, in one of the first Jewish suburbs in Jaffa, Neve Zedek,] because the houses were so close together, the toilets were built one beside the other and, what is more, the houses are at the back of the courtyard and the toilets at the front, near the street entrance. Thus in walking the streets of Neve Zedek, one passes a long row of outhouses.[12]

Even more compelling evidence of the centrality of the German Colony to the Jewish one that was subsequently to erase it is found in a letter of 1904: "To the highly esteemed Mr. Wolfson: In light of the great increase in Jaffa's Jewish population, there is a desire to establish a new Jewish quarter following the model of the German quarter in Jaffa."[13] The project outlined in the minutes of the first meeting of the Achusat-Bayit Association and later realized in construction carried out by the association finally exceeded the German Colony. It also filled a number of Herzl's prescriptions. Free-standing houses would be placed on lots of not less than 570 square meters; streets would be wide and tree-lined; there would be public gardens, paving with sidewalks, a central sewerage system, piped water from wells, and street-lighting. The new community was to be "a Jewish urban center in a healthy spot, beautifully arranged and ordered according to all the rules of hygiene."[14] There was no synagogue planned for the new community. The center was monumentalized not by a place of worship but by a gymnasium or lyceum for Jewish boys, the Gymnasia Herzliya, named in honor of Herzl. It was rendered by its architect, Joseph Barsky, in a "patriotically Hebrew style."[15] A massive central block is flanked by arms with a double arcade. The arcade had round-headed arches on the ground floor and pointed ones on the second. For the most part, however, the suburb was constituted of less-pretentious, single-family dwellings, many with red-tile roofs and classicizing details.[16] As specified, these faced tree-lined boulevards, reproducing the bourgeois German suburbs of Europe and Jaffa.

The European appearance of the suburb marked its elevated status. Arthur Ruppin, a remarkable Zionist administrator of the Jewish National Fund, used this image to raise money for further colonization: "In contrast with the pitiful Arab villages, with their huts of baked clay, the Jewish colonies, with their wide streets, their strong stone houses and their red-tiled roofs, look like veritable oases of culture."[17] "Red roofs" were then powerful markers of European difference. Now "red roofs" signify alien colonization. The continued ideological power of "red roofs" is indicated by the use of the epithet in the political struggles over Jewish settlements in the occupied territories.[18] Ruppin also recognized the importance of a prestigious Jewish community to the project of Jewish control of Jaffa. In a letter to the central office of the Jewish National Fund in Cologne of July 21, 1907, he wrote: "As far as Jaffa is concerned, it is especially important to build high-quality, hygienic homes for Jews of the middle-class. I think I would not be exaggerating if I said that the founding of a proper Jewish quarter is the best way for the Jews to take over Jaffa financially."[19] Red roofs contributed to the establishment of Jewish control of Palestine.

Altneuland was by no means the template for all aspects of the new suburb. Herzl's utopia was religiously and ethnically integrated. The projected suburb in Jaffa was to be completely segregated. The minutes of the first meeting of the Achusat-Bayit Association specified that residents were to be "100% Hebrew."[20] Subsequent regulations strictly prohibited selling or renting accommodation to Arabs. This contrasted not only with Herzl's vision but also with practices elsewhere in the Middle East and North Africa. The new European suburbs of Cairo, Istanbul, and other cities were accessible also to local elites.[21] The space of Jewish exclusivity in Jaffa was to expand. The strategic importance of securing land for further development is analyzed by the historical geographer, Yossi Katz:

> The land purchases displayed a clear intention to outflank northern Jaffa (the Menshieh quarter) and reach the seashore, which lay about one kilometer from the Tel Aviv center. The Tel Aviv leaders saw this corridor as a necessary condition for strengthening and developing Tel Aviv and they therefore invested a great deal of capital in acquiring land leading towards the seashore. The corridor would indeed turn out to be exceedingly advantageous. It blocked all possibility of Jaffa developing northwards and enabled Tel Aviv to expand freely to the north and west and to develop the seafront. The extension to the seashore was completed by 1913.[22]

The ideological location of the Tel Aviv development is implicated in its financing. The traditional institutional sources of support for Jewish immigration to Palestine were either religious or Zionist. The *hallukah* was a religious subsidy provided to Jews who came to Palestine that they might die in the Holy Land. Levied in the countries of the emigrants' origins and distributed equally among all emigrants, irrespective of need, it provided little more than a meager means to await death. Communities thus supported tended to reproduce the European ghetto in its architectural form and in its religious zealousness. Early immigrant communities, like Meah Shearim, built in Jerusalem in 1874, were usually constructed as island blocks around a communal court, on the model of the ghettos of eastern Europe.[23] In contrast, Zionist organizations, which received funds from Jews in Europe and America, tended to focus their funds on agricultural colonies, *moshavot* and *kibbutzim*.[24] As Ruppin made clear, the possession of a fertile land lay at the ideological core of Zionism: "[Agriculture] is not just one of the branches of production: it is also the fountain of youth, in which we renew ourselves in the physical and spiritual sense after centuries of crippling life in the cities, remote from the soil."[25] Fund-raising was most persuasively directed to the extension of Jewish farming.[26] The agrarian communities tended to the socialist.

Though less emphasis was given to urban development, Tel Aviv did receive some Zionist institutional support. Ruppin described the historical situation:

> When I came to Palestine for the first time, in the year 1907, I found there a poor, small Jewish Company calling itself Achusat-Bayit, which issued a project to build a Jewish suburb near Jaffa. If I had, in those days, turned to private capital to help in the building of this section, no one would have had a penny for such a mad enterprise. It was only because I was able to persuade

> the Jewish National Fund to extend a loan for the building of this section that Tel Aviv, of which we are so proud today, could be founded. National settlement must pave the way for private investment.[27]

Nevertheless, private capital as well as Zionist funding was always involved in the development of Tel Aviv. Tel Aviv, and communities like it in Haifa and elsewhere, depended on private capital. They tended to be secular like the kibbutzim, but committed to a capitalist economy rather than socialism. Their form, in consequence, could not remain ideal for long.

After World War I and with the replacement of Ottoman control by the British Mandate, Jewish immigration to Palestine increased exponentially. Tel Aviv absorbed half of all Jewish investment in Palestine, most of it private.[28] In 1921 Tel Aviv was officially separated from Jaffa and incorporated as a township. Patrick Geddes, the Scots sociologist, architect, and urbanist, and his follower Richard Kauffmann, along with his colleague Lotte Cohn, worked on plans for Tel Aviv.[29] These plans preserved the middle-class, Garden City spirit of the prewar scheme. They divided the extension of the city into lots appropriate for private, single-family housing, preserved a wide public beach front, and ensured the ventilation of the city by opening broad boulevards to the Mediterranean.[30]The thoroughness with which the space of Jaffa was colonized is suggested by Sir D. M. Stevenson's account of his visit to Tel Aviv in 1927: "[Tel Aviv was] beautifully laid out on land which I was told had been a few years previously little better than a desert, but now formed the center of acres upon acres of orange groves."[31]Arab Jaffa's old orange groves, so famous in the nineteenth century, were reimagined as new ones of Jewish Tel Aviv.

In the 1930s Tel Aviv began to exceed Herzl's vision in its modernity. The architecture of the novel remained trapped in the German eclecticism of the nineteenth century; the architecture of the real Tel Aviv embraced that of the German avant-garde. In the late 1920s and 1930s the architectural cutting edge was commonly identified in Palestine with the Bauhaus. Established by Walter Gropius at Weimar and later moved to Dessau, the Bauhaus attracted an international cadre of gifted artists and architects. The Bauhaus advocated ahistorical form and raised the functional to the level of a new aesthetic.[32] One of the earliest manifestations of the new architecture was the workers' housing project at Weissenhof. There, white, flat-roofed houses and low-rise apartment blocks presented Germany with an ideal environment for the modern working-class family. The project had its detractors. It was denounced by Paul Bonatz, a conservative local architect, as looking more like a "suburb of Jerusalem" than one of Stuttgart.[33] The Nazis later distributed postcards in which figures from a Middle Eastern souk overlaid a photograph of the Weissenhof quarter. The postcard was titled "Arab Village."[34] The new architecture was identified by the fascists as Jewish and oriental. Censured in Germany as Semitic, it was subsequently condemned in the Soviet Union as petit bourgeois and in the United States as Bolshevik.[35]

A historian of Modern architecture might well ask, what could be more appropriate for the New Society than a new architecture that was already identified as Semitic, as well as liberal-capitalist and as socialist?[36] The new architecture was embraced as the building form of choice for Tel Aviv.[37] Tel Aviv's rapid expansion in the 1920s and 1930s as well as its lack of an acceptably non-Arab architectural vernacular provided the necessary space for the full realization of the Modern. Indeed, Tel Aviv came as close as anywhere else in the world to materializing the White City—the truly modern city—envisioned by architects like Le Corbusier and Walter Gropius. Some architects who contributed to the whitening of Tel Aviv had established significant reputations in Europe before immigrating to Palestine. Most famous among these was Erich Mendelsohn, whose Columbus Haus in Berlin epitomized Modernity.[38] But, as the architectural historian Alona Nitzan-Shiftan concludes, Mendelsohn's commitment to developing a pluralistic modernism that was as relevant to the Arabs as to the Jews led to his marginalization in Israeli architectural politics: "In blatant opposition to Mendelsohn's reliance on Arab collaboration, for the Chug the success of the Zionist project was independent of, and consciously indifferent to, Arab culture. Putting the 'New Hebrew' rather than 'the Semite' at the core of Zionist identity, their Zionist enterprise focused inward—working, building and populating the Land of Israel, as well as reviving its (secular) Hebrew culture."[39] The Chug, or Circle, was a group of young, socialist architects who had been educated in a liberal tradition and trained in Europe under the influence of the Bauhaus and the other master-inventors of the new architecture.[40] Arieh Sharon, a founding member of the Chug, was a Bauhaus graduate. Others, like Ze'ev Rechter, educated in Italy and France, were committed Modernists before establishing themselves in Palestine. Ze'ev Rechter's Engle House of 1933 was the first building on pilotis in Tel Aviv (fig. 51). It brought to Tel Aviv the Le Corbusian villa and, more importantly, the commitment to ventilating buildings from below.[41] The

51. Tel Aviv, Engle House, 1933, the first building on *pilotis* in the city. Photo courtesy of Rechter Archive, Tel Aviv.

new architecture, identified in Palestine as Bauhaus architecture, was promoted as the appropriate architectural expression of the new state. Indigenous forms, first ignored in favor of European garden suburbs, were subsequently replaced as the local architecture by an imported modernity.[42] It is darkly ironic that the first exclusively Jewish modern city, inhabited largely by the victims of European racism, was also the first full urban expression of European Modernism.

The rewriting of Jaffa as Tel Aviv was completed after World War II. In 1950 Tel Aviv became officially Tel Aviv–Yafo; the state sanctioned the appropriation of the ancient port of Jaffa (Yafo) by its former suburb, Tel Aviv.[43] The port of Jaffa was closed in 1965, on the inauguration of the modern port at Ashdod, about twenty miles to the south. Jaffa was emptied of its Palestinian inhabitants as well as its fishing and trading traditions. Racist graffiti have obliterated the ancient Arabic street names. In spring 1998, Israeli friends could not name a restaurant in the vicinity of Tel Aviv serving Palestinian cuisine. The stone shops and houses of Old Jaffa have been converted into studios for Israeli artists and craftsmen and boutiques for the sale of their productions. The fishing quays are tourist restaurants. Old Jaffa is erased; it is now the historical theme park of new Tel Aviv.

By the late 1960s, time and the second generation of Modernist builders had turned the White City gray.[44] The earlier buildings were not maintained. Stucco skins disintegrated, open balconies had been crudely enclosed, strip windows divided and louvered. More disfiguring was the imposition of grisly new structures, like the enormous, banal Shalom Mayer Tower shopping and office complex which tragically replaced the landmark of the first suburb, the Gymnasia Herzliya, or the ghastly recasting of Genia Averbouch's elegant Dizengoff Circle of 1935 as a concrete underpass. Bauhaus was replaced with Brutal.[45] Massive fortresses of exposed concrete displaced athletic white structures tethered to earth by their pilotis. From the late twenties, concrete had been the material of choice for new construction. Palestine was without a local supply of steel and wood. Stone was expensive. Further, stone quarries and the stonemason's craft were largely under Arab control. Building in stone involved dependence on Arab-controlled materials and Arab labor. With the construction of the Jewish-owned Nesher cement factory in 1926, cheap Jewish-supplied building material became as available as unskilled Jewish labor. The choice of concrete was economic and ideological, not aesthetic.[46] In the 1960s the rawest form of this new material was mythologized: exposed concrete was appropriately heroic, like the Israeli nation; it was nonelite; it "seems to suit and convey—and even basically contribute to—the Israelis' no-nonsense way of doing things."[47] In the photographs published in monographs and architectural journals, these buildings don't look too bad. In life they are ugly and menacing. Architects did not initially realize how badly concrete would weather.[48] Characteristic is the Municipal Center, built on open, public space, in 1966, by Menachem Cohen (fig. 52).[49] This massive gray block, streaked with run-off grime and gridded with bureaucratically scaled windows is elevated on an overpass podium and confronts a vast expanse of concrete with the unlikely label "piazza" on published plans. This ominous space is not social but political. It attracts human occupants only for organized events—political rallies and holiday celebrations. The building is only sought out by those who look for the bleak memorial to the assassination of Prime Minister Yitzhak Rabin in the alley behind it (fig. 53). The site is not mentioned in many guidebooks.

52. Tel Aviv, Municipal Center, view of the main façade. Photo by author.

53. Tel Aviv, alley behind the Municipal Center, memorial to the assassination of Prime Minister Yitzhak Rabin. Photo by author.

Tel Aviv Hilton. Opened in 1965, the Tel Aviv Hilton is an excellent example of Tel Aviv's second generation of modern architecture in all ways but one—it is not a bad building, but a distinguished one (figs. 54 and 55).[50] In the early 1970s the eminent architectural critic, Ada Louise Huxtable, wrote a denunciation of the stifling standardization of the hotel industry. She included a critique of "predictable Hiltons around the world, with a few notable exceptions such as the Istanbul Hilton and the Tel Aviv Hilton by architects Skidmore, Owings and Merrill and Jakov [Ya'acov] Rechter, respectively."[51] That the Tel Aviv Hilton is an aesthetically satisfying building is due in part to its design and in part to its location. Its architect, Ya'acov Rechter, is the son of Ze'ev Rechter. The Tel Aviv Hilton is as invested in the Western modernity of the 1960s as his father's Engle House was in the European Modern of the 1930s. It exhibits the commitment to form as an expression of structure and the disdain for applied ornament that the son shared with the father.[52]

54. Tel Aviv, Tel Aviv Hilton, view from the southeast. Photo courtesy of Rechter Archive, Tel Aviv.

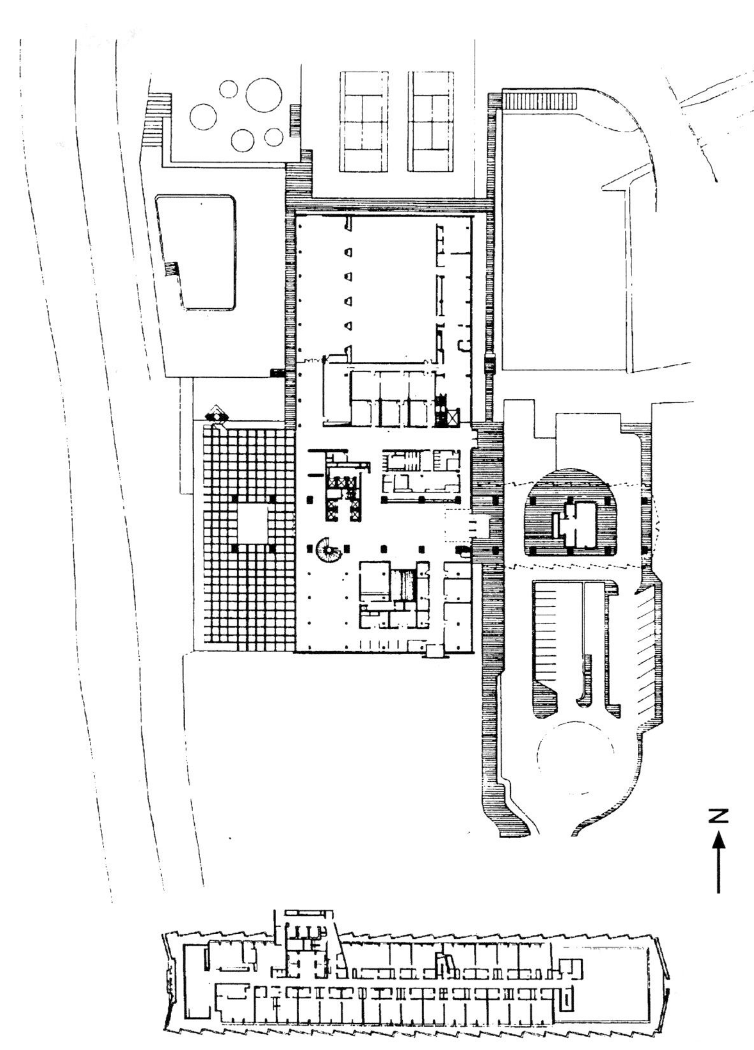

The program of the hotel follows the successful Hilton International model: public and service spaces in a horizontal base and guest rooms in a tower above (fig. 56). But here that program takes an unusually expressive form. The base is not a broad podium from which the tower block rises; rather, a lateral section of space crawls under the belly of a powerful superstructure that rises with apparent independence, supported on massive pier-pilotis and monumental triangular cradles. The tower block extends two massive bays beyond the low shelf of space both to the east and west. The extension toward Tel Aviv serves as a porte cochere for the arriving guests. The symmetrical extension at the opposite end toward the Mediterranean covers a deck that confronts the sea. The roughly pebbled, gray-stuccoed piers and the exposed concrete of the superstructure, textured by the impression of the wooden formwork that molded it, exaggerate the primal mass of the building.[53] The craggy quality of the hotel is accentuated by the angled plan of the guest rooms. To ensure a view of the sea from each of the

55. Tel Aviv, Tel Aviv Hilton, detail of the southeast corner. Photo courtesy of Rechter Archive, Tel Aviv.

56. Tel Aviv, Tel Aviv Hilton: *A*, plan of the ground level; *B*, plan of a typical guest room floor. Drawings courtesy of Rechter Archive, Tel Aviv.

446 rooms in the hotel's east-west oriented tower, they are angled fifteen degrees to the west.[54] The view of the sea and the West was every guest's privilege. The view of the city and the East was offered to no one.

The interior of the Tel Aviv Hilton maintains the heroic scale of the exterior while refining its surfaces. The double-storied monumentality of the porte cochere, briefly interrupted by a dropped ceiling at the entrance, is dramatically continued the entire length of the building (fig. 57). The great piers supporting the tower are lightened by the substitution of dark marble revetment for gray stucco. The floors and walls are also faced with marble. The giant coffers of the belly of the guest room block are carried through from exterior to interior. The perspectival recession of both the piers and the coffers dramatize the distance from the front to the back of the structure. The glazed entrance is duplicated in the plate glass at the opposite end of the lobby, so that the length of the building serves to focus the gaze on the Mediterranean and theatricalize its proximity. The lounge, bar, and shops that occupy the extension of the base to the south are less massively scaled.

The interior decoration of the Tel Aviv Hilton had the consistency of the Nile Hilton. But, in contrast to that earlier member of the chain, it was not historically thematized. Despite the thematic naming of the public rooms—for instance the main restaurant was titled King Solomon's Grill Room—the decor was insistently Modern. The principal designer, Dora Gad, was a prominent architect and interior designer of the first generation of Jewish Modernists in Palestine. Born in what is now Romania and later trained in engineering and architecture in Vienna, Dora Gad emigrated to Palestine in 1936. Her views on the importation of European forms to the region were summarized in the catalogue of an exhibition devoted to her work:

> [T]he modernism that she had absorbed was an impenetrable barrier for the romantic-oriental outlook which characterized quite a few of the previous generation of architects. The Arab world which she met in Palestine did not seem to her to present itself as a model for imitation because the comprehensive outlook of modernism, in which every design object expresses the social and cultural qualities of its designer, does not allow one to detach a

57. Tel Aviv, Tel Aviv Hilton, view of the interior. Imagine this interior without heavy draperies, shrubs, and bulky furniture. Photo by author.

> form from its content. Anyone not wanting to live in an Arab society and to adopt its culture, customs and its attitudes is not entitled to take its design-form language and use it as he wishes.[55]

Earlier attempts to invent historical Jewish architectural forms had inevitably involved contamination with motifs associated with Arab vernacular or elite buildings. Abstraction was the only alternative. Gad expressed her commitment to the local both as non-Arab and as nonhistorical: "Ornamented Arab furniture no longer catches the eye. . . . I am trying to impart to the Hilton an Israeli character, but without Israeli clichés. I believe that real artists create original works by means of an Israeli prism through which our light, color, and rhythm of life are reflected. The Hilton will not have a dominant Mediterranean atmosphere. The Negev will be the theme."[56] She "incorporated in her scheme blocks of stone from King Solomon's Mines, coral from Eilat and local ceramics," but the desert theme that she identified was never explicitly figured. Gad's abstraction evaded direct quotation of the autochthonous Arab culture of Palestine. Abstraction also offered an escape from religious reference. Gad, as an European intellectual and a secular Jew, scrupulously avoided religious thematization. At the Tel Aviv Hilton, she pressed the management unsuccessfully to name the principal dining room King Solomon's Mines rather than King Solomon's Grill Room. She apparently wished to move the emphasis from a person to a place, from a powerful figure of the religious past to a specific site that could be visited in the secular present.

Abstraction, however, allowed commentators to impress their own desired meanings on the decoration. The most commonly invented theme was, not surprisingly, biblical. The description in the *New York Times* is typical: "Architects and other experts responsible for building and decorating the hotel have leaned heavily and tastefully on biblical references. The magenta, yellow and orange colors of fabrics found with ancient scrolls have been reproduced in the hotel's curtains and carpets. Israeli art can be found in tapestries, pottery and sculpture, while motifs representing Israeli culture and history, from the copper of King Solomon's mines to ancient stones of the Sea of Galilee, are used throughout the building."[57] The decoration remained an abstraction. Reference was made only allusively in the earth tones and bold forms of the hangings, carpets, and furnishings that she designed or selected. Prominent in the decorative scheme were the sculptures of Dani Karavan, one of Israel's best known artists.[58] Karavan invested bronze solid geometries with the dangerous spirituality of origins. Gad's designs and Karavan's muscular works equally complemented Rechter's in-your-face building.[59] The forceful Modernity of the architecture and the interior decoration of the Tel Aviv Hilton contributed to the hotel's high social status. The hotel also, of course, came equipped with the standard Hilton amenities. All rooms had private balconies, thermostatic temperature control, circulating ice water, and direct-dial telephones. There were also extensive convention facilities that could accommodate about a thousand delegates.

The second factor contributing to the status of the Tel Aviv Hilton was the hotel's commanding site. Like the Hiltons of Istanbul and Cairo, the Tel Aviv Hilton was sited like a great civic monument: isolated and in a public park. Its detachment allowed it to be seen from a distance and as a whole, emphasizing it presence. The Tel Aviv Hilton was constructed on prime property in a prime location. The older, southern part of Tel Aviv which abutted Jaffa had declined into slums. New construction occurred along the coast to the north. In Tel Aviv the most modern section of the city seems always to have been the wealthiest.[60] The new Hilton was located in this preferred, northern part of the city, on a slight rise directly on the sea front. In addition to conventional outdoor leisure facilities—tennis courts, a children's playground, and a large, heated, saltwater swimming pool with underwater portals for watching the swimmers—the Tel Aviv Hilton is the only hotel in the city with its own directly accessed beach.

The Tel Aviv Hilton's remarkable building and its unique site promised success. Success, however, did not come immediately. Arab-Israeli hostility dampened both touristic and business interest in Israel. Local use of the Hilton was apparently also discouraged by one of the early managers, who insisted that jackets and ties be worn in the restaurant. Informality in business attire, and all the more in leisure wear, is de rigueur in Israel. The manager was deemed a snob, and the Hilton was avoided. Optimism after the 1967 War and a change of managers increased the new hotel's popularity and profits.[61] Since the Six Day War, the Tel Aviv Hilton has been the principle locus of the city's haut monde. In the 1970s the hotel was so popular that lobby and lounge seating had to be booked in advance.[62] As in Cairo, Athens, and Istanbul, the Hilton was the point of convergence of Israeli and foreign elites. In 1998 it was still the most prestigious hotel in Tel Aviv.

The high status of the hotel, assured by the quality of its building and by its location, came at considerable cost. The site on which the hotel was constructed was a public park, a garden that erased two distinct histories. The northern section had been occupied by a British army camp; the southern part by a late-nineteenth-century Muslim graveyard. The appropriation of this public area caused a bitter debate.[63] Opposition issued from the government's contribution to the project as well as from the project's usurpation of one of Tel Aviv's few open spaces. In its announcement of the hotel's opening, the *New York Times* included a comment on the controversy provoked by its construction: "A complex financing arrangement that saw the Government put up guarantees for a substantial share of the development cost brought cries of favoritism from other hotel owners. A communist bid to bring the controversy under full Knesset (Parliament) scrutiny missed by four votes."[64] The government of Israel had approached Hilton International with a proposal for a new hotel in 1960. Hilton agreed to participate in the project, on condition that the government would provide the building and guarantee its completion. The four-and-a-half-acre seafront site in Independence Park was appropriated for the building. The American Israel Basic Economy Corporation (AMIBEC), which had been formed by American Jews to initiate and fund business development in Israel, established the Israel Hotels International Corporation, with its home office in Delaware—Israel Hotels International Corporation was the institutional owner of the new Hilton.[65] The Israeli government provided a loan and guaranteed earnings. According to the *Times*, the Tel Aviv Hilton was the biggest project ever undertaken by a private corporation in Israel.

The minister of finance, Pinchas Sapir, was quoted as saying, "[I]t is rare that the political importance of an enterprise coincides with its economic importance, as is the case with the Tel Aviv Hilton."[66] The hotel's economic significance is obvious. Tourism was central to Israeli development. The commercial value of Holy Land pilgrimage was fully appreciated already in Herzl's New Society. Steineck points out to his visitors that "[a]t Nazareth or Bethlehem . . . one is reminded of Lourdes in the Pyrenees.

There is the same vast tourist traffic—the hotels, hospices, convents."[67] But the New Society also recognized that Palestine's climate and waters would make it a leisure haven. "[T]he medicinal hot springs and the beautiful situation of Tiberias attracted visitors from Europe and America who had always sought perennial spring in Sicily or Egypt. As soon as first-class hotel accommodations were available in Tiberias, the tourists had streamed thither. Experienced Swiss hotel-keepers had been the first to recognize the climatic advantages and scenic beauty of the spot, and prospered accordingly."[68] Both these quotes acknowledge the importance of good hotels to the stimulation of tourism. In the end, an American, not a Swiss, hotelier recognized the potential of Tel Aviv, not of Tiberias. The Tel Aviv Hilton addressed the resort and business sides of Palestine's attraction. Later, the Jerusalem Hilton would answer the pilgrim's desire.[69]

As in London and Rome, the Tel Aviv Hilton was economically important enough for its developers to contravene the city's overall plan. It was the first monumental structure to be placed directly on the public swath along the beachfront. Its site ensured that the resort character of the hotel could be maintained even in the center of the city: "One of the newest hotels in the worldwide chain of Hilton International, the 446-room, seventeen-story, air conditioned Tel Aviv Hilton was opened in 1965. A resort hotel in the center of the city, but away from the sound of its hustle and bustle, it is perfectly situated overlooking the Mediterranean and bounded on its other three sides by Independence Park."[70] The hotel was also the first broad high-rise to block the sea breeze of one of Tel Aviv's major east-west boulevards, stifling the ventilation of the city's core. It initiated the eradication of the Geddes plan that the present building boom along the sea front is driving to complete extinction.

Control of corporate development in Israel is notoriously lax. A study of urban planning systems in Israel provides "evidence for endemic failure."[71] Public interest has less chance in Israel than in England. Efraim Torgovnik describes the development of cities in Israel as "planning by deviation." It is inevitably subject to political machinations.[72] He writes: "The Bases of Deviation. National political considerations, such as an increased Jewish presence in Jerusalem, is one factor that led to the negation of [building codes and planning] procedure. Other factors included the state's need for foreign investment and tourism projects. In Israel it was not uncommon for the Ministries of Tourism and Finance to enter into agreements with foreign investors who wanted to build a high-rise hotel on a site formally designated as a public area."[73] Palestinian villages are under constant, daily surveillance to ensure that owners, under threat of confiscation, add no garage or porch to their residences. But Jewish settlers and corporate developers in Israel consistently overbuild, encroaching on occupied or public lands, with no adverse repercussions.[74]

If the economic significance of the Hilton is manifest, the political importance of the hotel to which Pinchas Sapir alluded is less apparent. It was articulated in the *New York Times:* "The Tel Aviv Hilton will be formally opened Tuesday, a triumph for the Israeli Government over the Arab boycott."[75] A subsequent issue of the *New York Times* elaborated on the implications of the Tel Aviv Hilton for the Arab boycott of Israel:

> Premier Levi Eshkol today warmly acknowledged the determination of the Hilton organization in defying the Arab boycott by building a hotel in Tel Aviv. . . . Mr. Eshkol read from a letter written by Conrad Hilton four years

> ago to the Arab boycott committee. Mr. Hilton told the committee, Mr. Eshkol said, that its efforts to bring pressure against the hotel chain ran "absolutely counter to the principles we live by. . . . As Americans, we consider Arabs and Jews our friends and hope ultimately we can all live in peace with one another," Mr. Hilton wrote. "There was no threat from Israel when we opened our hotel in Cairo," he added.[76]

Curt Strand, former president of Hilton International, also reflected on the delicacy of the international politics in which the Tel Aviv Hilton was embedded:

> [W]e were threatened by governments of various Arab countries, including Egypt, that we would lose our agreements with these hotels and we must abide by the Arab contract. We drafted a letter for Mr. Hilton's signature. He wrote to these boycott committees (today it would be illegal for him to write to them but then it was perfectly legal) saying that we didn't invest in Egypt, we didn't invest in Tel Aviv. We were performing a management service which accrues to the benefit of the countries concerned. We took no part in politics and we were only in the tourism business.[77]

But the Tel Aviv Hilton was politics. It was the international politics of investment capital and Arab-Israeli hostility. And it was the local politics of investment capital and entrepreneurial usurpation of the space of the dead and of the dispossessed.

Jerusalem.

The Tel Aviv Hilton was built in a city with a shallow history. Old Jaffa is, after all, now only virtual. The Jerusalem Hilton, in contrast, occupied a landscape structured by centuries of spiritual deposit.[78] The West particularly privileges one moment of that past: the Roman period, more specifically the time of the latest and largest of the Jewish temples of Jerusalem. This was the temple of Herod the Great, begun around 20 B.C.E. and completed about 62 C.E. During this era, Jerusalem was one of the great city-showplaces of the eastern provinces of the empire, complete with palaces, a theater, hippodrome, and amphitheater.[79] But Herod's new temple was the city's greatest spectacle. It was a magnificent structure, elaborately adorned and surrounded by colonnades and courts of increasing exclusivity, sequentially excluding gentiles, women, laymen, and finally admitting only one priest once a year. Herod set this temple complex on a colossal podium, a platform larger than any other known in the Greco-Roman world. For Jews the temple was a site of unparalleled sacredness, the center of religious life and unquestioned sign of the Jewish state.

In 66 C.E., the Jews revolted against Rome. In the process of suppressing the uprising, Herod's new temple was devastated. In Rome this void was rendered as permanent theater: the great marble reliefs of the Arch of Titus display booty from the absent temple, including its great menorah.[80] A second Jewish revolt was suppressed between 132 and 135 C.E. The emperor Hadrian also marked his conquest through erasure. Jerusalem itself was eliminated. Its name was eradicated, all Jews were expelled from the city upon pain of death, its sacred center was desolated. Even with the advent of Christianity, the Temple Mount was left a ruin. For Christians, the temple's destruction was important proof of New Testament prophecy. Their commitment to maintaining the temple's absence is indicated by the ferocity of their opposition to Emperor Julian's attempts to rebuild it.[81] From the Middle Ages the only part of the temple that was accessible to the Jews was the west wall of its great podium, named the Wailing Wall. Here Jewish pilgrims lamented the loss of their temple and the loss of their state. The simultaneous destruction by the Romans of both the Jewish temple and the Jewish state assured the identity of the two; the absence of the one stood for the absence of the other until the twentieth century—for many within the Jewish radical religious right it still does, even today.

Christian pilgrims also make this same Jerusalem, the Jerusalem of the first years of the first millennium C.E., the object of their desire. This was the Jerusalem inhabited by the historical Jesus. The locus that perhaps best represents Christian pilgrimage is Jesus' empty tomb. Since the fourth century, the site was identified by most Catholic and Orthodox Christians with the Church of the Holy Sepulchre.[82] In the nineteenth century, when Protestant Christians became increasingly interested in Palestine, they found the Holy Sepulchre too material for their more cerebral piety. The unflattering report of Jerusalem by Samuel Wheelock Fiske, a traveler of the mid-nineteenth century, exhibits the Protestant aversion to the tactility of religious shrines:

> The town itself . . . is a filthy, muddy, Oriental town, full of dogs and vermin, and intolerable smells, habitable by decent people only on Mt. Zion and near the Jaffa gate. The so-called sacred places have been described a thousand times, and even if they had not been, are not worth the trouble, as no one now believes in their genuineness. . . . [Y]ou are thankful to know that Calvary and the Holy Sepulchre could not possibly have been where the Greeks and Catholics locate them, and quarrel so fiercely about their possession that the Turk is obliged to interfere as a peacemaker in these *Christian* brawls.[83]

The Protestants required a more idyllic, contemplative site for Jesus' burial. This they located in a charming garden, complete with a nearby skull-shaped mound. The Protestant plot is known as the Garden Tomb.[84] For believers, one or the other of these tombs is proof of the resurrection of Jesus and promise of their own bodily salvation. Christian pilgrims go to Jerusalem to experience the presence of God embodied in a material absence.[85] Jerusalem is the object of pilgrimage for the marks left behind by a once manifest divinity.

The popular primacy given to the Jerusalem of Herod's temple and Jesus' life is demonstrated by the remarkable model of Jerusalem staged at the Holy Land Hotel (fig. 58).[86] The construction of the Holy Land Hotel model has been overseen by distinguished Israeli archaeologists, first Michael Avi Yonah and now Yoram Tsafrir. It was built and is continuously renewed and augmented by craftsmen working with authentic materials—Jerusalem stone and marble for the buildings, ceramics for trees and roof-tiles, and true gold leaf for adornments of the temple and palaces. The model was begun at the urging of the hotel's proprietor in the early 1960s. Between the Arab-Israeli War of 1948 and the 1967 War, Jerusalem was a city brutally divided, like Berlin. The old city, part of the Jordanian domain, was inaccessible to the Jews. The model was intended to provide Israelis with access to the city that was forbidden them. It was a means of visually mastering the whole of Jerusalem in the absence of a direct experience of the old city.

The Holy Land Hotel model represents a Jerusalem of the first century C.E. untouched by Arabs. After Jerusalem bloodlessly capitulated to Umar in the seventh century, the Temple Mount, left desolate by Christians, became Al-Haram al-Sharif, "the Noble Sanctuary," a locus of Muslim holiness (fig. 59).[87] The Muslims put the residual numinousness of the site back to work with new construction. Al-Aksa Mosque (c. 639–640) and the remarkably beautiful Dome of the Rock (c. 691) appropriated the holiness of this ancient site for the new religion and contributed to the site's generation of a new set of religious narratives—notably the ascent of Mohammed to heaven. Al-Haram al-Sharif is one of the few constructed spaces in the world that can compete in its serenity with nature. These buildings and their stories are absent from the Holy Land Hotel model.

58. Jerusalem, Holy Land Hotel model of Jerusalem before 70 C.E., view from the southwest toward the Temple Mount. Photo by author.

59. Jerusalem, view of Al-Haram al-Sharif from the Mount of Olives before the construction of the new Hilton. Photo by author.

The substitution of a past Jerusalem for the present one in the Holy Land Hotel model is an altogether reasonable historical and archaeological exercise. The Rome represented in the model of the city in the Museo della Civiltà Romana is that of Constantine. Gorham Phillips Stephens selected fourth-century B.C.E. Athens for his model of that city.[88] The problem remains: in the case of Jerusalem, the model of the past city has become for some the model of its future. The radical religious right wishes to cleanse the Temple Mount/Al-Haram al-Sharif of its venerable Islamic monuments. The substitution of Jewish sacrality for Islamic sacrality at the site began in 1967. On June 10, 1967, during the 1967 War, the old city was taken by the Israelis. Moshe Safdie, Israel's best known architect, describes the moment:

> Within an hour [of first breaching the defenses of Jerusalem], the soldiers had reached the [Wailing] Wall. The words of the announcer moved a nation: "I cannot believe it. Here it is, I am seeing the Wall. The great stones. Everyone around me is touching the Wall. They are crying. I'm crying myself." Within forty-eight hours, Jerusalem had become a unified city. Bulldozers moved in and razed the concrete walls that had divided it. They also razed the Maghariba Quarter that had surrounded the Western Wall, creating a large open space in front of it. To this day it is not clear who ordered the bulldozers in.[89]

The medieval Magharib Quarter or Moors Quarter was the site of a mosque and Muslim shrine of Shaikh'A'id, the Afdaliyya Madrassa of the twelfth century. The area had been designated as a Muslim holy place by the League of Nations in 1930. The destruction of these monuments was symptomatic of the religious right's aggressive appropriation of sacred space.[90] The unnecessarily brutal opening of the archaeological tunnel in September 1996 by the then prime minister, Benjamin Netanyahu, is another example. Right-wing radicals regard these episodes as a preface to the destruction of the Dome of the Rock and Al-Aksa Mosque. Extreme groups with both nationalistic and sectarian motivations plan the destruction of the Muslim buildings and the reconstruction of the temple. At least two dozen attacks have been launched against the Dome of the Rock by anti-Muslim fanatics since the Israeli occupation of Jerusalem in 1967.[91] In the early 1980s a small group of Jewish settlers, members of the Gush Emunim, firm in the belief that their actions would precipitate a movement for national redemption, gathered the explosives and the intelligence necessary to blow up the structure. They even set up cameras to film the destruction. Ironically their plot was foiled when another, less diabolical attack by an independent Jewish radical resulted in the tightening of security in the area. The plan of those associated with the Gush Emunim was uncovered only after some of their members were arrested for their murders of Palestinian mayors and Palestinian college students.[92] Their attempt to appropriate the Temple Mount/Al-Haram al-Sharif through the erasure of the Muslim presence is documented in a book written by a member of the group. The attitude

toward the Dome of the Rock and the Al-Aksa Mosque is revealed in a chapter titled "Clear Away the Abomination!"[93]

If the radical right seeks the immediate and material reconstruction of the temple, the traditional Orthodox Jewish community awaits its messianic restitution. In the meantime, Orthodox Jews remember their loss at the Wailing Wall. They also attempt to minimize the pollution of the Temple Mount by discouraging the unclean—women, gentiles, ritually unpurified Jews—from visiting it. Safdie describes the situation:

> At the ramp leading today to the Temple Mount, or as the Muslims call it the Haram esh-Sharif, there is a sign in several languages, put up by the chief rabbinate, forbidding Jews to enter the grounds of the Temple Mount. One may enter the Temple only when one is pure. In the past one purified oneself with the ashes of the red cow. As red cows have disappeared, with them went the means of purification. Only the High Priest may enter the Holy of Holies (the specific location of the chamber housing the tabernacle) and only on Yom Kippur. The exact location of the Holy of Holies is also uncertain, so the entire area of the Temple Mount is out of bounds to Orthodox Jews, to eliminate the possibility of an unpure person going near it. Jews pray at the Wall because it is all that is left to them of the Temple. The wall has become the holiest place for Jews, Orthodox or not—a remnant of the truly holy Temple itself, where the presence of God was believed to reside.[94]

It is not only Jews who are discouraged from ascending to Al-Haram al-Sharif. All visitors who seek access to the sacred precincts are, indeed, harassed at its main entrance by Orthodox Jews who accuse them of defiling holy ground. Both the Orthodox and the radical right, in their distinctive ways, attempt to erase the sacred space of the Other.

Since the 1967 War and the Israeli annexation of the old city of Jerusalem and its suburbs, the function of the Holy Land Hotel model has shifted. It no longer serves as an ersatz experience of the old city. Now, for the radical fringe, it gives plastic form to the outrageous political and ideological desires of a city without Islam. More innocently, it provides Jewish and Christian tourists with the city that most of them really want to experience. The villas within the walls, the market places, Herod's palace, hippodrome and theater, the storehouses, the great fortified Antonia at the corner of the Temple Mount, and, dominating the whole, the temple itself. The site now occupied by the Church of the Holy Sepulchre, traditionally identified by the Catholics and eastern Orthodox sects as the site of Jesus' crucifixion and burial, is clearly located in the model outside the city's Second Wall as a quarry with a skull-shaped outcrop. The site of the Garden Tomb, further to the north, is also identifiable in the miniature. The Holy Land Hotel model gives Jewish and Christian tourists an overview of the city and the sites they came to see. This Jerusalem, like many of the set itineraries for the city, does not include the Dome of the Rock and Al-Aksa Mosque.[95]

The Jerusalem Hiltons.

Negotiations for the first Jerusalem Hilton began in the immediate aftermath of the 1967 War. In September 1968 the *New York Times* announced Hilton International's agreement to build a hotel in Jerusalem that would almost double the city's first-class accommodations.[96] The following month, the

New York Times provided further information about the project: "A $6-million hotel to be built with private capital and an Israeli government loan will start to rise soon in Jerusalem. The 300-room hostelry, to be named the Jerusalem Hilton, will be the second Hilton hotel in Israel. Hilton International has operated the Tel Aviv Hilton since 1965. The Jerusalem building will be built near the Israeli Knesset (Parliament) by a group led by Lt. Col. John Furman, an investment banker."[97]

There was opposition both to the disruption of the city's profile by a high-rise and to the use of public land for a luxury hotel.[98] Nevertheless, the hotel was constructed. It was opened on December 31, 1974 (figs. 60 and 61). The architect was again Ya'acov Rechter. It was reported in *Architectural Record* that the slender high-rise was "shaped to complement the convention hall [a low, fan-shaped building], which was designed in the late fifties by his father, architect Ze'ev Rechter."[99] It was noted in the same article that "[t]he younger architect, like most thoughtful Israeli architects and planners, is opposed in principle to the construction of towers on the hills surrounding Jerusalem. He believed, however, that the Hilton should be an exception."[100] Ya'acov Rechter tells the story of the building's conception.

60. Jerusalem, Jerusalem Hilton under construction. Photo courtesy of Rechter Archive, Tel Aviv.

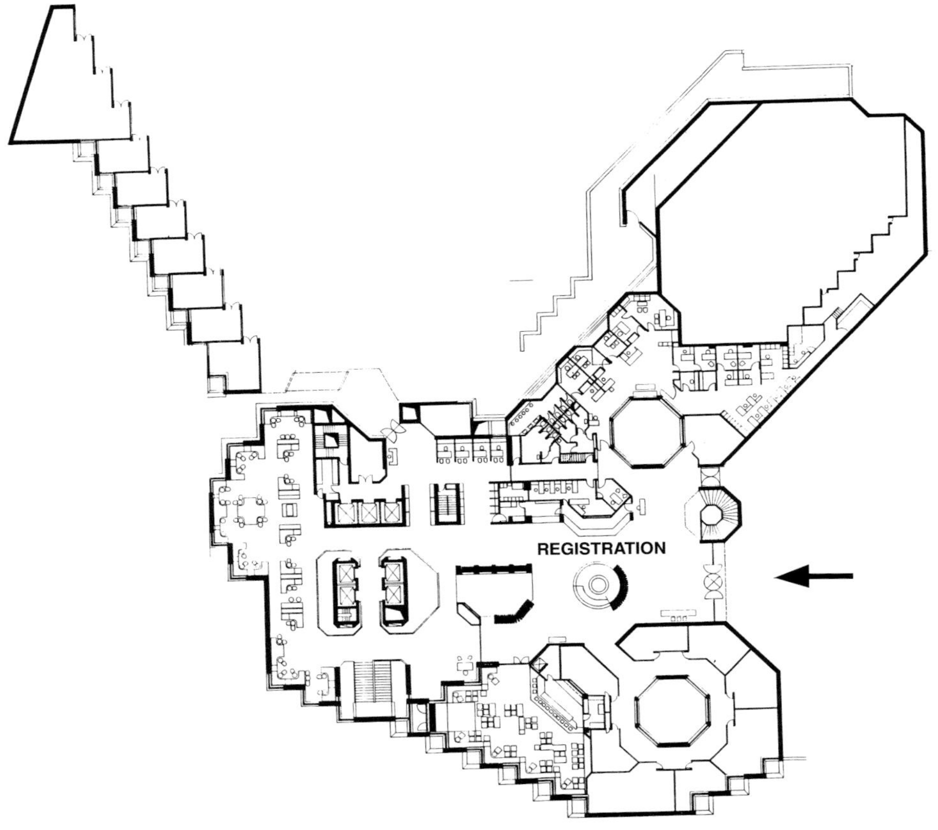

In Jerusalem the site was selected by a group of Chicago investors organized by Philip Klutznik. These investors entered into an agreement with Hilton. The first sketch or proposal was very schematic. We took it to a first meeting in New York, with the Hilton people and the investors. At this first stage of the process of crystallizing an idea, the hotel was schematic, not a specific shape. It looked very modern; it didn't have much to do with Jerusalem. Then Mr. Dimitry [Emmanuel] Gran made a plea: "This is JERUSALEM!" he said. "This is our most important hotel. You must do something that suggests the city." They gave us an office, and we worked the plan into a group of three round forms. Important were the openings of the angles, the angles were open for fenestration and balconies. These were covered with vaults of conical section, which are functional. They are structural, tectonic, not decorative. Walls are stressed; glass is kept to a minimum. I did a sketch and a section, and brought it to Dim Gran, and he almost cried. He was so happy. We started to work on this project, and developed it quite well. A Turkish architect [Ali Kolsal] briefly took over the Hilton architectural office from Gran, who had become ill. There was a meeting for the final project, with all the details, held in Tel Aviv, and I thought that Gran was coming. Charlie Bell, director of

61. Jerusalem, Jerusalem Hilton, plan of the entrance level. Photo courtesy of Rechter Archive, Tel Aviv.

62. Jerusalem, Jerusalem Hilton, now the Crowne Plaza Jerusalem Hotel, interior, originally by Dora Gad, now thoroughly remodeled. Little of the 1974 interior decoration survives, apart from the central lobby sculpture by Dani Karavan. Photo by author.

> food and beverage, came, and the Turkish architect, but not Dim Gran. During the first meeting, when we were sitting together, the Turkish architect was called to the telephone. He came back and told us that Gran was dead. I cannot say that not being able to see the final Jerusalem project killed him, but he cared greatly for it. It was very sad. We [Israelis] count by wars. In 1974, there was a low feeling in the country, almost like now. So we did not have a grand opening.[101]

The depression in Israel after the Yom Kippur War of 1973–1974 made festivity problematic, just as the unraveling of the Peace Accords by the Likud government muted Israel's fiftieth-anniversary celebrations in 1998.

The presence of the new hotel was, however, celebrated in the local press. The description of the new Hilton in the *Jerusalem Post* suggests how closely this late member of the Hilton chain conformed to its earlier siblings. The new Hilton boasted the latest technology: "The Jerusalem Hilton, latest link in the world-wide chain of plush hotels, can probably lay claim to being Israel's most modern hostelry in architectural conception and equipment."[102] In addition to cutting-edge technology, the new Hilton was a showplace of local culture.

> [T]he newest Hilton is not just a palace of polished steel and polychrome plastic. A respectable slice of the $24 million investment went to assure that the decor blend with the environment, and top Israeli talent was commissioned to work in association with the design department of Hilton International. Dora Gad, one of the designers, had designed the prize-winning Jerusalem Museum. She had also been responsible for laying out two major folklore exhibitions at the Museum on the art of Bukharan and Moroccan Jews, and this is reflected in some of the themes of the Hilton's decor. . . . [T]he Hamsah Grill has a ceiling of "inverted copper cones" and a patio dominated by Ya'acov Agam's gas-fire-and-water fountain sculpture. Bezalel Shatz did the iron grillwork and *hamsah* motif. Ziona Shimshi used an oriental motif in the Judea Bar, including 4,000 separately made tiles arranged in Turkish flower motifs.[103]

There were three separate sculptural pieces by Dani Karavan (fig. 62): "One, a large sphere, is situated in the center of the entrance hall, representing the centrality of Jerusalem. Inscribed around it are passages from the Psalms and the Prophets. It is complemented by a copper prism jutting from a nearby wall, suggesting a sun-dial and the timeless quality of Jerusalem, and a large square bronze relief—a triptych depicting the Holy City's role as the shrine of the three great monotheistic faiths."[104] As in Tel Aviv, the

abstraction of the decoration allowed a great deal of scope in its interpretation. Karavan's sculpture was most poetically described by Klaus-Hartmut Olbricht as based on traditional models of the cosmos, which came from the culture and art of the old Orient. The bronze sculpture in the Jerusalem Hilton, he suggests, is a meditation on the recent and tragic history of Israel as well as a rendering of the sacredness of the ancient, multireligious city.[105]

The Jerusalem Hilton also had its trademark interior shopping mall: "[T]he Hilton boasts of what is probably the largest hotel shopping arcade in the country—24 units that include banks, airline offices, a car rental bureau and a variety of top-grade shops."[106] But most important, the Jerusalem Hilton was sited in a commanding location, next to the Knesset, the Israeli parliament, on the highest site in the city: "The Hilton occupies a site of 21.4 dunams [about five and a half acres] on Jerusalem's highest hill."[107] Its monumental height makes it the first building that meets the traveler arriving from the airport on the Tel Aviv–Jerusalem highway. And of course: "The design . . . gives each of the 420 rooms a panoramic view of Jerusalem and, depending on floor level, considerably beyond. The crowning view was reserved for the three 'royal apartments' on the top 19th floor—the highest residential quarters in the capital."[108]

The Jerusalem Hilton was dramatically different and dramatically the same as the Tel Aviv Hilton. Both buildings had a sculptural quality that invited a figurative reading. The Tel Aviv Hilton, straddling the lobby with its massive legs, might have been invented by the Empire to attack the troops of the Federation in *Star Wars*. The Jerusalem Hilton's three vertical towers of differing heights bundled on a podium have been interpreted as the three major religions with a stake in Jerusalem. To me it has the shape of a set of ballistic missiles on a launching pad. The Jerusalem Hilton's conically sectioned window-bay vaults serve as functional relieving arches; they also allude to the architectures of the city's premodern past. The figurative character of both buildings derives from the bold muscularity of the structures' articulation. The assertive buttresses at the base of the Jerusalem Hilton and the powerful cradle supports in Tel Aviv convey mimetically a sense of architecture as structure. The differences between the two Hiltons are equally apparent. The Jerusalem Hilton's columnar verticality, its warm, smooth, stone facing, and its lobby's focus on itself in the form of Dani Karavan's great global sculpture contrast with the Tel Aviv building's treatment as a horizontal slab, its rough, gray, exposed concrete surface, and the transparency of its lobby.

Some of these differences were predetermined. From the time of the British Mandate, in an effort to maintain the special character of the city, Jerusalem's building code required that its new structures be clad with Jerusalem stone.[109] Whether a quarter-inch skin of stone lends a new building the same integrity as an old one constructed with three-foot-thick rock walls is questionable. Nevertheless, the injunction does ensure the city a modicum of visual coherence. If the surface of the Hilton followed code stipulations, its elevation did not. Like the Tel Aviv Hilton, the hotel displaced the master plan of the city in which it was constructed. It usurped public park land. It also disrupted the cityscape with its dominant height. The elevation of the Hilton was not, of course, an aesthetic decision. The hotel's height was required by the number of rooms that needed to be sold and the view that was needed to sell them. The Holy Land Hotel offered its guests a view of the city of their desire. The model allowed the hotel's visitors to see and thus experience a Jerusalem to which, before the 1967 War, they had no access. After the 1967 War, the Jerusalem Hilton offered its guests a remarkably similar sort of view of Jerusalem: the old city, miniaturized by distance and seen from above.

The old Jerusalem Hilton is now the Crowne Plaza Jerusalem. The new Jerusalem Hilton, built by Moshe Safdie, was opened in 1998. The new hotel is posed as a giant horse-shoe magnet opposite the great Jaffa Gate of the old city. The hotel is part of a larger building project for the very wealthy that dramatically erodes the green belt that the British mandated for the old city. The building itself offers a new synthesis of the luxury resort and grand urban hotel. The massive portico that introduces the structure opens to a multistory lobby encircled with broad-arched galleries producing grand internal vistas. It is a Piranesi version of the Guggenheim (fig. 63). The details of the building are high-tech and exquisitely wrought. The best rooms open into the horseshoe, on to the pool in its center, and beyond to the old city. The best view of Jerusalem is not offered by a rooftop restaurant to a dining public but is, rather, produced by a rooftop club house exclusively for guests residing in the elite executive floors of the hotel. Now hotels, like airplanes, have clearly demarcated first and coach classes.

63. Jerusalem, the new Jerusalem Hilton, opened in 1998, lobby interior. Photo by author.

In other ways, the new Jerusalem Hilton seems to mark a return to a more traditional conception of hotel space. It is located in the heart of the new city, not in the most elite segment of its periphery. Its lobby is monumental, with an impressive architectural gesture at its core. Its rooms open into a garden courtyard as well as on to a more distant view. The new Jerusalem Hilton might even be compared with its neighbor, the old King David Hotel. The King David was to Jerusalem what Shepheard's was to Cairo. The *New York Times* of April 13, 1930, reported:

> A hotel as magnificent as the famous Shepheard's in Cairo, is being built in Jerusalem by a new company, the active head of which is Charles Bachler, the "hotel king" of Egypt, managing director of the Egyptian Hotels Company, which controls Shepheard's, the Continental-Savoy and other leading caravanserais in and around Cairo. . . . Its site embraces five acres overlooking the Jaffa and Zion Gates and the Tower of David, and it is within a few hundred yards of the North wall of the old city. The building will be the largest in Palestine, and will be surrounded by gardens, tennis courts, lawns and parks. Central steam heating and electric refrigeration are features which have not been common to the Holy Land. About 200 rooms are projected.[110]

Externally, the King David Hotel is a massive beaux arts palazzo with rusticated arcades that allude to deep history. Internally, this history is specified as biblical. The great lobby of the hotel is a series of generous and elaborately ornamented rooms (fig. 64). Its original Swiss decorator wished to "evoke, by reminiscence, the ancient Semitic style and the ambiance of the glorious period of King David."[111] This was the hotel of Herzl's New Society, built and owned by the Jewish-Egyptian Mosseri family and rendered in an exotic orientalist form that integrated Judaism with the East. This hotel was used by the British as an administrative center after World War II. A bomb placed by the Jewish terrorist organization, Irgun Zvai Leumi, destroyed one wing of the building and killed ninety-one individuals on July 22, 1946.[112] In the recent renovations of the King David, the original decoration, which makes allusions to Assyrian and Babylonian building forms, has been thoroughly restored. The original furnishings, specially designed in the same historical style, have also been reproduced. The guest rooms have been completely and sumptuously remodeled. The delicate complexity of the

64. Jerusalem, King David Hotel, lobby interior. Photo by author.

decoration and furnishings of the hotel as well as the human scale of its spaces makes the King David extremely appealing. Here orientalist forms, rather than suggesting colonialist exploitation, add nostalgia to the attractions of the hotel.

The orientalist King David Hotel might even be read as a reminder of the ethnic and religious concord of Herzl's New Society. In Israel, egalitarianism remains only a dream. The Modern and postmodern Hiltons, in contrast, represent that act of the New Society that was always also performed in Israel: the imposition of the West on the East. The Hiltons are, as Herzl had Joe Levy say, "heralds of [Western] technical civilization in the Orient."[113] The list of Hilton Hotels at the beginning of this chapter documents the political and cultural location of the Tel Aviv and Jerusalem Hiltons. The Istanbul Hilton, which looks at Asia from Europe, is listed under "Western Asia." In contrast, the Tel Aviv and Jerusalem Hiltons, which participate in Israel's definition as Western, are located in "Europe."

Rome, Cavalieri Hilton, fountain at the bottom of the grand staircase.

[Rome] is the city of illusions. This is the city, after all, of the church, of government, of movies. They're all makers of illusion. I'm one too. So are you. And now, as the world dies through over-population . . . the last illusion is at hand, and what better place than this city which has died so many times and was resurrected so many times to watch the real end from pollution, overpopulation. It seems to me the perfect place to watch, if we end or not.

—GORE VIDAL, IN FREDERICO FELLINI'S *ROMA*

I had never known Florence more herself, or in other words more attaching, than I found her for a week in that brilliant October. She sat in the sunshine beside her yellow river like the little treasure-city she has always seemed, without commerce, without other industry than the manufacture of mosaic paper-weights and alabaster Cupids, without actuality or energy or earnestness or any of those rugged virtues which in most cases are deemed indispensable for civic cohesion; with nothing but her tender-colored mountains, her churches and palaces, pictures and statues.

—HENRY JAMES, *ITALIAN HOURS*

5 Antispectacle: Rome and Florence

Rome. In Federico Fellini's 1960 film *La dolce vita*, the clouds behind the opening credits yield to two distant incoming helicopters. The militaristic allusion of the sequence is at first reinforced then subverted by an ominous load suspended from the first of the helicopters. As the helicopter comes into focus, the audience sees that the cargo is not a large piece of artillery, but rather a colossal Jesus, his arms outstretched and cape blowing. The incongruity of the flying Jesus is recognized in the ludic response of the witnesses below. The landscapes over which Jesus soars are similarly ambiguous. The helicopters first appear above the massive arches of the Aqua Felice. The monumental vestiges of the aqueduct identify the location of the narrative as Rome, where ancient ruins inevitably represent lost greatness. In the next cut, the helicopters fly over an anonymous modern wasteland. An emptiness that initially suggests the devastations of war is revealed as a vast construction site. The heroic longevity of the ancient is contrasted with a modernity that is a ruin even as it is built. The sequence ends with three scantily clad women, sunbathing on the roof of a modern apartment building. Beautiful female bodies introduce the moral signature of the film at the same time that they relieve the ugliness of the setting. They are approached for their telephone numbers by the occupants of the second helicopter, the journalist-protagonist of the film, Marcello, and his photographer-companion, Paparazzo.

These professional voyeurs divert their attention and ours from Jesus to unclothed Woman.

The beautiful female body functions as the principle object of attention in Fellini's film. At the same time that it offers the aesthetic redemption of modern space, the beautiful body transforms the function of the ancient monument from the subject of modern attention—touristic or scholarly—to the setting for modern pleasure. The dome of St. Peter's, the Baths of Caracalla, and the Trevi Fountain are mere backdrops for Anita Ekberg's remarkable body. Only one space in the film is itself objectified: the Via Veneto. The Via Veneto is, for Rome, a modern boulevard, constructed in the early twentieth century as a locus first for elite residences and then for elite fashion and leisure. It was a new, broadly curved, tree-lined avenue, contrasting in its elegance with the ancient, straight, and relatively narrow severity of the Corso, the traditional site of the horse races and carnival festivities into the nineteenth century (fig. 65). Fellini literally reconstructed the Via Veneto as the site of the carnivalesque in Rome (fig. 66). "The Via Veneto which [Piero] Gherardi rebuilt was exact down to the smallest detail, but it had one thing peculiar to it: it was flat instead of sloping. As I worked on it I got so used to this perspective that my annoyance with the real Via Veneto grew even greater and now, I think, it will never disappear. When I pass the Café de Paris, I cannot help feeling that the real Via Veneto was the one on Stage 5, and that the dimensions of the rebuilt street were more accurate or at any rate more agreeable."[1] Fellini believed that his stage set was more real than the actual Via Veneto; he also claimed that the actual Via Veneto remade itself after his model. "[I]n my film I invented a non-existent Via Veneto, enlarging and altering it with poetic license, until it took on the dimensions of a large allegorical fresco. The truth is that, in response to *La dolce vita*, Via Veneto has transformed itself and has made a violent effort to come up to the image I gave it in the film."[2]

65. Sketch plan of Rome, by author: *A*, Cavalieri Hilton; *B*, Vatican; *C*, Castel S. Angelo; *D*, Stazione Termini; *E*, Colosseum; *F*, Monument of Victor Emmanuel II; *G*, Excelsior Hotel; *H*, American Embassy; *I*, Spanish Steps; *J*, Hassler Hotel; *K*, Pantheon; *L*, Trevi Fountain; *1*, Via Veneto; *2*, Corso; *3*, Via dei Fori Imperiali.

66. Federico Fellini, *La dolce vita*, 1960, view of the Via Veneto set.

The Cavalieri Hilton was planned to initiate Fellini's spectacle rather than to imitate it. The Hilton was intended, like Fellini's segment of the Via Veneto, to act as *the* modern foreground in Rome on which beautiful bodies would be displayed against a panoramic backdrop of the premodern city. The Hilton's conception of a spectacularized modern space for Rome dated to 1950, thereby preceding Fellini's filmic representation by nearly a decade. However, the moment at which the Cavalieri Hilton might have authored Rome's rewriting passed before it could be constructed. The Cavalieri Hilton opened only in 1963, three years after Fellini had remade the city. This chapter explores the Cavalieri Hilton's failure to remodel Rome.

The gala opening of the Cavalieri Hilton was planned for early June 1963. Starlets, politicians, journalists, were flown in by chartered planes from the United States. An invitation to the affair suggested its lavishness. "Benevenuto! To the Eternal city and its newest hotel, the Cavalieri Hilton. In the following pages you will find the complete schedule of events for the international opening of the Cavalieri Hilton. Our program has been planned to give you a taste of the traditions, customs, contrasts and culture of Rome." For the grand banquet the Hilton ballroom was adorned with a monumental globe of the world flagged with the Hiltons that had been opened or were being prepared for openings. The globe was attended by young women dressed in the national costumes of those countries in which Hilton was opening hotels in the same year (fig. 67). In addition to a variety of formal and informal receptions, meals, and ceremonies at the Hilton, the three-day agenda included sight-seeing, a poolside fashion show, dinner at the well-known restaurant Da Meo Patacca, a treasure hunt, and luncheon "at the historical Villa Mufi in Frascati, largest of the picturesque towns of the Castelli Romani in the Alban Hills," and a "Soiree de Gala at the Rome Opera House sponsored by the Cavalieri Hilton for the benefit of the Italian Red Cross (black tie)." The invitation ends with an appeal to its recipient to return. "We hope you have enjoyed your stay with us as much as we have enjoyed having you. We hope, too, that you and your friends will

67. Rome, Cavalieri Hilton, ballroom before the opening ceremonies. Girls, dressed to represent the countries in which Hilton International hotels were opening in 1963, are photographed in front of a large globe. Flags on the globe marked the sites of Hilton hotels around the world. Photo courtesy of Cavalieri Hilton Archive, Rome.

return soon again to visit the Cavalieri Hilton in this magic city and this beautiful country."[3]

The pope died the day before the Hilton was to open. As reported in the *New York Times* of June 14, 1963, "The new Cavalieri Hilton Hotel here was introduced today to about 800 representatives of the Italian and foreign press. The event came a few days after the hotel opened to the public without fanfare. The lack of ceremony was in respect to Pope John XXIII."[4] The unveiling of the Cavalieri Hilton was, instead, shrouded. The opaque opening of the Hilton presaged the hotel's continued obscurity.

The ominous inauguration of the Cavalieri Hilton was the correlative of its invisibility. The hotel's architecture refused full Modernity and instead slipped into antispectacle. The Cavalieri Hilton is big. It takes the dramatic form of an eight-story zigzag (figs. 68, 69, and 70). It nevertheless lacks presence. The hotel was fixed on the eastern slope of Monte Mario, below its crest and a good distance from the access road. Those approaching the building feel as though they look down at its entrance. Seven white piers, emphasized by complementary flagpoles, at the central angle of the face appear to be Modernist signs of entrance, like the "flying carpet" porte cochere in Istanbul. This Modernist gesture is revealed as empty; the entrance is elsewhere. The hotel's fabric also contributes to its anti-Modern recessiveness. The building is realized in ornamentally laid red brick with travertine and white concrete elements.[5] The façade's deep earth tones as well as its horizontality allow the building to disappear despite its monumental size. The recent introduction of ivy and planters to the entrance façade has further domesticated the structure. For the approaching observer, the shape and coloration of the Hilton, as well as its location on the topography's incline, mask its scale. These same elements make the building invisible from a distance. The conspicuous Modernity of the Istanbul or Tel Aviv Hiltons is lacking in Rome.

68. Rome, Cavalieri Hilton, entrance façade during construction. Photo courtesy of Cavalieri Hilton Archive, Rome.

69. Rome, Cavalieri Hilton, view of the hotel from beyond St. Peter's. Photo courtesy of Cavalieri Hilton Archive, Rome.

70. Rome, Cavalieri Hilton, plan of the entrance level. Modified from a plan provided by the Cavalieri Hilton, Cavalieri Hilton Archive, Rome.

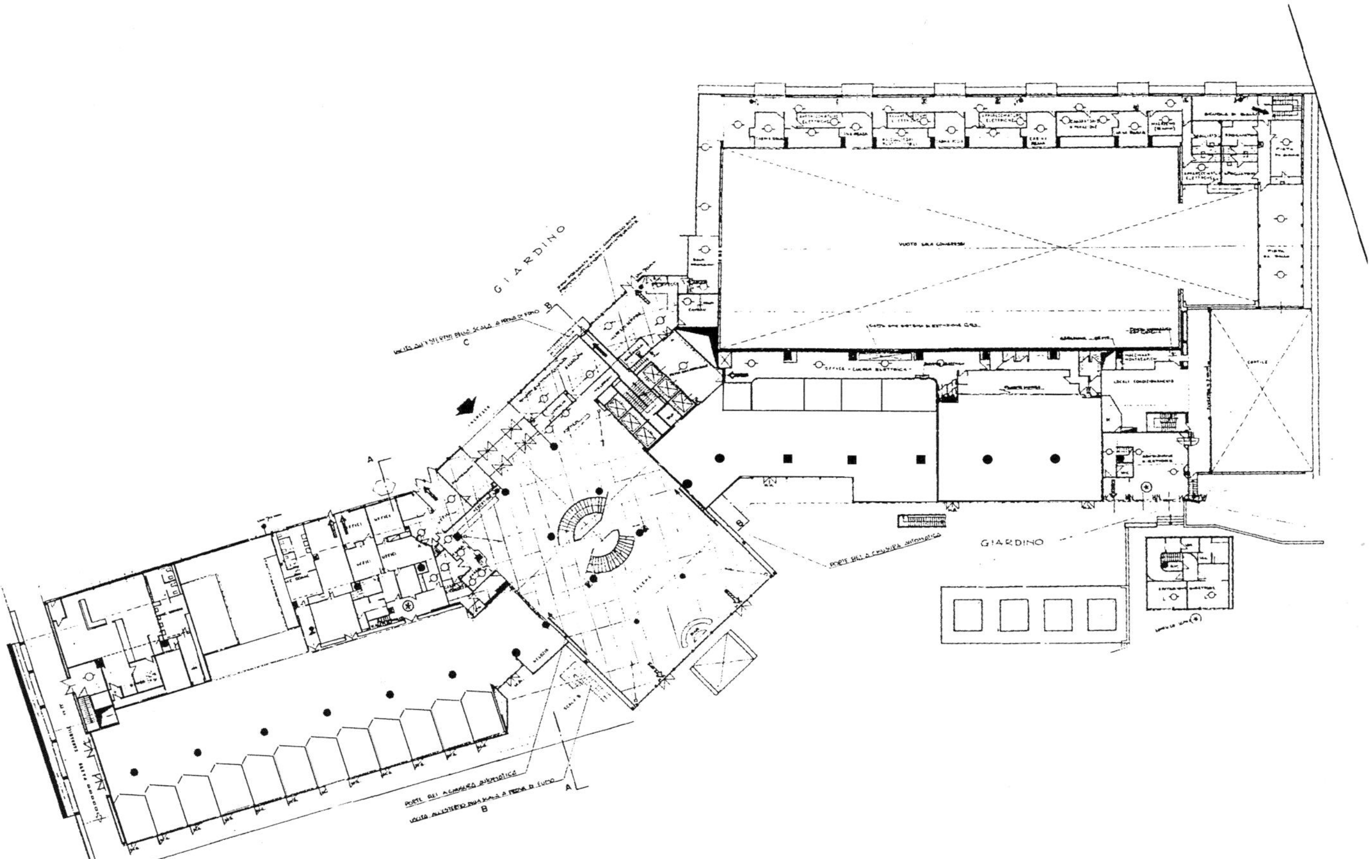

GIARDINO

GIARDINO

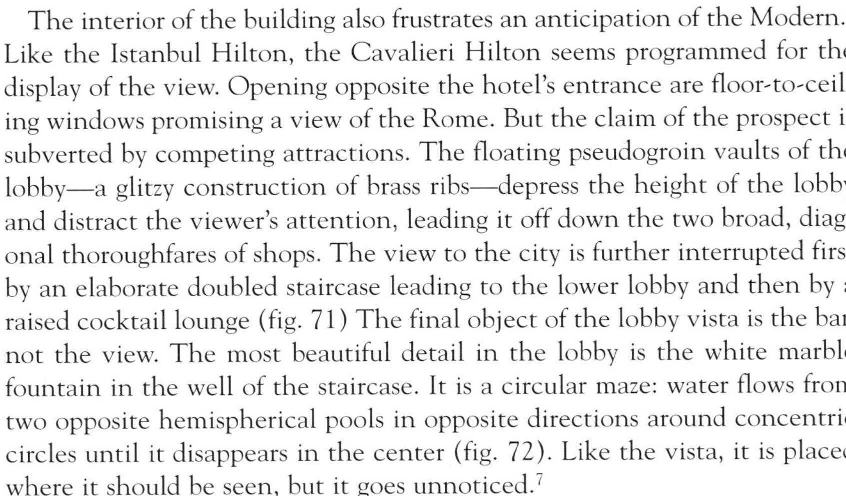

The interior of the building also frustrates an anticipation of the Modern.[6] Like the Istanbul Hilton, the Cavalieri Hilton seems programmed for the display of the view. Opening opposite the hotel's entrance are floor-to-ceiling windows promising a view of the Rome. But the claim of the prospect is subverted by competing attractions. The floating pseudogroin vaults of the lobby—a glitzy construction of brass ribs—depress the height of the lobby and distract the viewer's attention, leading it off down the two broad, diagonal thoroughfares of shops. The view to the city is further interrupted first by an elaborate doubled staircase leading to the lower lobby and then by a raised cocktail lounge (fig. 71) The final object of the lobby vista is the bar, not the view. The most beautiful detail in the lobby is the white marble fountain in the well of the staircase. It is a circular maze: water flows from two opposite hemispherical pools in opposite directions around concentric circles until it disappears in the center (fig. 72). Like the vista, it is placed where it should be seen, but it goes unnoticed.[7]

71. Rome, Cavalieri Hilton, view of the grand staircase and two levels of the lobby. Photo courtesy of Cavalieri Hilton Archive, Rome.

72. Rome, Cavalieri Hilton, fountain at the bottom of the grand staircase. The automobiles in the background are display models in a Fiat exhibition. Photo by author.

The architects of the Cavalieri Hilton were Ugo Luccichenti, Emilio Pifferi, and Alberto Rossa.[8] Luccichenti is the best documented of the collaborators. He established his practice under fascism in the 1930s. His office flourished with the building boom in the 1950s, doing considerable work for developers like the Società Generale Immobiliare, the owner of the Cavalieri Hilton.[9]

The interior and exterior space of the Hilton refused the spectacular aspects of Modernity while incorporating its technologies. The ballroom of the Cavalieri Hilton was vast, the largest space of its kind without columnar supports in Italy at the time of its construction. It had ice water piped to the rooms and air-conditioning throughout. As in the Athens Hilton, the public spaces were opulent. The lobby was vast. The program of the hotel also followed the successful Hilton formula. The rooms were spacious and well-appointed; each had its own balcony. There was an expensive rooftop dining room as well as restaurants of various levels of formality. The shopping mall was expanded. And most obviously, the hotel was planned to offer its patrons a view of the city both from their own rooms and from the public spaces. The view presented was magnificent. From the Hilton's rooftop restaurant, the Pergola, the guest was in visual control of Rome. At the center of the perspective were the Pantheon, SS. Trinità dei Monti, and the monument of Victor Emmanuel II. Rome may be experienced without leaving the Hilton. No less than Athens and Cairo, the Cavalieri Hilton offered the view as a commodity:

> Rome is a busy, bustling, dynamic city—with all the noise that must accompany such activity. But visitors have been everlastingly grateful for the chance to escape the traffic din since the summer of 1963, when the four-hundred-room, eight-story Cavalieri Hilton was opened on fifteen acres of landscaped pine and cypress woodland atop Monte Mario, about ten minutes from the heart of town. . . . *Il più bell'albergo di Roma*, the Italians call it—the most beautiful hotel in Rome. All Rome is spread out before you, and since the Cavalieri Hilton stands far above its surroundings, you'll be able to enjoy magnificent views from most guest and public rooms, cafes and restaurants. Italy is the country most Americans would like to be caught dead shopping in. . . . You might very well start off your expeditions right at the shopping

> gallery of the Cavalieri Hilton, where some of the leading downtown stores have branches. These include Cesari for table linens and lingerie, Perrone for gloves, Gucci for leather goods. . . . Downtown Roman shops are open from nine to one, closed until four, and open again until seven-thirty or eight at night. Shops in the Cavalieri Hilton are open until eight.[10]

This piece explicitly suggests that the Cavalieri Hilton, in contrast to Hilton's other hotels, offered its guests an escape from the city that they were there to experience. The text thus attempts to conceal the possibility that the view offered by the Cavalieri Hilton is too distant. Monte Mario frames the northwest flank of Rome. The Hilton shuttle takes a half an hour to get to the Via Veneto. For guests, if not for workers, the hotel is virtually inaccessible by public transport.[11]

In contrast to Istanbul and Cairo, Rome does not intimidate. Its attraction lies not in its exoticism, but in its embodiment of a Western tourist's own cultural identity. Distance from the ancient center was a liability rather than an asset. Nor was the Cavalieri Hilton, like the Istanbul Hilton, registering the site of a new city center, a new commercial or cultural core. The area around the Hilton on Monte Mario is indifferently residential. The place of the elites is the Corso during the day and the Via Veneto at night. Further, Rome had at its center well-established grand hotels with resources for post–World War II renovation. The Excelsior, built in 1906 in a voluptuous Italianate style, anchored the Via Veneto's development from a rural artery at the turn of the century to the core of urban nightlife in the 1950s and early 1960s.[12] In *La dolce vita*, the Excelsior is the stage for the confrontation of virile America and amoral Italy—Rex Barker, Anita Ekberg's fiancé in Fellini's movie and Tarzan in most others, decks Marcello Mastroianni with a single blow. In the 1970s the Excelsior was identified in the Touring Club Italiano guide as "probably the most luxurious and prestigious hotel in the city."[13] There were, in addition, small, exclusive hotels, most notably the Hassler, established at the highest point of the city center, at the top of the Spanish Steps, next to the church of SS. Trinità dei Monti. The Hassler, always a privately owned hotel, has maintained a family tradition of Swiss hostelry established in Italy in the eighteenth century. Eisenhower, Truman, Kennedy, and Eleanor Roosevelt are counted among its repeat clients.

The Excelsior presented to its patrons center stage in Rome's most current spectacle; the Hassler offered its guests a retreat to baroque Rome from which the premodern city might be surveyed from its center. Both establishments manifestly identified those who stayed in them as members of the elite. The hotels' visibility was shared by their clients. The Excelsior and the Hassler performed as Hiltons did other cities, but as the Cavalieri Hilton failed to do in Rome. The Cavalieri Hilton was less successful then its earlier siblings because it was less visible. Its invisibility was both optical and social. The confident Modernity of the earlier Hiltons was expressed as a dominant presence in the urban landscape. The Cavalieri Hilton's discretion made it illegible. You can see the Hassler from your balcony in the Hilton. From the Hassler you can only see the radio tower that rises behind the Hilton as a technological blemish on the city's western frame.

The Cavalieri Hilton exhibits the conventional Hilton International formula—superb view, lavish modernity, luxury accommodations. This formula did not, however, work in Rome as it had elsewhere. The Cavalieri Hilton was not in its early years as profitable as the chain's other hotels in

Europe and the Middle East. Its relative lack of financial success can be attributed to its not being seen.[14] Not only was the Cavalieri Hilton virtually invisible when it was built, but it was built too late. The Hilton missed the moment as well as the space in which the hotel might have performed as spectacle. The hotel was belated. The archives narrate the political and economic obstacles that deferred the Cavalieri Hilton's construction and thereby contributed to its failure to produce a modern spectacle. Like the city's underground metro system in Fellini's pseudodocumentary, *Roma*, the building of the Hilton was delayed by archaeological impediments and detained by politics. Further, its site was not only remote, but it was also emptied of its originating value by the speculative greed of Hilton International's partner. Hilton's local associate in the project was the Società Generale Immobiliare. One of the principle shareholders in the company was the Extraordinary Administration of the Holy See, that is, the Vatican.

John Houser's letter of September 1950 records the Rome Hilton as the first European Hilton International Hotel for which an agreement was signed. It also suggests a certain urgency related to the financing of the project:

> Well here is the first signed preliminary agreement—Rome. We are dealing with a powerhouse of a company [Società Generale Immobiliare] and I have full ECA [Economic Cooperation Administration] backing and other support in the Italian Government. Also enclosed is a plot plan of a site they own and want to use. It will offer real problems to an architect but hope it will work. If Bill Irwin is there give it to him and ask him to talk to Skidmore. . . . It is to be air-conditioned throughout and must be a beautiful building. They have agreed to employing an American architect associated with their staff of architects so unless something unforeseen comes up, Skidmore can have the job. . . . The timing is right to work these out but ECA may be forced to call a halt with the defense program underway and we had better get these things started if we intend to go ahead.[15]

Attached to Houser's letter was a copy of the "Memorandum of Understanding," which provided further specifications for both the building and its financing. Emphasis was again placed on producing a high-quality building, preferably by an American architect. "It is understood that, if possible, an American architect will be utilized, at least in a consulting capacity, in conjunction with Italian architects."[16] The architectural firm identified in Houser's letter was Skidmore, Owings and Merrill, the same company that soon after began work on the Istanbul Hilton. It is clear from the memorandum that the projected contract followed the Hilton model first drafted for the Caribe Hilton in Puerto Rico and later followed in Istanbul and Cairo. Società Generale Immobiliare was responsible for costs; Hilton corporation provided the specifications and operating expertise. Società Generale Immobiliare received two-thirds of the profits, Hilton one-third.

As in Istanbul, Hilton International secured the support of American officials in the city. The strength of this support is suggested by a memorandum sent in August by Theodore J. Pozzy, chief of the United States Travel Development Section, to Paul Hyde Bonner, special assistant to the chief, ECA Special Mission to Italy in Rome:

> As you know, both ECA/Washington and OSR are very anxious to increase first class accommodations in several of the capitals of Europe and up to now, it has been very difficult to find American firms interested in developing new hotel capacity on this side of the Atlantic.

> During the time I was in Washington in November, 1949, and April, 1950, I personally contacted Hilton Hotels International, with the backing of ECA/Washington and the Department of Commerce, in an effort to interest that corporation in European hotel problems. . . . Today we still feel that where necessary not only use of counterpart funds but also small allocations of dollars should be made to finance new hotel construction.
>
> I have again discussed this matter with Dr. Wilkinson who, as you know, represents both the Department of Commerce and ECA/Washington, and we both felt that strong support should be given by the Missions to American firms interested in building new hotels when it has been determined the investment is sound financially.
>
> Enclosed for your information is copy of Memorandum of Understanding between the Società Generale Immobiliare and Hilton Hotels International, Inc., which indicates that the project can be started at once, provided 50% of the funds is made available through the Marshall Plan. . . .
>
> The greatest help you can give to this project would be to contact the Italian government officials and encourage their favorable consideration of a loan of 50% of the total cost of the project, composed of counterpart funds and necessary ECA dollars to cover items which must be imported from the United States. Of course, it is entirely up to you to decide whether your approach to the Italian government is ethical and such a step is only a suggestion on our part.[17]

Plans for the Cavalieri Hilton seemed to progress rapidly. Italian architects were in New York consulting with Skidmore, Owings and Merrill in January 1951.[18] In November, Dr. Aldo Samaritani, managing director of the Società Generale Immobiliare, promoted the project at a meeting in the Bankers Club in New York. In his talk, he described his company as "the largest Italian group in building, real estate development and related fields," and he named the Vatican as one of the principal shareholders in the company. He identified Emilio Pifferi as the Italian architect who was designing the hotel in cooperation with Skidmore, Owings and Merrill. He suggested that the new hotel would open by Easter 1953.[19]

Attached to the transcription of Aldo Samaritani's remarks to the Bankers Club were a list of the hotel's specifications. The document indicates the prominence of the military and relatively low profile of postwar tourism in 1951. Although tourists were expected to be the hotel's principal clients in the summer, winter income would depend on local Romans, attracted to the hotel by its public areas. "Foreign business men, military and government officials are to be provided for throughout the year as semipermanent residents until transient trade warrants otherwise." His description of the new hotel shows that it was drawn to the Hilton template. Except for the hotel's corner suites, its four hundred guest rooms were to be identical, each fourteen by twenty-six feet, furnished as studios, and arranged for double occupancy. The public areas, like the individual guest rooms, were "to emphasize the view of Rome."[20] There were restaurants, a ballroom with its own entrance, a gourmet night club on the roof, a cocktail bar, and an American snack bar. Amenities were to include a heated outdoor swimming pool, cabanas, a Turkish bath and massage rooms, tennis courts, and facilities for such Roman games as *boccia*. There was to be both covered and open air parking.

There is, nevertheless, a note of austerity in the description. Each room was to have a balcony with a view; only half the rooms, however, were to have bidets in their bathrooms—an indication of an American clientele. Although the garden and leisure spaces outside the building were to be lavish, the interior areas were to be as effectively utilized as possible. "The hotel is to be planned to gain maximum efficiency of operation, particularly in layout and devices which will conserve labor. Rooms must be gracious in size but all areas must be utilized. The only leeway is in terraces and similar construction requiring minimum expenditure. American-type of centralized service is to be used as a key to the operation." Original specifications minimized public space, indicating that the lobby should be a "relatively small lounging area, chiefly used for access" to elevators, airline offices, and those shops which were to offer "the most attractive Italian handicrafts, wearing apparel, etc." The arrangement of the kitchens and laundry facilities were to be copied from the efficient design of the Caribe Hilton.

Despite these small austerities, the projected Cavalieri Hilton was the embodiment of Hilton International's formula for success. Rome was among the most important political and touristic sites in Europe. The hotel's projected location, not far from St. Peter's on Monte Mario, provided a controlling view of the city. The agreement called for an aesthetically significant Modern building planned by a distinguished American architect.[21] The local owner, with government subsidies, was to bear the cost of the land purchase as well as of the construction and maintenance of the structure. Hilton provided its name and experience in exchange for a third of the profits.[22] The owner was powerful and linked closely with the ruling conservative Christian Democrats and the Catholic Church. The Società Generale Immobiliare was one of the largest real-estate speculators and construction companies in Italy. A major shareholder in the company was the Vatican. Had a Modernist Cavalieri Hilton designed by Skidmore, Owings and Merrill opened in 1953, it would have been the first International Hilton constructed outside the Western hemisphere. The Hilton would have presented America as a spectacle in Rome before Hollywood's arrival.

The Cavalieri Hilton, constructed as originally planned, would have contributed to *la dolce vita* of post–World War II Rome, if not created it. In the 1950s and early 1960s ancient Rome became the new American film capital, or as Sam Steinman, columnist for the *Hollywood Reporter*, suggested, "Hollywood on the Tiber."[23] Rome offered American filmmakers a solution to their money problems. The historical city complemented by the modern production facilities at Cinecittà and good weather made Rome an appealing physical setting for movie making. More important, it had significant economic attractions. Labor was cheap. The profits that film studios had already made in Italy could not be transferred to the United States because of currency restrictions; however this large cache of lira could be used to support production in Italy.[24] The first effort, *Prince of Foxes* (1949), with Tyrone Power starring as Cesare Borgia, was followed by much more ambitious and highly successful efforts including *Roman Holiday* (1953) with Gregory Peck and Audrey Hepburn, *Ben Hur* (1959) with Charlton Heston, and *Cleopatra* (1963) with Elizabeth Taylor and Richard Burton. These movies "managed to transport much of the tinsel and glitter usually associated by Italians with Hollywood to Via Veneto and Cinecittà."[25]

The Cavalieri Hilton was not, however, produced when initially proposed. The Hilton Archives continue the narrative of the Hilton's belatedness. A letter from John Houser in Rome to Conrad Hilton at the end of May 1951 indicates that Hilton International discovered obstacles to construction that they hadn't suspected.

> We really walked into a hornets nest. . . . The confusion came from some effective work against the hotel by CIGA [Compagnia Italiana dei Grandi Alberghi] and others with hotels they felt were jeopardized. Their approach was to work against [the government] granting the loan to Immobiliare. They have a point in that the funds are limited and they would like to borrow to modernize, build, etc. The point is that interest rates from other sources than ECA or the counterpart funds are prohibitive and money is really scarce. The trouble from the ECA side was that they are trying to divert all possible money to guns and bullets and didn't really understand the importance of tourism in these times. They had originally planned 6 billion lira for tourism, then cut it to 3 and I found on arrival they were thinking it might be cut out [entirely]. We had quite some sessions which finally ended in their referring the matter to Washington with their recommendation for approval.
>
> The plan is to propose 750,000,000 lira this year and the same next year for our hotel. It will take the sting out of the grant in relation to the other hotels (and their political power is great) since it leaves something for the others. I have been in touch with Washington and Paris and they are working to get a strong affirmative reply. Dr. Wilkenson in Washington is the key and it might be wise for someone to call him to encourage his efforts. I feel sure the answers will be good.
>
> From this end conversations have been going on with certain government officials and their reaction is very favorable. Dr. Samaritani is tackling that side like a general and is planning receptions, meetings, etc., as soon as we get the ECA final answer.[26]

Initially money was the principal difficulty. Correspondence indicates that the project was held up by the protracted struggle to obtain low-interest government loans subsidized by American counterpart funds. In January 1952 John Houser still hoped to receive ECA support for the Hilton project: "In Rome [I] found that ECA has taken the position they have given us a commitment they will honor, *but* they have told the Italian Cabinet they are afraid of serious repercussions in our Congress if they finance a luxury hotel with counterpart funds while all emphasis must be on defense. It scares the Italians, but I'm going back to work it out."[27]

A letter written a few months later to Houser by E. Allen Fidel, chief of the U.S. Mutual Security Agency, Trade Division, of the Special Mission to Italy for Economic Cooperation, suggests that the ECA was not, after all, in a position to honor their promise to Hilton. The text begins with statistics on the growing number of tourists to Rome. The author comments, "I am not saying this to make you feel bad about the business you have lost by not having your hotel here, but because the record certainly makes the old story of the Rome hotel owners that no additional capacity is needed here sound absurd." The letter then specifies in some detail the amount of ECA funding available for projects and notes that Hilton's "chances of obtaining any of this money are about nil."[28] At the same time that efforts continued to secure cheap funds for building, advocates for the Hilton worked to promote the municipal construction of an access road to the proposed hotel. The Società Generale Immobiliare proposed that the city pay for the road that their company planned and later built.[29] Work also proceeded on the plans for the hotel. A complete set of drawings to a scale of 1:100 was expected by the end of October 1952.[30] Dr. Aldo Samaritani of the Società Generale Immobiliare remained particularly active:

> As you know, I have kept in constant touch with Government circles here in Rome, including Mr. Romani, and have left no stone unturned in order to

> expedite the procedure concerning the presentation of the law to Parliament. Dr. Ferrari Aggradi and other friends have given me invaluable help, as in the past. . . . We are at present doing our utmost in stimulating the clearance of the law in which we are interested. The outcome is still uncertain, and the going is very rough since at this delicate juncture the Government has a strong inclination to keep in the icebox all that is even remotely controversial. We have reasons for believing that the Prime Minister himself is favorably inclined, though on the other hand the counter pressures are still quite strong. I do not venture to make any forecast. We are, however, fighting with all the means we have. Meanwhile, the plans have been completed in a 1–100 scale, and a detailed cost estimate will be ready shortly. We continue to proceed on the assumption that the Hotel will be built, and are acting accordingly. . . . [In addition to efforts to secure a loan, progress was being made on road construction.] By the end of this month the executive plans for the new road leading from Viale Mazzini to Monte Mario, worked out on the actual location, will be presented to the City of Rome, together with the cost estimate for the bid from our Company for construction and financing the work. Here too we are proceeding with great caution, and have prepared a detailed justification for the job, based on the general needs of the area rather than on its usefulness in terms of the Hotel. Our preparations are so completed that we are ready to start the job within a few days after the project has been approved by the City.[31]

Even the American ambassador to Rome, Clare Booth Luce, was involved in the Hilton project. "I have inquired about the project you mention concerning a Hilton Hotel on Monte Mario here in Rome. I am told that counterpart funds are not available for tourism projects, and have not been available for such projects for some time. On the other hand, I am personally convinced that anything which will contribute substantially to Italy's ability to increase her tourist earnings is of the utmost importance to her economy. I would be very happy to discuss this further with you or with some of your people whenever the occasion presents itself. It may be that I can be of some help in furthering the project."[32]

A contract was finally signed in 1954. In a letter to Conrad Hilton concerning the contract, Houser outlines the state of the project.[33] The bulk of the letter is devoted to the financial arrangements for the hotel and to the concessions demanded of the government. Houser lists Hilton International's demands on the Italian government in order to lessen the blow of the real message of the letter: that the project will not go through without some direct American investment:

> Many concessions are needed from the Italian Government; for example, tax exemption for 25 years, assurance of the construction of the new scenic road, licenses and permits for building on the commanding site, rights to convertibility of profits to dollars, etc. To obtain these rights as well as to insure strong support from financial groups in Italy, Immobiliare has taken the position that there must be American investment in the hotel. . . . In my judgment, however, it would need to be [only] $500,000 in dollars and some extra participation in dollars or in frozen lira. Dollar investment in Italy has certain protection which could not be accorded to other forms of investment. Under the guarantee clauses of FOA designed to induce American investment abroad, it is believed possible to obtain Government guarantees for from ten to fourteen years. . . . The Italian Government is keenly feeling its stopping of ECA help and while their economy is increasingly strong, they are putting

> great stress upon the psychological and practical importance of American private investment which they understand is encouraged by our Government. This would be the first major American investment in Italy and might have a far-reaching effect politically and otherwise. . . . The importance of Rome as a focal point for travel in Europe becomes increasingly clear and while a downtown location would have more provable certainty of success from the outset, the Monte Mario site offers the possibility of developing one of the most famous hotels in the world and for attracting a substantial local business as well as business from abroad. The matter has been discussed with top political figures in Italy and they have promised their complete and full support if we are able to arrange the requested portion of financing from American sources.[34]

The search for dollar funding seems to have been directed toward the government rather than private investors. Houser testified before the Committee on Foreign Affairs of the U.S. House of Representatives in March 1954 in support of the House's joint resolution no. 350 for the promotion of international travel.[35] In July 1954 John Houser wrote to Conrad Hilton:

> DeGaspari's brother-in-law, Pietro Romani, Italy's High Commissioner for Tourism, who was here with us in the States a short while ago, has taken a great personal interest in the Cavalieri Hilton and has started to put pressure on Samaritani from that end. A new source of loan money for this hotel and perhaps others seems to be developing in Washington. The Agriculture Department has been authorized by the President to sell up to one billion dollars in surplus products abroad in exchange for foreign currencies. This foreign currency, we are now informed, will be available for international development including hotels. . . . We will discuss this with Stassen as soon as possible to see if from this source we can obtain a low-interest loan to take the place of the original ECA commitment on which they reneged.[36]

The possibility of financing the hotel with blocked funds of the American Motion Picture Companies in Italy was also considered at this time.[37]

Construction of the new Hilton in Rome was officially announced at the end of 1954.[38] The note in the *New York Times* of December 5, 1954, read: "Hilton in Rome—400-room, $7,000,000 hotel to be located on Monte Mario. . . . Blueprints that were ready for several years foresee a shopping center, swimming pools, tennis courts and vast gardens surrounding the main structure. The project still awaits examination by municipal authorities. A joint company, Italo-Americana Nuovi Alberghi, with the participation of the Hilton Hotels International, was incorporated here today. Its capital will eventually reach $3,000,000."[39] Nevertheless, construction still did not begin. Political opposition continued. Conrad Hilton ascribed local hostility to ideology. He projected the new hotel as the embodiment of American support of Italian democracy, contributing to the Italians' fight against communism by assisting in the country's economic and political stabilization. Conrad Hilton clarified the political thrust of the project in a press release:

> Commenting on the hotel Mr. Hilton said, "We feel privileged at being selected to participate in this project in the oldest center of Western civilization. We hope to contribute to mutual understanding and friendship between the Italian and American people. We expect the hotel to be an instrument which will play an integral part in the development of a large flow of foreign

> guests to Rome, with resultant economic and political benefits to the Italian people. . . . The Albergo Dei Cavalieri Hilton will be one of the world's finest hotels—an international symbol of comfort and service. It will be designed in the modern manner but with full respect for Roman artistic feeling and tradition," Mr. Hilton said. "The Italian people are making a valiant effort to destroy the remnants of the Communist enemy which only a few years ago threatened to engulf them. In their fight to remain free they are being strengthened by the economic benefits coming from a flow of foreign tourists. Hilton Hotels will strive through the facilities of its properties in the United States to increase this flow of guests to Italy," Mr. Hilton declared.[40]

Hilton established the effectiveness of his hotels in the fight against communism by emphasizing the left-wing opposition to the Hilton project. "Seven years after my first visit to Rome . . . I picked up a paper on my arrival in Chicago and read a headline: REDS BLOCK HILTON. . . . Communist members of the City Council in Rome had prevented the Italian company from getting the license to build the hotel."[41] The *New York Times* announcement of the government's final action on the Rome Hilton, though positive, seems to confirm Hilton's claims:[42] "In the face of Communist opposition the city council authorized today the construction of an American-owned hotel in Rome. By a vote of 42 to 23, Rome's Municipal Parliament ended an eight-year fight over a change in zoning regulations that would permit the construction of a hotel near the highest point of Mount Mario overlooking this city. . . . Most opposition to the hotel had come from Communists and fellow travelers. Others opposed a structure that would change Rome's skyline."[43]

Houser's correspondence suggests that money was the principal object and first obstacle in the construction of the Rome Hilton. The *New York Times* article reveals, however, that the site was at least as problematic as capitalization. Hilton's corporate partner in the project, Società Generale Immobiliare, seems to have presented the Monte Mario site to Hilton as theirs to offer. Apparently this was not the case.[44] The site was part of public land. How the land was to be developed had been under discussion for decades. From the first draft of the Italian government's Plan for Rome of the 1930s, Monte Mario had been designated as a green space, with a low population density, crowned by a *piazzale panoramico*, a great public piazza, that was to offer to the Roman public a superb view of Rome similar to that available from the Gianicolo. However, in collusion with the conservative Christian Democrats, Immobiliare secured Monte Mario for speculative building. Instead of minimal, low-density construction culminating in a generous space for Romans' leisure, Immobiliare developed relatively high-density housing with a minimal commitment to such infrastructural features as schools or parks. In place of the popular, public *piazzale panoramico*, they constructed the private, elite Cavalieri Hilton.[45]

The collaboration between Immobiliare and important government officials caused a scandal that led to highly publicized litigation.[46] Journalistic outrage and left-wing opposition further delayed the construction of the Hilton. Nevertheless, Immobiliare's profitable project for Monte Mario superseded that of the civic vision of the planners. The Società Generale Immobiliare's control of the area made the Hilton possible; it also made its immediate success impossible. Modern apartment blocks, like those in the opening sequences of Fellini's film, fill the space. The Hilton, like *La dolce vita*'s sunbathers, attempts to distract the audience from the relentless ugliness of modern urbanism. If Fellini's sunbathers succeed in their project, the Hilton fails in its. It does not manage to mask the banality of its surroundings. Immobiliare's exploitation of Monte Mario made it an impossible space for even the Hilton to redeem. Spectacle requires an appropriate frame. The Cavalieri Hilton, in contrast to the Hiltons of Istanbul, Cairo, Athens, Berlin, London, and Tel Aviv, never attained urban spectacle. By the time that the building was finished, *la dolce vita* was elsewhere. The Cavalieri Hilton remains hard to find. Even those Americans who know Rome well ask where the Hilton is.

Florence.

The Cavalieri Hilton's apparent lack of presence in Rome is contextualized by the Hilton's real lack of presence in Florence. Florence is, of course, one of the great tourist destinations of Italy. A high percentage of the canonical artworks that have been identified with the core of Western culture is preserved there. Certainly a larger number of famous Western paintings and sculptures can be looked at in Florence than in any other city of a comparable size in the world. Further, Florence provides its art with an appropriately historical setting. Its buildings are relentlessly premodern, shaped with an austerity deeply satisfying for northern, Protestant visitors. The museification of its churches also helps obscure its Catholic difference. For instance, the Brancacci Chapel, with its celebrated frescoes by Masolino and Masaccio, is no longer part of the church of Sta. Maria del Carmine, but rather the subsidiary space of a museum shop. It presents a perfect example of the commodified look. Only those who purchase admission may see—and then for no longer than fifteen minutes. Semipermanent screens sever the chapel from the body of the church. The church can no longer be viewed as a whole, either by those in the chapel who pay or by those in the nave who pray.

Florence is beloved by the tourist not only because it presents a wealth of art in what appears to be an authentically historical setting, but also because the city itself seems relatively coherent. Florence is small and neatly ordered. It has none of Rome's incomprehensible scale and complexity. A tourist can easily traverse the old city in a quarter of an hour. It is also geometrically ordered. The neat grid of the city's Roman origins survives. The rectilinear order of its originating plan was reinforced in the nineteenth century. The Piazza della Republica obliterated the city's intricate medieval center, including the Jewish ghetto. Florence's legibility is fostered by its frame, the Arno and the hills of its Tuscan landscape, so aptly described by Henry James in the passage quoted at the beginning of this chapter.

The Arno and those "tender-colored" hills, picturesquely adorned by the façade of San Miniato, are framed by the window that begins and ends E. M. Forster's *A Room with a View,* first published in 1908. The observer of the landscape from the room is the heroine of the novel, Lucy Honeychurch. Miss Honeychurch is a self-identified tourist. On a carriage ride outside the city, she is interrogated by her companions, an expatriate clergyman and a lady travel-writer:

> "So, Miss Honeychurch, you are travelling? As a student of art?"
> "Oh, dear me, no—oh, no!"

> ture that had stood on the same spot Galileo watched the stars from there during his sojourns in Florence.
>
> The city's building commission has so far rejected six sets of plans for a hotel near the tower and is now considering a seventh project.
>
> A member of the commission who opposes the project, Riccardo Gizdulich, said that the city administration and the central government's Superintendent of Monuments in Florence seemed favorable to it. Mr. Gizdulich, an architect and a spokesman for Italia Nostra, said the issue had become so controversial that the final decision would have to be made by the central authorities in Rome.[50]

The first phase of the controversy was ended with the unanimous rejection of the project by the city planning commission in October of the same year.[51] It was, however, revived nearly ten years later.

Harry Brewster owns the Villa Francesco di Paola. Though only a twenty-minute walk from the Ponte Vecchio, once inside the walls of the villa, a visitor feels herself in rural Tuscany. The villa was the patrimony of Mr. Brewster's grandfather, the nineteenth-century German sculptor Adolf Hildebrand. Mr. Brewster's other grandfather was the cosmopolite, Henry Bennet, a friend of Henry James; his grandmother was a descendent of the barons of Lewenhagen.[52] Born in a Roman palazzo, Palazzo Antici Mattei (the Palazzo Roccanera of *The Portrait of a Lady*), Harry Brewster now lives modestly in the converted barn of his own villa in Florence.[53] To pay his property taxes he rents both the villa and its farmhouse to wealthy foreign tenants. A graduate of Oxford University, where C. S. Lewis was his tutor, Brewster has written books on the archaeology of Asia Minor and, more recently, on his own remarkable family.[54] He writes in his study/living room, formerly a shed attached to the barn, which is now filled with books, most prominently the complete Loeb classical library. Though he was eighty-seven years old when I met with him in 1998, he daily walked his property, climbing the long, steep path to the site of the ruins of S. Donato a Scoperto. The medieval monastery had been destroyed because its view of the city was too perfect—the Florentines demolished the structures in anticipation of an attack on the city by the exiled Medici and their brutal Spanish allies.

This remarkable site would certainly provide a room with a view. Hilton International opened negotiations for this land above the Villa Francesco di Paola. In response, Mr. Brewster drafted a letter protesting the construction of a Hilton hotel in Florence that was endorsed by the directors of the major foreign academies in Florence—British, French, Dutch, German, European, and American:

> The undersigned foreign cultural institutes, which have their home in Florence and which live their life together with the city, mindful of the feelings of fraternal affection of those with whom the city has always shared their cultural work in the happy and in the sad times, [and] always assured of such fraternal interest, unite with other Florentine institutions and associations to express their shocked surprise in discovering that the inadmissible idea of the construction of a Hilton hotel on the slope of the Bellosguardo hill—one of the most admirable sites of Florence for its natural and extremely poetic beauty—may be under consideration.[55]

The *Nazione* reported that the Hilton hotel was to be constructed behind the church and convent of S. Francesco di Paola, near the ruins of the monastery of S. Donato a Scoperto. In the same article, Remo Ciapetti, the president of the Provincial Association of Tourism, promoted the project, arguing that there was not enough hotel space for tourists to Florence and that the city center itself could not accommodate more hotel construction. Building a major hotel outside the center would assure the demographic and economic balance of the city, as well as generate new jobs and a higher standard of living for Florentine workers.[56] This second battle and its conclusion were described by Mr. Brewster in an article in *Country Life:*

> No historic city in Italy of any size combines natural with artistic beauty to the extent that Florence does, and no other city but Florence has succeeded in preserving the essential elements of this harmony, at the cost, however, of unrelenting vigilance. . . . There exists a powerful, well-organized section of the Florentine population which is constantly clamoring for the execution of major works which would have catastrophic effects; for structural modifications to fine old buildings and for new houses to be built in protected areas. Their main argument for indiscriminate expansion is as follows: the conservation restrictions are exerting a stranglehold on the natural economic development of the city. If the Florentines are to enjoy a higher standard of living to which they have every right, then those facilities which are essential to trade and tourism should be promoted and not impeded, whatever damage might be caused to the historic monuments and to the character of Florence since, in any case, this potential damage is grossly exaggerated by sentimental aesthetes.
>
> On the basis of this argument, the Hilton Hotel project was about to be carried out four years ago. For the location of the gigantic new building, which would have dwarfed everything not only in its immediate neighborhood, the site of the Torre del Gallo had been chosen—an old tower on the Archetri hill, from which it is said that Galileo observed the stars through his telescope. It overlooks San Miniato, the Fortezza de Belvedere and the whole of Florence. The architectural features of the new building, whatever their merit from the point of view of modern architecture, would have clashed with that of every other building in the neighborhood. In addition, the vast hotel, which though it was designed to sprawl across the brow of the hill, would have been visible from everywhere and would have put out of proportion the historic edifices of Florence. It was argued, however, that to give an economic boost to the town it was of essential importance that there should be a Hilton Hotel in Florence. Nevertheless, Firenze Viva started an anti-Hilton campaign with the aid of public opinion both local and abroad. There was a worldwide outcry, and the battle was won, at any rate for the time being. There is always a danger of the scheme being revived. . . . [The opponents of the Firenze Viva, who seem to control the local government, don't realize, the author argues, that] the prosperity of the town depends primarily on the thousands of visitors who come every year, many of whom rent or buy property and settle in town or in the neighborhood precisely because of this unique quality which still survives. Any serious impairment of it is bound to prove counterproductive. Owing to the protean forms which the wrong kind of development tends to assume, constant vigilance and active counter measures are required. Firenze Viva has taken on this task, but it is seriously short of funds and adequate staff. Above all it needs the sympathy and interest of the foreign press, since it lacks the support of local newspapers.[57]

The local population and the local press apparently supported the development of a luxury hotel below the Torre del Gallo, but the foreigners who occupied the city to possess its authenticity successfully opposed construction.

In Rome, the Cavalieri Hilton was completed, though the process was so prolonged that spectacle eluded the project. The elites—the speculators and the corporations as well as the privileged guests of the Hilton—prevailed. The public lost—their parkland and their *piazzale panoramico*. In Florence, the Florence Hilton was never built. The elites—the owners of villas, contemporary cosmopolites, foreign academics—prevailed. The working Florentines lost—the labor of construction, service jobs, and Modernity. The Cavalieri Hilton is absent from Hollywood and Fellini's filmic and glitzy images of Rome. The Hilton is also absent from Alinari's authentic black-and-white stills of Florence.[58]

Appendix

"Memorandum of Understanding," August 29, 1950, signed by Dr. Aldo Samaritani and John W. Houser, attached to a letter of September 5, 1950, from John W. Houser to J. B. Herndon and R. J. Caverly, transcribed by Jean F. Hansen, secretary to Mr. Houser, from the Conrad N. Hilton College Archives and Library, University of Houston. This is the tentative contract agreement made between Hilton International and the Società Generale Immobiliare, describing their respective obligations to the project.

> A first-class hotel with about 400 guest rooms is to be built in Rome which will be named "Albergo dei Cavalieri, a Hilton Hotel." The objective is to create, through the mutual efforts and cooperation of the undersigned organizations, an outstanding hotel which will play an integral part in the development of a larger flow of foreign guests to Rome, with the resultant economic and political benefits to Italy. The hotel is to have all the facilities customary to a hotel of this standing and shall be operated on a level equal with famous hotels throughout the world.
>
> Plans and specifications for the building, furnishing and equipment of the hotel are to be mutually agreed upon. It is understood that, if possible, an American architect will be utilized, at least in a consulting capacity, in conjunction with Italian architects.
>
> The Società Generale Immobiliare will undertake as its responsibility the financing of the building, furnishing, and equipment of the hotel. The Hilton Company will join with the Società Generale Immobiliare to help, and arrange any financing in dollars or other foreign currency, needed for necessary imports. . . . Both parties will join together to seek the necessary approval of such a loan, both from the Italian Government and from ECA.
>
> Hilton Hotels International Inc. will enter into an agreement with Società Generale Immobiliare, under which they will use their regular staff to guide, advise and direct the planning, furnishing and equipping of the hotel, and in that connection will make available all facilities, purchase arrangements and so forth of

Hilton Hotels. Both no fee nor profit is to be charged for such work, but Hilton Hotels International Inc. will be reimbursed for all expenditures (such as traveling specialists and other out-of-pocket expenses), which are made in connection with the hotel and such expenditure shall be treated as a part of the cost of the building.

The agreement will further provide that after the hotel is completed, Hilton Hotels International Inc. will have the full responsibility for a period of 15 to 20 years (to be mutually agreed upon) for its operation and management.

The agreement covering operation of the property will probably take the form of a lease, but regardless of the form, the financial arrangement to be provided for will be a payment to Società Generale Immobiliare of 66⅔% of the gross operating profit. Hilton Hotels International's compensation for operation will be the remaining 33⅓% of the gross operating profit.

Dr. Aldo Samaritani, managing director, Società Generale Immobiliare di Lavori di Utilità Pubblica ed Agricola, Rome, Italy, remarks at a meeting in the Bankers Club, New York, March 14, 1951, from the Hilton Archives. This document describes the history and structure of the Società Generale Immobiliare.

Società Generale Immobiliare was founded in Turin in 1862, and moved its headquarters to Rome in 1870. It is, I dare say, the largest Italian group in building, real estate development and related fields. We have a share capital of 5.8 billion lire, equivalent to a little over 9 million dollars, assets of 12.6 billion lire, equivalent to approximately 20 million dollars, and a new worth of 8.9 billion lire, equivalent to some 14 million dollars. We hold real estate for a value in excess of 9 million dollars, and actually more, since it is evaluated in our current statement at 18 times its pre-war book value, while prices in the same period have increased about 50 times. Our principle shareholders include the Extraordinary Administration of the Holy See and Assicurazioni Generali of Trieste and Venezia, while the balance of our stock capital is held by some 10,000 individual shareholders. The Chairman of the Board of our Company is Mr. Bernadino Nogara, whose name I am sure is familiar to many of you. Another outstanding man, Mr. Eugenio Gualdi, is Vice-Chairman of the Board and General Manager. Our Board also includes Mr. Guido Treves. . . . [Description of the activities in all areas of building.]

To be perfectly frank with you, we could very well pause for a while at this stage and settle down to a comfortable and profitable routine. We are extremely conscious, however, of the responsibilities which industry and private initiative must face in order to play their full part in the recovery of Italy. The recovery accomplished by Italy to date, thanks both to generous American assistance and to the efforts of our own people, has been most remarkable. We still have, however, large numbers of unemployed, we have to raise living conditions, and we have to become strong enough to go our way without outside help. . . . [Discussion of slum clearance projects and note of the speaker's first meeting with John Houser.]

You are probably already familiar with the main features of that arrangement [the agreement between Immobiliare and Hilton signed on November 4, 1950]. Immobiliare owns the ground site, and will be responsible for the construction and equipment of the hotel. The cost of the job will be about six million dollars, and we hope that approximately one-half of it can be financed, under the terms of existing Italian legislation, out of the local currency proceeds of Economic Cooperation Administration aid. The Hilton International Corporation will manage the hotel, on a 15-year lease, will supply the working capital, and will operate it along the standards which have given to the Hilton Hotels a world-wide reputation.

We have been asked by many people in Italy how it is that there is no American participation in the capital investment of the venture. The answer is that we would, of course, have welcomed any such participation, but realized that the present unsettled world-wide conditions are not yet favorable to such developments. We feel that Mr. Hilton and his organization, in contributing their experience and know-how for the building and operation of the hotel, will make an investment which will be invaluable for the success of the enterprise, and will result in a definite increase in the flow of American and other visitors to Italy.

My friends and I have just come back from a flying visit to California, Chicago and Puerto Rico. We have visited most of the Hilton hotels, and have done a great deal of useful work with our friends of the Hilton organization. The plans for the hotel are being worked out on the basis of the functional requirements of the operation, and for this purpose we have retained as consultants the distinguished American architects, Skidmore, Owings & Merrill. The actual plans will, of course, be the responsibility of us of Immobiliare, and of our architects, under the direction of Architect Emilio Pifferi, who has already been introduced to you. My friends and I have spent some unforgettable days in Puerto Rico, in the company of Mr. Hilton, and have seen how effective the operation of that wonderful hotel, the Caribe Hilton, has been in putting Puerto Rico "on the map" as far as American tourism is concerned. Rome, of course, has always been "on the map", and a great magnet for visitors from all over the world. Yet, we are convinced that this hotel which will arise on what might be called "the balcony of Rome" will have such outstanding characteristics as to be a new and important factor in the tourist trade between our two countries. Mr. Hilton and his associates are putting their hearts into the project, and so are we. If all goes well, we hope to open by Easter 1953.

Eugenio Gualdi, president and general manager, Società Generale Immobiliare, Rome, letter to Conrad N. Hilton, in care of John W. Houser, April 15, 1954, from the Hilton Archives. This memorandum describes difficulties involved in financing the project. It was attached to a letter written by John Houser to Hilton, April 20, 1954.

I believe that we have now reached a point when most of the necessary prerequisites for action exist, or are within our grasp. Specifically:

1. Our company is willing and ready to contribute, in real estate and cash, approximately two-thirds of the equity investment which is believed to be necessary in order to place the venture on a sound basis. Since total required equity investment in the Hotel Corporation is envisaged in the amount of 3.2 million dollars, the share to be subscribed by Immobiliare would amount to approximately 2.2 million dollars.

2. We have now secured a firm undertaking from Banca Nazionale del Lavoro to underwrite the placement of bonds to be issued by the Hotel Corporation in the amount of 3.2 million dollars. The bonds would have a 10-year maturity, and carry the current interest rate of the Italian market, which is around 7.5%. The bond issue would cover all the required debt financing of the Corporation.

3. Various possibilities are being actively explored, with a view to cutting down the interest charge of financing and to extending its maturity. These include:

a. Pre-financing, for the first 5 years of operation, at a 4% rate of interest, covering the whole or at least one half of the entire debt requirement. This would involve utilization of blocked funds (covered by the so-called "Dubbing Certificates") of American Motion Picture Companies in Italy.

b. Possible availability of long-term Italian Government financing, at the interest rate of 2%, up to a maximum of some 800,000 dollars.

c. The raising of additional equity capital from Italian sources.

d. The replacement of one-half of the 10-year 7.5% bonds with a 25-year mortgage loan, carrying the same rate of interest. . . .

The one catalyst which is essential to set the wheels in motion, and to overcome all difficulties, is a significant, though not unduly large, American participation in the equity of the Hotel Corporation.

Mr. Houser will explain to you in detail why, in our considered judgment, which is shared by all our friends and well-wishers in Italian Government and financial circles, such a requirement is essential, both on substantive and psychological grounds. He will also convey to you our suggestion to the effect that we might begin by reaching an agreement in principle, concerning American participation and its ration to total equity, within a range set by a floor and a ceiling.

I am not unmindful of the fact that this approach may give rise to several questions in your mind, on grounds of principle and expediency, and I certainly would not wish to press you in the slightest way. I am convinced, however, that decision along those lines, in addition to leading to a prompt realization of the Rome Hotel plan, would have the widest psychological repercussions among Italian Government and business circles, as a first concrete example of cooperation between American and Italian private investors, within the framework of the policies sponsored by President Eisenhower's Administration. I am also confident that it would help to solve quickly the financial problem of the hotel venture even in the event that the American participation should fall short of its desirable optimum.

In conclusion, please rest assured that my associates and I will continue to press forward with determination, in all possible ways, toward the accomplishment of our joint objective. We are very happy to note your continued success in developing the Hilton chain throughout Europe and Middle East, and do hope that through our combined efforts and good-will we may soon announce to the world that the Cavalieri-Hilton in Rome is a reality.

Los Angeles, Beverly Hilton.

In our great Republic we deck no palaces for our dignitaries; official power is too short-lived to require a gorgeous dwelling place. We are not, however, without magnificent and spacious habitations; but these, under the name of HOTELS, are erected . . . not for a few of some exclusive caste or family, but for the traveling public of the whole nation and all nations; all may find a home in these palaces.

—ANONYMOUS, *GODEY'S LADY'S BOOK AND MAGAZINE*

The industry sells a fugitive product. At the end of a day's operation, any room not sold is a piece of merchandise that has perished.

—H. B. LOVE, *ESTABLISHING AND OPERATING A YEAR-ROUND MOTOR COURT*

6 The Commoditization of Space: Making Modernity

Hilton International hotels were remarkably successful. Least visible but most basic was the significant profit that they made both for their local owners and for the corporation.[1] More visible but less observed was the change that they marked on the urban landscape. The two effects were commensurate. The Hilton International hotels in Istanbul, Cairo, Athens, Berlin, London, Tel Aviv, and Jerusalem altered the cities in which they were built. Not only was the look of the city modified by a monumental Modern structure, but how the city was acted also changed. The urban topography was transformed by the representation in it of the success of American capital. Hilton International produced abroad an icon of American economic authority. That icon—the Hilton hotel—was effective outside America because it embodied the spatial paradigms dominant inside America. This chapter describes some of the shifts in American public space that contributed to the particular look of the Hilton.

My account of how Hilton hotels came to give material shape to mid-twentieth-century American capitalism should not be mistaken for a history of American hotels. Rather, I use the hotel as an indicator of the peculiarly American commoditization of culture in the twentieth century. A commodity is a thing or an activity with some use value that is exchanged. Commoditization is the process of making people and spaces as well as objects ever more vendable.[2] The awkwardness of the word "commoditization" aptly suggests the uncanniness of the rapid encroachment of capitalism into all spheres of the social since mid-century. Americans have been particularly adept at transforming things and activities into commodities—from automobiles at the beginning of the twentieth century to human body parts at its end. The development of hotels in the United States suggests how space fully participates in this incremental commoditization of our lives.

For the sake of conceptualization, I have identified two stages in the commoditization of built space. One is named for its mode of production, and the other is named after its symptom. The first is Fordist space. Fordist space was most clearly articulated during the decade of prosperity between the end of World War I and the Great Depression. The second space, the space of McDonaldization, which evolved from the first, was made manifest during the decades after World War II. The titles of both these spatialities bear class connotations. The terms suggest that I am discussing popular forms of building. That is only partially the case. Both Fordism and McDonaldization sponsored an elite aesthetic as well as a popular culture of mass consumption. Fordism and McDonaldization altered the consumer as they modified desire. Modernism is not only the invention of Edward Hopper and Jackson Pollock or Frank Lloyd Wright and Gordon Bunshaft, but also the product of Fordism and McDonaldization.[3]

Fordism gets its name from its greatest master, Henry Ford.[4] It identifies the continuous refinement of assembly-line production with its implications—on one side, ever greater efficiency and therefore larger profits; on the other, the increasingly mechanical dissection of labor and progressive alienation of the worker. It also registers Ford's remodeling of the worker. Ford's system, put in place by 1914, required workers whose wages were high enough, whose working hours were short enough, and whose desires were so directed that they would consume that which was being produced. In order for the new consumer society to flourish, the laborer who produced new commodities also had to be constructed to consume them.

By spatial Fordism I mean the expansion and remodeling of space for consumption by expanded numbers of modified consumers. As the public—the literate, consuming classes—increased, private space was redefined in relation to the public sphere by newly available commodities. For example, the Kodak Brownie camera, introduced in 1900, made visual archiving of the domestic self, once the prerogative of the wealthy, available to women and children as well as working-class men.[5] The domestic scene might then be shared beyond its immediate boundaries, changing the quality of intimate space.[6] The Kodak movie camera, on the market for the first time in 1923, further explored the domestic setting as the backdrop of the family narrative.[7] Also in the 1920s the radio inserted the public sphere into the living room.[8] Most dramatically, the Model T Ford extended the territorial compass of an increasingly mobilized middle class. The most obvious architectural product of this expanded space was at its lower end—the tourist camp. A less direct architectural product of increased middle-class wealth was found at its higher end—the large, urban hotel. The grand urban hotels of the 1920s offered new settings for the new American professional elites. These hotels provided a traveling middle class with a palatial setting. Just as importantly, they furnished the local community with a theatricalized space of public display and ritual.[9] The spaces at the two extremes, created in response both to new products and to the new wealth that those products generated, still pretended to the private. The tourist cabin was a miniaturized home often with cooking and washing facilities; the grand urban hotel was the surrogate palace of the upwardly mobile.

McDonaldization gets its name not from an individual entrepreneur, but from a fast-food franchise.[10] What Henry Ford did through cars for the first half of the twentieth century, the McDonald brothers and Ray Kroc represented with food in the second half.[11] McDonaldization is a convenient label for spatial shifts that are legible well before Ray Kroc began franchising hamburgers in 1955. McDonald's did not change the way America produced, as had Ford, so much as it exemplified the new ways in which America produced and the new ways in which that production was seen and consumed in the late forties and fifties. McDonaldization is a metaphoric signifier for the literal and figurative extensions of Fordism. It is shorthand for developments in production and consumption that were contingent on Fordism's products and consumers. The increased speed of production in the forties and fifties involved the refinement of Ford's assembly line. Features of Fordism were amplified—workers were further deskilled for the sake of increased efficiency in the production of consumable commodities and profit. McDonald's made this process newly visible. But McDonaldization denotes here more than just the greater rate at which commodities were produced. McDonaldization also both identifies a shift in the space of consumption and literalizes the creation of new appetites.

The most visible arena of McDonaldization was the American suburb. Ford's middle-class worker and affordable automobile were the essential ingredients of the postwar suburban explosion. In the 1950s, for the first time since the onset of industrialization, cities lost population to nonurban areas. Such cities as St. Louis, Buffalo, and Detroit lost between 35 and 47 percent of their inhabitants between 1950 and 1980.[12] Even industry moved closer to the golf course.[13] The middle-class suburbs provided the patrons targeted by McDonald's. McDonald's appropriated not only the deskilled worker but also the deskilled housewife. The McDonald's hamburger may well have been an improvement on the Campbell's cream-of-mushroom-canned-condensed-soup casserole. And there were no maître d's, no wine list, no odd forks, and no dress code with which to cope. McDonald's was both cheap and unchallenging. Further, the suburb dweller was already familiar with the disposable and, indeed, had developed a deep desire for the time-saving commodity. "Throwaway Living: Disposable Items Cut Down Household Chores," an article that appeared in *Life* in 1955, featured such items as disposable feeding bowls for pets, disposable barbecue grills, and disposable cooking pots.[14]

McDonald's represents the extension of the conveyer belt to include consumers. On one side of the counter, food was produced on an assembly line in record time and in record amounts. On the other side of the counter, food was ordered, paid for, and eaten just as efficiently. McDonaldization promoted the speed of experience rather than its extension. Just as critically, McDonaldization made the process of production on both sides of the counter visible. The space of McDonald's was immaculately clean, simple, brightly colored, and brightly lit. Its space was transparent—the food being processed was visible through plate glass windows to the consumers. The consuming consumers were visible through plate glass windows to potential patrons outside. The interior made public an anonymous private space. Simultaneously its exterior was utterly identifiable. The glass box with its golden arches successfully signified McDonald's to those in passing automobiles.[15] McDonaldization renders mass production as visual spectacle in the suburban landscape. Its architectural stage was Modern. The lodging place equivalent to McDonald's eating-place was the Holiday Inn.

Fordist space. American hotels have long been distinctly American. From the late eighteenth through most of the twentieth centuries, the United States dominated hotel design and technological innovation.[16] Benjamin Latrobe's project of 1797 for a hotel in Richmond, Virginia, is the one of the earliest conceptualizations of a "modern" hotel, complete with a theater and meeting rooms as well as lodging facilities.[17] In the early nineteenth century, the largest and technologically most advanced hotels were constructed in the United States. Nikolaus Pevsner, the German-Jewish father of English architectural history, noted that the first hotel to be treated as an architectural monument was the Tremont, built in Boston between 1827 and 1830.[18] Also according to Pevsner, the first mention of a hotel with baths in every room was the Mount Vernon, a resort hotel at Cape May.[19] This structure, begun in 1850, was purportedly the largest hotel in the world, with accommodation for over two thousand patrons. It was opened in 1853, but burned in 1856, before construction of the whole of the vast edifice was complete.[20] The first steel-frame hotels were built in the United States.[21] From the later nineteenth century, the most modern hotels of Europe depended on American technological advances. American dominance of the industry was broadly acknowledged.[22] Thomas Cook, father of modern tourism, took his first trip to the United States in 1872. He expressed his belief that "American hotels, where '*Iced Water* is *The Beverage of the Tables*,' [were] the best in the world."[23] At the beginning of the twentieth century, Louis Adlon, son of founder of the famous Adlon Hotel in Berlin, observed, "There is no question that America leads the world in hotels. . . . American hotels are a university in which European hotel keepers complete their education. Not all European hotel keepers, perhaps, but the best, the most progressive, the most up-to-date of European landlords come to America to study as an American art student goes to France to study art."[24]

The innovative character of the American hotel was related to its distinct social function. American commentators claimed the preeminence of American over European hotels with patriotic zeal. Their arguments commonly began with politics rather than technology. They assumed the superiority of the youthful American Republic, unencumbered as it was by an inheritance of European aristocratic snobberies—American hotels were better because they served a better, more democratic patron. The anonymous comment quoted at the beginning of this chapter expresses this idea with characteristic bluntness. In 1884 E. L. Godkin, editor of the *Nation*, emphasized American egalitarianism as the true source of the superiority of American hotels. Hotels in America were built not as in Europe exclusively for the rich and powerful but rather for the great American public.[25] American hotels functioned as public space for the private individual rather than as a private domain for the public aristocrat. There were economic as well as political grounds for the democratization of hotel space. Rather than being family-owned as in Europe, many of the most prestigious hotels in the United States were owned by stock companies. Hotels, like railroads were the objects of investment, a phenomenon little known in Europe.[26] Hotels had to show a profit rather than make a living for their owners. Their status depended on their financial return rather than on the prestigiousness of their guest list. The Tremont Hotel in Boston was as famous for its individual door locks, free soap in every room, and gas-lit public rooms as for its grand, classicizing façade.

European travelers record their surprise in ways that express their unfamiliarity with the American social order as well as with American social space. After a visit to the United States, Gilbert A. Chesterton, the English essayist, shocked by the public nature of American hotels, described them in traditional European terms of class disorder—carnival and revolution.

> But it was not merely the Babylonian size and scale of [the hotels that was remarkable], it was the way they are used. They are used almost as public streets, or rather as public squares. My first impression was that I was in some sort of high street or market place during a carnival or a revolution. True, the people looked rather rich for a revolution and rather grave for a carnival; they were congested in great crowds that moved slowly like people passing through an over-crowded railway station. . . . [These people] did nothing whatever except drift into it and out again. Most of them had no more to do with the hotel than I have with Buckingham Palace.[27]

Emphasizing the publicness of hotel space, Chesterton added: "Now an American gentleman invariably takes off his hat in the lift [elevator]. He does not take off his hat in the hotel, even if it is crowded with ladies. . . . The lift is a room, but the hotel is a street."[28] The American hotel's peculiarly social character was also the subject of comment in an article in *Chambers's Journal of Popular Literature* in 1854: "An American hotel is not a house: it is a town."[29]

The public character of the hotel in the United States, in contrast to Europe, was understood by Americans as the appropriate built expression of an expanding republic. The allusion to a Roman prototype in the description of contemporary hotels in *New York Times* in 1922 suggests its function as a marketplace of ideas: "[The lobby] constitutes a social organism of the first order, indispensable to the smooth running of our metropolitan civilization. The lobby fills a transcendent need in social life, commerce, politics and art. It is the nerve center of the community. It is a mirror of contemporary life. It is the confluence of the well known streams of humanity. The closest classical analogy is the Roman Forum, the chief point of difference being that lounging is so much more comfortable in the modern lobby."[30] The pretensions of a town were manifested in the magnitude and magnificence of its principal hotel.[31]

In the discussion of hotels, as in most contexts, the rhetoric of democracy was more radical than its practice. In hotels, as in politics, the "public" was for the most part white, male, and Christian. Women were banned from the bars of reputable hotels in the era before Prohibition, and, in some instances, they were not allowed in the lobby, but had separate entrances. It was observed that at the turn of the century in New York's best hotels "[f]or the unattached male there was companionship in the lobby or at the bar. For the married couple, the women companions and the few lone women who had the courage to travel about by themselves there was only the room, a place to leave unoccupied as much as possible."[32] For social intercourse there were solely women's parlors. Some hotels wouldn't provide rooms to single women.[33] Jews were commonly not accorded guest privileges.[34] Blacks were completely excluded, often even from service, except when strike-breakers were required.[35] Discrimination on the basis of religion and race remained in place much longer than the exclusion of women.[36] Of course, class remained a basic determinant of admissibility. In addition to room charges, dress codes, enforced at the will of the hotel staff, maintained the appropriate status of the clientele.[37] Guests of the better classes were assumed in virtually all discussions of distinguished hotels. Remarkably absent in hotel literature is any serious reflection on the exclusionary practices of the hotel industry.[38]

Nevertheless, the American commitment to profiting from as broad a segment of the population as possible—the democratization of the consumer—effected the innovations of American hotels. In 1923 L. M. Boomer, president of Waldorf-Astoria, Inc., America's most prestigious hotel consortium, published an article entitled "How We Fitted Ford's Principles to Our Business": "If anyone could be excused for feeling that modern methods of quantity production and of working to rigid specifications are not applicable to his business, it is the hotel man. And yet it is only by sedulously adopting Simplification that a big metropolitan hotel can over come the disadvantages of its complexities and exist at all."[39] Boomer described in some detail how his organization applied Ford's principles of standardization, simplification, and controlling the source of supply to servicing guests of the highest classes. But at the same time that he promoted Fordist principles, Boomer also recognized the necessity of masking them for his elite consumers: "Although Simplification is absolutely essential to our success, *it must not be manifest to the customer;* he must feel that the service he gets is not machine service, but individual. The rooms, for instance, cannot be uniform as cells in a penitentiary are uniform, even though they be standardized to a high degree of luxury."[40] Boomer's article was directed toward those American businessmen who were resisting the application of Fordist principles to their industries. Boomer argued that if Fordist practices could be applied within hotels—where the *appearance* of individual attention is essential to success—they could be beneficially exercised anywhere. Boomer's article suggests that the discriminating guest of 1923 still required uniqueness in the experience of a fine hotel in which he purchased space. His room had to be as individual as the service that he received. Boomer acknowledged the necessity of masking the homogeneity of the product at the same time that he promoted new homogenizing technologies.

In the same year that Boomer's article appeared, Roy Carruthers, the general director of the same celebrated Waldorf-Astoria, presented his formulae for the architecture of a successful hotel.[41] In a series of short articles in *Pencil Points* entitled "Hotel Architecture from a Hotel Man's Viewpoint," the author described American commercial and resort hotels between the World Wars.[42] American commercial hotels were, before World War II, the largest in the world.[43] In his essays, Carruthers articulated the profit value of architectural representation and the importance of signifying the difference between the urban and the nonurban, between the places of engagement and disengagement, between the sites of the familiar and of the less familiar.

Carruthers's distinctions between commercial and resort hotels began with the *look* of the building. The commercial hotel was conventional. "The commercial hotel has become standardized, . . . it is a simple dignified, light and airy building, arranged for the convenience and comfort of its guests, but usually with little individuality of character." His principal model for this "commercial" type was the Olympic Hotel, which at the time was under construction in Seattle, Washington (figs. 74 and 75). This cubic high-rise occupied an entire city block, extending the urban grid vertically. The hotel's status was indexed by allusions to Italian Renaissance *palazzi* in the monumental symmetry of its mass and the vaguely classicizing sculptural elaboration of its main facades. The interior, too, was familiar early-twentieth-century Florentine in its decor. Apparently the highly textured, visually rich historicism of the hotel's form was so familiar in urban America in the 1920s that Carruthers might describe it as nondescript.[44]

74. Seattle, Washington, Olympic Hotel, now the Four Seasons Olympic Hotel, view of the exterior. Modified from Roy Carruthers, "Hotel Architecture from a Hotel Man's Viewpoint," *Pencil Points* 4 (June 1923).

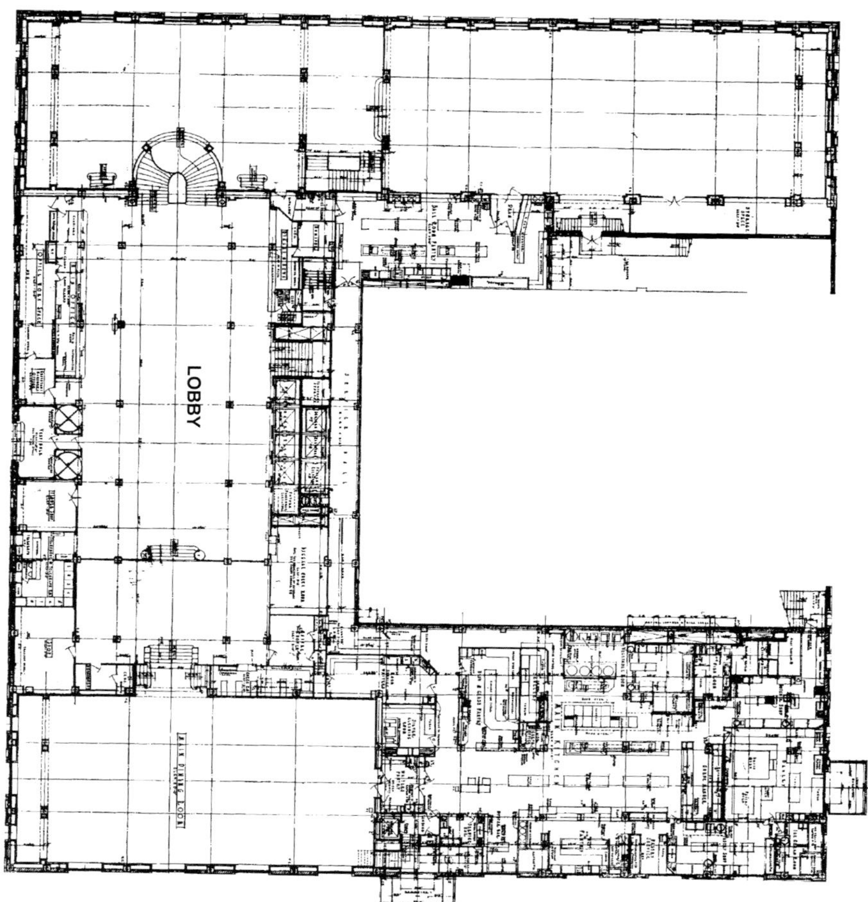

B.

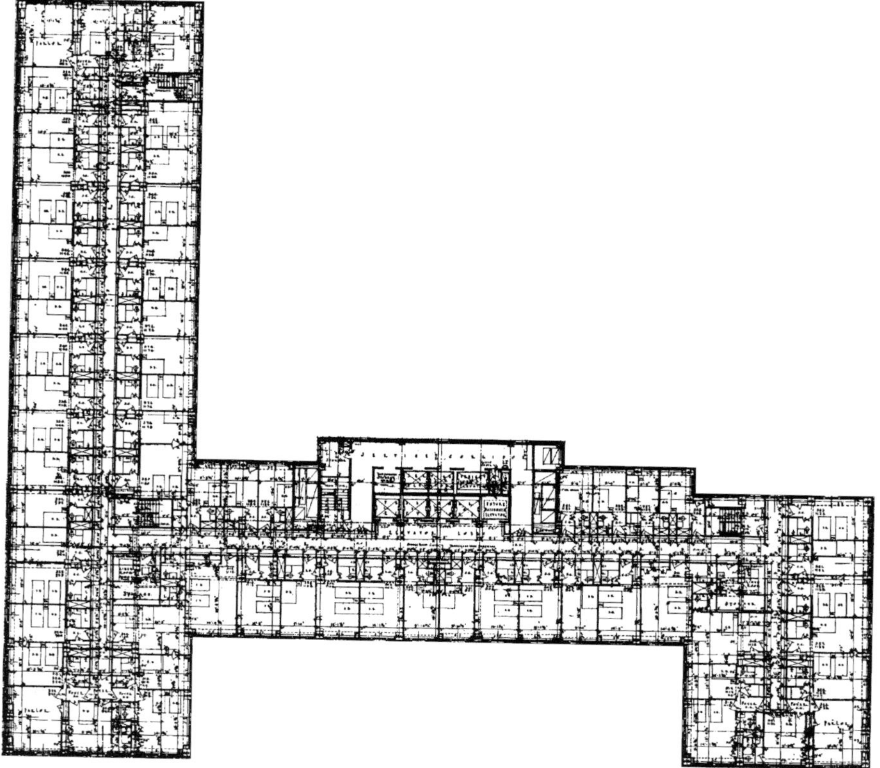

In contrast to the commercial hotel, Carruthers argued that the resort hotel should emphasize its alterity through its appearance. "The tourist hotel that is sufficiently different and interesting to become talked about, advertises itself, it attracts tourists. . . . Striking and appropriate design character is a very valuable asset to a tourist hotel."[45] "The idea expressed in the [small, successful] Samarkand [Hotel in Santa Barbara, California] is to combine the features of a stay in a private home with the advantages of residence in a hotel and the added attraction of an exotic atmosphere supplied by a dignified architectural treatment of Persian inspiration."[46] The Hotel Ponce De Leon, built in the 1880s, was identified as the first American tourist hotel that took style into account. Carruthers suggested that the architecture of the hotel was "in keeping with the atmosphere of its location."[47] The Hotel Ponce De Leon followed a grand, bilaterally symmetrical beaux arts plan. The style is beaux arts–conquistador, commonly known as mission style.

If the look of the building affected its revenues, the programming of its space was even more important. Carruthers emphasized the need for adequate areas for the staff.[48] Carruthers's concern for staff was practical. Before World War II, the more rooms a hotel had, the larger was the proportion of staff to guests and the greater its profit margin.[49] This changed dramatically only after the war, with the increased cost of labor. Carruthers made a number of other functionalist observations. The kitchen should be centrally located, ensuring direct accessibility to all the hotel's restaurants. "Sample rooms," assigned to traveling salesmen for the display of their wares to potential customers, should be on the second floor, near freight elevators, to facilitate the delivery of display trunks. These sample rooms should be large, airy, and equipped with beds that fold up into closets, so that the salesman can sleep in the room as well as use it to display his goods.[50] Carruthers also described recent technical and mechanical innovations. Modern improvements in plumbing and ventilation equipment allowed bathrooms to be built for the first time on an inside wall of the guest room, rather than on its outside wall. This arrangement provided the patron with a greater sense of privacy. The bedroom was isolated acoustically from the public corridor. The small anteroom generated by the width of the bathroom also visually and physically separated the bedroom from the hallway. Further, the inside bathroom allowed the outer wall to be more fully opened to the outside, introducing more light and air. One recently introduced innovation recommended by Carruthers was the "closet-door," or servidor. The servidor was a refinement of the door from the corridor to the guestroom. It had secondary doors on both sides, thus allowing the patron to hang clothing for dry cleaning or pressing at his convenience in its hollow interior and the valet to remove it from the exterior without disturbing the room's occupant. Carruthers pointed out that ease of pick-up also promoted the hotel's dry-cleaning business.[51]

The plans and views of two of the hotels that Carruthers discussed, the Bon Air–Vanderbilt in Augusta, Georgia, and the Olympic in Seattle, reveal a number of programmatic differences between commercial and resort hotels that go undiscussed by the author. The Bon Air–Vanderbilt was opened in 1892.[52] It was rebuilt and reopened after a devastating fire in 1922. It was famous as a haven for golfers. Complementing its rural site, the resort hotel was more expansive and more permeable than the commercial hotel (fig. 76). Unconstrained by the urban grid, it extended into the landscape, controlling the natural vista through incorporation. Terraces and

75. Seattle, Washington, Olympic Hotel, now the Four Seasons Olympic Hotel: *A*, plan of the entrance level; *B*, plan of a typical guest room floor. Modified from Roy Carruthers, "Hotel Architecture from a Hotel Man's Viewpoint," *Pencil Points* 4 (June 1923).

porches complement the multiplication of windows, contributing to the building's porosity. This penetrable exterior was exemplified by the monumental porte cochere that provided a prominent and inviting access to the building. The patron entered the hall on the ground floor and ascended to the main level of the hotel. Stairs and elevators opened to the main lobby, which revealed a view through the sun parlor built above the porte cochere to a view of the river. On the main axis of the public rooms, the vista extended over two hundred feet, back through the great dining room. On either side of the sun parlor, the lobby opened laterally to side porches and the terrace. In contrast to the penetrability of the resort hotel, the urban commercial hotel appeared impermeable. The entrance of the Olympic Hotel, a break in the heavily rusticated base of the structure marked by a marquee, was relatively small and remarkably defensive. Inside, the space was introverted. The main lobby was completely enclosed by service space along its longitudinal walls. The transverse axis presented the principal vista. This included the lobby in the center, a formal lounge to the left, and the Palm Room and main dining room to the right. This vista does not culminate beyond the walls of the structure, but rather it is theatricalized by elaborate monumental staircases marking changes in elevation along its route.

76. Augusta, Georgia, Bon Air–Vanderbilt: *A*, plan of the entrance level; *B*, plan of the second level. Modified from Roy Carruthers, "Hotel Architecture from a Hotel Man's Viewpoint," *Pencil Points* 4 (June 1923).

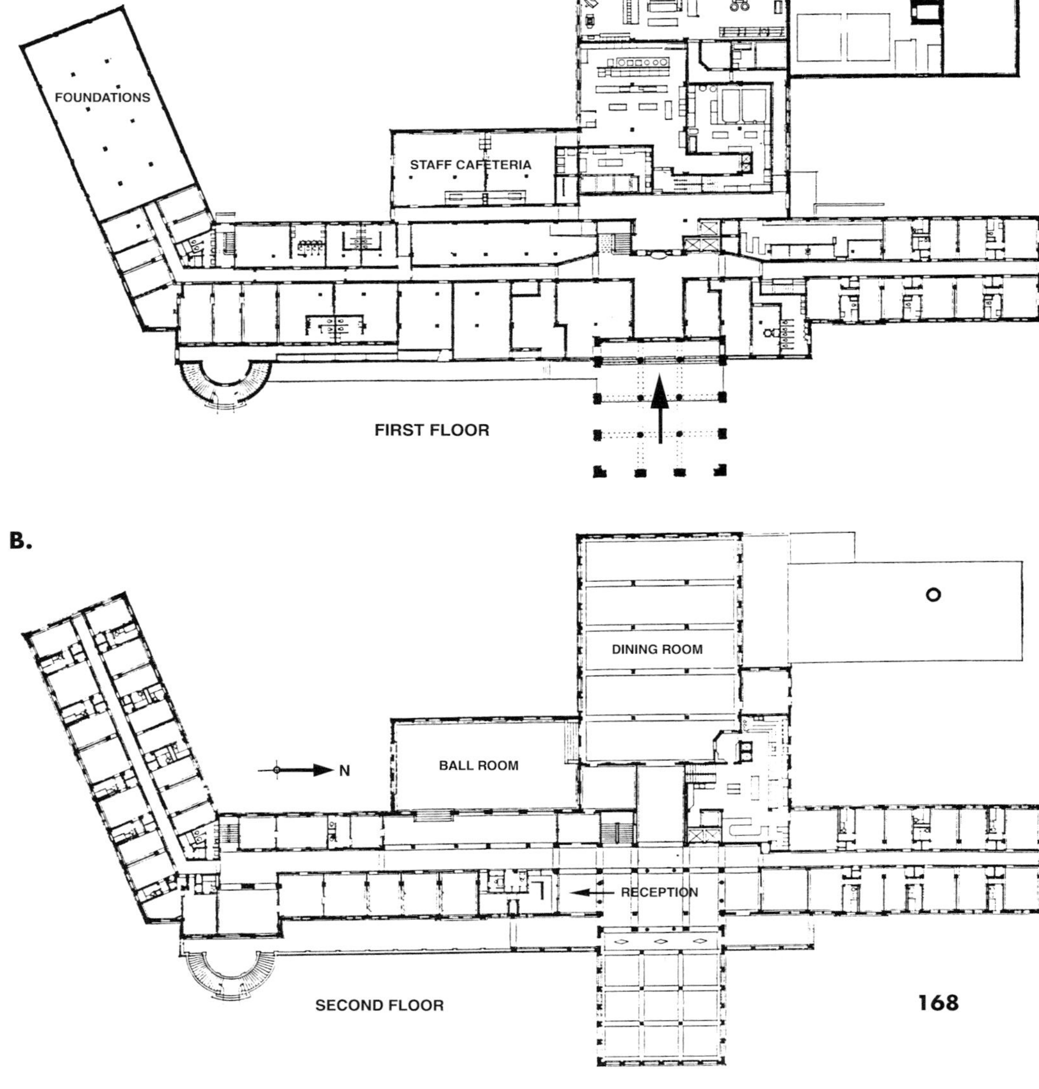

The different forms of the two hotel types corresponded to the distinct experiences they sold to their patrons. The commercial hotel met the spatial expectations of its guests; the resort hotel attempted to exceed them. The axial orderliness of the Olympic laid out its sumptuousness with clarity. The Olympic provided an appropriately luxurious setting for the traveler. Its lavishness indicated the status of both the city in which it located and the guest who temporarily resided there. As the formally ordered space of civic ritual, the hotel's luxury was also an index of the prosperity of local elites. In contrast, the architecture of the Bon Air–Vanderbilt manipulated and surprised its individual patrons. The encounter with the building was cadenced: the lavish porte cochere raised expectations of grandeur that were frustrated by the small, ground-floor entrance hall. Disappointment was superseded by delight as the guest ascended the stairs and witnessed the extended vistas framed by the dining room and sun porch. These vistas were not limited, as at the Olympic, to the sequential spaces of the interior; rather, they culminated in the picturesque landscapes for which the patron had come to the hotel.[53]

Also suggested by the plates of Carruthers's article, if not by his text, were the shared characteristics of major American hotels in the pre–World War II era. The author offered no comment on the size or arrangement of guest rooms. Nevertheless, the plans of the Olympic and Bon Air–Vanderbilt hotels indicate that bedrooms were generously scaled. In both hotels, doubles range from a little less than 200 to over 300 square feet. The average single is about 160 square feet. Ceilings were high. Rooms (Olympic) or suites (Bon Air–Vanderbilt) had their own bathroom. The coherence of the Olympic's plan allowed the bathroom to be located on the inside wall of the guest room. The openness of the plan and the consequent greater cost of a ventilation system may have determined the location of the bathroom on the hotel's outer wall in the Bon Air–Vanderbilt. With the widespread replacement of communal bathrooms with private ones in the 1920s, hotel guest rooms finally had to potential to became what they remain today, the domain of exquisite isolation.

In the mid-nineteenth century, hotel corridors were titled "flirtation galleries." Chambers wrote, for example, "What strikes us as rather remarkable, is the fact that the doors of these various sitting-apartments are generally wide open. I saw this everywhere. Passing by, you see highly-dressed ladies reposing on satin couches, or lolling in rocking chairs."[54] A good bit of this publicness persisted into the 1920s. The core of the hotel remained sumptuously communal. Both the Olympic and Bon Air–Vanderbilt had multiple, lavishly appointed public rooms for the presentation of the self to society: lounges and foyers, sundecks and porches. The hotel continued to be identified as a place in which women displayed themselves as an extension of their wardrobes.[55] The Olympic even had parlors in the principle corners of the building on each of the guest room floors. Libraries were also common in pre–World War II hotels. Most characteristic, however, was the spatial and ornamental opulence of the formal lobbies. Because of Prohibition, there were no bars. The few shops in hotels were treated as service spaces for the guests and inconspicuously located. In the Bon Air–Vanderbilt the barber and sundries shops were located on the ground level, off corridors leading to staff quarters. The space of the hotel before World War II still looked social rather than commercial and private.

Noticeably absent from Carruthers's discussion of hotels is an assessment of their occupants. His hotels' patrons are as invisible in his text as in his plates. He alludes to the traveling salesmen who will patronize the Olympic and to the families who will spend their vacations at the Bon Air–Vanderbilt. But the clientele remains uninvestigated. The absence of discussion of lavish suites, special kitchen and service arrangements on each floor, and sumptuous accoutrements supplements the absence of reference to the patrons. Carruthers is not concerned with the luxury of the establishment but rather with its efficiency. This preoccupation with the practical was the correlate of the prosperous middle-class patron for whom these hotels were produced. The hotels discussed by Carruthers were designed for the expanding American middle class, whose members remained essentially anonymous. Carruthers was manager of one of the world's great hotel establishments, the Waldorf-Astoria, a preferred New York locus of the extravagently wealthy, the American model and rival of the Savoy in London and the Ritz in Paris. But in his series of articles in *Pencil Points*, Carruthers did not discuss the temporary residences of the social elite but rather the lodging of the increasingly affluent middle class. As in Godkin's article, though less explicitly, American democracy is central to Carruthers's description of the architectural innovations of American hotels. That Carruthers left the guests undescribed is evidence of their middle-class character.

The anonymity of the client in the hotels presented by Carruthers is accentuated, by contrast, to the naming of patrons in the accounts of the world's grand hotels. In that genre of hotel biography, mentioned in the historiographic excursus that follows the last chapter of this book, the rich and famous replace the building as the subject of study. "The grand hotel is a place where people come and go, and nothing ever happens," observes the mysterious Dr. Otternschlag in *Grand Hotel*, MGM's 1932 Oscar-winning movie based on the novel by Vicki Baum. The film brilliantly unravels the lives of a prima ballerina, a baron, and an industrial magnate for our entertainment. The final degeneration of an already decadent elite is displayed in a fantasy architecture that combined premonitions of Wright's Guggenheim Museum and Portman's Hyatt Hotels. The film was an epitaph for its subject. The last of the grand hotels was the rebuilt Waldorf-Astoria in New York. The financial agreements were signed two days before the crash of the New York Stock Market in 1929. Construction continued despite the Depression and the hotel opened in 1931. It did not show a profit until 1944.

The Depression ended the era of civic hotels produced by stock companies of local shareholders. During the boom years of the 1920s a large number of such hotels had been constructed in cities with a population of around 50,000 as an appropriate status symbol of the town and as an appropriate space for civic events of the middle-class elite—coming-out parties, local balls, and political gatherings. These hotels, of which the Olympic is one, had been architecturally ambitious. They had provided the public stage for the display of the prosperity of those who invested in them along with their peers. However, the rising expectations for community hotels and the rising expense of building and maintaining structures that met such expectations made them unprofitable. Overbuilding also contributed to the multiple hotel failures that occurred during the Depression. Walter Irving Hamilton's book *Promoting New Hotels: When Does It Pay?* is devoted to the amusing but disastrous mistakes made by ignorant if civic-minded citizens who wished to construct a community hotel. "To sum it all up," he writes, "it has to be said that too many hotel projects have been floated on an artificially created wave of enthusiasm rather than on a calm appeal to business sense."[56] The charge of inadequate business practices rationalized the collapse of the confidence of the middle-class public. The middle-class ceremonies of civic life celebrated in these great hotels were curtailed by the Depression. When significant hotel building began again in the 1950s, ownership was neither individual nor communal, but rather corporate. Profit, rather than civic pride, determined construction. The need to appeal to a clientele of a certain class through a certain level of architectural presence had to be balanced against the profit margin.

Boomer's and Carruthers's articles provide a sense of American hotels at a particular moment—the decade before the Great Depression. The hotels of one of America's first great chains—Statler—allows the buildings of the 1920s to be understood in a broader context. The old Buffalo Statler, built in 1907, provides a preface to the 1920s. The new Buffalo Statler of 1923 supplements an understanding of the 1920s derived from Carruthers and Boomer. Two further Statlers, the Washington Statler, opened in 1943, and the Statler Center in Los Angeles, opened in 1951, trace the subsequent development of the urban hotel. They register stages in the emergence of the Modern hotel and its corporatization. Like the Olympic and the Bon Air–Vanderbilt, all of these Statler hotels were built for the mobile middle-class American. Their architectural development objectifies shifts in the construction of the desires of the middle class as well as changes in the corporate order. The financial and material strictures of the war years and the competition with novel forms of lodging in the postwar period contributed to a new emphasis on efficiency by the producer and a new acceptance by the consumer of the *look* of efficiency. A shift from Fordist space to the space of McDonaldization is traceable in this sequence of Statler Hotels.

As its title suggests, Rufus Jarman's biography, *A Bed for the Night: The Story of the Wheeling Bellboy E. M. Statler and His Remarkable Hotels*, represents Ellsworth Milton Statler as the model American Horatio Alger entrepreneur.[57] At the age of nine Statler labored as a coke stoker in a glass factory in Wheeling, West Virginia. At thirteen he shifted to the local hotel for a job as a bellboy. Working his way from desk clerk through pool hall manager and bowling-alley mastermind, he became a mass restaurateur, making his fortune first by offering all-you-can-eat for a quarter then promoting meal ticket books: six twenty-five-cent meals for the price of five. Statler then built and ran enormous temporary hotels, each with over two thousand rooms, for the Pan American Exposition in Buffalo in 1901 and the Louisiana Purchase Exposition in St. Louis in 1904. He invested the profits from this last enterprise in the design and construction of the Hotel Buffalo, in Buffalo, New York (later renamed Hotel Statler), which opened in 1907.[58] Here was the first major urban hotel to have a bath in every room. "A bed and a bath for a buck and a half" was Statler's slogan. It was also the first hotel to have ice water piped to each individual room, to have spaces under the door for the delivery of newspapers, and to have keyholes above the knob rather than below it so that patrons could locate it more easily. Statler did in his hotel what he had already done in his restaurants: provide a desirable product at a price low enough to attract large numbers of consumers. Managerial and technological innovations allowed him to offer privacy and comfort at a low profit margin to an expanded, middle-class clientele.

Three later Statler hotels, the new Buffalo Statler, the Washington Statler, and the Statler Center, Los Angeles, suggest a continuity of commitment to technological innovation as a means of realizing greater efficiency and thereby maximizing profits. This commitment also corresponded to the look of the building. The new Buffalo Statler, designed by the architectural firm of George B. Post and Sons, was built in 1923 (fig. 77). An article on the hotel in *Architectural Forum* began by applauding the new emphasis on efficiency that the building represented. "In studying the plans of many recently completed buildings of institutional and investment types, it becomes obvious that a fundamental change is taking place in the procedure of the architect's office."[59] The author noted that traditionally architects had begun with the form of the building and only later considered how its function might be fitted within that frame. The new Buffalo Statler indicated that finally function was studied before the form was determined. "[W]hile [the Hotel Statler in Buffalo] presents no radical departures or theoretical experiments, it is a structure most efficiently planned through the coordinated efforts of one of the world's most successful hotel organizations."[60]

After an initial paragraph praising efficiency, however, the article reverts to a more conventional presentation of the building. The bulk of the piece is devoted to describing the building's style and the details of its interior

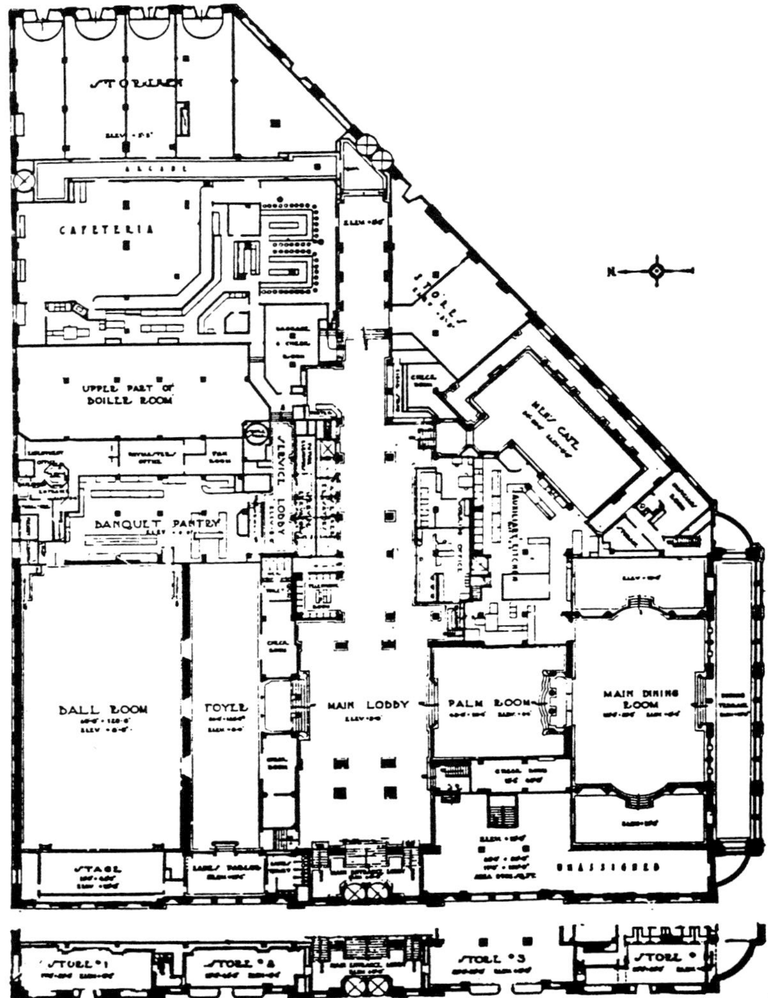

77. Buffalo, New York, Buffalo Statler, plan of the entrance level. Modified from "The Hotel Statler, Buffalo," *Architectural Forum* 39 (1923).

ornamentation. The hotel's look was as conservative as the article written about it. The basement to ballroom levels occupied the whole of the irregular five-sided block owned by the hotel. But this space of public rooms and service areas is visually dominated on the exterior by the rectilinear discipline of the hotel's sixteen-story, E-shaped guest room tower. Rendered in a "modified Georgian" style in red brick with terra-cotta trim, the massive geometry of the structure controlled the city center of Buffalo. The entrance was in the middle of the building's main face. Conventionally marked by a great marquee and revolving doors, it opened directly on to the principal street, Delaware Avenue. The public spaces of the Statler, like those of the Olympic in Seattle, were supremely formal. The sumptuous, high-ceilinged lobby opened transversely into a series of monumental spaces—to the north through an embellished foyer to the two-storied ball room and to the south through the Palm Room into the two-storied main dining room and beyond to the more intimate groin-vaulted dining terrace. This "interior architecture" was Italian Renaissance; the walls were Botticino marble, the floors terrazzo with brass striping, the furniture and fixtures appropriately historical. Each of the private dining rooms on the second floor were "given a special architectural effect." The service space was generous, including the full basement, a basement mezzanine, and a significant section of the first floor, but circulation patterns were complex and utility areas scattered. There were, for example, four separate major kitchens serving different parts of the hotel.

The efficiency vaunted in the article was more apparent in the guest rooms. These spaces were not quite as generously proportioned as those of the Olympic and the Bon Air–Vanderbilt. The smallest single was 144 square feet; the large doubles were just under 200. The sample rooms ("The third floor is entirely devoted to sample rooms, as the Hotels Statler specializes in service to commercial travelers") were, however, considerably larger. "Each room is provided with a disappearing bed. This has been done to make possible the full use of the room for business purposes during the day, and to eliminate any suggestion of its use as a bedroom." Guest rooms had a central ceiling light controlled by a switch and three room lamps. "Bathrooms are grouped on the double stack interior plan, providing the double bath unit with pipe space between and accessible by opening the back of the built-in medicine closets."[61] The same efficiency was exemplified in the planning of the hotel's garage, located across the street from the hotel. It contained a filling station and parking for six hundred cars. Its exterior was "in architectural agreement" with the new hotel. Its rusticated base, Doric pilasters framing double-storied arched windows, and overall symmetry made it look more like a bank than a car park. There is a disjunction between the historical formality of the hotel with its Georgian façades and Renaissance interiors and the functionalist rhetoric of its description. In response to a changed aesthetic as much as to new pressures of competition, the gap between historical style and rational planning was closed in the Statler Corporation's later buildings.

McDonaldization.

The motel did for transient accommodation what McDonald's did for eating.[62] Motels had their origins in public campsites provided for a new class of automobile travelers. In the 1920s many municipalities maintained free automobile campsites equipped with washing and cooking facilities. In civic journals such as *The American City*, municipal campsites were widely promoted: "Truly the towns through which these auto tourists pass have found that a municipal camp is a good thing. Each year sees more camps built. They are a good advertisement and they make friends. Further, they actually bring money to the town, for the guest at the municipal camp must have gasoline, tires, oil, picture post-cards, pancake flour, auto veils, goggles, candy, chewing gum, cigars, bolts, paint, overalls, and a multitude of other things."[63] During the Depression, the free municipal camp, occupied by destitute squatters, became a liability to the township rather than an enhancement. Municipal camps were closed. Public accommodations were superseded by private ones. These individually owned campsites were increasingly elaborated, first with simple cabins, then with fully equipped cottages. The campsite was superseded by motor courts and motels in the years after World War II. The motel was the built response to the desires of the newly mobile middle classes. Motel chains, usually begun at the initiative of an individual in the late forties and early fifties, were later corporatized. By the 1970s motel chains dominated the industry.

A study sponsored jointly by *Architectural Record* and *Hotel Management* provided an assessment of the motel in 1950.[64] It represented motels as a moral threat to the American traveling public: "Many are the euphemisms for their most profitable kind of business. We hear of one which turned away any travelers with luggage on Saturdays and Sundays. Conditions were so bad that in 1940 the Chief of the FBI published a popular magazine article tracing a number of crimes in lurid detail to tourist camps."[65] Alfred Hitchcock's movie of 1960, *Psycho*, exploited an ominousness that clung to the motel well past mid-century. The regulation of motels, the article went on to argue, was inadequate. Only one motel in twelve was recommended by the American Automobile Association, and only one in thirty was recommended without qualification. But the motel was less a threat to the public than to architecture. The failings of the motel were represented as commensurate with the absence of architecture. Fewer than 20 percent of motels were architect-built and only one motel out of a hundred had any "architectural interest or planned efficiency." The discrepancy between hotel and motel investments identified in the text allows the reader to appreciate the bias of its authors. "Costs per unit [in a motel], completely furnished, are now between $3500 and $5000, but horizontal construction is estimated at one third of the vertical. City hotel costs per room are $12,000 to $24,000 including full hotel facilities."[66]

A different perspective on the motel was presented by George Horne, who wrote of his travel experience for the *New York Times*, also in 1950:

> One who never before this year submitted himself to the blandishments of the modern and progressive motel operator returns from a four-week driving junket into the Middle West and Southwest convinced that the third and second-class hotel is doomed, and that the first-class hotel is going to have a run for its money in a terrifically competitive field. . . . [Motels] are modern, well-equipped, warm in winter, mostly clean, and well policed by look-alive national organizations. . . .They are on every major highway bisecting the nation, both the north-south and the east-west routes. They are adding new comforts for the weary traveler every season. . . . Spotless venetian blinds, tile flooring, perhaps over radiant heat, deep and comfortable lounge chairs, plenty of clothes closet space—it is all there. After showers, the family strolls through neatly landscaped walkways to the adjacent restaurant, where the food is . . . in fact surprisingly good.[67]

Hotels were expensive; motels were cheap. The relatively low price of motel rooms was the direct result of low capital investment and low operating costs. The semirural land on which motels were built was inexpensive; the urban sites of hotels were costly. Motel units were often prefabricated; individual owners commonly supplied most of their own labor; they were constructed to last ten to fifteen years. Hotels required architects and professional laborers; their materials were expensive and their building costs were high; they were designed as permanent fixtures in the urban landscape. Certainly the look of the motel was as important as the look of the hotel, but the desire that directed the gaze was entirely different. The visual signs sought by the middle-class, suburban consumer were not those of prestige, history, and community, but rather those of hygiene, accessibility, and privacy. The pleasures sought were popular and informal—a coffee shop with hamburgers and a swimming pool for the children—not elite and formal.[68] For those from the suburbs, the motel was a familiar territory.

The appeal of the motel to the middle-class traveling family resided in large part in what was avoided—most obviously, city traffic and parking problems, the high prices of accommodation, and tipping. But there were other, less quantifiable advantages. In motels, surveillance was minimal. The guest evaded the scrutiny and critique of one's self and one's companions by reception clerks, bellboys, and valets. Also eluded was a certain self-consciousness imposed by the formality of hotel space (the luxurious lobby, the opulent dining room, the overfurnished rooms) as well as the formality of hotel practices (the hierarchies of the staff, the rituals of luggage moving, the decorum of dining). The simplified architecture and the manifold signage of the motel was the material expression of this escape. Motels made themselves visible from the highway. The imaginative marquee, the cottages, and the swimming pool were displayed to the passing motorist. Well-groomed lawns, unbroken parking pavements, neat buildings constituted the motel's attractiveness. In contrast, the urban hotel-palazzo publicized the formalities of the traditional hotel. By the 1950s, this elaborate architecture was not an asset but a liability. McDonaldization not only brought new efficiencies to urban hotel practices, but also the appearances of efficiency to its architecture.

Hotels Statler Company published a comic book version of Ellsworth Statler's life in 1948. The magazine ends with a description of the progressive efficiencies of the hotel chain as part of a celebration of the American free-enterprise system (fig. 78). Earlier in the text there is a comment on the new Washington Statler: "Out of Statler profits—and the savings people invested in this company because its performance proved that it was a paying business—came the 850-bed Washington Statler, in 1943 . . . the most modern hotel in the United States."[69] The Washington Statler was the only major American urban hotel conceived and built between the onset of the Depression and the end of World War II. Hotels were built in Miami and Las Vegas during this time, but they tended to be small and unimaginative in their program if not in their décor.[70] An article in *Architectural Forum* at the beginning of 1953 summarized hotel development of the previous seven years:

> So as the 1945–52 era of necessitous building [i.e., the uncritical work of the postwar boom] nears its end, this might be a very good time to look at the record of the one building type where insistent demand vanished in 1929—the hotel. For two decades only Miami Beach has cried for more and more hotels for more and more vacationers. And so, perhaps characteristically, Miami Beach until this year has contributed little or nothing to progress in

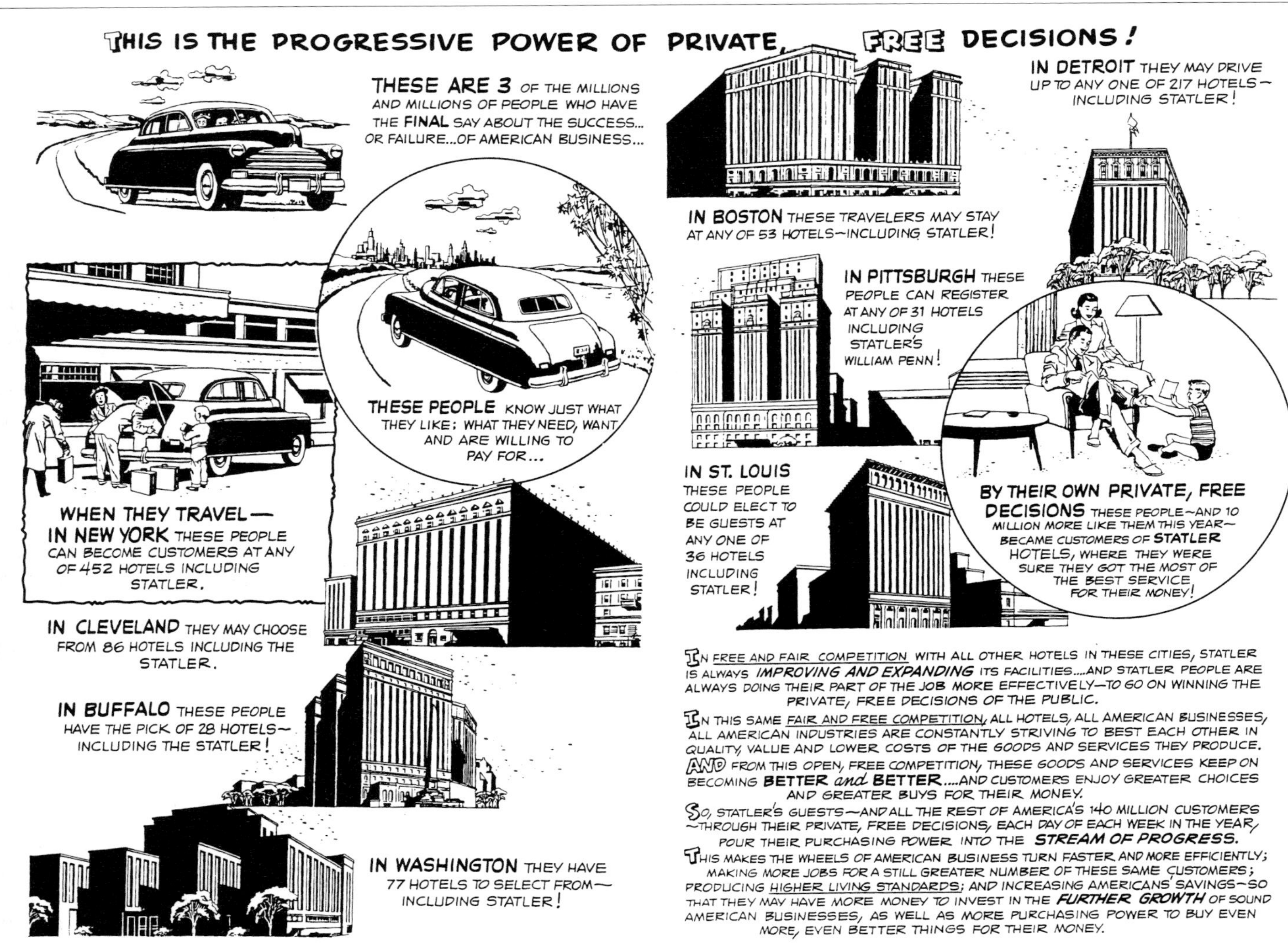

78. Two-page spread from *Ellsworth Statler* (Hotel Statler Co., 1948).

79. Washington, D.C., Washington Statler, now the Capital Hilton, view of the exterior. Modified from *Architectural Forum* 78 (1943).

80. Washington, D.C., Washington Statler, view of the Capitol Terrace. Photo modified from *Architectural Forum* 78 (1943).

> hotel design. But where there was no necessitous hotel building, architects, engineers and owners have been spurred to create a revolution in hotel design, construction and economics. . . . The milestones in this revolution are very few: The Statler in Washington; the Terrace Plaza in Cincinnati; the balconied El Panama and its offspring the Caribe Hilton.[71]

The Washington Statler, the first of the "revolutionary" designs mentioned in the article, might be claimed as the first Modern hotel on several grounds (figs. 79, 80, and 81).[72] The least noticed of these grounds is political. The Washington Statler connected the Statler Corporation intimately with the government. Jesse Jones, the Texas multimillionaire running the Reconstruction Finance Corporation and charged with lending money to stimulate business growth in the Depression, apparently promoted the hotel by promising to finance it to the amount of $5 million.[73] The White House Secret Service acted as consultants for the building's accommodation of a crippled president and his security. In consequence the Statler became *the* setting for official dinners during the war.[74]

The Washington Statler was also, from the beginning, talked about as modern. Efficiency, always a theme in writings on American hotels, is the

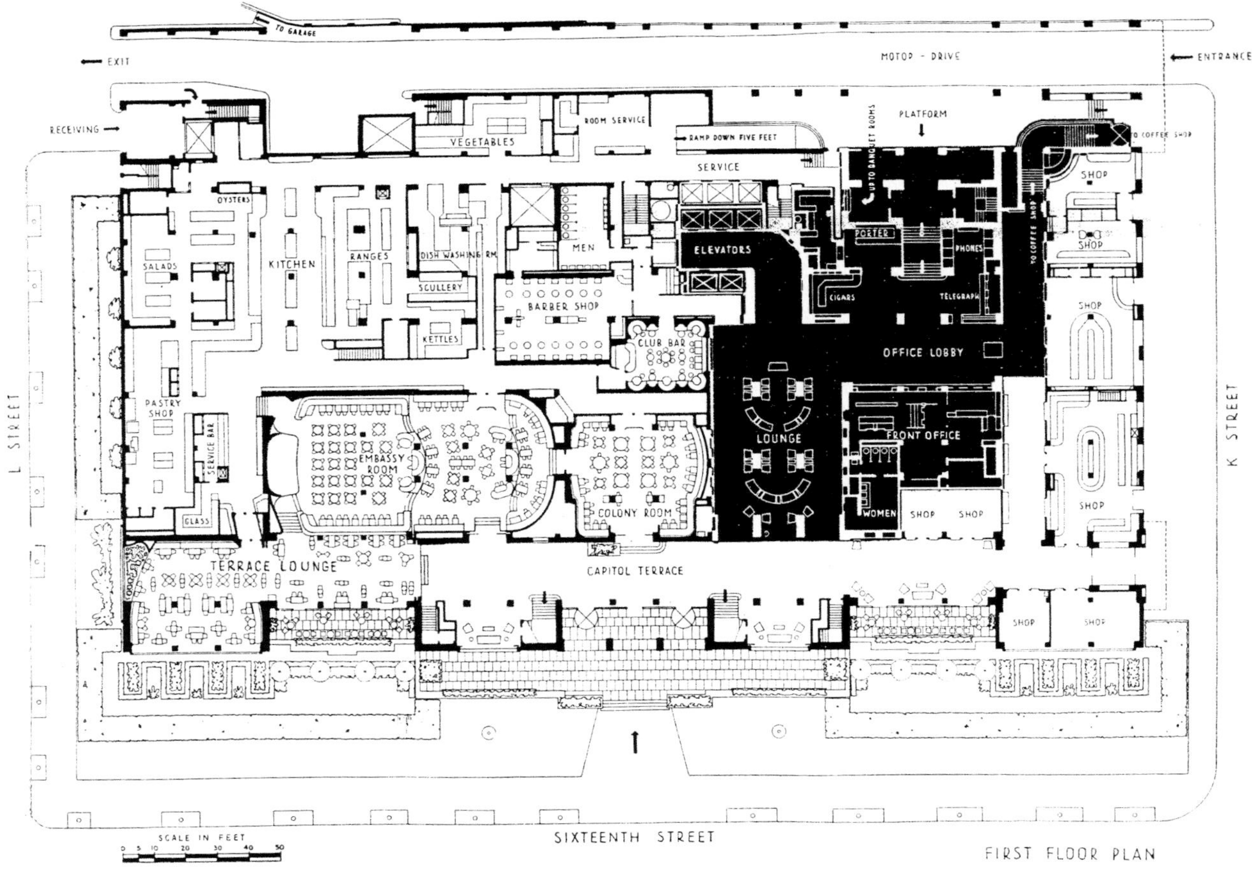

81. Washington, D.C., Washington Statler, plan of the entrance level. Modified from the plan provided by the Capital Hilton Archive.

principal subject in treatments of the Washington Statler. A special issue of *Hotel Monthly* devoted to the Washington Statler predicted that this undertaking would have "a profound effect on the future of hotel construction" because of its embrace of efficiency.[75] A long article in *Architectural Forum* insisted that "this hotel by Architects Holabird and Root sets the pace for postwar design."[76] The article identified three notable innovations in the hotel's design: "in the handling of incoming and outgoing guests without disrupting street traffic; in the most flexible guest rooms yet developed; and in the use of cold cathode tube lighting as a major decoration element." In all the articles on the Washington Statler, the feature of the hotel that was most emphasized was the shift of the main entrance from the front of the structure to its rear. The main entrance of the Washington Statler opened from a covered "motor-drive" at the back of the hotel.[77] Automobile passengers descended a broad staircase that was flanked by a tobacconist and a telephone and telegraph station rather than the traditional double-story marble columns. Almost immediately in front of the staircase was the reception desk. The short, transverse axis of the entrance hall was terminated by a bar at one end and shops at the other.

The principal pedestrian entrance on the Sixteenth Street face of the hotel was secondary. Though framed externally by fascist-classical piers, the vestigial quality of this access was revealed internally by the space into which it opened. The "Capitol Terrace," despite its rather grand name, served as a broad corridor rather than a lobby. The ornate interior gestures of the palatial hotel had disappeared. The articles on the building and the plans and photographs that illustrate them allow the reader to understand the Washington Statler as the first major urban hotel to respond to the new dominance of the automobile in American life. The texts' emphasis on efficiency and the illustrations' representation of the unadorned façades and rectilinear interiors of the hotel presented the Washington Statler as the first consistently Modern hotel. Efficiency was identified as Modernity. It was claimed that the Washington Statler's austerity made it popular: "[The Washington Statler became] the most glamorous thing in Washington principally because it has departed from the old hotel building tradition . . . with glass walls, efficient arrangements and absence of adornment."[78]

Modernity was, in the war years, the ideologically inevitable aesthetic of austerity. The building of a hotel was sanctioned by the desperate housing shortage in Washington in the 1940s.[79] The large number of rooms—850—were its apparent raison d'être.[80] The hotel was designed for conventioneers, politicians, and the military, not for salesmen. Sample rooms were eliminated. Guest rooms were smaller than they were in the Buffalo Statler. A small single was a little more than a hundred square feet. Further, the rooms had significantly lower ceilings. A minimum number of guest rooms was necessary to ensure the hotel's profitability. Consequently, room height was limited so that an additional floor might be realized within the strict building-height restrictions of the Washington construction code. Living rooms in a Levittown house were more generous than the bedrooms of the Washington Statler.[81] Lower ceilings also cut air-conditioning costs. The St. Louis Statler had been the first hotel to be fully centrally air-conditioned, but the Washington Statler added thermostats in each of the guest rooms for individual temperature control.[82] The introduction of horizontal windows and the elimination of ceiling lights helped mask the room's lowness.[83] Its smallness was further disguised by the use of the couch-bed and multiply functioning furniture. Each night table, for example, had a built-in four-channel radio and a lamp with a base that served as a telephone cradle.[84]

The Statler's concern with innovative efficiencies was displayed in the shape of the hotel itself. It was Modern in the simplicity of its forms. The rectilinear precision of its exterior blocks was undisturbed by obvious gratuitous detail. Only the surrounds of paired window bays, segments of reel moldings, and decorative balconies above the side entrances of the building relieved the underadorned surface of the structure. Its equally severe interior geometry was not significantly softened by the hotel's elaborate new lighting systems. The linear discipline of the hotel's architecture was emphasized by the abstract forms of its interior decoration. Furnishings and fixtures were also Modern. Flamboyances were eliminated. The texts and photographs of professional hotel and architecture journals represent the building as efficient; they also hide the hotel's eliteness.

The Statler did more than provide additional space for visitors in Washington, D.C. It also materially embodied status in the programming of its public spaces and in the quality of its finish. The look of efficiency was costly. The cream limestone of the building's skin was flawless. The hotel's lobby was sheathed in fine marble. The hotel's laminated furniture was particularly expensive to maintain. For the sake of this efficient-looking Modern furniture, cleaners were contractually assigned fewer rooms in their shifts than in other luxury hotels. The second floor of the building was devoted to ballrooms and private dining space. It was designed to receive appropriately the most prestigious of guests. A car elevator was installed to serve a single function. It delivered Franklin Roosevelt's limousine to the second floor where he and his wheelchair were discreetly deposited behind the curtains on the stage of the President's Ballroom. The ballroom's outer wall was constructed of specially reinforced concrete as protection against bombings. In the hotel's tower there was a private smoking room for the president's use, from which the White House could be seen.

The program of the Washington Statler was not, in other words, dictated by efficiency alone. That its elite elegance went largely unnoticed by commentators at the time of the hotel's opening during the war years suggests that austerity contributed to the ascendancy of efficiency as a dominant aesthetic. Features that rendered the building elite were tempered. Ornamental flourishes were minimized. The chrome crown on the model of the Chrysler Building reportedly planned for the hotel was eliminated.[85] Most remarkable, perhaps, the building's dramatic reorientation from the front to the rear of the building, represented in architectural criticism as a response to the automobile, was apparently imposed by the strict building codes of Sixteenth Street. Prominent commercial entrances were not allowed on the axis of the White House.[86] The form of the efficient was not only, as it was presented, a means of reducing expenditure; it was also the new style of the elite. The materials of the building were of the highest quality, and the program addressed the needs of Washington's politically and socially privileged. The Washington Statler became an object of study in the hotel world. In 1947 Rupert D'Oyly Carte, chairman of the board of the Savoy, and Hugh Wontner, its managing director, went to Washington "to see its latest hotel."[87] With the Washington Statler, Modernity superseded tradition as the index of the hotel's prestige. Efficiency had attained the status of art among both its producers and its consumers.

82. Los Angeles, Statler Center, now the Wilshire Grand Hotel, view of the architect's model. Photo modified from *Architectural Record* 109 (1951).

83. Los Angeles, Statler Center, plan. Modified from *Architectural Record* 109 (1951).

The Statler Center, Los Angeles, built in 1950–1951, pressed the look and the profitability of Modernism further.[88] Holabird, Root and Burgee, who designed the hotel in consultation with William B. Tabler, enhanced the programmatic and formal innovations of the Washington Statler (figs. 82 and 83). Automobiles were even more deeply inscribed in the plan of the Los Angeles hotel. Its main entry opened from Seventh Street, its principal access artery. Instead of the traditional, marquee-covered sidewalk entrance, the hotel had a covered drive-in space for taxicab drop-offs and pickups. There the patron entered into a low-ceilinged, irregularly shaped space flanked with a bar and shops and ascended by escalator to reception. A similarly protected entrance is located on the higher, Wilshire Boulevard level. There was, in addition, a third entrance off Francisco Street, specifically designed for travelers with their own automobiles and connected to the hotel's 465-car underground garage. This entrance was provided with its own small registration desk and elevator bank for the convenience of patrons arriving by car, who were thus provided direct access to their rooms.

Guest rooms were also further economized. There were more rooms (1,275) than in the Washington Statler, and they were smaller. The attraction of an individually controlled room heating and cooling system helped compensate the patron for the loss of space, as did the free television set—a new room accessory. To neutralize the effects of space reduction, further refinements were made to the furniture and the decor. Large wall mirrors gave the illusion of more space, as did the half lamps specially designed to be set into them. By appearing to be whole, rather than doubled, they contributed to the deception of depth. Furniture intended to "streamline" the appearance of the room and to save space was specially designed for the

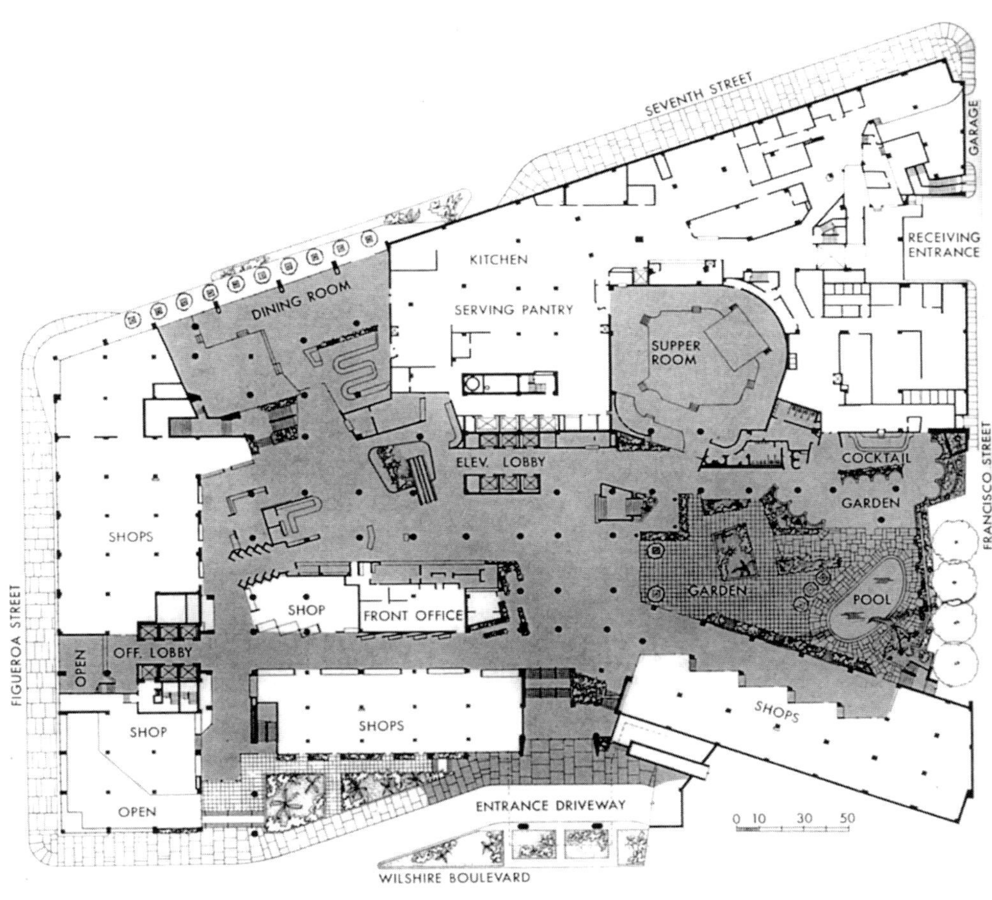
SEVENTH STREET
GARAGE
RECEIVING ENTRANCE
KITCHEN
DINING ROOM
SERVING PANTRY
SUPPER ROOM
ELEV. LOBBY
COCKTAIL
GARDEN
FRANCISCO STREET
SHOPS
SHOP
FRONT OFFICE
GARDEN
POOL
FIGUEROA STREET
OPEN
OFF. LOBBY
SHOP
SHOPS
SHOPS
OPEN
ENTRANCE DRIVEWAY
0 10 30 50
WILSHIRE BOULEVARD

hotel.[89] Most important was the interior's greater inclusion of the exterior. Used again from the Washington Statler were the large, horizontal guest room windows. But in Los Angeles the window offered not only light but also something of a view. In contrast to the traditional urban hotel arrangement, the arms of the hotel were splayed so that guests did not look directly into one another's rooms. Further, spaces in the interstices of the arms were planted, so that guests overlooked gardens rather than the roofs of the public and service spaces of the hotel's base. These windows and the sight that they invited were symptomatic of the new transparency that represents the most innovative aspect of this hotel.

The Modernity of the Washington Statler was of a classicizing sort. It was an austere and rectilinear definition of space that still emphasized the high quality and fine finish of marble and stone enclosure. Its volumes, both interior and exterior, were massive and symmetrical. Spatial hierarchies were clearly articulated. Continuing the tradition of the urban hotel, its plan remained introspective. The Statler Center was, in contrast, externalized and transparent. Carefully manicured lawns and gardens and a swimming pool were made as much a part of the interior of the hotel as possible. Solid limestone walls were replaced by glass. The pool area, garden, and cocktail bar were visually integrated to form the focus of visual excitement for the main lobby level. Seventy thousand square feet of shops provided the frame. In the Los Angeles Center, shops virtually replaced the lobby, though the substitution of commercial space for social space was differently represented by its producers:"The . . . design [of the lobby] has what might be termed a unique 'looseness'; which is intended to produce exactly the opposite of the frequently stuffy hotel lobby. Ahead of one making his way through there will always be a vista enhanced by appropriate greenery."[90] The apparent randomness of the piloti-like columns located in the public areas contributed to a sense of the independence of space from structure. Even the introduction of technologies for televising events into the Statler's ballroom—the first such facilities permanently installed in a hotel—might also be identified as part of the radical externalization of its form. Architecture had moved from being the subject of spectacle to being a diaphanous backdrop for its possibility.

In the late 1940s and early 1950s, Holabird, Root and Burgee exported their experience with the Statler Center in Los Angeles abroad for Intercontinental Hotels, Inc. Intercontinental was a wholly owned subsidiary of Pan American Corporation. Pan Am, at the time the largest American overseas carrier, entered the hotel business as a means of stimulating business and tourism that would in turn promote foreign air travel. Intercontinental's first hotel ventures were in South and Central America, following Pan American's most numerous airline connections.[91] The early Intercontinentals—in Caracas, Venezuela; in Maracaibo, Venezuela; and in Bogotá, Colombia—are all versions of the Statler Center in Los Angeles.[92]

Holabird, Root and Burgee's consultant on the Los Angeles project was William B. Tabler, an articulate observer of the efficiencies of modern architecture.[93] Tabler, trained as a civil engineer and an architect at Harvard, had worked for Holabird and Root on the Washington Statler in 1939. After serving as a construction officer in the navy, he was hired by the Statler Corporation. The senior vice president of the company, H. B. Callis, sent him on a tour of Statler hotels so that he might develop a critical list of suggestions for modernization. Later, Tabler's formula for hotel cost-effectiveness was published in *Architectural Forum*.[94] It was promised that by following Tabler's specifications for hotel design the owner would break even at 60 to 65 percent occupancy. Construction costs per room should be no more than $1,000 per dollar of the room charge. Bedroom floor space should be equal to or greater than combined service and common space. There should be less than one employee per guest room. Land cost should be no more than 10 percent of the building cost. Room sizes are 90–110 square feet for singles, 130–150 for doubles, and 160–180 for twins. According to Tabler, 70 percent of a hotel's profits came from room rental, only 20 percent from beverages, and none at all from food. Profits were to be maximized by introducing "repetitive economies."

As the hotel's economic well-being depended on its guest rooms, this space received Tabler's greatest attention. His "repetitive economies" were best "represented in Tabler's now famous bathroom. Plumbing is back to back and cut to a minimum. An elongated washbasin counter and angled toilet double as makeup table and chair; towel racks are next to the bathtub so that guests will dry themselves in the tub instead of using bathmats; a towel hook is placed so they will reuse hand towels instead of reaching for a new one (which Tabler points out can save $7,000 a year alone in laundering costs)."[95] Some traditionally important parts of the hotel were minimized. "The big hotel dining room with its long menus and lavish entertainment is becoming a thing of the past."[96] Still others were reconceptualized. The single great ballroom, now divisible by removable walls, was shifted out from under the guest room tower, freeing it from the grid of columnar supports. The modern hotel should have a single, central kitchen, avoiding redundant appliances and, more particularly, redundant labor. Construction should be as simple as possible, preferably cantilevered flat-plate slab construction with thin, porcelain enamel, sandwich curtain walls. Tabler's innovations presented hotel owners and their architects with a single, consistent message: the rising cost of labor requires the deployment of new technologies; a hotel's profitability depends on eliminating workers.

During the 1950s, air-conditioning, television, and self-service elevators became necessary features of the modern hotel. Other labor-saving mechanisms that have since become commonplace were just being introduced. Hilton and Sheraton had installed central reservation boards. Several chains had central accounting computers. In an effort to eliminate large numbers of operators, Hilton first experimented with direct-dial telephones in guest rooms in the Waldorf Astoria and the Pittsburgh Hilton. By the 1960s Tabler was prophesying the technological developments that would ensure the industry's continued profitability. Several of these are now familiar: message lights on guest room telephones, taped calls-waiting, information lists on the guest's television, and visual surveillance devices for the corridors and entrances. Other predictions suggested that literal McDonaldization was at least a conceptual possibility. Tabler forecast, for example, "kitchen conveyor belts carrying complete pre-frozen dishes under special quick-heating warmers out to waiters." Guests would not only eat the plasticized, but sleep on the throwaway. "Disposable items—towels, sheets, pillowcases, dishes and glasses—will further reduce the service of the traditional hotel. They must all be of acceptable quality (the airlines have shown the way here), of course, but they can help considerably in the relief of labor pressures."[97] Hotel space, like domestic space, was increasingly filled with the disposable as a response to the increasing cost of labor.[98]

Tabler's articles represent an essentially Modernist view of building. In Tabler's assessment of the hotel, technology not only eliminates human presence, it also displaces architecture. "Some day the weary traveler may be able to drive directly to his tower-floor bedroom, take his own ice cubes out of a refrigerator without waiting half an hour for room service, recline on a mattress adjustable to hard, medium or soft, in front of a radio-television screen that can also be turned on by the front desk to warn him of anything from an air raid to a noisy party. . . . Lounges in new hotels are being tucked off to the side out of the way of elevators and front desk, and reduced in size to discourage free-loaders from the street. Soon there may be no free seats at all."[99] Efficiency not only precluded the worker, but also excluded the public. The greater openness promised by Modernity was visual only, not social.

Statler Hotels, established through individual enterprise, was a public corporation by the second decade of the twentieth century and one of the first great corporate hotel chains.[100] In 1954 Statler was absorbed by Hilton. Hilton thereby became the largest hotel chain in the world, controlling some 37,000 rooms.[101] Tabler, who had worked for the Statler Corporation, became a significant figure in the Hilton Corporation. He contributed to the purest example of the American Modern hotel, the Beverly Hilton, which superseded the Los Angeles Statler Center in a mere five years (figs. 84 and 85). An article in *Architectural Forum* celebrating the hotel's opening was aptly titled "Motel in Cinemascope."[102] It described the hotel as having 450 super deluxe rooms, one thousand parking spaces, and 100,000 square feet of shops. Further:

84. Los Angeles, Beverly Hilton, at the juncture of Santa Monica and Wilshire Boulevards, view from the east. Photo by author.

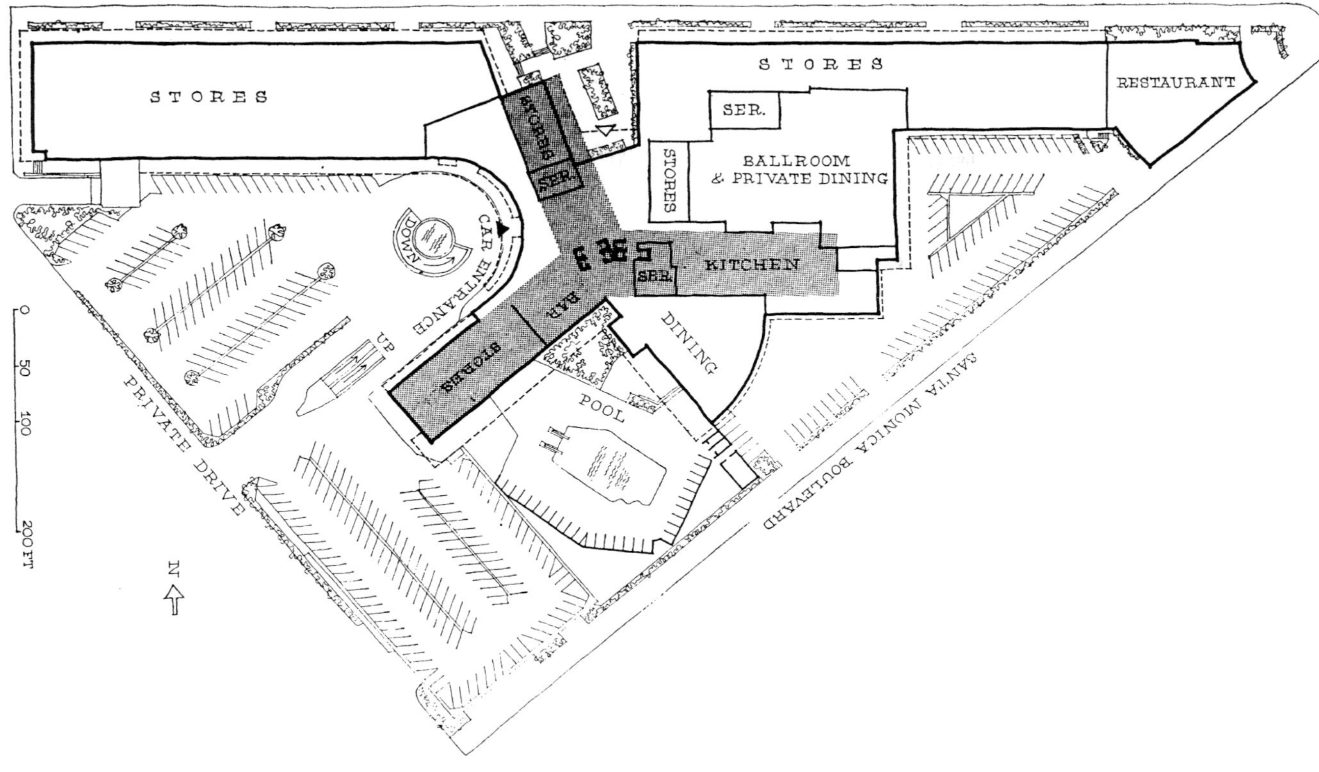

85. Los Angeles, Beverly Hilton, plan. Modified from *Architectural Forum* 104 (1956).

> There are six restaurants and bars, ranging from an English pub in the basement to a gourmet's paradise on the roof, plus banquet rooms freely derived from Versailles, Oslo, the Caribbean, the Mediterranean and the Bosphorus. In back, the customary palm trees and bathing girls adorn the customary king-size, free-form pool nestled in a rainbow of *cabanas*. A press agent summed it up: 'The queen of the Hilton Empire . . . the most beautiful hotel on earth.' A week-long, $500,000 coronation was held, with more than the customary number of searchlights, aquacades, blimps, rose petals and girls on technicolor elephants.[103]

Richard Nixon, then vice president of the United States, cut the ribbon marking the opening of the hotel. The gala was well attended by foreign diplomats as well as local movie stars. The "queen of the Hilton Empire" was adorned with spaces named for Hilton's international far-flung territories.

The Beverly Hilton was designed by Welton Becket and Associates, with William B. Tabler again acting as a consultant. Gone was the stone facing. The steel-frame structure had a stucco skin painted white with particolored partitions between the balconies. The Beverly Hilton was the sole occupant of a large triangular block formed by the juncture of Santa Monica and Wilshire Boulevards. The bar at one side of the lobby was surrounded with shops. Boutiques and airline offices also lined the Wilshire Boulevard face of the building. Slender white pilotis supported the arcades on the shop side and at the main entrance to the building. It had a grand ballroom with an automated floor that could rise, fall, or slide away to reveal a skating rink. The stage, it is said, originally had a monumental, backlit mosaic on a

Christian theme, which was soon walled over. Darnoc, "Conrad" spelled backward, was a liquor produced by Hilton to serve to special guests. The coffee shop on the lower level had "its own view of the Esther Williams Swim Club." At the time of its construction, the eight-story hotel was the tallest building in Beverly Hills. When it was first built, it was possible to see the Pacific Ocean to the west; on smogless days it is still just possible to make out the famous Hollywood sign against the Hollywood Hills to the northeast. But there never was a very meaningful vista. The panorama from L'Escoffier, the roof restaurant, was described in *Architectural Forum* as an "unmatched view of movie studios, oil wells and general suburban sprawl" (fig. 86).[104] Nevertheless, each room of the broad V-shaped guest block had its own balcony. The hotel constructed a gaze without an object. The balcony performed other functions. It might be argued that the balcony advertised a privacy so complete that it included exterior space. But the balcony also prefigured the public display of the guest to those outside. Balconies, in any case, promised an opulence of individual experience at the same time that they marked its repetitive identity.

86. Los Angeles, Beverly Hilton, view of L'Escoffier, the hotel's rooftop restaurant. Photo courtesy of Beverly Hilton Archive.

The Beverly Hilton's form was indeed a "motel in cinemascope." Motel Modern raised to the level of an elite urban-resort hotel was introduced into the sprawl of Los Angeles as a site of luxury. The new aesthetic—an aesthetic of efficiency, regularity, and standardization—achieved at the Beverly Hilton what it had already attained in Modern painting: elite status. This authoritative representation of a McDonaldized spatiality as elite was more than the consequence of a genealogy of American hotels. The Beverly Hilton's form depended directly on Hilton's earliest experiment abroad—the Caribe Hilton in Puerto Rico, which opened in 1949 (figs. 87 and 88). The design of the Caribe Hilton was the result of a competition held by Hilton Corporation, as the operating company, and Puerto Rico Industrial Development Company, the hotel's owner. The product was described in an article in *Interiors* entitled "The Caribe Hilton: An Object Lesson in What You Can Do with $7,000,000":

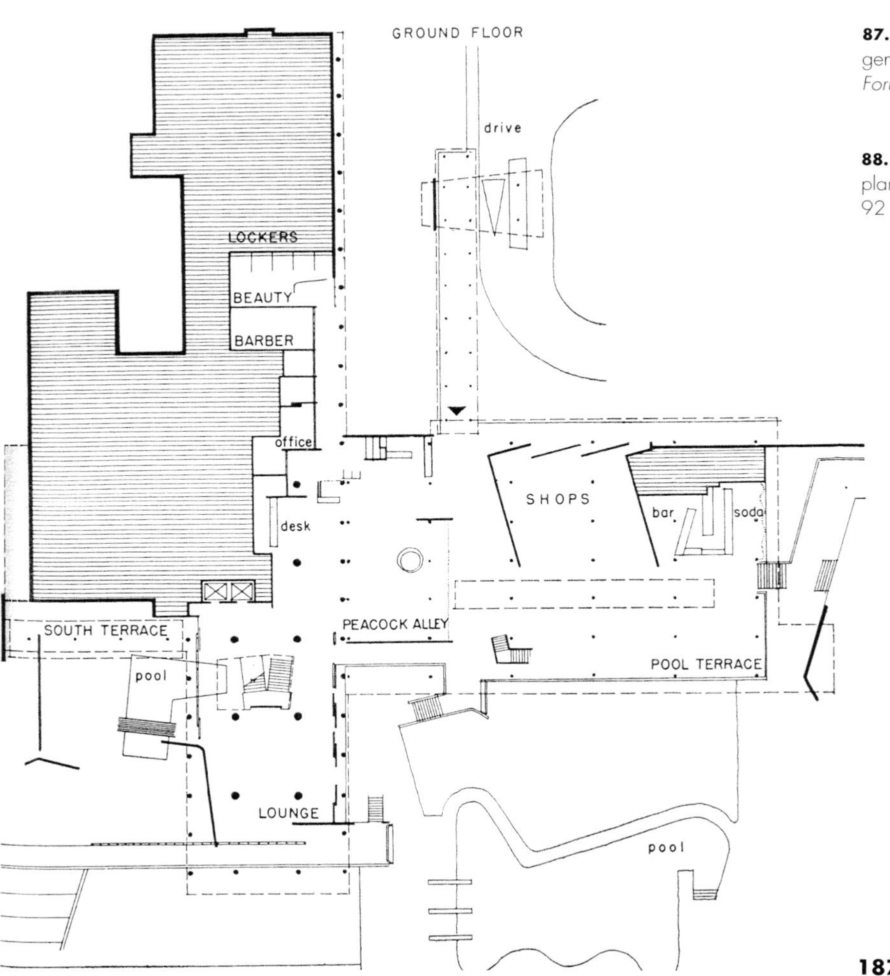

87. San Juan, Puerto Rico, Caribe Hilton, general view. Modified from *Architectural Forum* 92 (1950).

88. San Juan, Puerto Rico, Caribe Hilton, plan. Modified from *Architectural Forum* 92 (1950).

> The Caribe Hilton is a ten-story, air-conditioned, reinforced-concrete building. It was designed by the Puerto Rican architects, Toro, Ferrer, and Torregrosa, whose ideas on the subject were submitted in a competition. Final plans were drawn in collaboration with Warner-Leeds of New York, who designed the interiors and special furnishings, and with Hunter Randolph of Puerto Rico, who did the sumptuous landscaping. The furniture and assorted parts were supplied by Marshall Field and Company and shipped down in ten plane loads. This was the largest peacetime air shipment to a single consignee on record.[105]

Charles Warner and Oswardo Luis Toro had been friends and fellow students together at Columbia University's School of Architecture. Though they had talked about establishing an office together, Toro moved to Puerto Rico. When the Hilton competition was announced, Toro telephoned Warner and asked him to collaborate with him on a design for submission. Their successful entry was constructed in 1949.

The most prominent feature of the Caribe Hilton was its grid of balconies. It was the first major Modern hotel constructed with this external sign of the repetitive luxury of the hotel's interior space. The clear geometry of the balcony grid was dramatically framed and elevated on pilotis. The depth of the grid was activated by the diagonal of each room's outer wall, which optimized the occupants' view of the ocean. The guest room block stood over an expansive, two-story base. The public spaces were treated as unenclosed. "There aren't any doors; the lobby is part of the landscape."[106] "Guests alight from automobiles under [a] canopy. Walking through the open lobby to the registration desk, they shortly see the windswept view of the ocean past [a] sinuous swimming pool."[107] Glass curtain walls were the principle means by which openness was realized, but the asymmetries of the façade and the circulation patterns also made a contribution. Other optical devices contributed to the illusion of spatial freedom: "The lounge also contains one of those details whereby the outdoors is pulled indoors, but it surpasses all others of its kind by the thoroughness with which the joke is carried out. An extension of an outdoor pool flows under a glass wall and into the lobby, where it has a path of stepping stones leading across it to a patio. The bottom of the pool, according to plans, will be kept scrupulously muddy and disreputable, in conformance with the outdoor world it represents."[108] The Caribe Hilton, designed by a team of young, unknown architects, provoked one critic to comment, "This is the kind of hotel which should be built in Florida and California, but never has been."[109]

The spatial imagination of the Caribe Hilton was shared by one other contemporary structure—Edward Stone's El Panama Hotel in Panama City, Panama. In the Tabler tradition, El Panama economized on social space. A commentary on El Panama in *Architectural Forum* notes, "'All that big lobbies are good for,' one hotel planner said recently, 'is to attract old ladies who like to watch the passing parade'": [Stone's hotel was designed to] waste no space on public shelters. To make El Panama's lobby pay for itself, the architects turned the ground floor into one large public space. One part of it is the restaurant; another is the bar; a third is a lounge. None is separated from the other by more than a moveable trellis or a plant box, so that the restaurant, on busy days, can spill over into the lounge; so that the bar rather than the 'big clock' becomes the landmark in the lounge, ticking off profits rather than minutes while people wait to meet their friends."[110] Stone is commonly credited with introducing a Modern openness to the resort hotel. "'I told Frank Lloyd Wright that we had designed a hotel without windows, without doors and without corridors,' says Architect Ed Stone. 'But that was an exaggeration, of course.'"[111] A large part of its openness may be attributed to its "egg-crate brise-soleil" private balconies, another original feature ascribed to Stone.[112] In Stone's architectural résumés, the year listed for El Panama is inevitably 1946.[113] In fact, the hotel was only opened in 1951, two years after the Caribe Hilton. In Talbot Hamlin's magisterial four-volume *Forms and Functions of Twentieth-Century Architecture*, prepared under the auspices of the Columbia University School of Architecture in 1952, the Caribe Hilton was presented as the latest word in hotel construction; the El Panama does not appear.[114] Perhaps El Panama's originary aura proceeded from Stone's prominence in the architectural world. In an article entitled, "Beehive in the Tropics," *Life* magazine gave El Panama a seven-page, full-color spread in 1952.[115] From then on, El Panama was the regarded as the model of the American luxury hotel abroad.[116] Whether the prototypical American space was El Panama or the Caribe Hilton, both are easily distinguished from the first generation of hotels designed by Holabird and Root and Burgee and Associates, and built by Intercontinental in South America.[117] None of these had private balconies, and all had more conventional, formal entrances. They were variations on the Statler Center theme.

The Caribe Hilton was the prototype for the Beverly Hilton, the Istanbul Hilton and the other first-generation Hilton international hotels. It was also the progenitor for Hilton's contractual arrangements with hotel owners in third world countries. Conrad Hilton gives the Caribe Hilton an almost mythological status in his autobiography, *Be My Guest:*

> [I]n 1942, I had dreamed that some day [entering a world-wide stage] might be possible. I had thought then of a quotation I'd read stating that if business didn't cross frontiers, armies would. But it was an unreal, impractical time to pursue such dreams, with frontiers already topsy-turvy and flying armies crossing borders until they hardly seemed to exit at all. . . . Again, on V-J Day, after I had prayed that my generation would be given light and courage to help confirm the peace our sons had won, my mind had toyed with a vision of hotels . . . being used to draw the peoples of the world into closer understanding. . . . The dreaming and praying led to opportunity. A chance now came along to work toward it. Both the State Department and the Department of Commerce suggested that the Hilton organization could make a substantial contribution to the government program of Foreign Aid by establishing American-operated hotels in important world cities. These hotels could stimulate trade and travel, bringing American dollars into the economies of the countries needing help. Besides, and this pleased me especially, they felt that such hotels would create international good will.
>
> Providentially a chance presented itself almost at once for testing the idea and laying out a blueprint which, when it proved itself, we could follow in subsequent operations. The Puerto Rico Industrial Company, a government agency, wrote letters to six or seven American hotel men stating the desire of Puerto Ricans to build a hotel in San Juan with their own capital, providing they could interest an American hotel man in furnishing and operating it. I replied at once in their own graceful Spanish tongue and with all the enthusiasm I felt. However, I expressed my sincere belief that providing the building was not enough. They must also furnish and equip it. Then it would be their hotel. We in turn would provide consultants on architectural design and, dur-

ing building, furnishing and equipping. We would then come in with operating capital, managerial controls and techniques, extensive worldwide advertising, sales promotion and publicity programs, to insure that any hotel in a given area would produce the highest volume of profit. We would operate their hotel under a long-term percentage rental agreement with renewal options, two-thirds of the gross operating profits to go to the owners and one-third to us. We would also hire Puerto Ricans for a large percentage of our staff and work out a program of on-the-job training in our United States hotels where their own people could learn the best we knew in techniques of modern hotel management. . . . [T]hey wrote back at once accepting my terms.[118]

Although he had built hotels in his native Texas, Conrad Hilton established himself as a hotelier of note after the Depression by buying up distinguished older hotels from owners who were without the means to renovate their properties. Curtis O'Keefe, the antagonist of Arthur Hailey's novel, *Hotel*, is a thinly disguised Conrad Hilton:

> "Excuse me, sir, Mr. Curtis O'Keefe?"
>
> The hotelier nodded, with a hovering half smile, his face composed, the same face which beamed benignly from a half-million book jackets of *I Am Your Host*, a copy placed prominently in every hotel room of the O'Keefe chain.[119]

The setting of the novel, the grand St. Gregory Hotel, retains the opulent public space of the prewar era. O'Keefe surveys the possibilities of its commoditization:

> In the arcade beneath the lobby he observed a choice area occupied by a florist shop. The rent which the hotel received was probably around three hundred dollars monthly. But the same space, developed imaginatively as a modern cocktail lounge (a river-boat theme!—why not?) might easily gross fifteen thousand dollars in the same period. The florist could be relocated handily. Returning to the lobby, he could see more space that should be put to work. By eliminating part of the existing public area, another half-dozen sales counters—air lines, car rental, tours, jewelry, a drug-store perhaps—could be profitably squeezed in. It would entail a change in character, naturally; the present air of leisurely comfort would have to go, along with the shrubbery and thick pile rugs. But nowadays, brightly lighted lobbies with advertising everywhere you looked were what helped to make hotel balance sheets more cheerful. Another thing: most of the chairs should be taken away. If people wanted to sit down, it was more profitable that they be obliged to do so in one of the hotel's bars or restaurants.[120]

The St. Gregory is saved from O'Keefe at the last minute by an eccentric millionaire, Albert Wells, who predicts postmodernity. "I do know one thing, miss—just like always, the public's going through a fad. Right now they want the slickness 'n the chrome and sameness. But in time they'll get tired and want to come back to older things—like real hospitality and a bit of character and atmosphere; something that's not exactly like they found in fifty other cities 'n can find in fifty more. Only trouble is, by the time they get around to knowing it, most of the good places—including this one maybe—will have gone."[121] Like Conrad Hilton, O'Keefe buys hotels in the United States and builds them abroad: "Curtis O'Keefe had never understood the point, which his critics made, that it was possible to travel around the world, staying at O'Keefe Hotels without ever leaving the U.S.A.

Despite his attachment to foreign travel, he liked familiar things about him—American décor, with only minor concessions to local color; American plumbing; American food and most of the time—American people. O'Keefe establishments provided them all."[122] In the novel, the traditional values associated with individualism—acted out in the refined desires of the consumer and acknowledged by the manager—are coded in the spatial opulence of the St. Gregory. In contrast, the Modernity of the O'Keefe hotel represents the corporate uniformity that is expected by its banal patrons. And it makes a greater profit for its owner. But the novel itself is Modern. It is a literary soap opera. Despite the narrative importance of the space of the St. Gregory, it remains underdescribed and therefore unimaginable. The St. Gregory has a transparency that is, in the text, ascribed to O'Keefe's hotels. The thick space of Henry James, like the thick space of the prewar hotel, is absent.

Architectures of tourism.

In 1950 an article in the *New York Times* commented on the Modernity of the Caribe Hilton and other international hotels under construction by American hotel chains:

> Hotel building on a world-wide scale is accelerating rapidly to meet the pressing demands of air travel and the new big business of tourism. And this increasing hotel construction is giving modern architecture a powerful stimulus. . . . These hotels are being built in the modern style not because of any altruistic esthetic interest on the part of management but because acceptance of modern architecture is good, hard-headed business. It means an absolute minimum of unproductive space (the presence of which can wreck a hotel's profit); economy deriving from efficient planning of service areas; neat, attractive interiors which can be easily maintained. . . . Hotels have to meet the requirements of the businessman or stopover traveler, interested in quick laundry and valet service, and simultaneously fill the vacationist's desire for days of lolling relaxation and nights with diverting entertainment.
>
> Modern architecture is oriented to the human scale. There is no attempt to impress with grandiose effects or to awe with ostentatious display. Ceilings are brought to comfortable, rather than soaring, levels (an economical as well as psychological change.) There is luxury without pretentiousness. . . . Elaborate columns, gilt swags, heavy draperies, are out—the direct beauty of materials is played up. In guestrooms fussy wallpapers, chintzy chairs, Louis Quinze desks, gloomy rugs and dark woods give way to walls of clear color. . . . Balconies, private terraces, outdoor dining and dancing areas, swimming pools with adjacent bars for food and drink are becoming standard wherever climate permits—and everywhere buildings are oriented and opened out to give the tourist the most desirable and spectacular view.[123]

The author misidentifies the aesthetic imperative of touristic architecture as purely functionalist. The simple forms of the space and the transparency of their effect expressed a new aesthetic that had its equivalent in the modified tourist of the fifties. Postwar touristic practices, like the spaces in which they were accommodated, were distinctly Modern.

The popular definition of tourism has remained relatively stable. At least since the eighteenth century, tourism has been that which travelers other than oneself do.[124] As Goethe wrote with disdain in 1787: "To acquire an intimate knowledge of Rome, its atmosphere, its art, and to feel natural and at home, one must do as I am doing, live here and walk about the city day after day. The impressions of a mere tourist are bound to be false."[125] Tourists are those who inhibit your access to authenticity at the same time that they are unable to recognize it. Recently, an American colleague of mine in Rome commented to me, "I wouldn't mind so much that tourists get in the way if they would only see what they looked at."

Although the contemptuous conception of the tourist has persisted, the practices of tourism have shifted dramatically. Leisure travel before the late eighteenth century was undertaken by a small elite; its purpose was literary in character and self-improving in intention.[126] From the mid-nineteenth century, leisure travel was transformed. New modes of transport introduced by industrialization were sold in bulk to those who had already profited from industrialization. The well-to-do or aristocratic, private leisure excursion was superseded by the well-enough-to-do, private, semiprivate, or group tour. The territory of leisure travel expanded along with the colonial power and military authority of England, France, and Germany first into the Near East and then beyond. For Europeans, America was also an exotic destination; conversely, for Americans, northwest Europe was a primary site for experiencing difference. In the late nineteenth century, Thomas Cook and Son pioneered the package tour.[127] Cooks provided their tourists with both transportation and accommodation. The successful promotion of travel as pleasure produced the first generation of Western European hotels in Mediterranean and Middle Eastern territories—hotels like the Pera Palas in Istanbul and Shepheard's in Cairo. Travel was increasingly routinized; tourism from the turn of the century through the 1920s was an extension of Fordist space. Package tours and guidebooks manifest the systematization of travel.

The guidebook standardized the narrative for group travel. Its archetype was the *Baedeker*.[128] In E. M. Forster's *Room with a View*, first published in 1908, the heroine, Lucy Honeychurch, finds herself confronting a great church in Florence without her *Baedeker*: "Tears of indignation came to Lucy's eyes—partly because Miss Lavish had jilted her, partly because she had taken her *Baedeker*. How could she find her way home? How could she find her way about in Santa Croce? . . . A few minutes ago she had been all high spirits, talking as a woman of culture and half persuading herself that she was full of originality. Now she entered the church depressed and humiliated, not even able to remember whether it was built by the Franciscans or Dominicans."[129] This passage identifies two stable features of travel narration in the form of a guidebook: our dependence on our guidebooks and our disdain for others who rely on them. A comparison of two Baedeker texts—*Italy: Handbook for Travellers* by K. Baedeker (1877) and *Baedeker's Touring Guide: Italy* (1962)—suggests how radically the narrative of travel changed over nearly a century, as well as how radically it stayed the same.[130] The *Baedeker* of 1877 states its purpose in its preface: "The objects of the Handbook for Italy . . . are to supply the traveler with a few remarks on the progress of civilisation and art among the people he is about to visit, to render him as independent as possible of the services of guides and valets-de-place, to protect him against extortion, and in every way to aid him in deriving enjoyment and instruction from his tour in one of the most fascinating countries in the world."[131] Of this three-volume edition on Italy, 332 pages in a nine-point font in volume 2 are devoted to Rome. There is one map of the city, plans of a dozen buildings, and a fold-out panorama of the city. The volume is prefaced by a very serious 30-page discourse on Roman art by a German professor. The introduction to Rome includes a 15-page history of the city as well as a list of libraries, reading rooms, artists' studios, hotels, and restaurants. Half the inventory of shops are art-related: "Antiquities," "Cameos," "Casts," "Colors and Drawing-Materials," "Copies of Ancient Bronzes and Marbles," "Engravers," and so on. Guiding itself is organized topographically. The tourist is methodically moved through the city and its monuments. The buildings and their treasures are itemized. Over a thousand words are devoted to Sta. Maria Maggiore, for example; the architecture of the monument and its history are described in small print; details and individual objects are enumerated in tiny type.

By 1962, the three volumes on Italy had been reduced to one. The guide begins apologetically: "Our Touring Guide to Italy, of which this is the first edition, is in spite of its new form a real 'Baedeker,' combining the traditional reliability and editorial experience of the century-old firm of Baedeker with the requirements of modern means of travel. . . . To meet the requirements of road users, railway routes have been replaced by a description of roads."[132] The editors also introduce a claim of authoritative objectivity: "All the information supplied in our books is objective and impartial." Rome is done in 26 pages. There is one map and an ornamental sketch as a headpiece. In the little over one page that is devoted to the history of the city, fascism goes unmentioned. The monuments are still deployed as topographical itineraries, but they are selected for a traveler staying only three days in the city. Sta. Maria Maggiore can be seen in five sentences.

As the reorganized *Baedeker* demonstrates, tourism was streamlined in the post–World War II years. Americans, unable to travel for economic reasons during the Depression and for political ones during World War II, inundated Western Europe. New means of transport and new means of financing travel stimulated tourism. In 1955, *Life* reported: "U.S. tourists take off by hundreds of thousands in biggest ever vacation exodus. . . . There are 70 passenger liners plying the Atlantic. . . . Almost all ships have been solidly booked for months. Airlines were reaching an entirely new category of transatlantic traveler with installment travel-now-pay-later plans, and with tours that enabled people to see Europe and get back without taking more than two or three weeks from their jobs."[133] Touristic travel might be likened to the fins of a Cadillac—even excesses become aerodynamic. The plane replaced the ocean liner, the suitcase replaced trunks. After the war the limited vacation time of middle-class travelers combined with their considerable wealth and large numbers contributed to the McDonaldization of travel sometimes labeled leisure migration.[134] Package tours became the most common mode of traveling experience. By the 1980s tourism had become the world's largest nonfood industry, outstripping oil production.[135]

America exported the aesthetic of Modernity to create abroad the demand already felt at home—for a space of transparent pleasure. This was a site of familiar comforts—air-conditioning and swimming pools. It was also the locus from which the alien might be watched as spectacle in a new way—from a distance. The suburban escape from the American city was distinctively rendered as the elevated view of the foreign one. The tourists' destination was changed by Modernity: the safe and distant view, the view from above, was the privileged object of desire. The hotel that both created and best satisfied that desire was the Hilton.

Istanbul Hilton, view from the southeast at night (detail), 1955.

Epilogue

Monopoly is a game of vicious property speculation. Its object is to bankrupt your friends by building hotels and charging exorbitant rents. Park Place and Boardwalk, the most expensive properties on the original Monopoly board, were, indeed, the locations of the great hotels of Atlantic City before World War II. According to Monopoly's corporate Web site, the game has a simple, entrepreneurial origin.[1] It was invented in 1934, deep in the Depression, by an unemployed worker named Charles B. Darrow, in Germantown, Pennsylvania, who was desperate for cash because his wife was pregnant. The tokens were charms from his wife's bracelet.[2] He offered it to Parker Brothers in 1935; it immediately became the best-selling game in America.[3] Darrow, as licensee, became a multimillionaire—a truly Horatio Alger story.[4] An alternative history is offered by Ralph Anspagh, inventor of the game Anti-Monopoly.[5] According to Anspagh, Monopoly originated around 1910 and was played through the 1920s by antimonopolists as a means of ridiculing laissez-faire capitalism. Quaker teachers in Atlantic City, to whom Darrow, a salesman, was introduced by his wife, taught him the game. It was this version that Darrow pirated from the Quakers and presented to Parker Brothers.

Monopoly furnishes a curious analogy to the history that I described in the last chapter. The Anti-Monopoly version of the historical narrative allows the game's origins to be identified with the frenzy of land speculation in the United States at the beginning of the century and of hotel building in the 1920s. Its early commercial popularity coincided with widespread hotel bankruptcies in the 1930s. The urban space of the game is a space without airports, only railroad stations; it is a space in which churches, universities, and sports are not yet commoditized. The board retained its original integrity through the 1950s; in the 1960s it began to be marketed abroad. Like *Reader's Digest*, Donald Duck, and Hilton International Hotels, Monopoly helped naturalize American capitalist practices in foreign cultures.[6]

Monopoly's evolution in the 1980s and 1990s suggests the effects of postmodernity. Universities, sports, and even religion have been colonized by the game. The space of Atlantic City has been replaced with that of any one of seventy-eight American college campuses. Sports, in Monopoly as in real life, have also been commoditized. There are NFL, World Cup and Nascar versions of Monopoly. You can also play the Christian game, Bibleopoly.[7] Postmodern nostalgia, the desire to retrieve the felt authenticity of earlier experience, is exploited by the Heritage version of the classic Monopoly game, available for only $105. Postmodern anxiety about the loss of community is addressed by producing game boards with local addresses. The consumer may chose from any one of thirty cities or six states. The elimination of a real topography is completed in the transference of the game to an electronic format. Monopoly can be found in video forms and on the Web. The corporation itself, like the games it produces, has lost its traditional site. In 1968 Parker Brothers became a wholly owned subsidiary of General Mills Corporation, a corporation recognized for its food products, not its toys. Since 1991 Parker Brothers has been a division of Hasbro, Inc. Parker Brothers has lost its identity in a global market. The same thing has happened to Hilton International.

In 1967 Hilton International was sold to Trans World Airlines. In 1988 Hilton International was bought by a British firm, the Ladbroke Group, best known for its interests in gambling. The older staff members of Hilton International hotels consistently name this corporate shift as the loss of family. A longtime employee at the Nile Hilton commented:

> In the old days the Hilton was a family. Now it is different. Now young people graduate from university and they immediately want to be general managers. They want to take everything and to give nothing. When I was an assistant manager, I did not dare pass through the lobby. Now everyone goes through the lobby. We were prompt and we were loyal. I received many offers, but I refused them. It is easy to read books, but it is hard to live through experience. I have attended more than nineteen courses while I have worked here, to keep my mind developing. I have been to seminars in the United States, Canada, and Austria. Since Ladbrokes, I have not been to any seminars.[8]

The same sense of loss was conveyed by a member of the staff at the London Hilton:

> In the early years, the discipline of the hotel was very strict; the dress codes were dictated—the correct shoes, the uniforms, no smoking even in the staff canteen. We worked eight-hour shifts, six days a week. But there was great camaraderie; the young people became great friends. There were always parties to go to. And there was tremendous commitment to the hotel. The first manager was Louis Vouille, from a French hotel family. He had a real presence. He was general manager for about fourteen or fifteen years. Every morn-

> ing he walked around the hotel and said good morning to those in every department. One of my fellow-workers, now a part time member of the staff, used to say, "Here comes father.[9]

"Family" here represents Hilton not only as security, nurture, and status, but also as structural clarity, hierarchy, serious training, and discipline. The dissolution of "family" is characterized not only by accusations of younger coworkers' irresponsibility and the company's lack of commitment to their employees, but also by a language of dislocation and directionlessness.

The lament over the erosion of family values is both overly familiar and ideologically suspect. But the pervasiveness and the politics of the sense of personal loss have a powerful spatial equivalent. American Modernity of the 1950s and early 1960s constructed Hilton International hotels as superior expressions of rationality and order. Hilton's Modernity was most readily identified in its material forms—the low ceilings and plate glass, the simple lines of Danish-American furniture (made in England), the thematized abstraction of the decorative panels in the guest rooms, the nonfigural sculpture by well-known local artists. These formal features were only some of the more obvious effects of the dazzling standardization of the object of desire that radically changed American society from the end of the forties through the fifties. Hilton contributed to that Modernity by giving it an elite form. Like abstract expressionism, Hilton hotels refined the elementary and the efficient and sold it to the highest echelons of society. Hilton made less more costly than more. The clarity and transparency of the building, its efficient plan and manifest structure gave spatial utterance to the supple forms of American entrepreneurial expansion.

Domestic Hiltons of the 1950s contributed to the remodeling of American cities. Along with corporate structures—great icons like Lever House and the Seagram Building—the reconceived hotel fostered the American acceptance of Modernism as an elite aesthetic. That aesthetic provided the rationale for the transformation of the American urban landscape in the 1950s and 1960s. But the Hilton's most dramatic effect was abroad. International Hiltons introduced American Modernity into the fabric of many of the major cities of the world. The new Hiltons in Istanbul, Cairo, and Athens were unprecedented. They were dominant in their siting, scale, and whiteness and extraordinary in their Modernity. Like the grand hotels of the nineteenth century, the Hiltons occupied the most prestigious sites in the city. But in contrast to their predecessors, the status and meaning of the neighborhood often followed from the hotel's construction. Instead of fitting into an assemblage of deluxe structures as had the earlier grand hotels, the Hilton represented a dazzling intervention in the landscape.

Conrad Hilton's political project depended on his hotels' effective representation of Modernity. The Modernity of the Hilton spatialized American notions of a well-trained, well-disciplined workforce that employed the most efficient mechanisms to serve the traveler. That traveler increasingly cared less about the quaint peculiarites of the accommodation than about its modern comforts and conveniences. In the 1950s and 1960s, the Modernity of the Hilton dramatically inscribed the cities in which they were built with a monumental sign of an anticommunist, capitalist America. For their local investors and even for some part of the local populations, the Hilton hotel promised participation in an affluent postcolonial Western economy. The architecture of the Hilton hotels contributed to their utopic force. For Conrad Hilton, these hotels, these "little Americas," promised an excellent profit as well as world peace through the economic suppression of communism. The peace that Conrad Hilton envisioned was that of universal capitalism.

Conrad Hilton's dream came true. It has been named the globalized economy. But globalized capitalism has its own architectural forms. These forms are most famously rendered in Las Vegas and Disneyworld, but most familiarly found in the local supermall and up-market suburb. These forms—pastiches of historical motifs and high technology—have been adeptly described by Fredric Jameson and others. Classical complexities of pleasurable perversity constructed of Dryvit and draperies have replaced the cool austerity of Modernism with its dictates of functionalism and truth to materials. The monumental Modernity of the first generation of Hiltons has lost its authority. It no longer bears a utopic meaning. To remain fashionable, Hilton International remodels.

The Istanbul Hilton is symptomatic. The remarkable site occupied by the Hilton and its unrivaled grounds has helped the hotel sustain its privileged place among the city's hotels. Further, the exterior remains relatively intact. The owner's anxiety about the hotel's currency has been played out in its interior. The Modern, which Hilton introduced as elite form, has become the city's crude vernacular. In consequence, the hotel has been remodeled in an effort to distinguish the Hilton from that which it popularized. The Modernity of the interior is purged (figs. 14 and 15). The Klee-like fountain in the atrium has been replaced with a pseudo-Japanese garden. No ceiling goes unadorned. Elaborate plaster mouldings are everywhere. The simple domes of the reception and the atrium have been elaborated with painted floral decor. The great transverse lobby is now divided into three bays by dropped ceilings with pseudo-stucco ornament, marble parapets, and *mashrabiyyah* screens. The clear glazing of its clerestory has been replaced with ornate stained glass in heavy wooden frames. Neo-Victorian armchairs and couches in saturated brocades have replaced the spare forms and natural colors of the original furnishings. There are large ornamental jars, multiple oriental carpets, and potted palms. The Turkish tiles are almost all gone. If there is a theme, it is vaguely late-Ottoman-European-colonial. Most critically, as the patron enters the lobby, there is no unobstructed view east. The transparent space of Bunshaft's Modernity has been converted to the faux intimacy of the postmodern.[10]

The consistent Modernity of the original Hiltons elicited complaints of the "predictable Hiltons around the world."[11] In the fifties and sixties, however, that predictability was remarkably different. Modernity distinguished the Hilton from its local setting and gave the hotel its political force and ideological content. The loss of Modernity through the embrace of the new eclecticism of the postmodern is an index of Hilton International's loss of identity. These hotels no longer represent the technological sophistication and economic power of America. They are owned by a British betting firm and they mask their technologies with ornamental swags and mahogany ionic columns. The changed space of the hotel materially articulates the changed structure of the lives of both those who labor in it and those who play there. The felt loss of authenticity and order—of "family"—is a spatial gap that is unfilled by the pleasure of unequivocal imitation and the excitement of apparent luxury.[12] But the cold war is over. The political message, like the architecture of a building, is no longer clear.

Historiographic Excursus and Bibliographic Note

My discussion of Hilton International Hotels does not fit neatly within any of the disciplinary subgenres of hotel history. It is certainly not a biography of Conrad Hilton. Conrad Hilton already has a biography by Whitney Bolton, *The Silver Spade: The Conrad Hilton Story*, with a foreword by Conrad Hilton (New York: Farrar, Straus and Young, 1954). Conrad Hilton's own remarkable autobiography, *Be My Guest* (1957; Englewood Cliffs, N.J.: Prentice-Hall, 1987), compensates for Bolton's lack of critical analysis, providing remarkable insights into the subject's activities and motivations. A copy of this autobiography was once standard equipment in a Hilton hotel guest room, always placed on the bedside table along with the King James version of the Bible. Both official and unofficial biographies of hotelmen tend, in any case, to be encomiastic. Among the better examples of the genre are Michael Bird's *Samuel Shepheard of Cairo* (London: Michael Joseph, 1957), Rufus Jarman's *A Bed for the Night: The Story of the Wheeling Bellboy E. M. Statler and His Remarkable Hotels* (New York: Harper, 1952), and Robert O'Brien's *Marriott: The J. Willard Marriott Story* (Salt Lake City, Utah: Deseret Book Co., 1977).

This text is also not a conventional history of a hotel. Most hotel histories are narrativized guest registers with a little institutional information thrown in. In such works, the aura of rich and famous patrons veil the building and its workers. The Waldorf-Astoria has had several biographies, including Edward Hungerford's *Story of the Waldorf* (New York: G. P. Putnam's Sons, 1925) and Horace Sutton's *Confessions of a Grand Hotel: The Waldorf-Astoria* (New York: Henry Holt, 1953). Other examples of the genre, such as Hedda Adlon's *Hotel Adlon: The Life and Death of a Great Hotel*, transl. Norman Denny (London: Barrie Books, 1958), Stanley Jackson's *The Savoy: The Romance of a Great Hotel* (London: Frederick Muller Ltd., 1964), and Nina Nelson's *Shepheard's Hotel* (New York: Macmillan, 1960), are characteristically devoted to the hotel's owners or their famous patrons and the great affairs that they occasioned.

Even those volumes that treat hotels more broadly tend to depreciate architecture in their texts, if not in their plates. The lavishly produced volume by Jean d'Ormesson, David Watkin, Hugh Montgomery-Massingberd, Pierre-Jean Rémy, and Frédéric Grendel, *Grand Hotel: The Golden Age of*

Palace Hotels, an Architectural and Social History (New York: Vendome Press, 1984) is, despite its title, almost exclusively about the exclusiveness of the grand hotel's clientele. David Watkin's brief essay in the volume, "The Grand Hotel Style," 13–25, does provide a summary of the architectural history of hotels. But as Jean d'Ormesson makes clear in the book's introduction, the status of the grand hotel does not depend on architecture. "Every grand hotel has its legend, and that is what makes its heart beat and gives the place its identity. . . . The legends on which grand hotels throve belong . . . to the vestiges of Atlantis, that vanished continent formerly known as *society*. Snobbery, needless to say, is no stranger to the world of grand hotels" (8).

Other works of this particular genre appeal to their audience's desire for gilt by association. Willi Frischauer's *An Hotel Is Like a Woman: The Grand Hotels of Europe* (London: Leslie Frewin, 1965) is as much an expression of his own status as a longtime guest of the grand hotel as about the beautiful people whose lives he recounts. The hotels he selects are exclusively European. They were all opened between 1870 and 1910 and nearly half were established in preexisting mansions or palaces. Those located in countries occupied by Axis powers during World War II all served as local Nazi headquarters. His suggestive title is indicative of his treatment of his favorite hotels as great ladies. Such books provide considerable factual information. By the assumptions and exclusions of their authors, they also allow insight into spatial practices of the elite. In my book, the distinguished guest makes no personal appearance.

Another, much smaller genre of hotel writing treats the hotel's architectural history. The best introduction to hotels as a particular kind of structure is a chapter on hotels in Nikolaus Pevsner's *A History of Building Types*, Bollingen series 3519 (Princeton, N.J.: Princeton University Press, 1976), 169–92. Pevsner's volume seems to be arranged according to the building type's cultural status. The first chapters treat national monuments and government buildings, the last two present shops and factories. His chapter on hotels comes late in the volume; it is appropriately located between "Prisons" and "Exchanges and Banks." His survey of the hotel moves masterfully from the inns of the late middle ages to Butlin's Holiday Camp at Minehead in the 1970s, charting functional changes in the plan and ordering the styles of the superstructure. It treats the evolution of form. An earlier essay of the same sort, written by John Wellborn Root, appeared in volume 3 (96–130) in a 4-volume work entitled *Forms and Functions of Twentieth-Century Architecture*, edited by Talbot Hamlin (New York: Columbia University Press, 1952). This piece, which ends with the Caribe Hilton, is useful not only as a discussion of the architectural development of hotels but also as a primary source.

Although the style of Hilton hotels is assessed in my book, form is not considered independently of its social consequences. My interest in the institutional and economic implications of the Hilton associates this work more closely with a few older hotel histories, such as Jefferson Williamson's classic, *The American Hotel: An Anecdotal History* (New York: A. A. Knopf, 1930), and Friedrich Rauers, *Kulturgeschichte der Gaststätte* (Berlin: Metzner, 1942). These very useful books are not, however, seriously concerned with the architectural effects—material and political—on the urban landscape. Those effects form the core of my volume.

Authors in several disciplines provide models for how buildings—if not hotels—express political or economic aggression: urban critics like Michel de Certeau, *The Practice of Everyday Life* (Berkeley: University of California

Press, 1984), M. Christine Boyer, *The City of Collective Memory: Its Historical Imagery and Architectural Entertainments* (Cambridge: MIT Press, 1994), and Mike Davis, *City of Quartz: Excavating the Future of Los Angeles* (New York: Verso, 1990), and his *Ecology of Fear: Los Angeles and the Imagination of Disaster* (New York: Metropolitan Books, 1998); social geographers like David Harvey, *The Condition of Postmodernity: An Enquiry into the Origins of Cultural Change* (Oxford: Basil Blackwell, 1989); materialist sociologists like Henri Lefebvre, *The Social Production of Space*, transl. Donald Nicholson-Smith (Oxford: Basil Blackwell, 1991), and his *Writings on Cities*, transl. and ed. Eleonore Kofman and Elizabeth Lebas (Oxford: Basil Blackwell, 1996); and cultural commentators like Jürgen Habermas, *The Structural Transformation of the Public Sphere*, transl. Thomas Burger (Cambridge: MIT Press, 1989), and Fredric Jameson, *Postmodernism, or The Cultural Logic of Late Capitalism* (Durham, N.C.: Duke University Press, 1990). I also hope that the impulses of classic works by Michel Foucault, such as *Discipline and Punish: The Birth of the Prison*, transl. A. Sheridan (New York: Random House, 1979), and Walter Benjamin, *The Arcades Project* (Cambridge, Mass.: Harvard University Press, 1999), are apparent in the text.

Notes

Notes to the Introduction

The epigraphs are taken from Conrad N. Hilton, *Be My Guest* (1957; Englewood Cliffs, N.J.: Prentice-Hall, 1987), 265, and V. N. Volosinov, *Marxism and the Philosophy of Language*, transl. Ladislav Matejka and I. R. Titunik (1929; Cambridge, Mass.: Harvard University Press, 1986), 13. Hilton's autobiography, first published in the 1960s, continued to appear in new editions. Quoted throughout is the 1987 edition.

I am grateful to Nicole Epstein for her critical reading of the preface.

1. For brief corporate histories of Hilton, see Daniel R. Lee, "How They Started: The Growth of Four Hotel Giants," *Cornell Hotel and Restaurant Administration Quarterly* (May 1985): 22–32, and Carol I. Keeley, "Hilton Hotels Corporation," in *International Directory of Company Histories*, ed. Tina Grant (Detroit: St. James Press, 1998), 19:205–9.

2. In his autobiography, Hilton represents himself as a hotel gigolo. His description of his desire for the Sir Francis Drake in San Francisco is characteristic: "The Sir Francis Drake was 'right.' Twenty-two stories at Powell and Sutter Streets . . . and a reputation for elegance and taste. While I had loved my dowagers, gotten tremendous satisfaction from building my own dream girls, this was like marrying into the social register. This lady had a family tree. What would have been a hopeless courtship before the depression turned now into a possibility. As a matter of fact, when I went wooing, the Hucking-Newcomb Hotel Company, which owned the property, treated me as if I had come to take an elder spinster daughter without a dowry off their hands." Hilton, *Be My Guest*, 179.

3. Caribe Hilton, San Juan, Puerto Rico, 1949; Istanbul Hilton, 1955; Continental Hilton, Mexico City, 1956; Berlin Hilton, 1958; Habana Hilton, 1958; Trinadad Hilton, Port of Spain, 1960; Royal Hilton, Teheran, 1963; Cavalieri Hilton, Rome, 1963; London Hilton, 1963; Hong Kong Hilton, 1963; Rotterdam Hilton, 1963; Amsterdam Hilton, 1963; Athens Hilton, 1964; Tunis Hilton, 1965; Tel Aviv Hilton, 1966; Paris Hilton, 1966; Barbados Hilton, Bridgetown, 1966. There were other Hiltons in these years. For example, the Madrid Hilton, the first Hilton in Europe, was opened in 1953, but it was not designed under Hilton direction; the Queen Elizabeth in Montreal, opened in 1958, though managed by Hilton, had been built by the Canadian National Railway; similarly, Hilton took over the management of the El Panama in Panama City soon after its construction.

4. A great deal has been written about the cold war. A good introduction with bibliography is Walter L. Hixson, *Parting the Curtain: Propaganda, Culture and the Cold War, 1945–1961* (New York: St. Martin's, 1997). There are a number of studies that consider the effect of the cold war on a specific genre, such as Woody Haut, *Pulp Culture: Hardboiled Fiction and the Cold War* (London: Serpent's Tail, 1995). For art, the most important study remains Serge Guilbaut, *How New York Stole the Idea of Modern Art: Abstract Expressionism, Freedom, and the Cold War*, transl. Arthur Goldhammer

(Chicago: University of Chicago Press, 1983).

5. Reading *Life* magazine from the 1950s provides a sense of how intolerable phenomena were made commonplace. For example, on the domestication of the nuclear holocaust, "Facing the Fallout Problem," *Life*, February 28, 1955, 24–26; "H-Bomb Hideaway: Completely Equipped Family Shelter to Bury in Backyard for $3,000," *Life*, May 23, 1955, 169–70; or best, "H-Bomb Shelter Tests Texas Family: Volunteers Survive Three Damp, Dull Days below Ground," *Life*, July 11, 1955, 69–70. This last shelter was part of a model-home exhibition.

6. David Halberstam, *The Fifties* (New York: Fawcett Columbine, 1993), offers an informative and entertaining introduction to the period from an American perspective.

7. Original *I Love Lucy* shows were produced from October 15, 1951, to September 24, 1961. David Marc and Robert J. Thompson, *Prime Time, Prime Movers: From* I Love Lucy *to* L.A. Law*–America's Greatest TV Shows and the People Who Created Them* (Boston: Little, Brown, 1992), 26–29. The episodes were popular abroad as well as in the United States.

8. A number of important hotels have been omitted. Most notably, the Caribe Hilton, the first of Hilton's enterprises abroad and an important prototype, is relegated to a small part of the final chapter. The recent thorough reconstruction of the hotel meant two things. First, I could not visit the site before the hotel reopened at the end of 1999 (and it is against the principles of architectural historians to write at any length on a building that has not been experienced). Second, now that the work is completed, the hotel is so changed that it would offer little understanding of the original. Other Hiltons, like the Habana Hilton (1958) and the Teheran Hilton (1963), are also absent from this study because of present political difficulties of access.

9. These eight hotels also marked cities that I either know reasonably well or felt that I should know reasonably well.

10. American Modern was also the form followed in the concurrent proliferation of American embassies and consulates. Lois Craig and the Staff of the Federal Project, *The Federal Presence: Architecture, Politics, and Symbols in United States Government Building* (Cambridge: MIT Press, 1978). U.S. embassies are discussed in relation to the Athens and London Hiltons. I use "Modern" with a capital "M" to refer to the dominant set of architectural styles from the Bauhaus and Le Corbusier in the 1920s to the work of architects like Gordon Bunshaft and Phillip Johnson in the 1950s and 1960s. I use "modern" with a lower case "m" in conventional historical periodization. The modern, broadly from the late eighteenth through the sixties of the twentieth century, followed the early modern and preceded the postmodern.

11. When the Habana Hilton opened in 1958, it was identified as the tallest building in all of Central and South America. Michael M. Lefever and Cathleen D. Huck, "The Expropriation of the Habana Hilton: A Timely Reminder," *International Journal of Hospitality Management*, 9 (1990): 15.

12. Michel de Certeau, *The Practice of Everyday Life* (Berkeley: University of California Press, 1984); Mike Davis, *City of Quartz: Excavating the Future of Los Angeles* (New York: Verso, 1990), and *Ecology of Fear: Los Angeles and the Imagination of Disaster* (New York: Metropolitan Books, 1998); David Harvey, *The Condition of Postmodernity: An Enquiry into the Origins of Cultural Change* (Oxford: Basil Blackwell, 1989); Henri Lefebvre, *The Social Production of Space*, transl. Donald Nicholson-Smith (Oxford: Basil Blackwell, 1991), originally published in French as *Production de l'espace* (Paris: Editions Anthropos, 1974), and *Writings on Cities*, transl. and ed. Eleonore Kofman and Elizabeth Lebas (Oxford: Basil Blackwell, 1996). Also see the bibliographic note at the end of the text.

13. Orhan Pamuk, *The Black Book* (New York: Harvest, 1996); Theodor Herzl, *Old New Land*, intro. Jacques Kornberg, transl. Lotta Levensohn (Princeton, N.J.: Markus Wiener Publishers, 1997); Henry James, *Italian Hours* (Hopewell, N.J.: Ecco, 1987); Federico Fellini, dir., *La dolce vita* (1960) and *Roma* (1972).

14. I do not read Arabic or Hebrew. Though I read German, Italian, French, and, painfully, modern Greek, locating sources was difficult. I attempted to find colleagues in each city to contribute assessments of the local reception of Hilton based on local documentation. This proved more difficult than I had initially supposed.

15. In downtown sites, shops had been included on the ground-floor periphery of hotels, just as they were in office buildings. The Palmer House in Chicago provides an

example of this kind of plan. In contrast to the Hilton's international hotels, however, these shops were not integral to the program of the building.

16. The extravagance of glass was particularly salient in the Middle East, where plate glass and its aluminum casing had to be imported.

17. The visibility of the guest was not shared with the staff. Only those with assigned positions in the lobby were ever to appear there.

18. George Bradshaw, "The View from a Tall Glass Oasis: The Subliminal Pleasures of Hilton Hotels," *Vogue* 146 (July 1965): 126.

19. These observations are based on two notebooks in the Conrad N. Hilton College Archives and Library, University of Houston, which document the advertising campaigns for Hilton by Needham and Grohmann. Vol. 1 covers the years 1947–1957; vol. 2 includes the years 1958–1962.

20. The term "commoditization" is discussed at the beginning of chapter 6.

21. A servidor is a refinement of the door from the corridor to the guestroom. It has secondary doors on both sides, thus allowing patrons to hang clothing for dry cleaning or pressing at their convenience in its hollow interior and the valet to remove it from the exterior without disturbing the room's occupants. For a discussion of this and other technologies of service, see chapter 6.

22. In his monograph on McDonald's, John Love makes the unsupportable claim that McDonald's was the first American corporation to sell things abroad. "In 1970, when McDonald's made its first big push abroad, it was indeed treading on foreign soil. Aside from the international oil companies . . . retailing was primarily a native business." *McDonald's: Behind the Arches* (Toronto: Bantam Books, 1986), 417.

23. Derek Howard Aldcroft, *The European Economy, 1914–1970* (New York: St. Martin's, 1978), 144, provides a usable description of the Marshall Plan: "Recognition of the relative ineffectiveness of the relief program [introduced at the end of World War II] was one factor prompting a change in policy in 1947. But the shift was probably conditioned more by the turn of political events, in particular the expansionist policy of the Soviet Union including its hardening line over Germany which eventually culminated in the blockade of Berlin. Fear of social and political disturbances and the threat of communist regimes in the west played no small part in the formation of the new aid program. When the new offer was first announced in June 1947, by Secretary of State George Marshall, it became clear, for political reasons, that it would be confined mainly to western Europe. . . . The funds were to be administered on the US side through the Economic Cooperation Administration, while on the European side 16 nations joined together to form the Organization for European Economic Cooperation (OEEC), which had the tasks of estimating national requirements and dividing the aid among members, while acting as a clearing-house for national economic plans so as to avoid countries working at cross-purposes. The Marshall Plan came into effect in April 1948 and was designed to last for four years, though in actual fact it was merged into the Mutual Defense Assistance program in 1951 after which the emphasis shifted to military rather than economic aid." Counterpart funds, from which support for Hilton sometimes came, are explained by Alec Cairncross, in *Economic Ideas and Government Policy: Contributions to Contemporary Economic History*, Routledge Explorations in Economic History 1 (London: Routledge, 1996), 108–9: "Marshall Aid took the form predominantly of grants but also included loans and 'conditional aid' (i.e. aid provided in support of intra-European trade). Payments for the goods supplied by the United States were paid (in local currency) into a 'counterpart fund' of which the United States kept 5 per cent, nominally to cover administrative costs. The rest could be used for domestic purposes with ECA approval." For a review of the exportation of American management models and technology, see Matthias Kipping and Ove Bjarnar, eds., *The Americanisation of European Business: The Marshall Plan and the Transfer of US Management Models* (London: Routledge, 1998). Among the flurry of fifty-years-later assessments of the Marshall Plan are Albert O. Hirschman, *Crossing Boundaries: Selected Writings* (New York: Zone Books, 1998), which also includes a more personal perspective in the author's "Fifty Years after the Marshall Plan: Two Posthumous Memoirs and Some Personal Recollections," 33–43.

24. Most notably by Serge Guilbaut, *How New York Stole the Idea of Modern Art*. Guilbaut treats painting and to a lesser degree film, particularly in France. He also documents the contemporary opposition to American cultural hegemony, notably from the left in both France and Italy. For a positive treatment of American hegemony, see

Stephen Spender, "We Can Win the Battle for the Mind of Europe," *New York Times Magazine*, April 25, 1948, 15, 31–35.

25. Anonymous, "Architecture for the State Department," *Arts and Architecture* 70 (1953): 16–18. There are also important scholarly treatments of architecture as foreign policy: Craig et al., *The Federal Presence*, esp. chap. 8; and Ron Theodore Robin, *Enclaves of America: The Rhetoric of American Political Architecture Abroad, 1900–1965* (Princeton, N.J.: Princeton University Press, 1992).

26. The still common understanding of ideology as a consciously constructed agenda of political persuasion was popularized in the West during the cold war as a description of Marxism. A second, more sophisticated definition of ideology issues from a Euro-Marxist analysis of Western capitalism: ideology masks inequities in the social order by naturalizing them; ideology is thereby a means by which the order of the status quo is maintained. For the classic formulation, see Karl Marx and Frederick Engels, *The German Ideology*, ed. C. J. Arthur (New York: International Publishers, 1986); also classic are Raymond Williams, "Ideology," in *Marxism and Literature* (New York: Oxford University Press, 1977), 55–71, and more recently, Terry Eagleton, *Ideology: An Introduction* (London: Verso, 1991). I have found the critique of the reification of consciousness and the insistence on the materiality of the sign in the construction of ideology offered by Volosinov, *Marxism and the Philosophy of Language*, extremely useful.

27. The *Economist* expanded on the profit motive. "The fact that American hoteliers' wage bills are much higher (despite lower staff-to-guest ratios) and their average profits correspondingly lower, may account in part for the interest of American hotel chains in Europe." "London's New Hotels," *Economist* 197 (December 3, 1960): 1048.

28 Hilton, *Be My Guest*, 267.

29. Hilton, *Be My Guest*, 237.

30. *Hiltonitems*, "The President's Corner" (July 1955), 3.

31. *Hiltonitems*, "The President's Corner" (May 1958), 1.

32. For the inappropriateness of condescension toward Africans and Asians, see Hilton, *Be My Guest*, 276.

33. Keeley, "Hilton Hotels Corporation," 207.

34. Lawrence M. Hughes, "Hilton's 'Private Statesmanship' Shapes World-Wide Hotel Empire," *Sales Management: The Magazine of Marketing*, October 19, 1956, 39.

35. Fredric Jameson, *Postmodernism, or The Cultural Logic of Late Capitalism* (Durham, N.C.: Duke University Press, 1990). For me, Jameson's account of postmodernity is still the most compelling.

36. Because of the dominance of literary criticism in the field of the postcolonial, materiality is sometimes reduced to an abstraction of language. For example, in Bill Ashcroft, Gareth Griffiths, and Helen Tiffin, *The Post-Colonial Reader* (London: Routledge, 1995), 391: "'[P]lace' in post-colonial societies is a complex interaction of language, history and environment. . . . [It is characterized by a] sense of displacement, of the lack of a 'fit' between language and place. . . . The theory of place does not simply propose a binary separation between the 'place' named and described in language, and some 'real' place inaccessible to it, but rather indicates that in some sense place *is* language."

Notes to Chapter 1

A number of individuals contributed significantly to this chapter. Carol Herselle Krinsky generously shared with me material she had collected for her excellent monograph on Gordon Bunshaft, *Gordon Bunshaft of Skidmore, Owings and Merrill* (New York: Architectural History Foundation, 1988). Those at the Istanbul Hilton who were particularly helpful included Kees Hartzuiker, the general manager of the Istanbul Hilton, Yavuz Erdem, the engineer who has overseen the Istanbul Hilton since its construction, and particularly Ali Kolsal, architect in charge of interior design. I also benefited from a long walk and conversation with an old friend and fellow Byzantinist, Doğan Kuban, whose exceptional knowledge of the city is reflected in his *Istanbul, an Urban History: Byzantion, Constantinopolis, Istanbul* (Istanbul: Economic and Social History Foundation, 1996). I want also to thank Sina Unel, native of Istanbul and author of the off-Broadway play, *Pera Palas*, for his supportive comments on this chapter.

The epigraphs to this chapter are from Le Corbusier (Charles-Edouard Jeanneret), *Journey to the East*, ann. and transl. Ivan Zaknic (Cambridge: MIT Press, 1987), 83–85, and Orhan Pamuk, *The Black Book* (New York: Harvest, 1996), first published as *Kara Kitap* (Istanbul: Can Yayinlavi, 1990), 14–18.

1. Speros Vryonis Jr., "Byzantine Constantinople and Ottoman Istanbul: Evolution in a Millennial Imperial Iconography," in *The Ottoman City and Its Parts: Urban Structure and Social Order*, ed. Irene A. Bierman, Rifa'at A. Abou-el-Haj and Donald Preziosi, Subsidia Balcanica, Islamica et Turcica 3 (New Rochelle, N.Y.: Caratzas, 1991), 13–52.

2. Evliya Çelebi, *Narrative of Travels [Seyahatname]*, transl. Joseph von Hammer (London: Oriental Translation Fund, 1934; reprint, New York: Johnson Reprint Corporation, 1968), 68–69.

3. Le Corbusier, *Journey to the East*, 149–52.

4. John L. Stoddard, *Lectures: Constantinople, Jerusalem, Egypt*, 10 vols. (Chicago: Shuman, 1910), 2:108.

5. For a detailed discussion, with bibliography, of the history and politics of the development of Galata, Pera, and the suburbs north of the Golden Horn, see Stephen T. Rosenthal, *The Politics of Dependency: Urban Reform in Istanbul* (Westport, Conn.: Greenwood Press, 1980); for the architectural expression of this development, see Zeynep Çelik, *The Remaking of Istanbul: Portrait of an Ottoman City in the Nineteenth Century* (Seattle: University of Washington Press, 1986), 31–49.

6. Edwin de Leon, *Thirty Years of My Life on Three Continents* (London: Ward and Downey, 1890), 133.

7. De Leon, *Thirty Years*, 130–31.

8. Published in the official newspaper *Takvim-i Vekayi*, transl. Rosenthal, in *The Politics of Democracy*, 51.

9. For remarkable photographs of Istanbul at the turn of the century, see Diana Barillari, *Istanbul, 1900* (New York: Rizzoli, 1996).

10. Robert Hichens, *The Near East: Dalmatia, Greece and Constantinople* (London: Hodder and Stoughton, 1913), 187–95.

11. Hichens was obsessed with the veil. "Many Turkish women come to the bazaars only to meet their lovers. They cover a secret desire by a pretense of making purchases. . . . I have watched these subtle truants passing in their pretty disguises suggestive of a masked ball. They look delicate and graceful in their thin and shining robes, like dominoes, of black or sometimes of prune-color, with crape dropping over their faces and letting you see not enough. . . . One day I was in the upper room of a photographer's shop when two Turkish women came in and removed their veils, standing with their backs to the English infidel. One was obviously much younger than the other, and seemed to have a beautiful figure. I was gazing at it, perhaps rather steadily, when, evidently aware of my glance, she turned slowly and deliberately round. For two or three minutes she faced me, looking to right and left of me, above me, even on the floor near my feet, with her large and beautiful blue-gray eyes. She was lovely." Hichens, *The Near East*, 206–9. The veil as seduction is a leitmotif in Western travel accounts of the East. Le Corbusier provides an excellent example: "As for the women, I hated them for three weeks not wanting to grant them anything at all! . . . Now it seems to me they are ravishing despite and also because of that second skirt flung over their heads, that makes an impenetrable veil. You will find real coquettes underneath. I bet you, you old bony fakir, that almost all of them are young, adorable, with ivory cheeks a little full and with the innocent eyes of gazelles—delicious! After all, these veils conceal a penetrable mystery." Le Corbusier, *Journey to the East*, 129.

12. Çelik, *The Remaking of Istanbul*, 134–45.

13. The movie, unfortunately, was shot at Burnham Beeches, Buckinghamshire, United Kingdom, rather than the Pera Palas in Istanbul. For a description of the affair, Nathalie de Saint Phalle, *Hôtels littéraires:Voyage autour de la terre* (Paris: Quai Voltaire, 1991), 181–83.

14. Sina Unel, *Pera Palas*. I thank the author again here for reading this chapter.

15. De Saint Phalle, *Hôtels littéraires*, 181–83.

16. Çelik, *The Remaking of Istanbul*, 146.

17. Çelik, *The Remaking of Istanbul*, 102, 144, 146; Kuban, *Istanbul*, 392, 410; Barillari, *Istanbul, 1900*, 19.

18. The announcement that Hilton would build a three-hundred-room hotel in Istanbul appeared in the *New York Times,* April 8, 1951, II 23:4. Construction began the following winter.

19. A description of the gala opening concludes this chapter.

20. "Tourist Hotel for Istanbul, Turkey," *Architectural Record* 113 (January 1953): 103–16; P. R. B., "Hilton Hotel, Istanbul," *Architectural Review* 113 (March 1953): 119–20. "Hôtel à Istambul," *L'architecture d'aujourd'hui* 25 (January–February 1954): 31–33; "Hotel in Istanbul," *Architectural Review* 118 (November 1955): 290–96; "Hilton's Newest Hotel," *Architectural Forum* 103 (December 1955): 120–27; Paul Bonatz, "Hilton-Hotel Istanbul," *Baumeister: Zeitschrift für Baukultur und Bautechnik* 53 (August 1956): 535–51; V. M., "Hotel Hilton, en Estambul," *Informes de la construccion* 9, no. 88 (February 1957): n.p.; *Bauen-Wohnen* (Zurich) 12 (April 1958): 105–40, esp. 119–20; "Hotel Hilton, Istanbul, Turquie," *L'architecture d'aujourd'hui* 26 (September 1961): 64–65. The hotel was also written up by hotel trade journals such as *The Hotel Monthly* 63 (November 1955): 24–27.

21. For an excellent consideration of Bunshaft and a review of the literature, see Krinsky, *Gordon Bunshaft.* Bunshaft had spent two months in Turkey, where he led a fieldwork study that resulted in a major set of recommendations to the Ministry of Public Works: "Tourist Hotel for Istanbul, Turkey," *Architectural Record* 113 (January 1953): 107. For Sedad Eldem, see *Sedad Eldem: Architect in Turkey* (Singapore: Concept Media Pte, 1987), which includes contributions by Hans Hollein, Suha Özhan, Sibel Bozdogan, and Engin Yenal.

22. Nathaniel Alexander Owings, *The Spaces in Between: An Architect's Journey* (Boston: Houghton Mifflin, 1973), 104.

23. Interview with Ali Kolsal at the Istanbul Hilton, November 21, 1997.

24. Interview with Yavuz Erdem at the Istanbul Hilton, November 24, 1997.

25. "Special features relate the hotel to its location. Most important is construction in reinforced concrete, the material of choice in countries lacking substantial steel technology and construction expertise; any steel used at the Hilton was designed with unusual economy." Krinsky, *Gordon Bunshaft,* 54.

26. Ernst Danz, *Architecture of Skidmore, Owings and Merrill,* intro. Henry Russell Hitchcock (New York: Praeger, 1963), 10. If Le Corbusier is considered the touchstone of critical analysis of this building, it might be suggested that the Istanbul Hilton combines the programatic conception of the Unité d'Habitation with the aesthetic sensibility of the Villa Savoye.

27. Peter G. Rowe, *Making a Middle Landscape* (Cambridge: MIT Press, 1991), esp. 93–94; Fred E. H. Schroeder, *Front Yard America: The Evolution and Meanings of a Vernacular Domestic Landscape* (Bowling Green, Ohio: Bowling Green State University Popular Press, 1993), 139–53.

28. Conrad N. Hilton, *Be My Guest* (1957; Englewood Cliffs, N.J.: Prentice-Hall, 1987), 265, as discussed in the introduction.

29. Henry-Russell Hitchcock and Philip Johnson, *The International Style: Architecture Since 1922* (1932; New York: Norton, 1966). The text was written for the Museum of Modern Art in New York as a catalog for the most important early exhibition of European Modern architecture in the United States.

30. Ada Louise Huxtable, "A Personal Inquiry," *Istanbul Hilton Magazine* 1 (fall 1970): 1.

31. James P. O'Donnell, "Istanbul," *Saturday Evening Post,* November 3, 1956, 104, refers to the marquee as a "potato chip caught in a high wind."

32. Hilton, *Be My Guest,* 264–65.

33. Seena Hamilton, "Hilton's International Expansion: Instrument in World Development," *Hotel Gazette,* March 1, 1958, 17.

34. "Hilton's Newest Hotel," *Architectural Forum* 103 (December 1955): 123.

35. "Americans See 'New Woman' in Turkey," clipping in from the *Chicago Tribune Magazine* (n.d.), Conrad N. Hilton College Archives and Library, University of Houston (hereafter Hilton Archives).

36. Mubin Manyasig, *Hiltonitems,* October 1955, 9.

37. Cathleen Baird Huck [Cathleen D. Baird], "Egypt's Modern Hotels: From the Historic Shepheard's to the Nile Hilton" (master's thesis, University of Houston,

1994), 84, goes so far as to suggest that the Hilton's "early preservation efforts of classical culinary traditions in Egypt and Turkey" provided a new status to foods that might otherwise had been lost through neglect.

38. O'Donnell, "Istanbul," 104.

39. For further discussion of the commoditization of space, see chapter 6.

40. George McGhee, former U.S. ambassador to Turkey, provides an American perspective on this and other aspects of Turkish politics affecting relations between the two countries: *The US-Turkish-NATO Middle East Connection: How the Truman Doctrine Contained the Soviets in the Middle East* (New York: St. Martin's, 1990), 163–65.

41. The *Hilton Hotels Around-the-World Travel Guide* promotes the great bazaar in Istanbul as a major tourist attraction. It then adds, "Fascinating as the Bazaar is, you might enjoy the convenience of shopping right at your hotel." Richard Joseph, *Hilton Hotels Around-the-World Travel Guide*, foreword by Conrad N. Hilton (Garden City, N.Y.: Doubleday, 1966), 35.

42. For the development of an aesthetic of efficiency, see chapter 6.

43. Rufus Jarman, *A Bed for the Night: The Story of the Wheeling Bellboy E. M. Statler and His Remarkable Hotels* (New York: Harper, 1952), 8.

44. *New York Times*, January 3, 1954, II 19:1.

45. *Hiltonitems*, July 1955, 5.

46. *Hiltonitems*, July 1955, 5.

47. For travelers' descriptions of the paradigmatic terrace of Shepheard's Hotel in Cairo, see chapter 2.

48. "Cet hôtel sera le plus haut bâtiment d'Istambul. Il est appelé à devenir un centre de grande activité, tant en ce qui concerne la diplomatie que le tourisme et le commerce." "Hôtel à Istambul," *L'Architecture d'aujourd'hui* 25 (January–February 1954): 30–31. Or again, "The hotel is situated in beautiful Belleview Park on a high promontory overlooking the 25-mile-long Bosphorus Strait. . . . The eleven-story edifice, highest in this ageless city of mosques and minarets, will be operated by Hilton Hotels International, Inc., under a lease with the Turkish Republic Pension Fund." *Hiltonitems*, July 1955, 3.

49. "Tourist Hotel for Istanbul, Turkey," *Architectural Record* 113 (January 1953): 107. The italics are mine.

50. Hilton, *Be My Guest*, 264.

51. On October 21, 1997, I wrote the following to the editor of the *New York Times*: "In doing research on the early Hilton International Hotels of the 1950s and 1960s, I encountered the following statement of fact in the *New York Times*, November 4, 1951, II 17:8: 'The Istanbul Hilton, to rise in a park overlooking the Bosphorus, within ten miles from the Russian border, will be operated by Hilton Hotels International, Inc. . . . ' Looking at a map, it seems to me that the closest Soviet land mass to Istanbul—the Crimea—is over three hundred miles away. Before I use this apparent misstatement in a discussion of the ideological construction of geography, I thought that I should check with the editorial staff of the *Times*." I have never received a reply.

52. John W. Houser, letter to Conrad N. Hilton, August 27, 1950, Hilton Archives.

53. Robert Gandt, *Skygods: The Fall of Pan Am* (New York: William Morrow, 1995), details government involvement in the airline industry but does not put aviation into a broader cultural context. For a general discussion of airlines and tourism, see Anthony Sampson, *Empires of the Sky: The Politics, Contests and Cartels of World Airlines* (New York: Random House, 1984), 110–14.

54. Hilton, *Be My Guest*, 223–30, 238–41.

55. John W. Houser, letter to Conrad N. Hilton, June 23, 1951, Hilton Archives. This passage is briefly discussed in Huck, *Egypt's Modern Hotels*, 83.

56. The government's involvement was also acknowledged elsewhere. "The steadily expanding global network of hotels which carry the Hilton name abroad and are operated by Hilton Hotels International, the wholly-owned subsidiary of Hilton Hotels Corporation, had their inception at the suggestion of the United States government." Hamilton, "Hilton's International Expansion," 16.

57. Hilton, *Be My Guest*, 233.

58. John W. Houser, letter to Conrad N. Hilton, from Ankara, June 6, 1951, Hilton

Archives.

59. Characteristic is the press release made by George C. McGhee, U.S. assistant secretary for Near Eastern, South Asian and African affairs on October 27, 1950, which praises Turkey's progress toward democracy and its willingness to defend itself and others against the communist threat through its involvement in the Korean War and NATO. The statement also outlines the economic, military, and cultural contributions being made by the United States to Turkey. "Turkey, the United States, and the Free World," *[U.S.] Department of State Bulletin*, November 6, 1950, 739–41. Also relevant, the State Department press release of May 16, 1950, and the statement of Acting Secretary James E. Webb of May 19, 1950, *[U.S.] Department of State Bulletin*, June 5, 1950, 869–70.

60. *[U.S.] Department of State Bulletin*, November 6, 1950, 740.

61. *New York Times*, March 30, 1951, 41:2.

62. *New York Times*, February 4, 1955, 2:8. The article explains, "The Mutual Security Act of 1951 set up a $200,000,000 revolving fund for guarantees to stimulate the flow of American capital to foreign countries. Investors are protected against the risk that their funds will be confiscated or that they will not be able to withdraw them in dollars."

63. See the relevant chapters below.

64. George S. Harris, *Troubled Alliance: Turkish-American Problems in Historical Perspective, 1945–1971*, American Enterprise Institute—Hoover Policy Studies 33 (Stanford, Conn.: Hoover Institution on War, Revolution and Peace, 1972), 49–84.

65. Harris, *Troubled Alliance*, 125–47.

66. The Hilton contract, developed for the Caribe Hilton, is discussed in greater detail in chapter 6.

67. For the Habana Hilton, see Michael M. Lefever and Cathleen D. Huck, "The Expropriation of the Habana Hilton: A Timely Reminder," *International Journal of Hospitality Management* 9 (1990): 14–20. The Habana Hilton was opened in 1958. Its owners were the Caja de Retiro y Asistencia Social de los Trabajadores—the pension fund of the Catering Workers' Union. Batista fled Cuba after Castro's invasion on New Year's Eve 1959. I have found no discussion of the fate of the Teheran Hilton under Khomeini.

68. United Nations Center on Transnational Corporations, *Negotiating International Hotel Chain Management Agreements: A Primer for Hotel Owners in Developing Countries*, UNCTC Advisory Studies, ser. B, no. 5, comp. Felix G. N. Mosha and Charles J. Lipton (New York: United Nations, 1990).

69. I have not been able to discover the place and date of publication of this text. The copy quoted is found in the album from the Istanbul gala in the collection of the Hilton Archives.

70. Conrad N. Hilton, address at the opening of the Istanbul Hilton, June 1950, Hilton Archives.

71. Hilton, *Be My Guest*, 265.

72. "Collector's Item," *Hiltonitems*, May 1956, 4.

73. For an old and brilliant reading of *Reader's Digest*, see Ariel Dorfman, *The Empire's Old Clothes: What the Lone Ranger, Babar and Other Innocent Heroes Do to Our Minds* (1983; New York: Viking Penguin, 1996), 135–73.

74. J. P. McEvoy, "New Hotels for Old Countries," *Reader's Digest* 67 (October 1955): 141–45.

75. Danz, *Architecture*.

76. Duncan MacMillan, "Miró's Hidden Legacy," *Studio International* 196 (1984): 5–6.

77. For a collection of essays dealing in detail with this project and with earlier bibliography, see Robert Bruegmann, ed., *Modernism at Mid-Century: The Architecture of the United States Air Force Academy* (Chicago: University of Chicago Press, 1994).

78. Robert Bruegmann, "Military Culture, Architectural Culture, Popular Culture," in Bruegmann, *Modernism*, 79–101.

79. Lois Craig and the Staff of the Federal Project, *The Federal Presence. Architecture, Politics, and Symbols in United States Government Building* (Cambridge: MIT Press, 1978), 442.

80. SOM also continued to be involved with Hilton. They originally had the contract for the Rome Hilton. "Designers of the new hotel will be the New York architectural firm of Skidmore, Owings & Merrill, which has designed several of America's most outstanding modern-style buildings. Construction will be by Sogene, an Italian concern, with Hilton representatives acting in an advisory capacity." Arthur Foristall, press release, November 23, 1950, Hilton Archives.

81. Hamilton, "Hilton's International Expansion," quotes $1,300,000 as the first year's profit.

82. Dora Jane Hamblin, "In Nineteen Lands, Instant America," *Life*, August 30, 1963, 68. Surprisingly, the Turks spent more traveling abroad than they made from tourists in Turkey, at least through the mid-sixties. Z. Y. Hershlag, *Turkey: The Challenge of Growth* (Leiden: E. J. Brill, 1968), 259.

83. Interview with Yavus Erdem at the Istanbul Hilton, November 24, 1997, with Ali Kolsal translating.

84. White cement is a variant of Portland cement, which produces a white concrete for architectural purposes. Adam M. Neville, *Properties of Concrete* (New York: J. Wiley, 1996), 77. I am grateful to Ewan Byars, lecturer in concrete technology at the University of Sheffield, for this definition and reference.

Notes to Chapter 2

My work in Cairo was greatly facilitated by Max F. Maurer-Loeffler, general manager and vice president for food and beverage for the Middle East and Africa, and Jutta Al-Husani, director of interior design for the hotel, and Galal Hamdy, human resources manager. I also was able to meet with several of the nearly twenty members of the Nile Hilton staff who have been at the hotel since it opened in 1959, including Seham Abdul Khalek, telephonist, Suliman Kahoul, health club manager, retired, and Sadik Khari, laundry manager. I also want to thank Thomas John, general manager of the Helnan Shepheard Hotel, for providing photographs of the old Shepheard's. In Athens, Elly Hadziotis, director of public relations, was kind enough to consult with me. I am indebted to Michael Lefantzis, who generously shared with me his collection of Greek sources dealing with the Athens Hilton. He himself is working on the history of the *perception* of architecture in Greece from 1948 to 1970. I also learned a great deal from conversations with Argyro Loukaki.

The epigraphs for this chapter are from Samuel Wheelock Fiske, *Mr. Dunn Browne's Experiences in Foreign Parts* (Cleveland: H. P. B. Jewett, 1857), 194–95, and William Morton Fullerton, *In Cairo* (London: Macmillan, 1891), 6–7.

1. Yiva French, *Blue Guide: London* (New York: Norton, 1994), 61, the page on which the topographical tour of the city begins. Alta Macadam, *Blue Guide: Florence* (New York: Norton, 1995), 65, the page on which the topographical tour of the city begins.

2. Veronica Seton-Williams and Peter Stocks, *Blue Guide: Egypt* (New York: Norton, 1993), 190, the page on which the topographical tour of the city begins.

3. Janet L. Abu-Lughod, *Cairo: 1001 Years of the City Victorious* (Princeton, N.J.: Princeton University Press, 1971), 102. This book provides an excellent analysis of the city's historical topography.

4. Abu-Lughod, *Cairo*, 104. Much of this additional edge, initially incorporated into the royal domain, was subject to flooding until the construction of the low dam at Aswan at the beginning of the twentieth century stabilized the Nile's banks.

5. Le Corbusier (Charles-Edouard Jeanneret), *Journey to the East*, ann. and transl. Ivan Zaknic (Cambridge: MIT Press, 1987), 172. The italics are Le Corbusier's.

6. Douglas Sladen, *Oriental Cairo: The City of the "Arabian Nights"* (London: Hurst and Blackett, 1911), 3–4.

7. Sladen, *Oriental Cairo*, 10, 44.

8. On similar subjects, Olivier Richon, "The Imageless Sanctuary: Piazzi, Smyth, the Pyramid and Photography," *Block* 15 (1989): 32–42.

9. Sladen, *Oriental Cairo*, 45.

10. Robert B. Ludy, M.D., *Historic Hotels of the World: Past and Present* (Philadelphia: David McKay, 1927), 276–78. Ludy's "all accounts" does not include

Mark Twain's negative reaction to the hotel as expressed in *The Innocents Abroad* (1869; New York: Oxford University Press, 1996), 615. Another description is found in Charles G. Leland, *The Egyptian Sketchbook* (London: Hurd and Houghton, 1874), 59–60.

11. A geography of power was written into Shepheard's site, as it was into the Hilton's location. "[Napoleon] rode into Cairo on Wednesday, July 25, 1798, and took over a brand-new palace which Mohammad Bey al Elfi had built at great expense but had not yet occupied. It stood in its own gardens in the place which eventually became the site of Shepheard's Hotel, and that too is a little bit of Cairo melodrama, because European occupation began on that particular spot and really ended there when Shepheard's was burned down in 1952." James Aldridge, *Cairo* (Boston: Little, Brown, 1969), 159. According to Cathleen Baird Huck [Cathleen D. Baird], "Egypt's Modern Hotels: From the Historic Shepheard's to the Nile Hilton" (master's thesis, University of Houston, 1994), 87, Shepheard's ruins were still intact in 1990.

12. After its opening in 1841, Shepheard's was frequently rebuilt and remodeled. It was reconstructed in 1891 and enlarged in 1899, 1904, 1909, and 1927. Nina Nelson's *Shepheard's Hotel* (New York: Macmillan, 1960) is typical of the hotel-history genre. It is a celebratory inventory of the famous people who stayed in the hotel and the executives who ran it. It is not a critical assessment of the hotel's architecture or the site's history. Her description of the structure is limited: "It was to be in the Italian style of the period with a covering of thick stucco. Once again the hotel emerged in the form of a rectangle enclosing a courtyard with fountains and palms, and what was to become the famous terrace replaced the balcony. . . . The main ground-floor passage looked like a picture gallery for it was hung with delightful paintings of Egypt by such eminent artists as Lamplough, Linton and Talbot together with etchings, lithographs and drawings of state occasions at Shepheard's. When the building was completed it ranked as one of the most elaborate hotels of the day" (57).

13. The ballroom was remodeled in a pharaonic style in the 1930s by the French architect Jean Riboult. Nelson, *Shepheard's Hotel,* 143.

14. Edwin de Leon, *Thirty Years of My Life on Three Continents* (London: Ward and Downey, 1890), 159–62, describing Shepheard's as it was in the 1850s.

15. "New Shepheard's on the Nile's Bank," *London Illustrated News,* August 10, 1957, 225, with photographs. Huck, *Egypt's Modern Hotels,* 87.

16. *New York Times,* November 12, 1953, 42:4.

17. The *New York Times,* August 18, 1956, 19:2, announced that Hilton had initiated international scholarships at Cornell University's School of Hotel Administration. "The first winner of the annual scholarship is Capt. Ahmad E. Gaafar of Cairo, a retired Egyptian Army officer."

18. Two documents in the Hilton Archives refer to the complex financial conditions of the Nile Hilton. Robert J. Caverly, in a letter to Conrad N. Hilton dated December 5, 1958, related that he met Dr. Mansour to review details of the funding while he was in Berlin. Mansour apparently had to go to his board to request an extra $90,000 (added to $105,000) to cover preopening expenses. "Efforts to complete formation of our Egyptian company have been long and complicated. Final formation of the company affects the amount of U.S. dollar capital which we will have to invest in Cairo, and also our ability to borrow funds locally." Fifteen days later Gregory R. Dillon wrote the following memorandum to Conrad N. Hilton: "With respect to Cairo, an Egyptian corporation is being formed in which 46/50ths will be owned by our Panamanian subsidiary. This is to avoid the tax on dividends which Hilton International would be subject to if it held the stock. By having the Egyptian money flow to Panama we avoid United States tax and are not subject to Panamanian tax, since the income is derived outside of Panama. This money will then be available tax-free for further development elsewhere in the world." Huck, *Egypt's Modern Hotels,* deals with financial arrangements of Cairo in greater detail.

19. For a discussion of the economics of the Nasser government, see Robert Mabro, *The Egyptian Economy, 1952–1972* (Oxford: Clarendon Press, 1974).

20. Conrad N. Hilton, *Hiltonitems,* October, 1955, 2.

21. *Hiltonitems,* October, 1955, 2.

22. *Hiltonitems,* October, 1955, 2.

23. Naguib Mahfouz, *Palace Walk,* transl. William Maynard Hutchins and Olive E.

Kenny (New York: Doubleday, 1990), 166–67, originally published in Arabic in 1956.

24. Suliman Kahoul, health club manager, retired, interview at the Nile Hilton, November 17, 1997.

25. Seham Abdul Khalek, telephonist, interview at the Nile Hilton, November 16, 1997.

26. *Since 1959* (Cairo: Nile Hilton, 1994), 3.

27. *Since 1959*, 3.

28. Interview at the Nile Hilton, Cairo, November 17, 1997.

29. Interview at the Nile Hilton, Cairo, November 17, 1997. For me, Cairo will always be a city of weddings. The night I first arrived in Cairo, the broad strip between highway lanes on the way from the airport to the city was lit with wedding parties having their pictures taken in front of the statues that monumentalize the thoroughfare—a colossal Ramses and the equally amplified images of a more recent politics. When I arrived at the Hilton, the lobby was also filled with a wedding celebration, complete with trumpets, bagpipes and multitudes of guests. It was difficult to communicate at reception, but it didn't matter. Everyone embraced the spirit of the occasion.

30. Richard Joseph *Hilton Hotels Around-the-World Travel Guide*, foreword by Conrad N. Hilton (Garden City, N.Y.: Doubleday, 1966), 97.

31. "Nile Hilton Opens in Cairo," *Hotel Monthly* 67 (April 1959): 40.

32. Perhaps the emphasis of 1960s travel brochures on the antiquities of ancient Egypt masked the irrational fear of the Arab that seems lodged in Western bourgeois consciousness. It still comes as a surprise to many of my acquaintances that I feel safer on my own in old Cairo, Istanbul, or Damascus than I do in many parts Durham, North Carolina. These feelings are no delusion. I am safer in old Cairo, Istanbul, and Damascus than in certain sections of Durham.

33. "Nile Hilton Opens in Cairo," *Hotel Monthly* 67 (April 1959): 40. What about the mosaics of San Marco? Perhaps the author meant "the world's largest *modern* Venetian glass mosaic."

34. "Nile Hilton Opens in Cairo," *Hotel Monthly* 67 (April 1959): 40.

35. Joseph, *Hilton Hotels*, 99–100.

36. Joseph, *Hilton Hotels*, 100. The italics are mine.

37. Lincoln Barnett, "Egypt the Oldest Nation," *Life*, October 1, 1956, 78–98, and "Egypt's Eras of Splendor," *Life*, November 26, 1956, 106–17; Helen Gardner, *Art through the Ages* (New York: Harcourt-Brace, 1959), in which there are twenty-four pages devoted to ancient Egypt and three to Islamic Egypt.

38. Joseph, *Hilton Hotels*, 96.

39. William Dudley Hunt Jr., *Total Design: Architecture of Welton Becket and Associates* (New York: McGraw-Hill, 1972). I have had a long-term aversion to Becket's work, based on the contextual insensitivity and abject ugliness of the North Carolina Mutual Life Building in Durham, North Carolina, built in 1965. This prejudice was aggravated by Hunt's monograph devoted to Becket's production. Hunt catalogs the corporate structure of the company and provides a chronological list of buildings; it offers no formal or historical analysis. Its presentation is also shockingly sexist. The volume includes dozens of images of men from each of the major sections of the firm, all of whom are carefully identified. In the entire volume there are only three images of women, not one of whom is named. The book also embodies a condescension toward the Other of the sort that I have otherwise not found in my research on Hilton, counter to my expectations. In discussing the interior design of the Hilton in the Philippines, Hunt writes: "But perhaps the greatest surprise of all was when Maas [the interior designer] quickly discovered, as he puts it, 'All of these people are hep.' No problems here like those of Cairo, where thousands of workmen were required to handle the simplest construction. Manila had up-to-date contractors, equipped with modern machinery, and trained workmen in all of the usual building trades." But they were insensitive to local products: "As Maas puts it, 'These people are educated and sophisticated, and they like good things. But at that time, if it was local, it just couldn't be good or exciting.' He started collecting antique Spanish furniture, which before him had been extremely cheap. He also began the local production of furniture. . . . Maas found the quality of all of this work very good indeed, but the artisans did the same designs over and over, out of the same materials. They felt no calling to be either experimental or inventive. . . . Eventually, he found an American woman who had

been working with the Filipino weavers and other artisans, helping them to adapt their native ability and the wide array of materials available to new designs and methods. She had found a Chinese who was teaching the Filipinos silk-screen printing. . . . And she had started some of the artisans on experimental work in various materials. Maas teamed up with these people" (70–72). The "American woman" and the "Chinese" remain nameless.

40. Hunt, *Total Design*, 21–22.

41. Robert Sheehan, "Portrait of the Artist as Businessman," *Fortune*, March 1967, 144, 146.

42. For a discussion of the Beverly Hilton, see chapter 6.

43. "Two Kinds of Hilton Hotels," *Architectural Forum* 104 (April 1956): 125.

44. For a thorough discussion of the finding of the parts of the Kritios Boy and their reconstruction, Jeffrey M. Hurwit, "The Kritios Boy: Discovery, Reconstruction, and Date," *American Journal of Archaeology* 93 (January 1989): 41–80. I am indebted to the author for the image of the Kritios Boy reproduced here.

45. Partial caption from an advertisement in the *Washington Post*, November 22, 1992. For more learned examples of the folding together of democracy and art, see *The Good Idea: Democracy and Ancient Greece: Essays in Celebration of the 2500th Anniversary of its Birth in Athens* (New Rochelle, N.Y.: A. D. Caratzas, 1995).

46. Patricia Storace in *Dinner with Persephone* (New York: Pantheon Books, 1996), 71, provides an amusing instance of the reification of ancient Greek democracy in its art and amusingly debunks it. In the passage, Mr. Angelchild, a journalist, compares Greek and Egyptian art, concluding that "'[T]heirs is an art of slavery, ours of freedom!' . . . [The author then comments] In fact, to call classical Greece, an ethnically based androcracy, a 'democracy' is just a little more meaningful than calling China a 'people's republic.'"

47. Johann Joachim Winckelmann, 1717–1768, commonly identified as the father of art history, is also perhaps the most important formulator of the Greek Ideal. His work, *Gedanken über die Nachahmung der griechischen Werke in der Malerei und Bildhauerkunst* (Dresden: Waltherischen Handlung, 1755), might be seen as the manifesto of the Greek Ideal. It was widely translated and read throughout Europe and the United States in the eighteenth century, e.g., *Reflections on the Painting and Sculpture of the Greeks: With Instructions for the Connoisseur, and an Essay on Grace in Works of Art*, transl. Henry Fusseli (London: A. Millar, 1765). For an excellent assessment of Winckelmann, see Alex Potts, *Flesh and the Ideal: Winckelmann and the Origins of Art History* (New Haven, Conn.: Yale University Press, 1994). For effects of the Greek Ideal and for bibliography, see David Constantine, *Early Greek Travellers and the Hellenic Ideal* (Cambridge: Cambridge University Press, 1984), and Nicole Loraux, *The Invention of Athens* (Cambridge, Mass.: Harvard University Press, 1986).

48. For a suggestive reference to the use of versions of the classical for the articulation of very different political positions, see Robert Eisner, *Travelers to an Antique Land: The History and Literature of Travel to Greece* (Ann Arbor: University of Michigan Press, 1991), 71; for a recent discussion of the effect of the Greek Ideal in Greece itself, see Yannis Hamilakis and Eleane Yolouri, "Antiquities as Symbolic Capital in Modern Greek Society," *Antiquity* 70 (1996): 117–28. Sheila Dillon brought this article to my attention.

49. Nicholas Biddle, *Nicholas Biddle in Greece: Journals and Letters of 1806*, ed. R. A. McNeal (University Park: Pennsylvania State University Press, 1993), 48. The trope that modern Greeks are in no way related to ancient Greeks has a long scholarly history.

50. M. Christine Boyer, *The City of Collective Memory: Its Historical Imagery and Architectural Entertainments* (Cambridge: MIT Press, 1994), 158, assesses the ambivalent position of Greeks in the nineteenth and twentieth centuries: "[Although Greeks might be] the living ancestors of Europe upholding the role of Ur-Europa, they were simultaneously blamed for being immature and backward children held down by their ancient past. This placed nineteenth-century Greece in an impossible position: it was to be the standard of civilization in the abstract sense, but judged in reality to be a humiliated Oriental vassal clearly inferior to—and in the end dependent on—the more modern Europe. This bind, moreover, served Eurocentric purposes and legitimated the plundering of Greece's past." See also Helen Angelomatis-Tsougarakis, *The Eve of the Greek Revival: British Travellers' Receptions of Early Nineteenth-Century Greece*

(New York: Routledge, 1990).

51. For a useful description of Greece's construction as non-European and the role played by anthropology in that construction, see Michael Herzfeld, *Anthropology through the Looking-Glass* (Cambridge: University of Cambridge Press, 1987).

52. Savas Kondaratos, "The Parthenon as Cultural Ideal: The Chronicle of Its Emergence as a Supreme Monument of Eternal Glory," in *The Parthenon and Its Impact in Modern Times,* ed. Panayotis Tournikiotis (Athens: Melissa Publishing House, 1994; distributed, New York: Abrams, 1996), 19–52.

53. For Lord Elgin's theft of the Pantheon's sculptures, originally intended for the decoration of his new country estate, see Jacob Rothenberg, "The Acquisition of the Elgin Marbles, the Years 1799–1806," in *The Parthenon,* ed. Vincent J. Bruno (New York: Norton, 1996), 128–70. Also, Brian F. Cook, "Lord Elgin and the Acquisition and Display of the Parthenon Sculptures in the British Museum," in *Parthenon-Kongress, Basel,* ed. Ernst Berger, Referate und Berichte 4. bis 8. April 1982, 2 vols. (Mainz: Philipp von Zabern, 1984), 326–28. For Winckelmann's use of Greek form as well as the later political use of Winckelmann in German politics, see Suzanne L. Marchand, *Down from Olympus* (Princeton, N.J.: Princeton University Press, 1996), esp. 10.

54. The last two decades have, however, shown an increased awareness of what has been lost. Efforts to save what remains have been enhanced. Serious discussion of the now removed medieval structures on the Acropolis is found, for example, in Richard Economakis, ed., *Acropolis Restoration: The CCAM Interventions* (London: Academy Editions, 1994).

55. Robin Francis Rhodes, *Architecture and Meaning on the Athenian Acropolis* (New York: Cambridge University Press, 1995), 1–2.

56. The title of an even more recent book on the Acropolis suggests that this historical vacuum will be filled: Jeffrey M. Hurwit, *The Athenian Acropolis: History, Mythology, and Archaeology from the Neolithic Era to the Present* (New York: Cambridge University Press, 1999). Unfortunately, only twelve pages—the epilogue entitled "Restoration"—of this three-hundred-page book deal with the fifteen centuries of additions to the Acropolis made by Christians and Muslims, and then only in terms of their elimination. (291–302). The author writes a sophisticated apology for the modern destruction of alternative pasts: "Paradoxically, it is even true that the very way the Acropolis was cleared and its monuments restored—the 'decontamination' of the place by the demolition of the small mosque within the Parthenon, the Frankish Tower, and every Turkish house, the re-erection of columns blasted over by the explosion of 1687, and so on—is as much a part of its cultural history as the actions of ancient or Medieval builders. . . . And if the Acropolis as the nineteenth century remade it, and as the current admirable restoration program will essentially leave it, ignores almost everything but its Classical efflorescence, we must also concede that any other possible Acropolis we might choose to reconstruct would be no less an artifice, no less a selection that future scholars, with a different ethos and a different agenda, might fault" (302). This observation does not, however, obviate the scholarly obligation to document that which is lost or to acknowledge the ideological reasons for its disappearance.

57. The most complete monographic treatment of the city is Alexander Papageorgiou-Venetas, *Athens: The Ancient Heritage and the Historic Cityscape in a Modern Metropolis,* Archaeological Society at Athens Library 140 (Athens: Archaeological Society at Athens, 1994). Many of the observations that follow are based on Papageorgiou-Venetas's impressive compendium of information about the city. See also Eleni Bastéa, "Athens," in *Streets: Critical Perspectives on Public Space,* ed. Zeynep Çelik, Diane Favro and Richard Ingersoll (Berkeley: University of California Press, 1994), 111–24.

58. *Hotel Grande Bretagne, Athens* (Athens: A. Georgiadis, 1997).

59. Bastéa, *Athens,* 115.

60. Ludwig Ross, *Erinnerungen und Mittheilungen aus Griechenland* (Berlin: R. Gaertner, 1863; reprinted as Subsidia byzantina 20, Leipzig: Zentralantiquariat der Deutschen Demokratischen Republik, 1982), esp. 28–31, 149–50.

61. Pausanias, *Guide to Greece,* transl. Peter Levi (London: Penguin, 1979), 1 n. 37. The description of Fourmont's collection of over three thousand inscriptions in Greece in *Historie de l'Académie Royale des Inscriptions et des Belles Lettres,* vii (Paris: Imp.

royale, 1733), 344–58, reflects on the textual character of early Western Europeans' way of "seeing" Greece.

62. For a provocative assessment of the American School's work on the Agora, see Argyro Loukaki, "Whose Genius Loci? Contrasting Interpretations of the Sacred Rock of the Athenian Acropolis," *Annals of the Association of American Geographers* 87, no. 2 (June 1997): 306–30.

63. Papageorgiou-Venetas, *Athens*, 302.

64. According to Michael Lefantzis, Marshall Plan funds were used to construct the Stoa of Attalos.

65. John W. Houser, vice president and general manager, letter to Conrad N. Hilton, February 1, 1951, Conrad N. Hilton College Archives and Library, University of Houston (hereafter Hilton Archives).

66. The documentation of the relationship between Hilton and various branches of the U.S. Government is most complete for the Rome Hilton. See chapter 5.

67. John W. Houser, letter to Conrad N. Hilton, from Ankara, June 6, 1951, Hilton Archives. The confidential cables mentioned in the passage were not, unfortunately, included in the Hilton Archives file.

68. Economic Cooperation Administration, *European Recovery Program: Greece* (February 1949), 32–33.

69. In discussing the luxurious scale of the public space in the Athens Hilton, Elly Hadziotis, director of public relations, commented that the "hotel was lucky to have as its owner a wealthy man who wanted to leave a monument to himself." Interview at the Athens Hilton, November 27, 1997.

70. The authors of a study made in the sixties of the demographic and ecological problems of Athens, contended that "the legislation and administration are too inefficient and inadequate to prevent 'illegal' building on a large scale." This might be translated to suggest that influential parties could disregard building codes. "Capital of Greece," *Ekistics* 23, no. 128 (July 1966): 38.

71. Scully, "The Athens Hilton: A Study in Vandalism," *Architectural Forum* 1, no. 119 (July 1963): 101–2.

72. Eric Pick, telephone interview, October 31, 1997.

73. "Athens Hilton Hotel Opens," *New York Times*, April 23, 1963, 16:3.

74. "Athens Hilton," *Architektonike* 15–16 (May–August 1959): 39–41.

75. For the Caribe Hilton, see chapter 6.

76. At least, not that I have discovered.

77. Fax to the author from Spryos Staikos of December 22, 1997. Capitalization is Spyros Staikos's.

78. Telephone interview with Spyros Staikos, October 29, 1997. They had also been scheduled to visit the Habana Hilton in 1958, but hostile relations between Castro and the United States prevented the visit.

79. Telephone interview, October 29, 1997.

80. Telephone interview, October 30, 1997.

81. Hilton advertisement (November 1978). I am grateful to Michael Lefantzis for a photocopy of this publication.

82. See Helen Fessas-Emmanouil, "Prestige Architecture in Post-War Greece: 1945–1975," *Themata chorou + technon/Design + Art in Greece* 15 (1984): 34–73, esp. 54–56, for a very positive scholarly assessment of the Hilton's role in the "Modernists' triumph [in Greece] in the late 50s and early 60s." According to the author this triumph "did not entail a total loss of interest for 'tradition' and 'history.'"

83. I am indebted to Michael Lefantzis, who undertook the survey, for this information.

84. Joseph, *Hilton Hotels*, 10–11.

85. A. G. Xydis, "Auspicious Collaboration of Art and Architecture: the Work of Yannis Moralis 1959–1963" (in Greek) *Architectoniki* 7, no. 42 (November–December, 1963): 6–15.

86. Of course, Clement Greenberg would have regarded everything about the Hilton as kitsch. Clement Greenberg, "Avant-Garde and Kitsch," *Art and Culture: Critical Essays* (1939; Boston: Beacon Press, 1961), 3–21.

87. Papageorgiou-Venetas, *Athens*, 98.

88. Telephone interview with Charles Warner, October 29, 1997.

89. Joseph, *Hilton Hotels*, 10–11.

90. "[I]n 1961, 1,180,000 people in the Athens Basin area had no easy access to any kind of public open area." For further comments on the demographics, distribution of wealth, circulation patterns, air pollution, and land values in Athens, see "Capital of Greece," *Ekistics* 24, no. 140 (July 1967): 95.

91. "Hotel Is Spoofed by Athens Revue," *New York Times*, August 10, 1963, 9:1.

92. The *New York Times* reported that "a woman said over the phone in poor English that these acts were to 'warn foreign tourists that our patience is running out.' Opponents of the regime who are abroad have called for a tourist boycott of Greece as long as the present Army-imposed regime is in power." *New York Times*, May 23, 1969, 6:1, and May 24, 1969, 3:1.

93. From *Kathimerini*, quoted by Vincent Scully, "The Athens Hilton: A Study in Vandalism," *Architectural Forum* 119 (July 1963): 101–3, quotation on p. 101.

94. Hilton advertisement (November 1978).

95. Telephone interview with Charles Warner, October 29, 1997.

96. Scully, "Athens Hilton," 100–103. Scully's article was noted by the Greeks. For example: "Critique of the Hilton," *Architectonike* (July–August 1993): xxix: "In the last volume of the authoritative American architectural periodical, *Architectural Forum* (119, July, 1963) a caustic critique against the Hilton Hotel in Athens was published by Vincent Scully, professor at Yale University. The same critique [Scully's article] was published in Greek in the weekly periodical *Tachidromos* 487 (August 10, 1963)." This note appeared in Greek; the rough translation is my own. I am grateful to Michael Lefantzis for this reference. Scully's article is also discussed by Papageorgiou-Venetas, *Athens*, 76–79.

97. Scully, "Athens Hilton," 101.

98. Scully, "Athens Hilton," 101.

99. Scully, "Athens Hilton," 101–102.

100. Scully, "Athens Hilton," 101.

101. Le Corbusier (Charles-Edouard Jeanneret), *Journey to the East*, ann. and transl. Ivan Zaknic (Cambridge: MIT Press, 1987), 209. The chapters on Athos and the Parthenon were not included in the author's first attempt to publish this work in 1912. For Le Corbusier's use of what he learned from the Parthenon, see Richard A. Etlin, "Le Corbusier, Choisy and French Hellenism: The Search for a New Architecture," *Art Bulletin* 69 (June 1987), 264–78.

102. Papageorgiou-Venetas, *Athens*, 12–16.

Notes to Chapter 3

I would like to thank two concierges of the Inter-Continental Berlin, who worked in the hotel from its earliest days as a Hilton, Dieter Werner and Peter J. Meyer, for the unpublished information about the hotel that they provided. I am indebted to many at the London Hilton on Park Lane who provided me information on the hotel, including David M. B. Irving, partially retired director of conferences and banqueting, Andreas Jersabeck, general manager, Ray Pask, chief engineer, Paula Scallon, marketing manager, Pam Weerry, reservations, and Vincent Zammattio, head waiter. I am also indebted to Stuart Holdsworth, of Cameron Holdsworth Associates, Civil and Structural Engineers, who has worked extensively on the Hilton, Susan Scott, Savoy Hotel archivist, and Ruth Jacobs, public relations manager, Langham Hilton. I am grateful for the access I had to the library of the Royal Institute of British Architects. I would also like to thank Richard Dill, former vice president for international affairs, German Public Broadcasting, Deborah Broderson for commenting on drafts of this chapter, and Mariatte Denman for finding mistakes in my German.

The epigraphs for this chapter are from Len Deighton, *Funeral in Berlin* (New York: G. P. Putnam's Sons, 1964), 26, and Steen Eiler Rasmussen, *London: The Unique City*, intro. James Bone (1934; reprint with addendum 1978; Cambridge: MIT Press, 1982), 407.

1. The original Berlin Hilton is now the Inter-Continental Berlin.

2. Walter Benjamin, "A Berlin Chronicle," *Reflections: Essays, Aphorisms, Autobiographical Writings*, ed. Peter Demetz, transl. Edmund Jephcott (New York: Schocken Books, 1978), 3.

3. Hedda Adlon, *Hotel Adlon: The Life and Death of a Great Hotel*, transl. Norman Denny (London: Barrie Books, 1958). The author was the daughter-in-law of the founder.

4. For a lively denunciation of the Hohenzollerns, see Anthony Read and David Fisher, *Berlin: The Biography of a City* (London: Hutchinson, 1994), 12. The authors comment: "For more than 500 years, Berliners were forced to kowtow to anyone wearing a uniform. . . . Civilians, no matter how rich or clever or exalted, were regarded as a lesser species whose primary duty and principal function was to serve and support the army."

5. T. H. Elkins with B. Hofmeister, *Berlin: The Spatial Structure of a Divided City* (London: Methuen, 1988), 45–46.

6. Anne Armstrong, *Berliner: Both Sides of the Wall* (New Brunswick, N.J.: Rutgers University Press, 1973), xviii.

7. Gerhard Keiderling, *Berlin 1945–1987: Geschichte der Hauptstadt der DDR* (Berlin: Dietz Verlag, 1987), provides a chronicle of the cultural politics of (East) Berlin, including reconstruction projects.

8. Alan Balfour, *Berlin: The Politics of Order, 1737–1989* (New York: Rizzoli International, 1990), 164.

9. For changing Soviet attitudes toward Modernism, see *Design, Stalin and the Thaw*, ed. Susan E. Reid, special issue of *Journal of Design History* 10, no. 2 (1997).

10. For example, *Baedeker's Berlin* (Hamburg: Karl Baedeker, 1954), 126, devotes a single sentence to the monument. In *Berlin Brandenburg: Ein Architekturführer* (Berlin: Ernst and Sohn, 1990), 65, it is relegated to a footnote.

11. For a discussion of the postreunification debate over the possible reconstruction of the Schloss and the destruction of the Palace of the People that replaced it, see Brian Ladd, *The Ghosts of Berlin: Confronting German History in the Urban Landscape* (Chicago: University of Chicago Press, 1997), 47–70.

12. On (East) Berlin's elimination of West Berlin, see Balfour, *Berlin*, 164.

13. Alan Balfour assesses the function of Columbus Haus within the changing conditions of Berlin from the building's conception in 1931 as the representation of a utopian Modernity through its absorption into Albert Speer's project for the Palace of the Reich Marshal in 1939 and its use as a Nazi prison to its destruction after the war in 1957. Balfour, *Berlin*, 108–51. See also Kathleen James, *Erich Mendelsohn and the Architecture of German Modernism* (Cambridge: Cambridge University Press, 1997).

14. The literature on the Berlin Wall is vast. For a useful discussion and bibliography, see Ladd, *Ghosts of Berlin*.

15. Departments of the Central Committee of the SED and the Central State Statistical Office of the GDR, *Successful Path of Developing an Advanced Socialist Society in the GDR: Facts and Figures* (Berlin: Central State Statistical Office, 1981), 118. The West German press, in contrast, recorded the complaints that were made in the East about the government's inability to provide appropriate building plans or even an adequate supply of construction materials. "Building Costs High in the Zone," *Frankfurter Allgemeine Zeitung*, April 18, 1955, 5.

16. Balfour, *Berlin*, 168–77. For architectural competitions, see Frank Russell, ed., *Architecture in Progress: Internationale Bauausstellung Berlin, 1984* (New York: St. Martin's, 1984), 1, which "presents an interim account of the competitions, both open and invited, which have so far been concluded by the Internationale Bauausstellung Berlin 1984 (IBA). IBA's vast and ambitious program for the rebuilding of four important areas in West Berlin . . . which collectively encompass sixteen separate competitions, began with the first project for Prager Platz in 1978 and was due to culminate with the 'City as Exhibition' in 1984."

17. Harold Hammer-Schenk, "Historische Einführung," in *Synagogen in Berlin: Zur Geschichte einer zerstörten Architektur*, 2 vols., ed. Rolf Bothe, Berlin Museum exhibition catalog (Berlin: Verlag Willmuth Arenhövel, 1983), 1:22–70.

18. Heinz Heineberg, "Aspects of City Centre Development in the 'Two Germanies:' The Examples of West and East Berlin," in *Essays for Professor R. E. H. Mellor*, ed. William Ritchie, Jeffrey C. Stone, and Alexander S. Mather (Aberdeen:

Department of Geography, University of Aberdeen, 1986), 154–55.

19. This comparison is made in a useful and sustained way by Klaus D. Wiek, *Kurfürstendamm und Champs-Élysées: Geographischer Vergleich zweier Weltstrassen-Gebiete*, Abhandlungen des 1. geographischen Instituts der Freien Universität Berlin 11 (Berlin: Dietrich Reimer, 1967), 17–20.

20. *New York Times*, April 10, 1955, 13:3. For an explanation of counterpart funds, see the introduction, note 23.

21. Peter Davey, "Outrage," *Architectural Review* 205 (1999): 25. The architects were Patzschke, Klotz, and Partner. The author denounces the building's retroness. "Why the rich like retro is a puzzle. . . . You can understand affection for such things when a building is really old. . . . Yet people who would never dream of wearing anything but pure wool, silk, leather or linen, who would never stoop to fake jewelry or fur, are apparently only too happy to patronize Disneyfied versions of the past."

22. Conrad N. Hilton, *Be My Guest* (1957; Englewood Cliffs, N.J.: Prentice-Hall, 1987), 237.

23. Polly Houser, letter addressed "Dear Friends," Sanatorium am Bodensee, Uberlingen, Germany, July 30, 1958, Conrad N. Hilton College Archives and Library, University of Houston (hereafter Hilton Archives).

24. *New York Times*, April 19, 1955, 10:5.

25. *Der Tagesspiegel*, April 19, 1955, 8, my rough translation, as are all quotations from German newspapers included in this chapter, unless otherwise noted.

26. Walter Henry Nelson, *The Berliners: Their Saga and Their City* (New York: David McKay, 1969), 371–72.

27. *BZ am Abend*, April 19, 1955, 5.

28. According to Anthony Haden-Guest, Charles de Gaulle objected to the construction of the Berlin Hilton, but no explanation of the French leader's opposition is offered. *The Paradise Program: Travels through Muzak, Hilton, Coca-Cola, Texaco, Walt Disney and other World Empires* (New York: William Morrow, 1973), 142–43.

29. "Es ist bedauerlich, dass der erhebliche Aufwand finanzieller (Gesamtbaukosten: 27,3 Millionen DM) und propagandistischer Art keine allseits befriedigende Lösung zur Folge gehabt hat." "Technische Einrichtungen im Berliner Hilton-Hotel," *Bauwelt* 50 (1959): 438–39.

30. "The Hilton, like the Europa Center, was put up with a lot of public funds and its construction caused a storm of protest from other Berlin hoteliers, all of whom felt left out in the cold." Nelson, *Berliners*, 371–72.

31. "Hilton: Sei gross," *Der Spiegel*, March 2, 1964, 66–77.

32. John W. Houser, letter to Conrad N. Hilton, May 21, 1954, Hilton Archives.

33. *Der Tagesspiegel*, November 29, 1959, 19.

34. "Hilton: Sei gross," *Der Spiegel*, March 2, 1964, 66–77.

35. *Der Tagesspiegel*, November 29, 1959, 19. Some sense of how the operating costs were covered is provided in a letter from Houser to Hilton: "[The Berlin Hilton] is now open and ready for business. The forecast of occupancy for the early part of 1959 is not encouraging, and we should be prepared for possible operating losses during the first part of the year at least. Working capital and financing of china, linen, glass, and silver has been advanced by Hilton International in the form of dollar funds—additional working capital is needed immediately and there may be further requirements if operating losses are experienced. We have begun to explore the possibility of obtaining loan commitments from West Berlin banks, with the thought that we could repatriate dollar funds already advanced, and also use the loan as a source of further working capital for the hotel." John W. Houser, letter to Conrad N. Hilton, December 5, 1958, Hilton Archives.

36. *New York Times*, May 5, 1955, 10:1.

37. *New York Times*, May 10, 1955, 46:2.

38. "Berlin Hilton in Stichworten," [1958], courtesy of Dieter Werner.

39. Polly Houser, "Dear Friends."

40. "Technische Einrichtungen im Berliner Hilton-Hotel," *Bauwelt* 50, no. 14 (1959): 438–39.

41. Polly Houser, "Dear Friends."

42. According to Charles Bell, air-conditioning was promoted by Hilton even in relatively northern climates because it addressed problems of noise and pollution as well as cooling. Despite Hilton's best efforts, air-conditioning was resisted in Rotterdam and Amsterdam as well as in Berlin.

43. *Die Zeit*, December 5, 1958, 10.

44. K. Landsberg, "Berlin Hilton," *Die Innenarchitektur* 7 (January 1958): 237–47; *Bauwelt* 50 (January 1959): 438–39; *Baumeister: Zeitschrift für Architektur, Planung, Umwelt* 56 (January 1959): 150–53; "Hotel Hilton à Berlin," *L'Architecture francaise* 211–12 (March–April, 1960): 211–12; "Hotel Hilton à Berlin," *L'Architecture française* 241–242 (September–October, 1962): 38–41.

45. *Der Tagesspiegel*, November 29, 1959, 19.

46. Peter J. Meyer, interview in Berlin, April 25, 1996.

47. "West Berlin Greets New Berlin Hilton," *Hotel Monthly* (February 1959): 36–39.

48. "Berlin Hilton in Stichworten."

49. Richard Joseph, *Hilton Hotels Around-the-World Travel Guide*, foreword by Conrad N. Hilton (Garden City. N.Y.: Doubleday, 1966), 20.

50. *Der Tagesspiegel*, November 29, 1959, 15.

51. For a more complete list of the contributing artists, see *Der Tagesspiegel*, November 29, 1959, 13.

52. "Berlin Hilton in Stichworten."

53. *Der Tagesspiegel*, November 29, 1959, 13.

54. "West Berlin Greets New Berlin Hilton," 36–39.

55. "West Berlin Greets New Berlin Hilton," 37.

56. Polly Houser, "Dear Friends."

57. The desire to escape the fear of the present is articulated by Polly Houser: "Afternoon concerts from our neighbor [the Zoo] give this newest International Hilton a light and gay feeling, no matter how sober the world surrounding it." In "Dear Friends."

58. The term "decorated shed" was coined by Venturi et al. in the early seventies for a Las Vegas architecture of the late fifties and sixties. The metaphor is still relevant on occasion outside Las Vegas, though now useless within it. "Where the architectural systems of space, structure, and program are submerged and distorted by an overall symbolic form. This kind of building-becoming-sculpture we call the *duck* in honor of the duck-shaped drive-in 'The Long Island Duckling,' illustrated in *God's Own Junkyard* by Peter Blake. Where systems of space and structure are directly at the service of program, and ornament is applied independently of them. This we call the *decorated shed*." Robert Venturi, Denise Scott Brown, Steven Izenour et al., *Learning from Las Vegas: The Forgotten Symbolism of Architectural Form* (1972; rev. ed. Cambridge: MIT Press, 1986), 87.

59. "Berlin Hilton in Stichworten."

60. For "duck," see note 58 above. The façade of the Hilton still calls attention to itself. "The façade design with its chessboard grid shows an extreme degree of ornamental effort for the unambitious neutrality of its period." Peter Güttler, Joachim Schulz, Ingrid Barmann-Kompa, Klaus-Dieter Schulz, Karl Kohlschütter, and Arnold Jacoby, *Berlin–Brandenburg: Ein Architekturführer* (Berlin: Ernst and Sohn, 1990), 71.

61. "'Nun erst recht!' Über die neue Stadtautobahn ins Berliner Hilton," *Die Zeit*, December 5, 1958, 10.

62. Joseph, *Hilton Hotels*, 16.

63. "West Berlin Greets New Berlin Hilton," *Hotel Monthly* (February 1959): 37. The italics are mine.

64. "Berlin Hilton in Stichworten."

65. Dieter Werner, concierge, Berlin Hilton, letter to the author, August 5, 1996, my translation.

66. *New York Times*, November 29, 1958, 42:5; November 1, 1958, 29.1; December 1, 3:6.

67. If I have done the math correctly, DM 100 in 1958 was equivalent to $180 in 1999. "'Nun erst recht!'"

68. *Der Tagesspiegel*, November 29, 1958, 13.

69. *Frankfurter Allgemeine Zeitung*, December 2, 1958, 5.

70. *Frankfurter Allgemeine Zeitung*, December 1, 1958, 4.

71. *New York Times*, December 1, 1958, 3:5.

72. *Frankfurter Allgemeine Zeitung*, December 1, 1958, 5.

73. *Telegraf*, December 2, 1958, 3.

74. "Hilton Enters Berlin," *Hiltonitems*, May 1955, 4.

75. "President's Corner," *Hiltonitems*, May 1958, 1.

76. "'Nun erst recht!'"

77. A great deal has been published about the plans for the new Berlin. For example and for bibliography, see Werner Suss, ed., *Hauptstadt Berlin*, vol. 3, *Metropole im Umbruch* (Berlin: Arno Spitz: 1996); for an insightful critique of the process of reconstruction, see Andrea Huyssen, "The Voids of Berlin," *Critical Inquiry* 24 (1997): 57–81.

78. Still the best description of London is Rasmussen, *London*. Many of Rasmussen's biases are written into the present text. Essential also is Nikolaus Pevsner, *Buildings of England: London*, vol. 1, *The Cities of London and Westminster*, rev. Bridget Cherry (Harmondsworth, United Kingdom: Penguin, 1973). For an excellent social and political overview, see Roy Porter, *London: A Social History* (Cambridge, Mass.: Harvard University Press, 1995).

79. Samuel Wheelock Fiske, *Mr. Dunn Browne's Experiences in Foreign Parts* (Cleveland, Ohio: H. P. B. Jewett, 1857), 20.

80. Ford Madox Ford, *The Soul of London* (London: Rivers, 1905), 7–8.

81. Maurice Anthony Ash, *A Guide to the Structure of London* (Bath, United Kingdom: Adams and Dart, 1972), 3, begins his discussion of London by questioning his subject's existence: "The question would then ask itself: this place of history, of kings and queens, that has become a fun-city—how real is it?"

82. For a recent treatment with bibliography, see Stephen Porter, *The Great Fire of London* (Phoenix Mill, United Kingdom: Sutton, 1996).

83. John Summerson, *Sir Christopher Wren* (New York: Macmillan, 1953), 69–76, suggests that Wren executed the plan in five days.

84. Wren did not appreciate all aspects of French architecture. In a letter about Versailles, he commented: "Not an inch within but is crowded with little Curiosities of Ornaments: the Women as they make here the Language and the Fashions, and meddle with Politicks and Philosophy, so they hold sway also in Architecture." Quoted by Summerson, *Sir Christopher Wren*, 71.

85. Thomas F. Reddaway, *The Rebuilding of London after the Great Fire* (London: Jonathan Cape, 1940), provides a detailed assessment of the reconstruction.

86. For an excellent general discussion, see John Summerson, *Georgian London* (Harmondsworth, United Kingdom: Penguin, 1978). For a more detailed discussion of the residential development of private estates in London in the eighteenth and nineteenth centuries, particularly the properties of the Foundling Hospital and the dukes of Bedford, see Donald J. Olsen, *Town Planning in London: The Eighteenth and Nineteenth Centuries* (New Haven, Conn.: Yale University Press, 1964).

87. Peter Smithson's interview for "Controversial Building in London," *Architectural Forum* 114 (March 1961): 81.

88. John Summerson, *The Architecture of Victorian London* (Charlottesville: University of Virginia Press, 1976), 1.

89. C. H. Holden and W. G. Holford, *The City of London: A Record of Destruction and Survival* (London: Architectural Press, 1951).

90. Porter, *London*, 344.

91. Sir Patrick Abercrombie, *Greater London Plan 1944*, a report prepared on behalf of the Standing Conference on London Regional Planning by Professor Abercrombie at the request of the minister of town and country planning (London: H.M.S.O., 1945).

92. But not, for some, committed enough. Lewis Mumford presented a virulent attack on modern urbanism as infertile (literally) and pathological. He argued that in order to promote necessary population growth, the population needs to be decentralized and housed in single-family dwellings. Couples living in a flat in the "necropolis" are unlikely to have more than one child. Specifically, Mumford criticizes the Forshaw-

Abercrombie Plan for "reducing the proportion of single-family houses to apartments, [and] it likewise falls short in setting a standard for open spaces." Lewis Mumford, *The Plan of London County* (London: Faber and Faber, [1945?]), 29.

93. Abercrombie, *London Plan*, chap. 12.

94. Abercrombie, *London Plan*, 119.

95. Abercrombie, *London Plan*, 116.

96. Abercrombie, *London Plan*, 119.

97. Donald L. Foley, *Controlling London's Growth: Planning the Great Wen, 1940–1960* (Berkeley: University of California Press, 1963), 61–79.

98. Thomas Hall, *Planning Europe's Capital Cities: Aspects of Nineteenth-Century Urban Development* (London: Chapman and Hall, 1997), 91.

99. Critiques of a lack of London planning are often made. Deyan Sudjic, "Metropolis," in *Metropolis: New British Architecture and the City*, ed. Linda Brown and Deyan Sudjic (London: Belmont Press, 1988), 1–4.

100. A fuller discussion of Monopoly is found in the epilogue.

101. Carol Kennedy, *Mayfair: A Social History* (London: Hutchinson, 1986).

102. This particular execution, which occurred on June 28, 1654, was well recorded because it was attended by the ambassadors of Catholic countries who had protested it to Cromwell. The Venetian secretary described the execution in the following terms, "[I]n a fashion worse than barbarous, when he was only half dead, the executioner cut out his heart and entrails and threw them into a fire kindled for the purpose, the body being quartered, one for each of the quarters of the city." John Southworth's parts were, however, never distributed to the various parts of London, but rather bought from the hangman by the Spanish ambassador for forty shillings, sewn together again and embalmed. The reassembled corpse was then smuggled out of England to the English Catholic College at Douai in France. The body was lost during the French Revolution but rediscovered in 1929, during urban renewal. It was returned to England. Southworth was beatified in 1930 and sanctified in 1970. E. E. Reynolds, *John Southworth, Priest and Martyr* (London: Burns and Oates, 1962). The corpse is on display in Bentley's magnificent neo-Byzantine Westminster Cathedral. Annabel Wharton, "Westminster Cathedral: Medieval Architectures and Religious Difference," *Journal of Medieval and Early Modern Studies* 26 (1996): 523–55.

103. Simon Jenkins, *The Selling of Mary Davies and Other Writings* (London: John Murray, 1993), 1–12, offers an amusing tale of the construction of the Grosvenor Estate and its final dismantling by the Major government's 1993 Housing and Urban Development Act. This act "was supposedly aimed at extending home-ownership and releasing established tenants from the bondage of bad landlords. If a few noble babies were tossed out with the bath water, so be it." For detailed information on both the history of the estate and the architecture of the square, see F. H. W. Sheppard, ed., *Survey of London*, vols. 39–40, *The Grosvenor Estate in Mayfair*, parts 1–2 (London: Athlone Press, for the London County Council, 1977 and 1980).

104. Sheppard, *Survey*, 1.

105. Quoted from Fello Atkinson, "U.S. Embassy Building, Grosvenor Square, London," *Architectural Review* 129 (April 1961): 252–58. See also "New U.S. Embassy for London," *Architectural Forum* 104 (April 1956): 138–45.

106. For Saarinen's façade sketch, see "London Embassy Competition," *Progressive Architecture* 130 (July 1961): 89–91. Also reproduced are the drawings of the other entrants: Stone, Stubbins, Sert, Anderson and Beckwith, Kump, Wurster, and Yamaski.

107. Quoted in "Controversial Building in London," *Architectural Forum* 114 (March 1961): 84.

108. Allan Temko, *Eero Saarinen* (New York: George Braziller, 1962), 31.

109. For a similar assessment, Ron Theodore Robin, *Enclaves of America: The Rhetoric of American Political Architecture Abroad, 1900–1965* (Princeton, N.J.: Princeton University Press, 1992), 153–55.

110. Reyner Banham, "Monument with Frills," *New Statesman*, December 10, 1960, 918–20.

111. "Room for More," *Economist*, June 6, 1964, 1155.

112. One of the great architectural abominations of the mid-twentieth century in

London is Seifert's Centre Point, a speculative venture that stood empty for many years, devastating the area. The building's evil social effects are considered by Jenkins, *Selling of Marie Davies*, 71–79. Its ugliness is described by Pevsner, *Buildings of England*, 371.

113. Porter, *Great Fire*, 356.

114. P.R.B. reported in *Architectural Review* 113 (March 1953): 120, that "Hilton Hotels International has been negotiating for the site of bombed Portman House (northwest corner of Portman Square) but this project is apparently held up pending Government approval, and a group associated with Hilton has subsequently been reported trying to gain control of Grosvenor House."

115. *London Hilton on Park Lane* (Hilton International brochure: n.d. [received April 1998]).

116. The Hilton is 405 feet high; St. Paul's Cathedral is 366 feet. Pevsner, *Buildings of England*, 116.

117. Description issued by Henry Bonner, director of public relations, Press Room, Infoplan Ltd., London, April 10, 1963.

118. "Cooling Facilities a Striking Feature of the London Hilton: A Towerful of Refrigeration," *Modern Refrigeration* (May 1963): 407–9. Information on kosher certification was provided by Vincent Zammattio, head waiter at the Hilton and on the staff of the hotel's restaurant from its opening, in an interview at the London Hilton, April 24, 1998.

119. "The Story of the Building," [1963?], [6], in-house description of the program and construction provided by the management of the London Hilton.

120. For a technical description of the foundation and basement-level construction, see "The London Hilton Hotel," *Builder* 204 (April 1963): 835. The basement was constructed from the top down. Concrete was poured for the highest level using the earth as formwork. After the concrete was dry, the ground below it was excavated and the next level prepared, and so on. It was claimed that this procedure "saved three to four months in construction time and meant the virtual absence of timber formwork for retaining walls, resulting in a saving in cost of approximately £100,000. See also, "Foundations for the Hilton Hotel, Park Lane," *Architect and Building News* 220 (July 1961): 14–16.

121. The Park Lane entrance and the main lobby housed a jeweler's, an art gallery, and a "Man's Shop," as well as desks for Avis Rent-a-Car, British European Airways, Michael Kent Theater Tickets, News Kiosk, Trader Travel, and Trans World Airlines. Anne Credson, public relations manager, London Hilton, "London Hilton Hotel: Facts at a Glance," [1963?].

122. Interview with David M. B. Irving, director of conferences and banqueting, in New York, April 24, 1998.

123. Interview with Vincent Zammattio, head waiter, at the London Hilton, April 24, 1998.

124. "The Story of the Building," [13].

125. Interview with Pam Weerry, Reservations, London Hilton, April 22, 1998.

126. Bonner, Description, 4.

127. Bonner, Description, 6.

128. "Roof Restaurant London Hilton Hotel," *Architectural Review* 134 (August 1963): 117–19, 121–22.

129. For the state of accommodation in London in 1960, see "London's New Hotels," *Economist*, December 3, 1960, 1047–48.

130. John W. Houser, letter to Conrad N. Hilton, Nice, September 20, 1950, Hilton Archives.

131. That the new Hilton was announced for London in the *Times* (London), May 30, 1951, 5d, suggests that these initial contacts were pursued.

132. Goronwy Rees, *The Multimillionaires: Six Studies in Wealth* (New York: Macmillan, 1961), 74–87; "Who's Who in Foreign Business," *Fortune* 59 (January 1959): 52; "Business Abroad: More for Santa Clore," *Time*, June 15, 1959, 91.

133. Some sense of the battle over the stock of the Savoy Hotel Group is conveyed in the reports of the *Times* (London), November 27, 1953, 8e, and December 6, 1953, 6e. The British Hotels and Restaurants Association reflected the concern of profes-

sional hoteliers in their public statement on the matter: "The council of the association . . . decided to place on record their profound concern at the attempts of outside interests to secure control of the Savoy Hotel Company, and expressed full support for the directors, managers, and staff who have built up the present predominant position held by this company in the hotel and restaurant industry not only in Great Britain but throughout the world." *Times* (London), December 3, 1953, 4d. For a chatty narrative of the takeover bid, see Edward Westropp, *The Way to Fortune* (London: Oldbourne Press, 1957), 181–84, 195.

134. *New York Times*, October 5, 1953, 29:8.

135. Announcements were made in the *Times* (London), May 14, 1957, 7a, and June 27, 1957, 10c. The latter article mentions that the freehold of the site had been acquired the year before by a property company controlled by Mr. Charles Clore.

136. *Times* (London), July 3, 1957, 6d and 10c. The same picture also appeared in professional journals, e.g., "Perspective View," *Architect and Building News* 212 (July 1957): 35.

137. Hilton management, sensitive to the sensibilities of its royal neighbors, does not allow its premises to be used by photographers looking for royal images.

138. For the inquiry, see *Times* (London), October 11, 1957, 13b; November 7, 1957, 7a; November 8, 1957, 14g; November 9, 1957, 4c; November 12, 1957, 13d; November 13, 1957, 2g.

139. It also appeared in the *Times* (London), September 14, 1957, 3b: "It was disclosed at a meeting of the London County Council yesterday that the council is to oppose the granting of a planning application. . . . 'It is not possible to give the full reasons for the objection in this answer but they stem fundamentally from the sheer height and bulk of the building,' he [Mr. Richard Edmonds, chairman of the LCC] said. The decision was not unanimous. Voting had been six to five in favor of the application not being granted."

140. *New York Times*, May 15, 1958, 6:6.

141. *Times* (London), April 29, 1959, 8g.

142. Porter, *Great Fire*, 356.

143. *Times* (London), April 13, 1959, 5d; April 29, 1959, 8g; June 17, 1959, 8b; *New York Times*, June 17, 1959, 58:2.

144. Rees, *Multimillionaires*, 87.

145. Shirley Green, *Who Owns London?* (London: Weidenfeld and Nicolson, 1986), 187.

146. He is mentioned in a few articles, including Graeme Shankland, "South Barbicon Office Towers, London," *Architectural Review* 131 (March 1962): 190–96, and J. M. R. "The New Scale in Office Blocks," *Architectural Review* 112 (September 1952): 197–98.

147. The resume reads: "Born, August 18, 1915. Education: School of Building, Brixton, London; The Polytechnic, 309 Regent Street, London. Career: Sidney Kaye, Eric Firmin & Partners; previously Sydney Clough, Son & Partners, 1931–39; Kaye and Newman, 1949–51; Lewis Solomon, Kaye & Partners, 1951–?. Major buildings: Euston Centre Development, London, London Hilton Hotel, Park Lane, Braunstone Warehouse, Leicester, J. F. S. Comprehensive School, Camden Road; Rubins & Shine House (Home for the Aged), 184 Ballads Lane."

148. Eric Firmin, "Obituary: Sidney Kaye," *Royal Institute of British Architects Journal* 99 (September 1992): 69.

149. Kaye discusses profit as evidence of aesthetics in Kate Wharton, "Talking to Sidney Kaye," *Architect and Building News* 7 (December 3, 1970): 50–51.

150. "Astragal: Notes and Topics," *Architect's Journal* 137 (April 1963): 858–59.

151. The architect did write a rebuttal, describing his original proposals and how they were changed under the pressure of economy and the London County Council. Sidney Kaye, "Hindsight at the Hilton," *Architect* 1 (February 1971): 34–37.

152. Edward Jones and Christopher Woodward, *A Guide to the Architecture of London* (London: Orion, 1997), 192.

153. "The Immediate Prospect," *Architectural Review* 123 (October 1960): 302.

154. *New York Times*, October 5, 1953, 29:8.

155. Rees, *Multimillionaires*, 87.

156. Rasmussen, *London*, 407.

157. *Times* (London), July 24, 1957, 3a.

Notes to Chapter 4

I feel privileged to have had the opportunity to interview two central figures in the development of Israeli architecture and design, Ya'acov Rechter, architect of both the Tel Aviv and Jerusalem Hiltons, and Dora Gad, who did the design work for the two hotels. Meetings were arranged by Michal Klein, director, social and business development of the Tel Aviv Hilton, who also provided me with much useful information about the Tel Aviv Hilton's history. I am particularly indebted to Rico de Schepper, general manager of the Tel Aviv Hilton. I am also grateful to other members of the Tel Aviv Hilton's staff, including Avi Varsano, concierge, Rahamin Even, assistant manager, and Michael Marinksy, banquet manager. My time in Tel Aviv was much enhanced by the company and insights of Ya'ael Meroz and Eric Zakim. Yoram Tsafrir taught me as much about the distress of politically liberal Israelis as about the Jerusalem of the Holy Land Hotel model. I want also to thank Inbal Ben-Asher Gitler for her reading of this chapter and for her (unsuccessful) attempt to lighten its political and aesthetic judgments.

The list of Hilton International conference and banqueting facilities that appears as the epigraph for this chapter is from Hilton International, *Incentive Destinations*, promotional brochure (1989), Conrad N. Hilton College Archives and Library, University of Houston (hereafter Hilton Archives).

1. Theodor Herzl, *Old New Land*, intro. Jacques Kornberg, transl. Lotta Levensohn (1902; Princeton, N.J.: Markus Wiener Publishers, 1997).

2. Herzl, *Old New Land*, 66.

3. Herzl, *Old New Land*, 205.

4. Herzl, *Old New Land*, 61–62. This passage makes an interesting comparison with the description of Istanbul, discussed in chapter 1, by Robert Hichens, *The Near East: Dalmatia, Greece and Constantinople* (London: Hodder and Stoughton, 1913), 187–95.

5. Herzl, *Old New Land*, 178.

6. Both events took place on May 9, 1998.

7. Mark Twain, *The Innocents Abroad, or The New Pilgrims Progress* (New York: Penguin Books, 1966), 453.

8. This difference was articulated by Arthur Ruppin in 1908: "Jaffa differs from, let us say, Jerusalem, in not being under the pressure of an ancient and unproductive settlement, hostile to all innovation; this city has therefore become the center of modern Jewish life in Palestine. . . . It is in Jaffa that we find the beginnings of a modern industrial development." Arthur Ruppin, *Three Decades of Palestine: Speeches and Papers on the Upbuilding of the Jewish National Home* (Jerusalem: Schocken, 1936), 5.

9. For an introduction to the early phases of Tel Aviv's construction, see Edina Meyer-Maril, "Europäische Stadtebauideen in Palästina, 1909–1939," *Architectura: Zeitschrift für Geschichte der Baukunst* 22 (1992): 138–43.

10. Herzl, *Old New Land*, 218.

11. Herzl, *Old New Land*, 71.

12. Quoted by Ruth Kark, *Jaffa: A City in Evolution, 1799–1917* (Jerusalem: Yad Izhak Ben-Zvi Press, 1990), 115.

13. Quoted by Kark, *Jaffa*, 129.

14. From the minutes of the meeting, June 3, 1907, quoted by Yossi Katz, "Ideology and Urban Development: Zionism and the Origins of Tel-Aviv, 1906–1914," *Journal of Historical Geography* 12 (1986): 406.

15. Catherine Weill-Rochant, "Tel-Aviv des années trente: Béton blanc sur la terre promise," *L'Architecture d'aujourd'hui* 293 (June 1994): 42.

16. For a discussion of the traditions of urbanism that affected the planning of Tel Aviv, see Meyer-Maril, "Europäische Stadtebauideen in Palästina, 1909–1939," 135–48.

17. From Arthur Ruppin's address to the Jewish Colonization Society of Vienna, delivered on February 27, 1908. Published as "The Picture in 1907," in Ruppin, *Three*

Decades, 9.

18. For an ideological assessment of "red roofs," see Daniel Bertrand Monk, review of Gilbert Herbert and Silvina Sosnovsky, *Bauhaus on the Carmel and the Crossroads of Empire*, *AA Files* 28 (1994): 94–99. This article begins with Shim'on Peres's 1991 attack on Itzhak Shamir's Likud government and Jewish settlements on the West Bank through reference to their "red roofs."

19. Quoted by Kark, *Jaffa*, 131.

20. Katz, "Ideology," 408.

21. Katz, "Ideology," 408–9.

22. Katz, "Ideology," 414.

23. Weill-Rochant, "Tel-Aviv," 41.

24. For the contribution of philanthropy, see Ran Aaronsohn, "Baron Rothschild and the Initial Stage of Jewish Settlement in Palestine (1882–1890): A Different Type of Colonization?" *Journal of Historical Geography* 19 (1993): 142–56.

25. "The Record of Twenty-Five Years," an address delivered before the 19th Zionist Congress, Lucerne, September, 1935, published in Ruppin, *Three Decades*, 284.

26. The distinction between institutional and private funds is not so clear as I have suggested. Irit Amit, "American Jewry and the Settlement of Palestine: Zion Commonwealth, Inc." in *The Land that Became Israel: Studies in Historical Geography*, ed. Ruth Kark, transl. Michael Gordon (New Haven, Conn.: Yale University Press, 1990), 250–71. Amit investigates American Jewry's interest in obtaining land in Israel while not committing themselves to immigration. Pre–World War I holding companies were formed to buy tracts of land in Palestine. "Each such company would work toward the establishment of its own moshava in Palestine. Company representatives would handle the purchasing of the land, and would find residents of Palestine [Arabs] to work it, plant crops and cultivate the soil for the first six to ten years. Once the groves bore fruit, the land would be apportioned into lots upon which the company members would settle" (251). After World War I, the process was renewed by the American Zion Commonwealth in Palestine. Settlement of the land was urged, but it was not mandatory. Agricultural land was sought, not urban. The block and lot were omitted from the title deeds, making them relatively flexible vehicles of exchange (255–56).

27. Ruppin, *Three Decades*, 147.

28. S. Ilan Troen, "Establishing a Zionist Metropolis: Alternative Approaches to Building Tel-Aviv," *Journal of Urban History* 18 (November 1991): 13.

29. It is worth noting that less than a decade later, another British town planner, Patrick Abercrombie, contributed to the Garden City conception of Haifa. Gilbert Herbert and Silvina Sosnovsky, *Bauhaus on the Carmel and the Crossroads of Empire: Architecture and Planning Haifa during the British Mandate* (Jerusalem: Yad Izhak Ben-Zvi, 1993), 189–204. Abercrombie was, in any case, an admirer of Geddes. He wrote an encomium to Geddes in *The Interpreter Geddes: The Man and His Gospel*, ed. Amelia Defries (London: Routledge, 1927), 322–25. For Geddes in Palestine, see Neal I. Payton, "The Machine in the Garden City: Patrick Geddes' Plan for Tel Aviv," *Planning Perspectives* 10 (October 1995): 359–81, or the restatement of the thesis in the same author's "Patrick Geddes (1854–1932) and the Plan of Tel Aviv: Modern Architecture and Traditional Urbanism," *New City* 3 (fall 1996): 4–25.

30. Meyer-Maril, "Europäische Stadtebauideen," 137–48. On May 25, 1925, Geddes wrote to Mumford concerning his urban plans: "I'm trying to save hundreds of thousands of £ in these small towns—& they are more than usually willing to let me—partly because Jews are intelligent—in appreciably higher proportion than gentiles! & partly because their difficulties are so great. I am adjusting all new city blocks to large ones, with *interior* bit[s] of garden village." *Lewis Mumford and Patrick Geddes: The Correspondence*, ed. and intro. Frank G. Novak Jr. (London: Routledge, 1995), 226. Also Troen, "Zionist Metropolis," 22–31. According to assessments of an international conference on modern architecture in Tel Aviv, appreciation of Geddes's contribution was universal. "His scheme for Tel Aviv, with commercial streets running between superblocks and divided into small plots and secondary streets, was unanimously praised for its underlying urban concepts. Even in the 1930s and 1940s, when the plots were filled with four-story apartment buildings raised on *pilotis*—rather than the smaller houses he had envisioned—Geddes's principle of freestanding buildings and incre-

mental parceling of the superblocks prevented the construction of large projects (including housing) and ensured the present cityscape of detached, medium-sized buildings surrounded by greenery." Esther Sandberg and Oren Tatcher, "White City Revisited," *Progressive Architecture* 75 (August 1994): 34.

31. Philip Boardman, *Patrick Geddes: Maker of the Future*, intro. Lewis Mumford (Chapel Hill: University of North Carolina Press, 1944), 360.

32. For a statement of the architectural principles of the Bauhaus, see Walter Gropius, *The New Architecture and the Bauhaus* (Cambridge: MIT Press, 1987). This manifesto was first published in English in 1936.

33. Richard Pommer and Christian F. Otto, *Weissenhof 1927 and the Modern Movement in Architecture* (Chicago: University of Chicago Press, 1991), 51.

34. Pommer and Otto, *Weissenhof 1927*, 207, n. 56.

35. Weill-Rochant, "Tel-Aviv," 41. For a useful discussion of architectural style as politics, see Susan E. Reid, "Destalinization and Taste, 1953–1963," in *Design, Stalin and the Thaw*, ed. Susan E. Reid, special issue of *Journal of Design History* 10 (1997): 177–201. Also note the discussion of Skidmore, Owings and Merrill's Air Force Academy in chapter 1.

36. Weill-Rochant, "Tel-Aviv," 41.

37. Winfried Nerdinger and René Block, *Tel Aviv: Modern Architecture, 1930–1939* (Tübingen: Wasmuth, 1994), is an essential source of analysis and photographs. The presentation of Modernism as ideologically innocent seems naive, as in, for example, a recent description of Munio Gitai Weinraub: "One of the few Israeli architects who attended the Bauhaus, he alone put into practice the Bauhaus ideal of designing things according to the way they were to be produced. . . . He sought to bring to the Jewish settlements in Palestine a transcendent modern architecture that would resist ideological frames and operate neutrally to serve basic human needs through elegance, progressive technology and infrastructural foresight." Richard Ingersoll, *Munio Gitai Weinraub: Bauhaus Architect in Eretz Israel* (Milan: Electra, 1994), 11.

38. Erich Mendelsohn's Columbus Haus was mentioned in my description of Berlin. For a discussion of the building as the representation of a utopian Modernity, see Alan Balfour, *Berlin: The Politics of Order, 1737–1989* (New York: Rizzoli International, 1990), 108–52. For Mendelsohn in Palestine, see Ita Heinze-Muhleib, *Erich Mendelsohn, Bauten und Projekten in Palästrina, 1934–1941*, Beiträge zur Kunstwissenschaft 7 (Munich: Scaneg, 1986).

39. Alona Nitzan-Shiftan, "Contested Zionism–Alternative Modernism: Erich Mendelsohn and the Tel Aviv Chug in Mandate Palestine," *Architectural History* 39 (1996): 147–80.

40. Ita Heinze-Greenberg, "Von Berlin nach Tel Aviv: Zur Immigration deutsch-jüdischer Architekten nach Palästina (1918–1948)," *Münster* 40 (1987): 113–16, English and French summaries, 175–76; Ingersoll, *Munio Gitai Weinraub*.

41. Jean-Louis Cohen, "International Style II: Una Terra Sancta fragile per i pilotis," *Casabella* 58 (1994): 48–49.

42. For a discussion of the politicization of architectural motifs, see Daniel Bertrand Monk, "Orientalism and the Ornament of Mediation," *Design Book Review: DBR* 29–30 (1993): 32–34.

43. Arnon Golan, "The Demarcation of Tel Aviv-Jaffa's Municipal Boundaries Following the 1948 War: Political Conflicts and Spatial Outcome," *Planning Perspectives* 10 (October 1995): 383–98.

44. Michael D. Levin, "The Second Generation of Israeli Architects," *Journal of Jewish Art* 7 (1980): 70–78.

45. Brutalism is an identity invented apparently by Alison and Peter Smithson to describe both their rejection of the overrefinements of the International Style and their assertion of the materiality of construction materials in the finished building. Alison Smithson and Peter Smithson, "The New Brutalism," *Architectural Review* (April 1954): 274–75. "Brutalism" came to refer to buildings that express their structure as mass. See Reyner Banham, *The New Brutalism: Ethic or Aesthetic?* (New York: Reinhold, 1966).

46. This is neatly laid out in relation to construction in Haifa by Herbert and Sosnovsky, *Bauhaus*, 224–25.

47. Amiram Harlap, *New Israeli Architecture* (East Brunswick, N.J.: Associated

University Presses, 1982), 38.

48. Interview with Ya'acov Rechter in his offices in Tel Aviv, May 6, 1998.

49. Massimo Dalla Torre, *Architettura contemporanea in Israele* (Rome: Officina Edizioni, 1969), 32.

50. "Hilton-Hotel, Tel Aviv," *Baumeister* 63 (March 1966): 229–35; "Hilton Hotel, Tel-Aviv," *Architectural Review* 140 (September 1966): 206–11; "Hôtel Hilton, Tel Aviv Israël," *L'Architecture d'aujourd'hui* 38 (April–May 1967): 72–73; "Hotel Hilton a Tel-Aviv," *L'Architecture français* 28, nos. 303–4 (November–December, 1967): 30–34; "Hilton-Hotel, Tel Aviv," *Baumeister* 63 (March 1966): 229–35.

51. Ada Louise Huxtable, "Stale Air and the Plastic Aesthetic," in *Kicked a Building Lately?* (New York: Quadrangle Books, 1976), 22.

52. "The Tel Aviv Hilton was conceived with the intention to create an exterior plastic object, rich in texture. But it would also be the mirror of its structure. The plastic elements are functional—they carry pipes and the like. The strength of the building comes from that concept." Interview with Ya'acov Rechter, Tel Aviv, May 6, 1998.

53. Unfortunately, in the next renovation it is planned to veneer the exterior piers with marble, like those of the interior.

54. With the later extension of the building, the hotel now has over six hundred rooms.

55. Ran Shchori, *Dora Gad: The Israeli Presence in Interior Design*, transl. Boaz Ben Menease and Richard Flanz (Tel Aviv: Architecture of Israel, 1994), 22.

56. Dora Gad, quoted by Shchori, *Dora Gad*, 131.

57. *New York Times*, September 12, 1965, X 25:1.

58. For Karavan's most monumental contribution to Tel Aviv, White Square in Edith Wolfson Park, see Volker Welter, "Von Jaffa nach Tel Aviv," *Bauwelt* 15 (1992): 854–55.

59. According to Michal Klein, Dani Karavan's principal sculpture for the Tel Aviv Hilton, designed for the ballroom, was given by Hilton International to the Tel Aviv Museum. It is not, unfortunately, on public display in the museum. Interview at the Tel Aviv Hilton, May 5, 1998.

60. Golan, "Demarcation of Boundaries," 385.

61. Interview with Ya'acov Rechter, Tel Aviv, May 7, 1998.

62. Interview with Michael Marinksy, banquet manager, Tel Aviv Hilton, May 11, 1998.

63. Shchori, *Dora Gad*, 132.

64. *New York Times*, September 12, 1965, X 25:1.

65. The investment in Palestine by American Jews who had no intention to immigrate and settle has a long history. Amit, "American Jewry," 250–71.

66. *New York Times*, September 12, 1965, X 25.1.

67. Herzl, *Old New Land*, 131–2.

68. Herzl, *Old New Land*, 159.

69. The business or leisure and religious motivations for hotel construction in Israel have periodically conflicted with the theocratic tendencies of the state's Religious Council. Demands that hotels observe completely Sabbath restrictions—which would mean no service, including elevators—have so far been successfully opposed. For example, the *New York Times*, November 17, 1968, 31, reported that "[t]he rabbis had demanded that the hotelmen correct such 'Sabbath desecrations' as smoking and writing or lose the rabbinical certificate that previously had been issued merely for keeping a kosher kitchen."

70. Richard Joseph, *Hilton Hotels Around-the-World Travel Guide*, foreword by Conrad N. Hilton (Garden City, N.Y.: Doubleday, 1966), 85–93.

71. E. R. Alexander, R. Alterman, and H. Law-Yone, *Evaluating Policy Implementations: The National Statutory Planning Systems in Israel*, Progress in Planning 20, ser. ed. J. Diamond and J. B. McLoughlin (London: Pergamon Press, 1983), 162.

72. Efraim Torgovnik, *The Politics of Urban Planning Policy* (Lanham, Md.: University Press of America, 1990), 77–78.

73. Torgovnik, *The Politics of Urban Planning Policy*, 147.

74. For official Israeli policies on the expropriation of Palestinian Arab land,

Michael Dumper, *The Politics of Jerusalem since 1967*, Institute for Palestine Studies series (New York: Columbia University Press, 1997).

75. *New York Times*, September 12, 1965, X 25:1.

76. *New York Times*, September 15, 1965, 3:3.

77. Curt Strand, president, Hilton Hotels International, retired, "An Oral History Interview," conducted by Cathleen Baird, University of Houston, October 21, 1992, and December 6, 1993, 17–18.

78. For an outline of the architecture of Jerusalem with many color plates, see David Kroyanker, *Jerusalem Architecture*, intro. Teddy Kollek (London: Tauris Parke, 1994). This volume epitomizes how deeply ideological an architectural survey can be.

79. Josephus, *Antiquities*, xv.7.1.

80. For a careful description and reconstruction of the *spolia*, see Leon Yarden, *The Spoils of Jerusalem on the Arch of Titus: A Re-Investigation*, Acta instituti romani regni suediae 8, 16 (Stockholm: Paul Åströms, 1991).

81. For a discussion and references, Annabel Wharton, "Erasure: Eliminating the Space of Late Ancient Judaism," in *From Dura to Sepphoris: Studies in Jewish Art and Society in Late Antiquity*, ed. Lee L. Levine, *Journal of Roman Archaeology*, Supplementary Series 40 (2000): 195–214.

82. For the tomb, Martin Biddle, *The Tomb of Christ* (Stroud, United Kingdom: Sutton, 1999).

83. Samuel Wheelock Fiske, *Mr. Dunn Browne's Experiences in Foreign Parts* (Cleveland, Ohio: H. P. B. Jewett, 1857), 157–58. The italics are Fiske's.

84. For Gordon's identification of the new site, see Charles George Gordon, *Reflections in Palestine* (London: Macmillan, 1884); also, Neil Asher Silberman, *Digging for God and Country: Exploration, Archaeology and the Secret Struggle for the Holy Land* (New York: Alfred A. Knopf, 1982), 152–53.

85. Glenn Bowman, "Christian Ideology and the Image of a Holy Land: The Place of Jerusalem Pilgrimage in the Various Christianities," in *Contesting the Sacred: The Anthropology of Christian Pilgrimage*, ed. John Eade and Michael J. Sallnow (London: Routledge, 1991), 98–121.

86. Michael Avi-Yonah, *Pictorial Guide to the Model of Ancient Jerusalem at the Time of the Second Temple in the Grounds of the Holy Land Hotel Jerusalem, Israel*, rev. Yoram Tsafrir (Herzlia: Palphot, [1987?]). I am grateful to Yoram Tsafrir for giving me a personal tour of the model and providing me with much of the information presented here.

87. Oleg Grabar, *The Shape of the Holy: Early Islamic Jerusalem* (Princeton, N.J.: Princeton University Press, 1996).

88. L. S. Meritt, *History of the American School of Classical Studies in Athens, 1939–1980* (Princeton, N.J.: American School of Classical Studies in Athens, 1984), 18.

89. Moshe Safdie, *Jerusalem: The Future of the Past* (Boston: Houghton Mifflin, 1989), 104.

90. Dumper, *Politics of Jerusalem*.

91. The contemporary political history of the Temple Mount/Al-Haram al-Sharif is presented by Roger Friedland and Richard D. Hecht, "The Politics of Sacred Space: Jerusalem's Temple Mount/al-haram al sharif," *Sacred and Profane Spaces: Essays in the Geographics of Judaism, Christianity and Islam*, ed. J. Scott and P. Simpson-Housley (Chicago: Kazi Publications, 1996), 21–61. For a not unbiased account of legal conflicts over the site, see Stephen J. Adler, "Israeli Court Finds Muslim Council Destroyed Ancient Remains on Temple Mount," *Biblical Archaeology Review* 20 (1994): 39.

92. This particular incident is narrated in some detail in Friedland and Hecht, "Politics of Sacred Space," 40–42.

93. Haggai Segal, *Dear Brothers: The West Bank Jewish Underground* (Woodmere, N.Y.: Beit-Shamai Publications, 1988), 50–60.

94. Safdie, *Jerusalem*, 106.

95. My niece, Brook Wharton, went on a Bucknell University–sponsored semester-around-the-world cruise in 1997. Of the three itineraries of Jerusalem offered to these American students not one included the monuments on the Al-Haram al-Sharif.

Judging from the pamphlets for tours available in various hotels, this absence is not anomalous.

96. *New York Times*, September 29, 1968, X 15:3.

97. *New York Times*, October 6, 1968, VIII 8:2.

98. "The Jerusalem Municipality and the speculators, including the Israel Lands Authority which acts in effect as the governmental land speculator, are all advocates of a compact Jerusalem punctuated by high-rise luxury residential clusters and a dense, concentrated commercial core. . . . The policy for developing tourism is standard the world over for promoting remote and undeveloped sites: foreign investment in hotels is encouraged by a series of public subsidies—public land (in Jerusalem's case, sometimes expropriated land) is sold at very favorable prices, low-interest government loans pay for up to 70% of the land and building costs, direct cash payments on a per-tourist per-day basis subsidize the hotels' operating costs, and tax-free profits are allowed to be taken out of the country without restriction." Arthur Kutcher, *The New Jerusalem: Planning and Politics* (London: Thames and Hudson, 1973), 91–93. The author offers a beautifully illustrated denunciation of the destruction of Jerusalem's skyline with high-rises.

99. "Building Types Study, 507: Hotels," *Architectural Record* 162 (October 1977): 120–22.

100. "Building Types Study, 507," 120–22.

101. Interview with Ya'acov Rechter, Tel Aviv, May 7, 1998.

102. "The Jerusalem Hilton—Where Decor Blends with the Environment," *Jerusalem Post*, December 31, 1974, 18.

103. "The Jerusalem Hilton—Where Decor Blends with the Environment."

104. "The Jerusalem Hilton—Where Decor Blends with the Environment."

105. Klaus-Hartmut Olbricht, "Sakrale Räume von Dani Karavan," *Die Kunst und das Schöne Heim* 88 (December 1976): 741–44.

106. "The Jerusalem Hilton—Where Decor Blends with the Environment."

107. "The Jerusalem Hilton—Where Decor Blends with the Environment."

108. "The Jerusalem Hilton—Where Decor Blends with the Environment."

109. "Town and Country Planning and Building Rules, 1947," sec. 41.66: "External, party and cross walls shall be constructed of sound, incombustible materials in a good workmanlike manner: Provided that nothing herein contained shall exempt or be deemed to exempt any building from the provisions of any authorized scheme prescribing that in the planning area in which such building is situated, the external walls of buildings shall be constructed of, or faced with, stone." Henry Kendall, *Jerusalem: The City Plan, Preservation and Development during the British Mandate, 1918–1948* (London: H.M.S.O., 1948), 89.

110. *New York Times*, April 13, 1930, III 8:1.

111. The decorator is quoted anonymously in a promotional brochure provided by the hotel. According to Robby Leon, guest relations assistant manager of the King David Hotel, the interior decorator was G. A. Hufschied, from Geneva. The architect of the hotel was also Swiss: Emil Vogt from Lucerne. I am grateful to Robby Leon for this information.

112. *New York Times*, July 23, 1946, 1:8; July 24, 1946, 1:8.

113. Herzl, *Old New Land*, 205, more fully quoted above.

Notes to Chapter 5

I am indebted to Harry Brewster. He is my reason for including Florence in this book. In Rome, I am grateful for the help of Donatella Peruzzi of the Hotel Excelsior and Sabina Galdiolo of the Hotel Hassler, and particularly to Grace Retondini, personal assistant to the general manager at the Rome Cavalieri Hilton, and Massimilliano Bellisoni, the Cavalieri Hilton's chief engineer.

The first epigraph to this chapter is transcribed from Federico Fellini's *Roma*, MGM/UA Home Video (1990); the second is from Henry James, *Italian Hours* (1909; Hopewell, N.J.: Ecco, 1987), 121.

1. Federico Fellini, *Fellini on Fellini*, transl. Isabel Quigley (New York: Da Capo,

1966) 81.

2. Fellini, *Fellini on Fellini*, 67–69.

3. Cavalieri Hilton Archive, Rome.

4. *New York Times*, June 14, 1963, 47:3.

5. Giuseppe Vindigni, "Albergo Hilton a Roma," *Costruire* 6 (May–June 1964): 21–30.

6. "The architecture of the interior, inspired by other constructions belonging to the Hilton corporation, is the work of the architects Franco Albini, Ignazio Gardella, Melchiorre Bega, and Andriano Alessandrini in consultation with Emmanuel Gran, director of interiors for Hilton International, and Inge Bech, the company's director of interior decoration." Vindigni, "Albergo Hilton," 22, my translation.

7. Grace Retondini suggested that the fountain was designed by Pier Luigi Nervi, to whom she also ascribed the staircase. Interview, Cavalieri Hilton, November 13, 1998.

8. The earliest complete set of plans that I found in the drafting office at the Cavalieri Hilton were dated 1963.

9. Filomena Pierdomenico and Mario Piersensini, eds., *Ugo Luccichenti architetto*, intro. Mario Manieri-Elia (Rome: Officina Edizioni, 1980). In revisionist histories of the creation of urban sprawl in Rome in the 1950s, his *palazzine*, or mansion-apartments, are identified as among the more interesting. Their façades certainly have a Mendelsohnian liveliness that distinguishes them from the functionalist blocks that generally characterize the new suburbs. Mario Manieri Elia, "Il contributo di Ugo Luccichenti," in *La palazzina Romana degli anni '50*, special issue of *Metamorfosi: quaderni di architettura* 15 (1990): 33–38. His dramatic deployment of strip balconies with repetitive protrusions to disrupt the planarity of the street façade appears arbitrary and certainly ornamental. These Modern mannerisms are echoed on the façade of the Cavalieri Hilton.

10. Richard Joseph, *Hilton Hotels Around-the-World Travel Guide*, foreword by Conrad N. Hilton (Garden City, N.Y.: Doubleday, 1966), 68–79.

11. The Hilton is difficult to access without an automobile. I arrived at the Cavalieri Hilton for the first time during a taxi strike. I took the underground to the last stop (S. Pietro) then the 999 bus up Monte Mario. Even then there was a ten-minute walk to the hotel. In a letter to Conrad N. Hilton, Houser emphasized the centrality of the site. He suggested that the Vatican is only a half mile distant. He further claimed that "the site is now a ten minute drive from downtown Rome, but a new, scenic road giving a more direct access is a prerequisite to carrying out the project." John W. Houser, letter to Conrad N. Hilton, Rome, April 20, 1954, Conrad N. Hilton College Archives and Library, University of Houston (hereafter Hilton Archives). Perhaps in 1954 the projected Hilton was a ten-minute drive to the city. Traffic is much worse now.

12. In the 1960s, the Excelsior was owned by CIGA (Compagnia Italiana dei Grandi Alberghi); now it is part of ITT Sheraton's "Luxury Collection" of hotels. See also Willi Frischauer, *An Hotel Is Like a Woman: The Grand Hotels of Europe* (London: Leslie Frewin, 1965), 64.

13. Touring Club Italiano, *Roma e dintorni* (Milan: Garzanti, 1977), 309.

14. There are, of course, other explanations. Charles Bell suggested that the Cavalieri Hilton "was built for big conferences. Europe wasn't ready for conventions. The Europeans never had conventions like those in the United States until recently." Interview, New York, June 23, 1997. One of the former general managers of the Cavalieri Hilton blamed its lack of financial success on the Italian trade unions.

15. John W. Houser, letter transcribed by Jean F. Hansen, secretary to Mr. Houser, and sent to Messrs. J. B. Herndon and R. J. Caverly, September 5, 1950.

16. The full text appears in the appendix to this chapter.

17. Memorandum from Theodore J. Pozzy to Paul Hyde Bonner, August 30, 1950, Hilton Archives, 2e.

18. "I just received a cable saying that the Italian architect will arrive in New York tomorrow. Skidmore's office will have men ready to start discussions with him but all of them are going to need specific advice as to just what we want the hotel to be. We are working on a list of requirements but before it is finished I feel that it is important that we get the best ideas possible. I have given J. B. a questionnaire just received from the Italians which is asking for our decision on many basic questions. It is illustrative

of the type of answers we are going to have to reach conclusions on within the next few weeks. I would particularly like your ideas as to what you would like to see in the Rome hotel, and would also like to have a clear right to call on any specialized experts in the Hilton organization to get the benefit of their thinking. J. B. will discuss this further with you. cc: Mr. J. B. Herndon, Jr." John W. Houser, letter to Conrad N. Hilton, January 23, 1951, Hilton Archives.

19. Dr. Aldo Samaritani, managing director, Società Generale Immobiliare di Lavori di Utilità Pubblica ed Agricola, Rome, Italy, remarks at a meeting in the Bankers Club, New York, March 14, 1951, Hilton Archives. A slightly abbreviated copy of the text appears in the appendix of this chapter.

20. Hotel specifications are listed in a memorandum attached to the transcription of Aldo Samaritani's remarks to the Bankers Club of New York. The information and quotes in this paragraph come from that memorandum.

21. "Designers of the new hotel will be the New York architectural firm of Skidmore, Owings & Merrill, which has designed several of America's most outstanding modern-style buildings. Construction will be by Sogene, an Italian concern, with Hilton representatives acting in an advisory capacity." Arthur Foristall, press release, November 23, 1950, Hilton Archives.

22. "Financial arrangements between the Italian and American companies follow the pattern successfully pursued by Hilton Hotels in connection with the Caribe Hilton in San Juan, Puerto Rico. The Hilton company will supply adequate working capital, operate the hotel and pay to Società Generale Immobiliare as rent $66\frac{2}{3}$ percent of the gross operating profit. The remaining $33\frac{1}{3}$ percent will be retained by Hilton Hotels International, Inc." Arthur Foristall, press release, November 23, 1950, Hilton Archives.

23. Quoted by Peter Bondanella, "America and the Post-War Italian Cinema," *Rivista di Studi Italiani* 2 (1984): 112.

24. Apparently Immobiliare hoped to use some of these monies to fund cheap loans for the construction of the Hilton. Documentation is included in the appendix to this chapter.

25. Bondanella, "America and the Post-War Italian Cinema," 112–13.

26. John W. Houser, letter to Conrad N. Hilton, from Rome, May 30, 1951, Hilton Archives.

27. John W. Houser, letter to Conrad N. Hilton, from Madrid, Spain, January 27, 1952, Hilton Archives.

28. E. Allen Fidel, chief, Mutual Security Agency, Trade Division, Special Mission to Italy for Economic Cooperation, letter to John W. Houser, June 5, 1952.

29. Dr. Aldo Samaritani, Società Generale Immobiliare, letter to John W. Houser, Rome, September 11, 1952, Hilton Archives.

30. Samaritani to Houser, September 11, 1952, Hilton Archives.

31. Dr. Aldo Samaritani, Società Generale Immobiliare, letter to John W. Houser, Rome, March 12, 1953, Hilton Archives.

32. Clare Booth Luce, American ambassador to Rome, letter to Conrad N. Hilton, Rome, June 8, 1953, Hilton Archives.

33. John W. Houser, letter to Conrad N. Hilton, Rome, April 20, 1954, Hilton Archives. The financial arrangements are discussed in detail. The land was valued at $1.6 million; the building and furnishings were estimated to cost $5 million. "This estimate is believed reasonable to accept since Immobiliare is one of the largest builders in Italy and also has completed two hotels in the last few years." Four hundred thousand dollars was to be reserved for contingencies. The total cost was projected at $7 million. Banca Nazionale del Lavoro was to underwrite a ten-year loan for $3,200,000 at $7\frac{1}{2}$% interest.

34. John W. Houser, letter to Conrad N. Hilton, Rome, April 20, 1954, Hilton Archives. For the view of Hilton International's Italian partners on the matter, see the memorandum of Eugenio Gualdi, president and general manager, Società Generale Immobiliare, to Conrad N. Hilton, April 15, 1954, in the appendix to this chapter.

35. John W. Houser, statement before the Committee on Foreign Affairs, United States House of Representatives during hearings on the H.R. joint resolution no. 350, March 3, 1954.

36. John W. Houser, letter to Conrad N. Hilton, July 16, 1954, Hilton Archives.

37. This strategy is mentioned in the letter of Eugenio Gualdi sent to Conrad N. Hilton in April, 1954, included in the appendix to this chapter.

38. The press release read: "The Società Generale Immobiliare, in co-operation with Hilton Hotels International, have formed the company to be known as Italo Americana Nuovo Alberghi, which will have an eventual capitalization of some $3,000,000. The hotel will be known as the Albergo dei Cavalieri Hilton and will cost approximately $7,000,000. It will include 400 guest rooms and a number of large function rooms and restaurants. Emilio Pifferi, a famous Italian architect, is presently consulting in Rome with John W. Houser, executive vice president of Hilton Hotels International, regarding the design and planning for the new hotel. The Albergo dei Cavalieri Hilton will be completely air conditioned. Its site is in the Monte Mario district of Rome in the northwestern part of the city. A shopping center, swimming pools, tennis courts and elaborate gardens are part of the project. It is expected that Rome's municipal government will build a new expressway from the heart of the city to the hotel itself and make other improvements in the area surrounding the hotel." Fred Joyce, publicity director, Hilton Hotels Corporation, Publicity Release, New York, December 13, 1954.

39 *New York Times*, December 5, 1954, 37:1.

40. Arthur Foristall, press release, November 23, 1950, Hilton Archives.

41. Conrad N. Hilton, *Be My Guest* (1957; Englewood Cliffs, N.J.: Prentice-Hall, 1987), 291. I was unable to find the article to which Hilton referred.

42. The PCI, the Italian Communist Party, recognized and opposed American cultural imperialism, conscious as they were of the anticommunist propaganda of popular American cinema. Stephen Gundle, "Il PCI e la campagna contro Hollywood (1948–1958)," in *Hollywood in Europa*, ed. David W. Ellwood and Gian Piero Brunetta (Florence: Ponte alle Grazie, 1991), 113–32. Stephen Gundle's new work on this subject, *Between Hollywood and Moscow: The Italian Communists and the Challenge of Mass Culture, 1943–1991* (Durham, N.C.: Duke University Press, 2000), had not yet appeared when this book went to press.

43. *New York Times*, September 26, 1958, 2:4.

44. Michele Valori, "I lavori per il Piano Regolatore di Roma: Quattro anni difficili," *Urbanistica* 28–29 (October 1959): 127–63, particularly, 140–43.

45. The Hilton might, however, be presented as the salvation of public space, though its "public" is distinctly configured. Grace Retondini, assistant to the general manager of the Cavalieri Hilton, contends: "The opposition—the communists and the socialists—has always argued that the Hilton has ruined Monte Mario, but the truth is that the Hilton has *preserved* it. We have this magnificent park which surrounds the hotel. The hotel is obviously a public establishment so anyone can come and enjoy the hotel and the beautiful park. We do have tennis courts where people come and play who are not guests of the hotel. And there is a swimming pool which is open to those from outside of the hotel. Especially in a city where it is not easy to find sporting facilities and high standards, the hotel makes a significant contribution. . . . The gardens and the views are still here because of the Hilton. And the Hilton is a public place, anyone can come here and have a drink and enjoy the view." Interview, Cavalieri Hilton, November 13, 1998.

46. The scandal is summarized in Michele Valori, "I lavori per il Piano Regolatore," 140–43. See also Italo Insolera, *Roma moderna: Un secolo di storia urbanistica, 1870–1970* (Turin: Einaudi, 1976), 112–14. I thank Stephen Grundle for this reference.

47. E. M. Forster, *A Room with a View* (New York: Barnes and Noble, 1993), 64.

48. *New York Times*, April 29, 1971, 40:3.

49. *New York Times*, May 11, 1971, 38:4.

50. *New York Times*, May 14, 1971, 22:4.

51. "The Florence Planning Commission has unanimously rejected a plan for construction of a Hilton International hotel on a hill dominating the city. The commission ruled yesterday that the $6.4 million project would spoil the landscape." *New York Times*, October 10, 1971, 4:8.

52. Harry Brewster, *The Cosmopolites: A Nineteenth-Century Family Drama* (Wilby, United Kingdom: Michael Russel, 1994), xii–xiii.

53. Brewster, *Cosmopolites*, 279.

54. Brewster, *Cosmopolites;* Harry Brewster, *A Cosmopolite's Journey: Episodes from a Life* (London: Radcliffe Press, 1998).

55. Firenze, 6 dicembre 1983

Pregiatissimo Signor Direttore della "Azaione," Firenze.

I sottoscritti Istituti Culturali stranieri che hanno la loro sede in Firenze e vivono la loro vita insieme a quella della Città; memori del sentimento di affettuosa fratellanza con cui la città ha sempre accolto la loro opera nei lieti e nei dolorosi momenti; tuttora certi di tale attiva fratellanza, si uniscono agli Istituti e alle associazioni fiorentine per manifestare la loro preoccupata sorpresa nel costatare che possa essere presa in consid erazione la inammissibile idea di costruire l'albergo Hilton sulle pendici del colle di Bellosguardo, uno dei luoghi fiorentini più ammirevoli per la loro naturale e altamente poetica bellezza.

Con distinti saluti e rigraziamenti,

Harvard University, I Tatti, Gene A. Brucker
Istituto Britannico (signature illegible)
Istituto Francese (signature illegible)
Istituto Germanico di Storia dell'Arte, Peter T (signature illegible)
Istituto Universitario Europeo (signature illegible)
Istituto Universitario Olandese(signature illegible)

I want to thank Professor Gino Cassagrande for correcting my translation.

56. *Nazione*, December 17, 1983, n.p.

57. Harry Brewster, "Florence under Attack," *Country Life*, April 24, 1975, 1030–32.

58. Fratelli Alinari, *Gli Alinari fotografi a Firenze, 1852–1920* (Florence: Arti Grafiche Bandettini, 1985).

Notes to Chapter 6

I am grateful to Eric Long, general manager of the Waldorf-Astoria Hotel in New York, and James Blauvelt, director of catering at the Waldorf-Astoria, for discussing with me the history and present of this largest of all luxury hotels. I am also grateful for the access I had to the Thomas Cook Archives.

The first epigraph to this chapter is from "Palace Homes for the Traveller," *Godey's Lady's Book and Magazine* 60 (May 1860): 465–66, quoted by Bayrd Still, *Urban America: A History with Documents* (Boston: Little, Brown, 1974), 153. The second is from H. B. Love, *Establishing and Operating a Year-Round Motor Court*, Industrial (Small Business) Series no. 50 (Washington, D.C.: U.S. Department of Commerce, 1945), quoted by Frederic Arden Pawley, "Motels," *Architectural Record* 107 (March 1950), 111.

1. "The Castellana Hilton in Madrid brought Spain more than $1 million worth of U.S. tourists in its first year of operation. The Istanbul Hilton, opened in 1955, is given large credit for an electrifying 60% increase in tourism that took place in the hotel's first year of operation. Egypt's President Nasser looks with favor upon the Nile Hilton—whose 1959 opening he attended personally—because it brings in $12 million in foreign currency annually into Egypt." Dora Jane Hamblin, "In Nineteen Lands, Instant America," *Life*, August 30, 1963, 68.

2. Still the best place to start thinking about the commodity is Karl Marx, "Commodities," in *Capital*, ed. Frederick Engels (New York: International Press, 1967), 35–83. For the relevance of the commodity to art-historical analysis, see Paul Wood, "Commodity," in *Critical Terms for Art History*, ed. Robert S. Nelson and Richard Shiff, (Chicago: University of Chicago Press, 1996), 257–80. Among the many useful assessments of the commodity are Arjun Appadurai, *The Social Life of Things* (New York: Cambridge University Press, 1986), and John Frow, *Time and Commodity Culture: Essays in Cultural Theory and Postmodernity* (Oxford: Clarendon Press, 1997). Anthropology continues to generate interesting discussions of the commodity; for example, William Pietz, "The Fetish of Civilization: Sacrificial Blood and Monetary Debt," in *Colonial Subjects*, ed. Peter Pels and Oscar Saleminck (Ann Arbor: University of Michigan Press, 1999), 53–82.

3. Painting continues to be celebrated as the principle index of Modernism. T. J. Clark, *Farewell to an Idea: Episodes from a History of Modernism* (New Haven, Conn.: Yale University Press, 1999).

4. For an excellent introduction to Fordism, see David Harvey, *The Condition of*

Postmodernity: An Enquiry into the Origins of Cultural Change (Oxford: Basil Blackwell, 1989), 125–40.

5. "The original Kodak camera had quite literally liberated photographers from the darkrooms of the nineteenth century and enabled people to step outside and casually take pictures. It democratized the craft of photography. Anyone, the first Eastman advertisements promised, could operate a Kodak camera. The Brownie expanded even that large group; everyone, it was claimed, could take good pictures with a Brownie, even children. Particularly children. . . . Advertisements for the Brownie were primarily directed at the children's market." Douglas Collins, *The Story of Kodak* (New York: Harry N. Abrams, 1990), 97.

6. The use of the camera in the redefinition of intimacy is, of course, found much earlier at a different social level. Carol Mavor, *Becoming: The Photographs of Clementina, Viscountess Hawarden* (Durham, N.C.: Duke University Press, 1999).

7. Collins, *Story of Kodak*, 136.

8. Westinghouse established KDKA in Pittsburgh in 1920 as the first broadcasting station as a means of marketing its radio receivers to a mass audience. Erik Barnouw, *A Tower in Babel: A History of Broadcasting in the United States*, 2 vols. (New York: Oxford University Press, 1966), 1:64–74.

9. For the political and intellectual arenas of the public, if not its physical space, see Jürgen Habermas, *The Structural Transformation of the Public Sphere*, transl. Thomas Burger (Cambridge: MIT Press, 1989).

10. The term "McDonaldization" has been addressed most tenaciously by George Ritzer, from his *The McDonaldization of Society* (Thousand Oaks, Calif.: Pine Forge Press, 1993) to his *The McDonaldization Thesis: Explorations and Extensions* (London: Sage Publications, 1998). At least in his earlier work, Ritzer seems to treat McDonald's as the virtual originator of the phenomenon that it names. Here I use the term paradigmatically. Changes in transient accommodation began before Dick and Maurice McDonald streamlined their food production in 1948.

11. John Love, *McDonald's: Behind the Arches* (New York: Bantam: 1986), 16, ascribes Fordism to the McDonald brothers. They developed the techniques of mass-produced food, but Ray Kroc took fast food to another level by franchising the McDonald's methods nationwide. For a postmodernist reading of McDonald's, see Allen Shelton, "Writing McDonald's, Eating the Past: McDonald's as a Postmodern Space," *Studies in Symbolic Interaction* 15 (1993): 103–18.

12. "Modernization," *Encyclopaedia Britannica Online* http://search.eb.com/bol/topic?eu=115569&sctn=16 (accessed June 8, 1999).

13. "From about 1950, with increasing frequency as the decade progressed, many traditionally urban corporations migrated to the suburbs. Rumor had it that the location of a new office was often determined by its proximity to the company president's golf club." Carol Herselle Krinsky, *Gordon Bunshaft of Skidmore, Owings and Merrill* (New York: Architectural History Foundation, 1988), 55.

14. "Throwaway Living: Disposable Items Cut Down Household Chores," *Life*, August 1, 1955, 43–44, suggests how familiar such throw-away items were in the mid-fifties.

15. The original McDonald's type—a red-and-white striped box framed by neon-lighted golden arches was designed by Stanley Clark Meston in 1952. The brick box with a low-profile, shingled, mansard roof was introduced in 1968. Alan Hess, *Googie: Fifties Coffee Shop Architecture* (San Francisco: Chronicle Books, 1986), 96–107.

16. Despite numerous errors of fact, still the best general history of American hotels is Jefferson Williamson, *The American Hotel: An Anecdotal History* (New York: Knopf, 1930). See also Nikolaus Pevsner, "Hotels," in his *History of Building Types*, Bollingen Series 35-19 (Princeton, N.J.: Princeton University Press, 1976), 169–92. American preeminence in the hotel trade is, however, commonly obscured by a Eurocentricity bred of European elitism and an American sense of cultural inferiority. "Much of life in an American hotel was and is European. The standards of service, of appointments and furnishings, the kitchens and dining rooms, were patterned after those of the hotels of the continent," writes Ludwig Bemelmans in his book promoting hotel careers in America. According to Bemelmans, Europeans "set the standards which to some extent remain, and . . . certainly established the mood of the modern hotel." He supports this claim with a photograph of the Ritz, captioned, "When American hotels were log cabins, the Ritz in Paris was already seeing French history made on the Place

Vendome." Ludwig Bemelmans, *At Your Service: the Way of Life in a Hotel* (Evanston, Ill.: Row, Peterson, 1941), 13–16. The Ritz, financed by an English consortium and established by refurbishing three baroque mansions, was opened only in 1896, three years *after* its archetype, the great Waldorf in New York. On a somewhat higher level, Stanley Jackson, biographer of the London's renowned Savoy Hotel, relates that its founder was inspired by his experience of superior hotels in the United States. He recounts how American technologies such as mail chutes and Otis lifts were the celebrated features of the renovations of the Savoy in 1903. Stanley Jackson, *The Savoy: The Romance of a Great Hotel* (London: Frederick Muller, 1964), 41. Nevertheless, the same author who documents the importance of American innovations in the earlier phases of the Savoy disdains those of his own moment in the early 1960s: "An hotel like the Savoy cannot guarantee survival by piping music and iced water through its arteries. Its appeal has deeper and more traditional roots" (288). Ice water, rightly regarded as an American peculiarity, was a particularly irritating referent for European hoteliers: it came to stand for all those other expensive innovations introduced to Europe by American competition after the war—notably, air-conditioning, direct-dial telephones, and radios or televisions in every room.

17. Talbot Hamlin, *Benjamin Henry Latrobe* (New York: Oxford University Press, 1955), 117–20.

18. Pevsner, *Building Types*, 175. A monograph was published on the hotel by William Harvard Eliot, *A Description of Tremont House* (Boston: Gray and Bowen, 1830).

19. Pevsner, *Building Types*, 177, expresses some scepticism. William Chambers and Robert Chambers, "The Large Hotel Question," *Chambers's Journal of Popular Literature* 10 (March 11, 1854): 152–53, gives a remarkable description of the Mount Vernon. It includes the comment "Among the luxuries of the place, is that every bedroom has a bath attached, with hot and cold water always laid on." The bridal suite is also noted as an American eccentricity.

20. Williamson, *American Hotel*, 244–45.

21. The first steel-frame hotel in New York was the New Netherland, built in 1893. Pevsner, *Building Types*, 182.

22. For American superiority in hotel technology and scale in the nineteenth century, Pevsner, *Building Types*, 188–89. Pevsner suggests that English and French accomplishments, including the great railroad hotels, can only be appreciated if "one forgets for a while the dimensions of American hotels." The greatest of these railroad hotels was Sir George Gilbert Scott's Midland Grand Hotel at St. Pancras. Scott's plans were accepted in 1866. The hotel was closed in 1935, largely because of the "lack of a sufficient number of private bathrooms and the difficulty of adding more." The solidity of the building's construction made it difficult to modify. Jack Simmons, *St. Pancras Station* (London: George Allen and Unwin: 1968), 81. See also Dan Cruikshank, "Gothic Revivalist," *Architects Journal* 206 (1997): 59–76.

23. Piers Brendon, *Thomas Cook: 150 Years of Popular Tourism* (London: Secker and Warburg, 1991), 143.

24. *New York Times*, May 9, 1909, V 9:1.

25. T. E. L. Godkin, "The Summer Hotels," *Nation*, September 11, 1884, 216–17.

26. Williamson, *American Hotel*, 13, cites the City Hotel in New York of 1794 as the first example.

27. G. K. Chesterton, *What I Saw in America* (New York: Dodd, Mead, 1922), 23–24.

28. Chesterton, *What I Saw*, 25.

29. William Chambers and Robert Chambers, "Things as They Are in America," *Chambers's Journal of Popular Literature* 22 (June 3, 1854): 342.

30. Eugene Lyons, "The Hotel Lobby as a Public Utility," *New York Times*, September 3, 1922, VII 2:2.

31. Karl B. Raitz and John P. Jones III, " The City Hotel as Landscape Artifact and Community Symbol," *Journal of Cultural Geography* 9 (1988): 17–36, provide bibliography as well as an analysis of the social and political function of the hotel, particularly in frontier regions of the expanding country.

32. *New York Times*, March 26, 1922, II 7:1.

33. See the amusing account of Mary Mortimer Maxwell, "The Woman Who Seeks

a Hotel in New York," *New York Times*, February 7, 1909, V 6:3. Elite hotels in Europe also excluded single women. Hedda Adlon, daughter-in-law of the founder of Berlin's most famous hotel, the Adlon, commented: "We only accepted single women as room guests at the hotel if they were well known to us or came with a special introduction. As a rule their visits were arranged in advance either by some member of their family or, in the case of businesswomen, by the secretariat of some firm which was known to us." Hedda Adlon, *Hotel Adlon: The Life and Death of a Great Hotel,* transl. Norman Denny (London: Barrie Books, 1958), 175.

34. An incident of this sort involving Mrs. B. Frank, sister of U.S. senator Isidor Rayner, was reported on page 1 of the *New York Times* in 1907. Mrs. Frank left the Marlborough-Blenheim Hotel in Atlantic City upon being told by the hotel clerk "that he had been instructed by the proprietors to refuse to give rooms to Jews. 'The policy of the house,' he said, 'is opposed to Hebrews.'" *New York Times,* May 18, 1907, 1:1. The *Times* reported in the same article: "It is well known that a number of Jews prominent in professional and business life, in response to inquiries regarding accommodations at leading Atlantic City hotels, have recently received in reply printed or engraved cards setting forth that 'The patronage of Hebrews is not solicited.'" Anti-Semitic practices were commonplace. Reported in the *New York Times,* December 27, 1923, 23:1, for example, was the case of Nathan D. Shapiro, attorney and member of the New York State legislature from 1914 to 1916, who was denied a room at the Traymore, Atlantic City, on the basis of his name. His chauffeur, who applied at the same time, was given a reservation. "This situation brings back to my mind a plan which I was considering when I was a member of the Legislature to permit owners of hotels, maintained principally for vacation purposes, to exclude legally Jews, provided that they notified the public in some direct, unmistakable form that Jews are not welcome. The Jews under those conditions, I am sure, would not be offended. In fact, Jews are very anxious to know just where they are not welcome, so that they may not trespass upon the sacred ground of some semicivilized people. I have also since been reliably informed that the Traymore Hotel in their nonbusy season are happy to have the Jews fill up their vacant rooms and merely exclude the Jews on days when Jewish patronage is not essential."

35. Discrimination against African American patrons is treated in some detail by Kevin Haynes, "Spatial Other: Hotels, Henry James, Property" (Ph.D. diss., Duke University, 2001).

36. *New York Times,* June 11, 1950, X 3:1, reported that the Greater Miami Airport Hotel then under consideration was planned in such a way that distinguished foreign visitors would not be embarrassed by local "Jim Crow" laws: "A portion of the hotel will be set up as an International House, in order to obviate the Jim Crowism of the region. There will be no restrictions in dining or other public rooms."

37. Of the Tremont, Williamson, *The American Hotel,* 28, writes: "Its management was the first to recognize, as a matter of policy, the fact that, in spite of all the shouting about liberty and equality—and there was a great deal of it then—there were upper, middle, and lower classes in America, and that the top layer was yearning for exclusiveness."

38 . John Harold Sherry, *The Laws of Innkeepers: For Hotels, Motels, Restaurants, and Clubs* (Ithaca, N.Y.: Cornell University Press, 1972), provides a compilation of court findings on various aspects of hotel affairs—from who must be admitted to who might be ejected for what reason. The legal treatment of homosexuals as represented in this volume is quite extraordinary.

39. Lucius M. Boomer, "How We Fitted Ford's Principles to Our Business," *System* 44, no. 4 (October 1923): 421.

40. Boomer, "How We Fitted," 421, my italics.

41. Roy Carruthers, "Hotel Architecture from a Hotel Man's Viewpoint," parts 1–3, *Pencil Points* 4 (June 1923): 22–25, 55; (July 1923): 39–46, 63; (August 1923): 52–60, 62. Carruthers's articles are neither particularly insightful nor particularly well written. They are, however, symptomatic. They also provide a useful set of plans and elevations of hotels from the early 1920s.

42. He also mentions in passing a third type, the residential hotel. Residential hotels were a peculiarly American phenomenon. Though well established in the nineteenth century, they became an increasingly popular alternative to apartments or single-family dwellings between World Wars I and II. They are described in greater detail by Lucius

M. Boomer, president of Waldorf-Astoria, Inc., in his *Hotel Management: Principles and Practice* (New York: Harper, 1925), 5–6: "Formerly, residential hotels did not differ greatly in layout, appointments and service features from the high type of transient hotels. Today, there is a rapidly growing number of apartment hotels, specially designed and equipped for residential purposes, and quite unsuitable for taking care of transients advantageously. The modern residential hotels consist of suites that may be rented furnished or unfurnished, often equipped with a kitchen or kitchenettes. . . . Most of these hotels maintain restaurants, and if a tenant desires, personal laundry service, in fact all the numerous services common to transient hotels are provided for tenants." It was certainly assumed that this kind of living would become increasingly popular. "Just as surely as the trend developed away from the private home and toward the apartment house, so will the ultimate step be away from the apartment house and toward the apartment hotel." So James S. Warren, editor of *Hotel Management*, hilariously mispredicted in "What the Typical Apartment Hotel 'Looks Like,'" *Hotel Management* (November 1930): 406–8.

43. Norman S. Hayner, *Hotel Life* (Chapel Hill: University of North Carolina Press, 1936), 62.

44. The Olympic is now a grand hotel. It underwent a $60 million renovation between 1980 and 1982, after a new management agreement was signed between the University of Washington's Board of Regents in partnership with the Urban Investment and Development Company and Four Seasons Hotels, Ltd. All the public rooms with historic designation were restored, and 450 guest rooms, a garden court, service areas, carriage entrance, and swimming and exercise areas were rebuilt or added. The Olympic Hotel was awarded the coveted *Mobil Travel Guide* Five-Star Award in 1996, one of only twenty-three hotels in the country to be so designated. Descriptions of its new prestigiousness, like the cover article that appeared in the *Seattle Times Magazine* (November 3, 1996), depict its architectural sumptuousness in the illustrations, but do not in the text emphasize the hotel's architecture as one of the factors contributing to its new status. I want to thank Elaine Griffin, director of public relations for the Four Seasons Olympic for providing photographs and information on the hotel.

45. Carruthers, "Hotel Architecture," part 1, 23.

46. Carruthers, "Hotel Architecture," part 3, 53.

47. Carruthers, "Hotel Architecture," part 1, 25.

48. "The architect . . . usually thinks too much of the bedrooms and not enough of the working parts of the hotel. . . . The importance of this part of the house can be understood readily when one realizes that the Waldorf-Astoria has fourteen hundred employees, an excess of two hundred over the capacity of the house for guests." Carruthers, "Hotel Architecture," part 2, 39. In another context, Carruthers also notes: "Provision must be made for the comfort of these employees and for their feeding and care. They must have lockers, shower baths and many other conveniences that need to be taken into account in making plans for a hotel." Carruthers, "Hotel Architecture," part 1, 55.

49. Hayner, *Hotel Life*. "According to data compiled by Horwath and Horwath and published in the 1928 edition of the Hotel Red Book the number of employees per 100 rooms, the annual sales per room and the investment per room increase consistently as the size of the hotel increases. Hotels over 1,000 rooms had more than three times as many employees per 100 rooms as hotels with less than 50 rooms. They also had more than ten times the annual sales and more than six times the investment per room" (62–63).

50. Carruthers, "Hotel Architecture," part 2, 45, 63.

51. Carruthers, "Hotel Architecture," part 2, 45.

52. I am grateful to Bill Babb, an editor of the *Augusta Chronicler* for historical information on the Hotel Bon Air–Vanderbilt. At present it is a retirement home.

53. In the 1917 advertising pamphlet for the Bon Air–Vanderbilt, there are no interior images of the hotel. Most of the photographs represent its golf course. *Hotel Bon Air, Augusta, Ga.* (Augusta, Ga.: The Hotel, 1917).

54. Chambers and Chambers, "Things as They Are," 340.

55. For the nineteenth century, see Godkin, "Summer Hotels," 218.

56. Walter Irving Hamilton, *Promoting New Hotels: When Does It Pay?* (New York:

Harper, 1930), 36.

57. Rufus Jarman, *A Bed for the Night: The Story of the Wheeling Bellboy E. M. Statler and His Remarkable Hotels* (New York: Harper, 1952).

58. "Hotels," *Architectural Forum* 92 (June 1950): 90–101.

59. "The Hotel Statler, Buffalo," *Architectural Forum* 39 (1923):11.

60. "The Hotel Statler, Buffalo," 11.

61. "The Hotel Statler, Buffalo," 13.

62. For bibliography, see John A. Jakle, Keith A. Sculle, and Jefferson S. Rogers, *The Motel in America* (Baltimore, Md.: Johns Hopkins University Press, 1996); for remarkable images of motels, as well as a summary history, see John Margolies, *Home Away from Home: Motels in America* (Boston: Little, Brown, 1995).

63. Arthur H. Carhart, "Where City and Nation Unite to Act as Summer Hosts," *American City* 22 (May 1920): 499. Also in the same issue, Thomas B. Reid, "Camp Grounds for Lincoln Highway Tourists," 502.

64. Pawley, "Motels," 111.

65. Pawley, "Motels," 111. The article is J. E. Hoover, "Camps of Crime," *American Magazine* (February 1940): 14–15, 130–32.

66. Pawley, "Motels," 111.

67. *New York Times*, April 30, 1950, II 15:4.

68. Margolies, *Home Away from Home*, 54, interprets the swimming pool and neat landscaping as signs of a somewhat different sort: "The irony in all of this was that these concrete oceans were seldom used. Their real function was symbolic; they were a visible icon used to make potential customers stop. . . . What was important about the pools, patios, and surrounding landscaping is that they represented a taming and refinement of the landscape as the motel building type became more refined and sophisticated."

69. Hotels Statler Co., *Ellsworth Statler* (n.p.: Hotels Statler Co., 1948), 9.

70. The Shelborne Hotel on Miami Beach by Igor B. Polevitzky and T. Trip Russel was one of the best of the new hotels. It had fewer then 150 rooms and no shops. Although the cocktail lounge, ground-floor dining room, and eleven of the thirteen rooms on each floor had ocean views, the hotel itself was not transparent. The side rooms, which had a limited panorama, were provided with a balcony as compensation. "The Shelborne Hotel, Miami Beach," *Architectural Record* 90 (July 1941): 41–46.

71. "New Hotels—Just Because They Are Better," *Architectural Forum* 98 (January 1953): 97.

72 The Washington Statler is now the Capital Hilton. I am indebted to Frank Otero, the general manager, and Michael Healy, the chief engineer of the building, who shared their remarkable knowledge of their hotel with me. The hotel was proposed in 1938, construction began in 1941, and the building was completed in 1943. It was financed by Metropolitan Life Insurance ($2 million) and Reconstruction Finance Corporation ($5 million).

73. For an amusing account of the hotel's origins, see David Brinkley, *Washington Goes to War* (New York: Alfred A. Knopf, 1988), 118–19.

74. Brinkley, *Washington Goes to War*, 253.

75. "Washington Statler," *Hotel Monthly* (March 1943): 1–53, reprinted in booklet form for the Washington Statler.

76. "Washington Statler," *Architectural Forum* 78 (June 1943): 61–76. For this firm's work for Statler, see Robert Bruegmann, *Holabird and Roche, Holabird and Root: An Illustrated Catalog of Works*, 3 vols. (New York: Garland, in cooperation with the Chicago Historical Society, 1991), 3, 344–50.

77. In the original plans for the hotel, the adaptation to the automobile was apparently even more radical. The *New York Times*, January 10, 1941, 34:6, reported "An unusual feature will be an automobile driveway through the center of the hotel from K to L Street, with entrances from this driveway to the grand ballroom and to the main lobby."

78. Jarman, *Bed for the Night*, 209–10; also quoted by Jack Eisen, "Metro Scheme," *Washington Post*, March 5, 1986, B2.

79. Washington's overcrowded conditions during the war, as well as the city's social life, are aptly described by Brinkley, *Washington Goes to War*.

80. The rooms were enlarged and their number reduced in subsequent renovations of the hotel. In 1976, at the same time that the name of the hotel was changed to the Capital Hilton, the inventory was reduced to 721 rooms, many with double bathrooms. In the major renovation costing $48 million in 1984–1986, room arrangement was completely changed; the number of rooms was reduced to 544. Interview with Frank Otero at the Capital Hilton, Washington, D.C., April 30, 1999.

81. In 1946, the living room in a Levittown house was 12 by 16 feet, or 192 square feet. This section might as well have been titled "Levittization" as "McDonaldization." The new efficiencies in building that William Levitt introduced in his construction of new suburbs for an expanded middle class after World War II decreased the workers' interaction in the production of buildings but increased both consumer satisfaction and his own profit. The assembly-line techniques invented for the construction of houses allowed Levitt to build thirty-six houses a day. Skilled labor was largely replaced by unskilled labor. Subcontractors, real estate agencies, and middlemen were eliminated. Houses were available for under $8,000. For an introduction to Levittown, see Herbert J. Gans, *The Levittowners: Ways of Life and Politics in a New Suburban Community* (New York: Pantheon, 1967).

82. Jarman, *Bed for the Night,* 274.

83. Jarman, *Bed for the Night,* 199.

84. Statler first installed radios in his Boston Hotel in 1925; in 1928, at the cost of a million dollars all his hotels were retrofitted with radios. For Statler and, on a smaller scale, other hoteliers, the radio "proved a most satisfactory method of providing the guest with entertainment in the privacy of their rooms." *New York Times,* January 30, 1928, 25:6; February 5, 1928, IX 4:7.

85. I heard this from a number of oral sources, but this planned adornment may be apocryphal.

86. Interview with Michael Healy in the Capital Hilton, April 30, 1999.

87. Jackson, *Savoy,* 238.

88. Now the Los Angeles Omni.

89. Jarman, *Bed for the Night,* 274–276.

90. "Statler Center, Los Angeles," *Architectural Record* 109 (March 1951): 98.

91. On the rise and decline of Pan Am, Robert L. Gandt, *Skygods: The Fall of Pan Am* (New York: Morrow, 1995).

92. "Hotels," *Architectural Forum* 92 (June 1950): 90–101.

93. See in addition: William B. Tabler, "Developing a Hotel: Clients and Finances Have Changed," *Architectural Record* 155 (May 1974): 146–47; "American Hotel Design Today," Statler Lectures (Amherst: University of Massachusetts, Department of Hotel, Restaurant, and Tourism Management, 1971), 1–6.

94. "Bill Tabler's Hotel Boom," *Architectural Forum* 107 (July 1957): 115–21.

95. "Bill Tabler's Hotel Boom," 118.

96. "Bill Tabler's Hotel Boom," 116.

97. William B. Tabler, "New Forces at Work on the In-City Hotel," *Architectural Record* 144 (July 1968): 134–37.

98. See above, note 14.

99. "Bill Tabler's Hotel Boom," 120.

100. *New York Times,* November 14, 1935, 19:4, quotes the then current Hotel Red Book, which indicated that there were, at that time, more than eighty groups in the United States operating three or more hotels under the same management. The three largest were the Knott Hotel chain of New York (9,825 rooms), American Hotel chain (9,305), Statler (7,700). An earlier *New York Times* article reported that Ralph Hitz, president of the Hotel New Yorker and National Hotel Management, Inc., argued for the necessity of hotel chain operation to stabilize the industry. "Out of the 18,523 hotels of twenty-five rooms or more in the United States and Canada, only 474 are operated as a part of chains of three or more hotels. This is slightly more than 2.5% of the hotels in the two countries." *New York Times,* January 2, 1934, 32:3.

101. *Business Week,* September 18, 1954, 186–90.

102. "Two Kinds of Hilton Hotels," *Architectural Forum* 104 (April 1956): 124–31; in the same issue, "A Look at Bedrooms," 132–37.

103. "Two Kinds of Hilton Hotels," 125.

104. "Two Kinds of Hilton Hotels," 127.

105. "The Caribe Hilton: An Object Lesson in What You Can Do with $7,000,000," *Interiors* 109 (April 1950): 74.

106. "Caribe Hilton: An Object Lesson," 74.

107. "Spectacular Luxury in the Caribbean—the Caribe Hilton Hotel," *Architectural Forum* 92 (March 1950): 98.

108. "Caribe Hilton: An Object Lesson," 77.

109. "Spectacular Luxury in the Caribbean," 98.

110. "El Panama: Hotel Made for the Tropics," *Architectural Forum* 94 (April 1951): 141.

111. "El Panama: Hotel Made for the Tropics," 139.

112. P.R.B., "Hilton Hotel, Istanbul," *Architectural Review* 113 (March 1953): 119–20.

113. For example, *Edward Durell Stone: The Evolution of an Architect* (New York: Horizon Press, 1962), 6, and Muriel Emanuel, ed., *Contemporary Architects*, 3rd ed. (New York: St. James Press, 1995), 927.

114. John Wellborn Root, "Hotels and Apartment Houses," in *Forms and Functions of Twentieth-Century Architecture*, ed. Talbot Hamlin, 4 vols. (New York: Columbia University Press, 1952), 3:96–130.

115. "Beehive in the Tropics: Hotel El Panama," *Life*, January 7, 1952, 50–57.

116. Charles Warner modestly makes no claim for the Caribe Hilton's priority. Nevertheless, he doesn't remember having any access to Stone's project. Telephone interview, April 21, 1999.

117. *Architectural Forum* 92 (June 1950): 101–4.

118. Conrad N. Hilton, *Be My Guest* (1957; Englewood Cliffs, N.J.: Prentice-Hall, 1987), 232–33.

119. Arthur Hailey, *Hotel* (Garden City, N.Y.: Doubleday, 1965), 77.

120. Hailey, *Hotel,* 50.

121. Hailey, *Hotel,* 101.

122. Hailey, *Hotel,* 247–48.

123. *New York Times,* June 11, 1950, X 3:1.

124. This definition was a theme of Dean MacCannell, *The Tourist: A New Theory of the Leisure Class* (New York: Schocken Books, 1976), that was further popularized by Jonathan Culler, "Semiotics of Tourism," *American Journal of Semiotics* 1 (1981): 127–40.

125. Johann Wolfgang von Goethe, *Italian Journey (1786–1788),* transl. W. H. Auden and Elizabeth Mayer (San Francisco: North Point Press, 1982), 373.

126. Judith Adler, "Origins of Sightseeing," *Annals of Tourism Research* 16 (1989): 7–29, argues that in the seventeenth and eighteenth century, "tourism" was discourse. The object of travel was intellectual and literary. Its purpose was political and professional, not relaxation.

127. Thomas Cook, a committed Methodist, organized his first excursions to benefit temperance meetings. "Thomas Cook saw tourism as his mission to humanity; it was a means of emancipation for large numbers of people whose work was drudgery and whose recreation was drink. The iron-willed John [Thomas Cook's son] was determined to forge a successful business, which could only be done, he believed, by attracting a 'select,' prosperous clientele." *Thomas Cook: 150 Years of Popular Tourism* (London: Secker and Warburg, 1991), 2.

128. Karl Baedeker published his first guide, modeled on Murray, in 1839. A. J. Norval, *The Tourist Industry: A National and International Survey* (London: Pitman and Sons, 1936), 40–41. For a classic analysis of the guide book, see Roland Barthes, "Blue Guide," in *Mythologies,* transl. Annette Lavers (New York: Hill and Wang, 1972), 74–78.

129. E. M. Forster, *Room with a View* (New York: Barnes and Noble, 1993), 21–22. The novel was first published in 1908.

130. Karl Baedeker, *Italy: Handbook for Travellers* (Leipzig: Karl Baedeker, 1877); *Baedeker's Touring Guide: Italy* (Stuttgart: Baekekers Autoführer-Verlag, 1962); also compare *Baedeker's Rome* (Basingstoke, United Kingdom: AA Publishing,1999).

131. Baedeker, *Italy*, v.

132. *Baedeker's Touring Guide*, 2.

133. "Europe, Here They Come," *Life*, June 27, 1955, 34–39.

134. József Böröcz, *Leisure Migration: A Sociological Study on Tourism* (Oxford: Pergamon, 1996), 51, offers this definition of tourism: "The tourism industry is that branch of the mass media in which not only the message but the receiver is physically transported through the communicative channel. Print, broadcast and travel media offer commercial ways in which curiosity—desire to know and be entertained—is satisfied. Tourism is the leisure migration of industrial capitalism."

135. Böröcz, *Leisure Migration*, 3.

Notes to the Epilogue

1. From the Web site http://www.monopoly.com/history/history.htm, accessed July 1999.

2. According to display descriptions in Pollock's Toy Museum, London.

3. According to the corporate narrative, Parker Brothers initially rejected Darrow's game. In response, Darrow himself assembled some five thousand handmade sets of the game that he then successfully marketed through a department store in Philadelphia. Parker Brothers subsequently changed its corporate mind and began producing the game in 1935 (http://www.monopoly.com/history/history.htm).

4. In its sixty-year history, over 200 million games have been sold worldwide. Over a billion little red hotels have been produced since 1935. The corporation holds trademarks on the tokens, on the images of Railroad, Community Chest, Chance, and on the Title Deed designs. Boardwalk and all four game board corners are also legally protected.

5. From the Web site http://www.antimonopoly.com/story.html, accessed November 1998. See also Ralph Anspagh, *The Billion Dollar Monopoly Swindle: During a David and Goliath Battle, the Inventor of the Anti-Monopoly Game Uncovers the Secret History of Monopoly* (Redwood City, Calif.: Ralph Anspach, 1999).

6. For a classic discussion of popular culture and imperialism, see Ariel Dorfman, *The Empire's Old Clothes: What the Lone Ranger, Babar and Other Innocent Heroes Do to Our Minds* (New York: Viking Penguin, 1996; first published in the United States by Pantheon Books, 1983).

7. These games are not authorized by Parker Brothers/Hasbro and so they do not bear the well-known red Monopoly bar.

8. Anonymity was requested.

9. Interview with Pam Weerry, Hilton reservations, London Hilton on Park Lane, April 22, 1998.

10. Similar changes have been made elsewhere. Jutta Al-Husani, interior design director at the Nile Hilton pointed out to me, for example, that when the Islamic ceiling panels in the lobby were introduced in 1978, the consistency of the original pharaonic theming of the hotel was compromised.

11. Ada Louise Huxtable, "Stale Air and the Plastic Aesthetic," in *Kicked a Building Lately?* (1973; New York: Quadrangle Books, 1976), 22.

12. This remodeling is, of course, not limited to Hiltons abroad. Brutalism has replaced Modernity at the entrance of the Beverly Hilton, and pseudopilasters and moldings cover up real marble at the Capital Hilton.

Index